NATIVISM AND SLAVERY

NATIVISM
AND SLAVERY

*The Northern Know Nothings
and the Politics of the 1850s*

TYLER ANBINDER

New York   Oxford
OXFORD UNIVERSITY PRESS
1992

For Jordana

Oxford University Press

Oxford   New York   Toronto
Delhi   Bombay   Calcutta   Madras   Karachi
Kuala Lumpur   Singapore   Hong Kong   Tokyo
Nairobi   Dar es Salaam   Cape Town
Melbourne   Auckland

and associated companies in
Berlin   Ibadan

Library of Congress Cataloging-in-Publication Data
Anbinder, Tyler Gregory.
    Nativism and slavery : the northern Know Nothings and the politics of
    the 1850s / Tyler Gregory Anbinder.
      p. cm.   Includes bibliographical references and index.
    ISBN 0-19-507233-2
    1. United States—Politics and government—1853–1857.   2. United
    States—Politics and government—1857–1861.   3. American Party.
    4. Nativism.   5. Slavery—United States—Anti-slavery movements.
    I. Title.
    E453.A52   1992
    320.973′09′034—dc20   91-43352

9 8 7 6 5 4 3 2 1

Printed in the United States of America
on acid-free paper

Preface

There are many people whose generosity in aiding my research and writing deserves recognition. The interlibrary loan staffs at Columbia University and the University of Wyoming helped me gain access to materials from far-flung repositories. I owe a special debt of gratitude to the reference librarians at Columbia University, whose tireless efforts helped me track down many research materials that would have otherwise eluded me. Beth Juhl, in particular, went beyond the call of duty in helping me answer countless mundane questions.

I would also like to extend thanks to the friends, colleagues, and teachers whose efforts contributed to the completion of this book. William Gienapp provided valuable suggestions concerning manuscript sources, and Jay Dolan answered questions concerning nineteenth-century American Catholicism. Thomas Jorge, Bud Moore, Karen Peterfreund, Ron Schultz, Christopher Shaw, James Shenton, David Stebenne, and Patrick Williams read the manuscript and offered valuable suggestions for its improvement. A number of teachers deserve special commendation. Clarence Walker, my undergraduate adviser at Wesleyan University, inspired me to enter the historical profession. Thomas Kessner provided two and a half years of employment as a research assistant, and the advice he gave me was of immense help when I began my own project. At Columbia, Rosalind Rosenberg and Eric McKitrick offered indispensable advice and assistance at every stage of my graduate career. Professor McKitrick, in addition, contributed his usual thorough and insightful comments on the manuscript. My dissertation adviser Eric Foner also deserves thanks. I developed an interest in the Know Nothings in his graduate seminar on slavery and the origins of the sectional conflict, in which I was given the unenviable assignment of critiquing his own work on nativism. Throughout the progress of my study, he provided invaluable guidance and advice, and his editorial skills improved every facet of this book.

During the final stages of manuscript preparation, Sharon Brown and Arlene Mascarenas helped compile my databases on Know Nothing members and officeholders. David Bovie provided able and enthusiastic research assistance, and his efforts were financed by the History Department of the University of Wyoming. A National Endowment for the Humanities Summer Stipend enabled me to undertake additional research when new Know Nothing minute books were discovered just months before the manuscript was ready to go to press. Karen Wolny at Oxford University Press and Stephanie

Sakson-Ford offered countless valuable suggestions for the improvement of the manuscript.

I owe a special debt to my family. My sister, besides enduring countless stories about the Know Nothings, worked late into the night guiding me through the intricacies of Lotus. My parents provided the moral and financial support which enabled me to embark upon such a time-consuming endeavor. Words cannot express my gratitude to them. Finally, my wife Jordana, in every way my most perceptive critic, read every page of every draft of the manuscript, and helped with every other aspect of its preparation. She also tolerated my unconventional work hours, as well as my inability at some points to concentrate on almost anything except the Know Nothings. This book is for her, with love.

Fort Collins, Colorado   T.A.
January 1992

Contents

Abbreviations Used in the Footnotes

AHR	*American Historical Review*
BPL	Boston Public Library
CG	*Congressional Globe*
CHS	Connecticut Historical Society
DCHS	Dauphin County Historical Society
HSP	Historical Society of Pennsylvania
HU	Harvard University
IlSHL	Illinois State Historical Library
InHS	Indiana Historical Society
InSL	Indiana State Library
JAH	*Journal of American History*
LC	Library of Congress
MHS	Massachusetts Historical Society
MVHR	*Mississippi Valley Historical Review*
NYH	*New York History*
NYHS	New-York Historical Society
NYHSQ	*New-York Historical Society Quarterly*
NYPL	New York Public Library
NYSL	New York State Library
OHS	Ohio Historical Society
SUNY-O	State University of New York at Oswego
UR	University of Rochester
WHS	State Historical Society of Wisconsin

Introduction

Although the United States has always portrayed itself as a sanctuary for the world's victims of poverty and oppression, anti–immigrant movements have enjoyed remarkable success throughout American history. None attained greater prominence than the Order of the Star Spangled Banner, a fraternal order referred to most commonly as the Know Nothing party. Vowing to reduce the political influence of immigrants and Catholics, the Know Nothings burst onto the American political scene in 1854, and by the end of the following year they had elected eight governors, more than one hundred congressmen, the mayors of Boston, Philadelphia, and Chicago, and thousands of other local officials. Prominent politicians of every persuasion joined the new party. Radicals such as Thaddeus Stevens, conservatives like former President Millard Fillmore, and notorious politicos including Simon Cameron all took the Know Nothing oath. After their initial successes, the Know Nothings attempted to increase their appeal by converting their network of lodges into a conventional political organization, which they christened the "American party."

Contemporaries were amazed that an organization with a ridiculous name and a proscriptive platform could attain such popularity, and they debated the causes of the Know Nothings' rise with great fervor. Yet until relatively recently, historians devoted little energy to the study of the Know Nothing party. Such neglect was somewhat understandable, because scholars who examined "the middle period" tended to focus on the causes and consequences of the Civil War. The Know Nothings seemed to have little impact on the sectional crisis, so students of antebellum America tended to mention the Know Nothings only in passing, if at all. Consequently, the Know Nothings became largely the province of county historical societies, whose members often presented papers that chronicled the local history of the mysterious order.[1]

1. Among the earliest of these local studies are George Schneider, "Lincoln and the Anti-Know Nothing Resolutions," *McLean County Historical Society Transactions* 3 (1900): 87–91; Hiram H. Shenk, "The Know Nothing Party in Lebanon County [Pennsylvania]," *Lebanon County Historical Society Papers* 4 (1906–9): 54–74; W. V. Hensel, "A Withered Twig: Dark Lantern Glimpses into the Operation of Know Nothingism in Lancaster Sixty Years Ago," *Journal of the Lancaster County Historical Society* 19 (1915): 174–81. For an example of the brief treatment the Know Nothings received from major historians, see Charles and Mary Beard, *The Rise of American Civilization*, 2 vols., rev. ed. (New York: Macmillan, 1934), II, p. 21.

Only in the late 1920s, when Richard Purcell's graduate students at Catholic University began to write dissertations on antebellum nativism, did the Know Nothings begin to receive serious scholarly attention. Just as Columbia University's William Dunning stimulated the study of Reconstruction, Purcell sparked interest in nativism, and by the late 1930s his students had produced theses examining the Know Nothings in nearly every state. The content of the studies produced under Purcell's tutelage rarely varied. His students described the history of anti-Catholicism in a particular state, recounted the Know Nothing party's success or failure in various elections, and applauded its quick demise. Although these studies assembled a good deal of factual information, they suffered from several limitations. In most cases, Purcell's students relied too heavily on the biased testimony of Know Nothing opponents when gathering evidence for their indictments. Furthermore, because they primarily sought to document the history of American anti-Catholicism in their works, Purcell's students rarely acknowledged that factors other than nativism might have contributed to the Know Nothings' remarkable success.[2]

That circumstances other than anti–immigrant sentiment contributed to the popularity of the American party became the theme of the subsequent generation of works treating the Know Nothings. Such suggestions were not entirely new. As early as 1907, John P. Senning had contended that a desire to preserve the Union, not a hatred of foreigners, had drawn voters to support the American party in the Midwest. Trends in Civil War scholarship may have inspired scholars to revive this argument in the 1940s. Rather than depict the war as an inevitable conflict between two distinctly different societies, revisionists in this period blamed the war on blundering politicians and irresponsible agitators. These scholars stressed that the nation's leaders had squandered opportunities for compromise during the 1850s, and cited the American party as a pro-Union alternative to the sectional organizations. The anti-Catholic harangues of the Know Nothings, concluded these historians, were to a large extent insincere diversions meant to deflect attention from the slavery issue.[3]

By the 1960s, historians no longer viewed the Civil War as a repressible conflict, but they continued to insist that religious prejudice could not explain the appeal of the Know Nothings. Following the lead of social scientists investigating the roots of bigotry, scholars came to believe that nativist attacks on

2. Mary St. Patrick McConville, *Political Nativism in the State of Maryland, 1830–1860* (Washington: Catholic Univ. Press, 1928); Sister Paul-of-the-Cross McGrath, *Political Nativism in Texas* (Washington: Catholic Univ. Press, 1930); Sister M. Evangeline Thomas, *Nativism in the Old Northwest, 1850–1860* (Washington: Catholic Univ. Press, 1936); C. J. Noonan, *Nativism in Connecticut* (Washington: Catholic Univ. Press, 1938); Mary de Lourdes Gohmann, *Political Nativism in Tennessee to 1860* (Washington: Catholic Univ. Press, 1938); A. G. McGann, *Nativism in Kentucky to 1860* (Washington: Catholic Univ. Press, 1944).

3. John P. Senning, "The Know Nothing Movement in Illinois, 1854–1856," *Illinois State Historical Society Journal* 7 (1914): 7–33; Harry J. Carman and Reinhard H. Luthin, "Some Aspects of the Know-Nothing Movement Reconsidered," *South Atlantic Quarterly* 39 (1940): 217–18; Allan Nevins, *Ordeal of the Union: A House Dividing, 1852–1857* (New York: Scribner, 1947), II, p. 401.

Catholics and immigrants reflected deeper, "fundamental tensions" within American society. David Brion Davis suggested that the American people used the threats created by imagined Catholic conspiracies to impose order and unity upon the bewildering social changes that characterized antebellum America. Following the lead of Richard Hofstadter, others suggested that "status anxiety" drove Americans to join the Know Nothings, because it allowed them to blame outsiders for their declining position in society. These scholars rejected the contention of the previous generation of historians who had attributed Know Nothing success to their pro-Union stance. Yet like their predecessors, they continued to deny that the Know Nothings' anti–immigrant, anti-Catholic program could have won the party such a huge following. Furthermore, they persisted in treating Know Nothingism as a fringe movement, undeserving of a major place in the story of the 1850s.[4]

By the end of the 1960s, however, the Know Nothings began to gain new prominence, thanks primarily to the emergence of the "new political historians." These scholars criticized the degree to which previous historians had concentrated on issues such as slavery and the tariff, contending that "ethno-cultural" divisions—such as religious affiliation and ethnic background—determined the partisan affiliation of most American voters. Not surprisingly, the new political historians gave unprecedented attention to the Know Nothings in their accounts of the 1850s. Noting that the Know Nothings emerged from the elections of 1854 and early 1855 with more momentum than the Republicans, the new political historians asserted that the traditional depiction of the collapse of the Whig party and the second American party system—one emphasizing the Kansas-Nebraska Act—could not be accurate. Instead, they posited that ethno-cultural issues such as nativism (epitomized by the Know Nothing party) destroyed the second party system. Only later, they said, did the Republicans establish themselves as the chief competitor to the Democratic party. Furthermore, these historians argued that the addition of nativism to the Republican agenda played a decisive role in the Republicans' eventual success.[5]

Many historians were convinced that the revisionists had discovered a

4. David Brion Davis, "Some Themes of Counter-Subversion: An Analysis of Anti-Masonic, Anti-Catholic, and Anti-Mormon Literature," *Mississippi Valley Historical Review* 47 (1960): 205–24; John Higham, "Another Look at Nativism," *Catholic Historical Review* 44 (1958): 147–58; Richard Hofstadter, *The Paranoid Style in American Politics and Other Essays* (New York: Knopf, 1965); Thomas J. Curran, "The Know Nothings of New York" (Ph.D. diss., Columbia University, 1963); Seymour Martin Lipset and Earl Raab, *The Politics of Unreason: Right Wing Extremism in America* (New York: Harper and Row, 1970), 53–59.

5. Michael F. Holt, *Forging a Majority: The Formation of the Republican Party in Pittsburgh, 1848–1860* (New Haven: Yale Univ. Press, 1969); Holt, *The Political Crisis of the 1850s* (New York: Norton, 1978); Ronald P. Formisano, *The Birth of Mass Political Parties: Michigan, 1827–1861* (Princeton: Princeton Univ. Press, 1971); Paul Kleppner, *The Third Electoral System, 1853–1892: Parties, Voters, and Political Cultures* (Chapel Hill: Univ. of North Carolina Press, 1979), William E. Gienapp, *The Origins of the Republican Party, 1852–1856* (New York: Oxford Univ. Press, 1987).

serious flaw in the traditional interpretation of the collapse of the second party system. But most found the ethno-culturalists' alternative even more unpersuasive. If nativism was so persistent, these skeptics asked, why then did it motivate voters so much more in 1854 than in any election before or since? Critics of the ethno-cultural interpretation also questioned whether nativism became an integral part of the Republican platform. Eric Foner admitted that most Know Nothings became Republicans, but insisted that "they were absorbed into a party which had made no concessions to them in its platform." Instead, he contended that like other Northerners, nativists eventually found the free-labor ideology of the Republican party irresistible. David Potter arrived at a similar conclusion in *The Impending Crisis*, although he stressed that nativism and anti-slavery both drew their strength from the same evangelical reforming impulse. The authors of several recent state studies have also found that the Republicans gained the votes of former Know Nothings without making concessions to them.[6]

In the past twenty years, then, the Know Nothings have moved from the periphery of historical scholarship to the center of the debate concerning the political crisis that led to the Civil War. Yet there is no general history of the Know Nothing party, and no work fully addresses the issues currently debated by historians. The most commonly cited book, Ray Billington's *The Protestant Crusade*, concerns itself primarily with nativism as a social phenomenon, and concentrates on the first forty years of the nineteenth century. Only Billington's concluding chapter considers the political activity of the Know Nothing party, and it is based solely on pamphlet and newspaper sources. Without utilizing the correspondence of the politicians involved, an accurate evaluation of the Know Nothings is impossible. A monograph does exist describing the Know Nothing party in the South, but contemporaries recognized that the Know Nothing party was "essentially a Northern party—all its great victories having been in that section." Furthermore, southern Know Nothingism bore little resemblance to its northern counterpart. The American party in most of the South ignored nativism. In fact, many southern states allowed Catholics to join the Know Nothing party. Furthermore, the history of the Know Nothing party in the South does not shed light on the collapse of the second party system, the extent to which nativism motivated antebellum voters, or the role of anti–immigrant sentiment in the rise of the Republican party.[7]

6. Eric Foner, *Free Soil, Free Labor, Free Men: The Ideology of the Republican Party before the Civil War* (New York: Oxford Univ. Press, 1970), 258; David Potter, *The Impending Crisis, 1848–1861* (New York: Harper and Row, 1976); Richard H. Sewell, *Ballots for Freedom: Antislavery Politics in the United States, 1837–1860* (New York: Oxford Univ. Press, 1976); Stephen E. Maizlish, *Triumph of Sectionalism: The Transformation of Politics in Ohio, 1844–1856* (Kent: Kent State Univ. Press, 1983); Dale Baum, *The Civil War Party System: The Case of Massachusetts, 1848–1876* (Chapel Hill: Univ. of North Carolina Press, 1984).

7. Ray A. Billington, *The Protestant Crusade, 1800–1860: A Study of the Origins of American Nativism* (Chicago: Quadrangle Books, 1938); W. Darrell Overdyke, *The Know-Nothing Party in the South* (Baton Rouge: Louisiana State Univ. Press, 1950); Philadelphia *Times* quoted in Philadelphia *News*, June 22, 1855.

This work fills this historiographic gap by presenting the first detailed survey of the Know Nothing party in the North. The study focuses to a great extent on state politics, in part because this was the arena in which the Know Nothings exerted the greatest influence, and in part because the organization differed tremendously from state to state. Nonetheless, certain broad themes and recurrent issues unify the story. The first is the role of the slavery controversy in the rise and fall of the Know Nothing party. Northern voters had grown increasingly disenchanted with the Whig and Democratic parties during the early 1850s, and this sentiment peaked after Congress enacted the Kansas-Nebraska bill. Many Northerners decided to abandon their old parties at this time in order to demonstrate their disgust with the new law, and the Know Nothings, who had acquired an anti-slavery reputation, attracted many of these disgruntled voters. Without the political crisis caused primarily by the Kansas-Nebraska Act, and the Know Nothings' anti-slavery reputation, the Know Nothings would never have enjoyed such phenomenal success. Slavery, not nativism, destroyed the second American party system. But because many Northerners chose to express their anti-slavery sentiment through the Know Nothing organization, the Republican party did not immediately benefit from the fallout over the Kansas-Nebraska Act. The slavery issue also contributed to the Know Nothings' speedy demise, because when the Order appeared to equivocate on the slavery-extension issue at its national convention in 1855, most Northerners abandoned the organization and joined the Republican party.

The depth of anti-Catholic sentiment in the United States forms a second theme of this study. Although the Know Nothings' anti-slavery stance drew many Northerners to the Order who would have ordinarily remained faithful to mainstream political parties, these citizens would not have become Know Nothings had they not also sympathized with its anti-Catholic agenda. Many in nineteenth-century America believed that Protestantism was responsible for the freedom and prosperity that the nation's inhabitants enjoyed. Conversely, Catholicism seemed hostile to everything they valued. The American people's devotion to "republicanism" inspired much of their anti-Catholicism, because they believed that the unlimited control which the Catholic hierarchy apparently exercised over its followers deprived Catholics of the independence necessary for participation in a republican government. Thus, while the devotion of the American party to nativism varied during its short lifetime, anti-Catholic sentiment never diminished during the mid-nineteenth century.

Although anti-Catholicism pervaded antebellum America, the Republican party's eventual success at recruiting former Know Nothings did not result from the addition of nativism to the Republican agenda. Some Republicans did advocate making concessions to nativists in order to secure their support and guarantee Republican ascendancy in the North. But in most cases, Republican leaders squelched these deals out of fear that they would cause more harm than good. Even when concessions were made, they were usually inconsequential gestures that failed to satisfy nativists and had little impact on the electoral balance. By 1856, the American party was dominated by conservative ex-Whigs who were concerned more about preserving the Union than the threat posed by immigrants. Consequently, the Republicans won the support of these voters primarily by moderating in certain states their radical views on slavery extension, and expanding their platform to include issues such as the tariff that appealed to conservative voters.

Finally, certain terms used in this work require brief clarification. First, anthropologists have come to understand "nativism" as a complex web of nationalism, xenophobia, ethnocentrism, and racism. Nineteenth-century Americans, however, used the term primarily to describe anti-immigrant sentiment. In order to maintain a consistency between my own words and those of the Know Nothings, my use of the term connotes the simpler, nineteenth-century definition. Second, Know Nothings attributed their origins to "Young Sam," whose uncle (the famous "Uncle Sam") had become discouraged about America's decline and had asked his nephew to start an organization that would revitalize the nation. Members consequently referred to their organization as "Sam" in correspondence and, as a result, this phrase appears from time to time in quotations. In addition, some historians object to use of the term "Know Nothings" to describe members of the Order of the Star Spangled Banner. They contend that this was a pejorative phrase coined by the movement's enemies, and that scholars should instead refer to the organization as the "American party," the name its members preferred.[8] Nonetheless, I have decided to utilize both terms. For one thing, the original members of the Order did not completely shun their popular name. One of the first newspapers to support the new movement was entitled the Boston *Know Nothing*, and even in 1856, the organization continued to call its political yearbook the *Know Nothing Almanac*. My prime motivation for using both terms, though, is the fact that the Know Nothings passed through two relatively distinct phases. During the first, from 1854 to 1855, they functioned as a secret fraternal order which attracted members with an anti-Catholic, anti-slavery, anti-party, and in most places anti-liquor agenda. Yet by 1856, a variety of circumstances had transformed the organization into one that ignored the slavery and temperance issues, minimized nativism, and instead stressed the maintenance of friendly relations between North and South. In order to distinguish between these two phases, I have referred to the organization in its initial phase as the Know Nothing party, and its members as "Know Nothings," because this term conveys the novelty and mystery that characterized the secret society. In its second phase I usually call it the American party and its adherents "the Americans."[9] Because this last term can easily cause confusion, I have used it sparingly, and whenever possible

8. See for example Paul Faler's review of Brian C. Mitchell's *The Paddy Camps: The Irish of Lowell, 1821–61* (Urbana: Univ. of Illinois Press, 1988), in *AHR* 94 (1989): 1172.

9. It should be noted that besides adding clarity to the narrative, this arrangement is historically accurate as well, because the conservatives who stressed Unionism over nativism were those who pressed most adamantly for the organization to drop its fraternal trappings and adopt the "American" label.

I refer to party members by one of their factional names: "North Americans," "National Americans," or "South Americans." In sum, then, my utilization of the term "Know Nothing" should in no way be considered pejorative. It has been utilized, along with these other terms, to enable the reader to comprehend more fully the intricacies of both antebellum politics and the history of American nativism.

When Charles B. Allen of New York City helped found the Order of the Star Spangled Banner, he set in motion what would become one of the most powerful nativist organizations America has ever known. Dramatically increasing immigration rates, escalating tension between Protestants and Catholics, and a reaction against the major political parties due primarily to the slavery issue all helped the Know Nothings enjoy unprecedented electoral success when they burst upon the American political scene in 1854. But divisions over slavery created an irreparable split in the organization. When party leaders attempted to appease Southerners by twice adopting platforms that preached acquiescence to the Kansas-Nebraska Act, most Northerners left the party. Those remaining in the Know Nothing ranks tried to attract new members by promising that their party would promote sectional harmony, but their 1856 presidential candidate, Millard Fillmore, carried only Maryland. This embarrassing performance further hastened the party's decline, and by 1860 the Know Nothings had disappeared. Yet despite their short life, the Know Nothings left an indelible legacy. First, the Know Nothing movement helped to destroy the second American party system. Know Nothing success also reflected the pervasiveness of anti-Catholicism in nineteenth-century America. Finally, the infusion of Know Nothings into the Republican party after 1856 transformed the Republicans into the nation's dominant political party. Although they prospered for only a brief period of time, the Know Nothings' story adds significantly to our understanding of Civil War–era politics and the history of American nativism.

NATIVISM AND SLAVERY

1

Immigration, Nativism, and Party Crisis

In 1854 the Know Nothing party burst upon the political scene with a swiftness unprecedented in American history. Yet the conditions that stimulated its growth had been developing for nearly half a century. European emigration to the United States increased dramatically after the War of 1812 and continued to grow in the decades that followed. In response to changes this influx of immigrants brought to American life, nativist political and fraternal organizations appeared in many major cities. However, even though these groups initially gained many adherents, they quickly declined in popularity, even while immigration continued to increase. Only when crises rocked the major political parties in the early 1850s did an overtly nativist political organization, the Know Nothing party, gain a national following.

Initially, it seemed unlikely that nativism would take root in the United States, because few Europeans emigrated to the country in the thirty years following the American Revolution. Military conflict on the Continent, as well as concern about the viability of the new republic, disrupted the previously steady flow of immigration. Once peace returned, however, immigration reverted to the pre-Revolutionary level of about 10,000 per year. Yet instead of stabilizing at that figure, immigration continued to increase steadily. Decade after decade, the pace of immigration quickened, peaking in 1854 when more than 400,000 Europeans settled in America. From 1845 to 1854, some 2,900,000 immigrants landed in the United States, more than had come in the seven previous decades combined. As a percentage of the nation's total population, the influx of immigrants from 1845 to 1854, amounting to 14.5 percent of the 1845 population, has never been surpassed.[1]

1. William J. Bromwell, *History of Immigration to the United States* (1856; rpt., New York: Arno Press, 1969), 14–15; *Historical Statistics of the United States: Colonial Times to 1970*, 2 vols. (Washington: U.S. Bureau of the Census, 1975), I, p. 106; David M. Potter, *The Impending Crisis, 1848–1861* (New York: Harper and Row, 1976), 241; Marcus Lee Hansen, *The Atlantic Migration, 1607–1860* (Cambridge, Mass.: Harvard Univ. Press, 1951), 3–225.

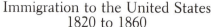

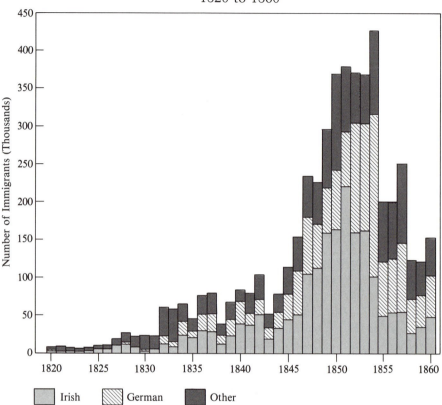

Immigration to the United States
1820 to 1860

Although Ireland and the German states supplied most of America's immigrants during the first half of the nineteenth century, the immigrants' backgrounds and the reasons for their emigration varied over time. Irish immigrants to the United States in the two decades after the War of 1812 tended to be Presbyterians or (to a lesser extent) Anglicans from the northern section of the island. The Catholics who emigrated were "the most enterprising, industrious, and virtuous part" of the Irish Catholic population: well-to-do farmers and middle-class city dwellers. Furthermore, the immigrants arriving in these years usually brought business or artisanal skills with them. Those without such skills had often been successful farmers, and a "substantial minority" of immigrants either bought farms when they arrived or worked in eastern seaboard cities until they saved enough money to buy farm land further west. "In general it is not the poorest who emigrate," noted one visiting Frenchman, but "chiefly . . . the middle classes . . . , comfortable tradesman, or small farmers, who, though already possessing some comforts, are anxious to better their conditions." Few ventured to the United States unless they had accumulated enough savings to finance a comfortable adjustment to their new home. The high cost of the Atlantic crossing also discouraged unskilled laborers and cash-poor tenant farmers from emigrating in this period.[2]

A variety of factors influenced the demographics of Irish immigration in the early nineteenth century. Irish craftsmen who could not compete with the flood of cheap goods from British factories in the early nineteenth century left to ply their skills in America. Textile manufacturers in northern Ireland adjusted to British competition with mechanization, transforming formerly independent artisans into piece or wage workers and convincing more artisans to emigrate. Because industrialization and the resulting economic displacement came to northern Ireland first, Protestants—who lived primarily in the north—outnumbered Catholics in early immigration to the United States.[3]

By the mid-1830s not only did the number of Irish emigrating to America increase dramatically, but their socio-economic background began to change as well. As southern and western Ireland surpassed the north as the chief source of Irish immigrants, Catholics came to constitute a majority of the voyagers, and unskilled laborers began to outnumber skilled emigrants. By 1836, almost 60 percent of Irish immigrants to America were classified as unskilled laborers, up from only 21 percent in 1820. Even the most remote areas of Ireland began sending immigrants to the United States in the 1830s and 40s, in part because transportation across the sea was becoming faster, safer, and (most important) cheaper, enabling poorer citizens to emigrate. Immigrants already in America also spurred emigration with their letters, which spoke of a land of freedom where failure was almost impossible.[4]

Nonetheless, the impetus for emigration resulted primarily from conditions in Ireland. As more and more of Ireland entered the modern free-market economy, cultural and familial ties which had discouraged emigration weakened. Over-population made land scarce, forcing fathers to institute primogeniture rather than divide property amongst their sons. As a result, noted one contemporary, "the younger branches of the family go to America . . . rather than make the farms smaller." Increasing discontent among Irish Catholics with the rule of the British may have also encouraged Catholics to abandon the persecution of Ireland for the independence of America.[5]

The extreme poverty that characterized life for most of the Irish provided the greatest incentive to emigrate. Over-population had made subsistence in rural areas increasingly difficult, and the decline in living standards after 1830

2. Kerby A. Miller, *Emigrants and Exiles: Ireland and the Irish Exodus to North America* (New York: Oxford Univ. Press, 1985), 194–95, 227–28 (quotation), 235, 240 (quotation), 264.

3. Miller, *Emigrants and Exiles*, 207–10, 227–35; Hansen, *Atlantic Migration*, 133–35; Oliver MacDonagh, "The Irish Famine Emigration to the United States," *Perspectives in American History* 10 (1976): 370–71.

4. Miller, *Emigrants and Exiles*, 195, 198, 200, 247, 264.

5. Hansen, *Atlantic Migration*, 89; Miller, *Emigrants and Exiles*, 199, 200, 203, 218–19 (quotation), 249, 252–53; MacDonagh, "Irish Famine Emigration," 369–71.

was "both rapid and dangerous." A traveler in western Ireland was shocked by the almost continuous sight of "wretchedly clad people inhabiting wretched homes, and carrying on a wretched and destructive tillage." Another visitor reported that in the average farmer's home "five or six half-naked children may be seen crouched near a miserable fire, the ashes of which cover a few potatoes, the sole nourishment of the family." This dire situation resulted in part from the deteriorating quality of the potato crop, which caused the traditional summer "hunger gap" before the harvest to lengthen each year. In addition, Irish farmers were continually forced to grow more cash crops to offset ever increasing rents, decreasing the amount of land available for potato farming and consequently increasing the farmer's hunger and privation.[6]

All these problems contributed to the terrible hardship that most Irish peasants faced, so when the potato blight struck in 1845, life there became completely unbearable. The potato blight was caused by a fungus which made the leaves of the potato plant turn black and crumble to ashes. Farmers thought at first that the potatoes themselves might be salvaged, but the seemingly healthy potatoes rotted soon after harvest. In 1845 the blight destroyed only 30 to 40 percent of the potato crop, and family and governmental relief efforts staved off starvation in most places. But the following year, the fungus reduced nearly the entire crop to "one wide waste of putrifying vegetation." The blight abated in 1847, but prospects had been so discouraging that few farmers had planted potatoes, and the resulting harvest brought in 90 percent fewer potatoes than in 1844. The 1847 harvest renewed the farmers' faith in the potato, and they again planted them in abundance. But this faith was rewarded with a harvest as disastrous as that of 1846. Each subsequent year until the middle 1850s brought potato harvests of less than half the pre-blight levels.[7]

Because severe poverty had gripped Ireland even before the potato crops failed, and so many of the Irish subsisted almost exclusively on potatoes, the consequences of the blight were bound to be disastrous. While suffering had been widespread in pre-famine Ireland, starvation had been rare. Now it became commonplace. A visitor surveying the horrible conditions found it amazing "not that the people died, but that they lived." It is estimated that between 1,000,000 and 1,500,000 Irishmen died either of starvation or starvation-related illness (out of a total pre-famine population of 8,000,000) during the famine. With friends and relatives dead or dying around them and the government doing little to relieve the suffering, another 2,000,000 decided to flee Ireland completely, and nearly three-quarters of that number came to America.[8]

6. MacDonagh, "Irish Famine Emigration," 361–66; Miller, *Emigrants and Exiles*, 204–6, 219.

7. Miller, *Emigrants and Exiles*, 281–82 (quotation); MacDonagh, "Irish Famine Emigration," 405.

8. Miller, *Emigrants and Exiles*, 286–93; MacDonagh, "Irish Famine Emigration," 406–10 (quotation); David H. Bennett, *The Party of Fear: From Nativist Movements to the New Right in American History* (Chapel Hill: Univ. of North Carolina Press, 1988), 63.

The famine immigrants were the most impoverished, destitute, unskilled group ever to arrive in the United States. Eighty to 90 percent of them were classified as unskilled laborers. Ninety percent were Catholics, as many as a third spoke only Gaelic, and few came with any savings. Contemporaries noticed these profound changes. As an Irish-American journalist put it, "the Irish [immigrants] of the present day . . . seem to be a different race of the Irish ten, 15, or 20 years since. . . . Dire wretchedness, appalling want and festering famine have tended to change their characters." These differences, along with the sheer magnitude of the migration, made the possibility of adjustment and assimilation far more difficult for the famine immigrants than it had been for their predecessors. As Oscar Handlin has remarked, "for a long time they were fated to remain a massive lump in the community, undigested, undigestible."[9]

Although they received less publicity than the Irish, nearly as many Germans emigrated to the United States during the mid-1800s. In fact, in the peak year of immigration, 1854, German emigration to the United States outpaced that from Ireland by two to one. Over-population played perhaps the most significant role in motivating Germans to emigrate. As land became more scarce and costly, many farmers chose to leave for the inexpensive, untaxed land that abounded in the New World. As in Ireland, industrialization and competition from England made it increasingly difficult for German artisans to earn a decent living. The growing unification of the German economy further aggravated the situation, as the removal of internal tolls and duties hurt artisans from the less industrially advanced sections of Germany in their efforts to compete with those from neighboring states (in Württemberg, for example, one in six weavers went bankrupt between 1840 and 1847). Incidental factors that contributed to Irish emigration, such as encouragement from earlier immigrants and cheaper transportation, also induced Germans to leave for America.[10]

As was the case with Ireland, German immigration to the United States grew to unprecedented levels in the decade ending in 1854. But while the potato famine caused the massive exodus from Ireland, the extraordinary growth in German immigration in the 1850s is more difficult to explain. Historians once attributed the increase to the revolutions of 1848. However, German emigration did not grow significantly from pre-revolutionary levels until 1852, long after authorities had quelled the uprisings. Furthermore, the sources of greatest emigration do not correspond to the areas of revolutionary unrest. Although the failure of the revolution did induce some well-known German radicals to emigrate, the preponderance of Germans emigrated for

9. Miller, *Emigrants and Exiles*, 295–99, 326 (quotation); MacDonagh, "Irish Famine Emigration," 418–30; Oscar Handlin, *Boston's Immigrants: A Study in Acculturation* (Cambridge: Belknap Press, 1959), 55.

10. Mack Walker, *Germany and the Emigration, 1816–1885* (Cambridge, Mass.: Harvard Univ. Press, 1964), 46, 49–50, 65, 138; Wolfgang Kollmann and Peter Marschalck, "German Emigration to the United States," trans. Thomas C. Childers, *Perspectives in American History* 7 (1973): 526–27.

many of the same reasons as their Irish counterparts. The potato crop also failed in Germany in the late 1840s, and although potatoes did not dominate the German diet, food prices and poverty rose dramatically as a result. Massive unemployment exacerbated these problems, reaching an unprecedented 17 percent by the mid-1850s. Southwestern Germany suffered most from these problems, and, consequently, most of Germany's emigrants to the United States came from this region.[11]

German emigration to America in the first half of the nineteenth century displayed many of the same characteristics as the Irish migration. As immigration progressed, fewer German immigrants brought either skills or money to America, and by the 1850s Catholic immigrants outnumbered Protestants. But unlike the Irish immigrants, Germans did not congregate in America's East Coast port cities. Arriving with more money than the Irish, most journeyed westward, either to such cities as Cincinnati and Milwaukee, or to western farming areas. Unlike their Irish peers, whose experience with the potato blight had soured them on farming, most German immigrants were determined to resume the agricultural life they had known in Europe.[12]

The tremendous influx of immigrants to the United States in the decade ending in 1854 presented, in the words of the New York *Tribune*, "a social phenomenon with few, if any, parallels." Indeed, the small immigrant enclaves that had previously existed in most American cities now grew nearly as large as the neighborhoods where native-born citizens resided. Theodore Parker reported with dismay that Suffolk County, Massachusetts, had become "a New England 'County Cork,' " while Boston was now "the Dublin of America." Similar complaints emanated from all American cities. By 1855, immigrants outnumbered native-born citizens in Chicago, Detroit, and Milwaukee, and the immigrant population would soon surpass the native in New York, Brooklyn, Buffalo, Cleveland, and Cincinnati. More than a third of the inhabitants of Boston, Pittsburgh, Albany, Rochester, and Troy were immigrants, and nearly that proportion lived in Philadelphia and Newark. In contrast, relatively few immigrants settled in the South, and only Baltimore, New Orleans, St. Louis, and Louisville received a significant influx of newcomers.[13]

The United States at its inception had looked favorably and even eagerly across the Atlantic for immigrants. In the Declaration of Independence the

11. Marcus L. Hansen, "The Revolutions of 1848 and German Emigration," *Journal of Economic and Business History* 2 (1930): 630–55; A. E. Zucker, ed., *The Forty Eighters: Political Refugees of the German Revolution of 1848* (New York: Columbia Univ. Press, 1950); Kollmann and Marschalck, "German Emigration," 523, 532–34; Walker, *Germany and the Emigration*, 44, 71–73, 129–33, 153–160; Hansen, *Atlantic Migration*, 284–90.

12. Walker, *Germany and the Emigration*, 46–48, 74, 160; Kollmann and Marschalck, "German Emigration," 530–31.

13. New York *Tribune* quoted in Edward K. Spann, *The New Metropolis: New York City, 1840–1857* (New York: Columbia Univ. Press, 1981), 24; William G. Bean, "Puritan Versus Celt, 1850–1860," *New England Quarterly* 7 (1934): 71; Harrisburg *Herald*, May 5, 1855; *Statistics of the United States in 1860 Compiled from the Original Returns of the Eighth Census* (1866, rpt. New York: Arno Press, 1976), lvii–lviii.

colonists complained that King George III had "endeavored to prevent the population of these States" by "obstructing the Laws of Naturalization of Foreigners" and by "refusing to pass others to encourage their migration hither." But this attitude began to change when Catholic immigrants began to outnumber Protestants. The first American settlers had brought from England an intense hatred of Catholicism, and every colony but Rhode Island passed laws that discriminated against them. While the framing of the federal and state constitutions after the American Revolution removed most legislative manifestations of American anti-Catholicism, popular antipathy toward Catholics continued unabated.[14]

Overt American anti-Catholicism did not re-emerge until the mid-1830s. In August 1834, a mob burned the Ursuline convent in Charlestown, Massachusetts, after a rumor spread stating that priests there were imprisoning a nun who wanted to leave her order. In the autumn of that year, artist/inventor Samuel F. B. Morse charged in a series of published letters that the monarchies of Europe had enlisted the aid of the Catholic Church to subvert the spread of democracy by sending Catholic immigrants to take control of the under-populated American west. A power base in the west combined with continuing Catholic immigration to the eastern United States would soon bring the country under the sway of Catholic despotism, Morse charged, which would prevent the spread of democracy and religious liberty to Europe. Morse claimed that the front for this operation was the Leopold Association, founded in Vienna in 1829 to finance the building of Catholic churches in America. By linking Catholicism (which most Americans had always despised) to immigration (which they had previously considered beneficial), Morse laid the foundation for decades of American nativism that would follow. Two other works also helped revive anti-Catholicism at this time. One, Lyman Beecher's *A Plea for the West* (1835), utilized a conspiracy argument similar to Morse's in denouncing the influence of Catholic schools on American children. The other, Maria Monk's *Awful Disclosures of the Hotel Dieu Nunnery of Montreal* (1836), with its lurid descriptions of illicit convent sexual practices, sold more copies in America than any other book until the publication of *Uncle Tom's Cabin*.[15]

Organizations designed to combat the purported threat posed by immi-

14. Marilyn Case Baseler, "Immigration Policy in Eighteenth Century America" (Ph.D. diss., Harvard University, 1990); Thomas More Brown, "The Image of the Beast: Anti-Papal Rhetoric in Colonial America," in Richard O. Curry and Thomas M. Brown, eds., *Conspiracy: Fear of Subversion in American History* (New York: Rinehart and Winston, 1972); Sister Mary Augustina Ray, *American Opinion of Roman Catholicism in the Eighteenth Century* (New York: Columbia Univ. Press, 1936).

15. Ray A. Billington, *The Protestant Crusade, 1800–1860: A Study of the Origins of American Nativism* (Chicago: Quadrangle Books, 1938), 70–76, 99–108, 122–27; Charles W. Frothingham, *The Convent's Doom; a Tale of Charlestown in 1834*, 5th ed. (Boston, 1854); Wilfred J. Bisson, *Countdown to Violence: The Charlestown Convent Riot of 1834* (New York: Garland, 1989), 107–25; Samuel F. B. Morse, *Foreign Conspiracy Against the Liberties of the United States* (New York, 1835).

grants and Catholics surfaced at this time. The first such group to gain prominence was the Native American Democratic Association (NADA), formed in
New York City in June 1835.[16] NADA candidates, running on a platform that
condemned the appointment of foreigners to office, the immigration of paupers
and criminals to America, and any encroachments by the Catholic Church,
polled 39 percent of the vote in the November 1835 New York City election,
although their ticket benefited from the fact that the Whigs ran no candidates.
Nativists formed similar organizations in Brooklyn, Cincinnati, New Orleans,
Washington, and Paterson, New Jersey. In some smaller towns these organizations claimed to have carried a few elections, but these undoubtedly came with
the help of one of the major parties. The following spring, the NADA nominated Morse as its New York mayoral candidate. This time, however, the Whigs
refused to abandon the field to the nativists, and as a result Morse captured just
6 percent of the vote. Few New Yorkers were willing to spurn the established
political parties for a nativist ticket. When Congress in 1838 took up the petitions of nativists concerning amendment or repeal of the naturalization laws,
the NADA had already faded into obscurity.[17]

Catholicism and immigration re-emerged as political issues in New York
after William H. Seward became governor of the state in 1839. Seward
learned that many Irish-Catholic immigrants in New York City kept their
children out of school because teachers used the Protestant King James Bible
(as opposed to the Catholic "Douay" version) as a reader, and because anti-
Catholicism pervaded the textbooks. The governor eventually proposed that
the privately run New York City school system remedy this situation by devot-
ing a portion of its funds to the formation of parochial schools, in which
immigrants "may be instructed by teachers speaking the same language with
themselves and professing the same faith." When New York City officials
balked, the governor suggested that the legislature pass a law mandating the
change.[18]

The school question became the paramount issue of the 1841 legislative
elections in New York City. Most Whigs adamantly opposed their own governor's plan, and when some of the usually pro-immigrant Democrats refused to
endorse Seward's proposal, Bishop John Hughes organized a third ticket

16. Some sort of association opposed to the increase of immigration existed in Schenectady
as early as 1832, but the only information I have uncovered concerning it is Chester Averill, *An
Address Delivered Before a Branch of the American Association at Schenectady, January 18, 1832*
(n.p., n.d.), BPL.

17. Leo Hershkowitz, "The Native American Democratic Association in New York City,
1835–1836," *NYHSQ* 46 (1962): 41–59; Louis Dow Scisco, *Political Nativism in New York State*
(New York: Columbia Univ. Press, 1901), 23–27; Sean Wilentz, *Chants Democratic: New York
City and the Rise of the American Working Class, 1788–1850* (New York: Oxford Univ. Press,
1984), 267–69.

18. Vincent P. Lannie, *Public Money and Parochial Education: Bishop Hughes, Governor
Seward, and the New York School Controversy* (Cleveland: Case Western Reserve Univ. Press,
1968), 1–102; Sister Marie Leonore Fell, *The Foundations of Nativism in American Textbooks,
1783–1860* (Washington: Catholic Univ. of America Press, 1941).

which included all the Democrats except those opposing Seward's proposal. When the votes were counted, all the Democrats supported by Hughes had won, while "the Whigs, with the help of the Native American party," defeated the Democratic candidates who lacked the bishop's support.[19] Seward then amended his proposal, asking that the legislature include New York City schools in the state's public school system, which would allow each city ward to elect school commissioners to determine its schools' curricula. A bill encompassing this plan passed the legislature in 1842, but opponents in New York City succeeded in electing commissioners who almost uniformly required reading of the King James Bible. By broadening the debate on immigration and Catholicism to include the sensitive area of education, Seward had opened a Pandora's box and unwittingly aided the revival of nativism.[20]

Nativists attempted to take advantage of the New York City school controversy by creating the American Republican party in June 1843. This organization called for a twenty-one-year probationary period before naturalization, repeal of the 1842 school law, reading of the King James Bible in all public schools, and the election and appointment of none but native-born Americans to public office. In the November 1843 elections the American Republicans surprised New Yorkers by polling 23 percent of the vote. For the mayoral election the following April the American Republicans nominated respected publisher James Harper (of Harper & Brothers), who promised that reform of the city government would be the priority of his administration. Embarrassed that the incumbent Whig mayor had governed the city as ineptly as his Democratic predecessors, the city's Whig press threw its support to Harper, and the backing of both nativists and these reformers carried the publisher to victory.[21]

Before Harper's administration could be tested, dramatic events in Philadelphia shifted the attention of nativists to that city. Inspired by Hughes's efforts, Bishop Francis Kenrick pressed Philadelphia school officials to allow Catholic students to use the Douay Bible during school Bible readings. The board voted down Kenrick's request, opting instead to allow Catholic children to leave the classroom. When a teacher in the predominantly Irish immigrant suburb of Kensington complained in February 1843 about the disruption caused by this policy, the Irish-American school director there ordered Bible reading stopped. The American Republicans of Philadelphia—who had to this point gained few adherents—capitalized on the ensuing Protestant pro-

19. This reference to the "Native American party" by the *Journal of Commerce* (quoted in Lannie, *Public Money and Parochial Education*, 189) refers not to an existing political organization, but to the nativist element within the electorate.

20. Lannie, *Public Money and Parochial Education*, 119–258; Billington, *Protestant Crusade*, 156, 164 n. 88. Similar controversies erupted in Philadelphia, Newark, Albany, and Detroit.

21. *Address to the People of the State of New York by the General Executive Committee of the American Republican Party of the City of New York* (New York, 1844); Ira M. Leonard, "The Rise and Fall of the American Republican Party in New York City, 1843–1845," *NYHSQ* 50 (1966): 162–70; Wilentz, *Chants Democratic*, 315–23.

test by electing their candidates to some of the county offices contested in March and April 1844.[22]

Heartened by these successes in Protestant wards, the American Republicans attempted to expand throughout the city. However, several attempts to organize in Kensington were violently rebuffed by its Irish-Catholic inhabitants, and skirmishes between the two groups in May escalated into a bloody three-day riot, in which two Catholic churches were destroyed by fire. In July, after Protestants saw Catholics delivering a wagon-load of guns to a Catholic church in suburban Southwark, another riot erupted. Protestants and Catholics each blamed the other for the bloodshed, but the conflict clearly aided American Republican candidates at the polls. In October, American Republicans won two congressional seats and swept their Philadelphia county nominees into office as well.[23]

While the Philadelphia riots galvanized nativists there, the bloodshed severely weakened the nativist coalition in New York City. Respectable Whigs who had flocked to the American Republican banner to bring about reform refused to have their names associated with the violent proceedings of the party in Philadelphia. "I shan't be caught voting a 'Native' ticket again in a hurry," vowed diarist George Templeton Strong after the riots. Nevertheless, Whig leaders did agree to back American Republicans running for local offices if they would support Whig presidential nominee Henry Clay. Clay and his running mate Theodore Frelinghuysen (who was selected in part because his militant Protestantism endeared him to nativists) lost New York and the election by the slimmest of margins, but the coalition did elect four American Republicans to New York congressional seats. Re-electing Harper proved much more difficult. The defection of Democratic American Republicans to their former party, Harper's inability to reform municipal government, Whig determination to offer a creditable opposition to the American Republicans, and the fallout over the Philadelphia riots all contributed to Harper's defeat in April 1845.[24]

Having won contests in Pennsylvania, New York, and Massachusetts (a coalition of Whigs and nativists had elected an American Republican mayor of Boston in early 1845), American Republicans organized a convention in an attempt to coordinate their various state organizations. The delegates attending the Philadelphia gathering spoke confidently of the future, renaming themselves the Native American party. However, local setbacks rendered the national organization superfluous. With their percentage of the vote declining rapidly after Harper's defeat, the Native Americans in New York ceased

22. Michael Feldberg, *The Philadelphia Riots of 1844: A Study in Ethnic Conflict* (Westport: Greenwood Press, 1975), 89–96.

23. Feldberg, *Philadelphia Riots*, 99–175; David Montgomery, "The Shuttle and the Cross: Weavers and Artisans in the Kensington Riots of 1844," *Journal of Social History* 5 (1972): 411–46.

24. Leonard, "Rise and Fall of the American Republican Party," 173–92 (Strong quoted p. 174); Spann, *The New Metropolis*, 37–41.

making nominations after 1847. Only in the Philadelphia area did the party continue to run candidates for office, winning one more congressional election and some minor local offices. But for this small group of Philadelphia die-hards, the Native American party disappeared. Nativist political organizations were unable to sustain voter loyalty once religious tensions had abated.[25]

Determined nativists did not abandon their cause. Rather than attempting to perpetuate their influence through political action, they opted to form semi-secret fraternal organizations. The most prominent of these, the Order of United Americans (OUA), had been founded in New York City in December 1844 by a number of American Republicans including Harper, attorney Thomas R. Whitney (who would later become a Know Nothing congressman), and other New York professionals. Their "code of principles" stated that the OUA had been organized "for the purpose of more effectually securing our country from the dangers of foreign influence," and called "the exclusion of the Bible from our public schools" the "most alarming" attempt at foreign influence attempted thus far. Yet the OUA eschewed the aggressive harangues of other nativist groups, and vowed instead to attract adherents to the nativist cause by advocating "love of country" and "patriotism." Furthermore, the OUA would not enter politics as a separate party, but would attempt to influence existing parties to carry out their goals.[26]

Slowly the OUA began to assert itself in New York politics. In the November 1849 New York City election, the OUA singled out the Democratic candidate for comptroller as undeserving of their vote, and although he still managed to win, he ran 1,000 votes behind the rest of the ticket.[27] By 1852, the OUA had grown large enough to draw the attention of politicians throughout the state. One New Yorker reported to Seward that the OUA had become "a pretty numerous class" and possessed "a force by no means to be overlooked," while another Seward spy stated that he was "doing all in his power to control the O.U.A. vote" and that if he succeeded, "it will give us 10,000 to 15,000 true and faithfull that can be relied on."[28]

Nativists had created other fraternal organizations in the 1840s. The most prominent after the OUA was the United Sons of America (USA), founded in

25. William G. Bean, "Party Transformation in Massachusetts with Special Reference to the Antecedents of Republicanism, 1848–1860" (Ph.D. diss., Harvard University, 1922), 228–35; *Declaration of Principles . . . of the Native American Convention . . . July 4, 1845* (New York, 1845); Feldberg, *Philadelphia Riots*, 168–72; Thomas R. Whitney, *A Defence of the American Policy* (New York, 1856), 252–56.

26. Whitney, *Defence of the American Policy*, 257–79; Jean Gould Hales, "The Shaping of Nativist Sentiment, 1848–1860" (Ph.D. diss., Stanford University, 1973), 12–18; Order of United Americans Scrapbook (quotations), NYPL.

27. This does not indicate that the OUA controlled only 1000 votes, but that 1000 OUA members usually voted Democratic. One year earlier, the OUA claimed to have 8000 members. Thomas J. Curran, "The Know Nothings of New York" (Ph.D. diss., Columbia University, 1963), 75; Hales, "Shaping of Nativist Sentiment," 12.

28. J. Sherwood to Seward, June 4, 1852, John W. Latson to Seward, April 22, 1852, Seward Papers, UR.

Philadelphia in 1845. In the Philadelphia area, it operated as the base for those Native Americans who objected to forming coalitions with the existing parties. The USA also boasted many members in Boston. Another group, the Order of United American Mechanics (OUAM), enjoyed a large following in Pennsylvania, with smaller contingents in New York, New Jersey, and a few other states. Primarily a workingmen's benevolent society, the OUAM limited its membership to "producers" by excluding merchants, professionals, and bankers. Criticizing primarily the economic impact of the immigrant on American life, the existence of the OUAM demonstrates that workingmen did not trust the more prominent nativist groups to address their concerns.[29]

As immigration to the United States soared during the late 1840s, these nativists became increasingly confident that their agenda would soon dominate political debate. In order to speed the arrival of that moment, the OUA through its organ *The Republic* began calling for a fusion of all nativist groups under the auspices of the OUA. Thus united, a great "conservative party" would spring to life, "*taking its cue from the doctrines set forth* by the Order of United Americans." The Native Americans felt that their organization should fill this role, but the OUA believed the Native Americans to be moribund, and continued to spurn direct participation in politics until a new party took shape. The Native Americans of Philadelphia attempted to demonstrate their vitality by convening a presidential nominating convention in July 1852. Dominated by delegates seeking a coalition with conservative Whigs, the convention endorsed Secretary of State Daniel Webster. When Webster died, "purists" opposing coalitions with outsiders substituted USA founder Jacob Broom. The "coalitionists" then threw their support to Democrat Franklin Pierce. Broom's dismal showing (2,685 votes out of 3,100,000 cast) dramatized the minute political clout of these nativist organizations.[30]

Nativists could not understand why, with immigration setting new records each year, their candidates could not make headway with the electorate. They failed to realize, however, that voters supported their tickets in large numbers only when religious controversies erupted or ethnic violence flared. Antebellum Americans were extremely loyal to their political parties, and when educational disputes ended and religious tensions died down, voters who had supported nativist candidates quickly returned to old allegiances. Furthermore, Whig connivance had played a major role in most previous nativist electoral victories. In some cases the Whigs had abandoned the field to the nativists, and at other times the two groups had formed coalitions. Unless some new religious crisis occurred, or the Whig party either disappeared or assented to a

29. Hales, "Shaping of Nativist Sentiment," 18–19; Leonard Tabachnik, "Origins of the Know-Nothing Party: A Study of the Native American Party in Philadelphia, 1844–1852" (Ph.D. diss., Columbia University, 1973), 215 ff.; Wilentz, *Chants Democratic*, 344; Bruce Laurie, *Working People of Philadelphia* (Philadelphia: Temple Univ. Press, 1980), 174–76.

30. Charles O. Paulin, "The National Ticket of Broom and Coates, 1852," *AHR* 25 (1920): 689–91; Lewis C. Levin to William Marcy, Oct. 15, 1852, Marcy Papers, LC; Curran, "Know Nothings of New York," 75–86 (quotation).

new coalition with one of the nativist organizations, nativism would continue to be a fringe movement on the American political scene.

Fortunately for the nativist cause, a political crisis developed in the 1850s that destroyed public confidence in the major parties and enabled nativist organizations to attract a substantial number of voters.[31] The most important element of this crisis was the demise of the Whig party, which began around 1850. In a very real sense, it was the discovery of gold in California that initiated the collapse of the Whig organization. As Americans flocked to California to stake their claims, Congress moved to speed the territory's admission as a state. Although Californians had voted overwhelmingly to exclude slavery from their boundaries, Southerners in Congress vowed to block California's admission as a free state unless Northerners reciprocated with certain concessions. These included repudiation of the Wilmot Proviso (which had sought to exclude slavery from all territories acquired during the Mexican-American War), a continuance of slavery in the District of Columbia, and, most important, a new fugitive slave law requiring Northerners to return runaway slaves to the South. Initially this compromise measure failed to win congressional approval, in part because President Zachary Taylor opposed it. When Taylor died, however, his successor, Millard Fillmore, endorsed it. Fillmore's support, combined with the division of the compromise measure into several smaller bills (which allowed congressmen to vote against some portions of the measure while endorsing others), changed enough Whig votes to enable the compromise to pass.[32]

Although most Americans were relieved that a sectional crisis had once more been averted, many felt that their own section had sacrificed too much. This was especially true in the North, where the fugitive slave law was immensely unpopular. The spectacle of black men and women being returned to the South without jury trial brought home to many Northerners for the first time the true barbarity of slavery. While few runaway slaves actually lost their liberty as a result of the statute, the isolated instances in which federal commissioners enforced the law caused outrage and indignation throughout the North. Furthermore, a section of the law empowered federal marshals to summon all citizens to aid in the enforcement of the law (usually in the form of local militia companies to quell popular protest), potentially forcing many Northerners who opposed slavery to aid in the rendition of runaways to the South.[33]

31. The relationship of this political crisis to the rise of the Know Nothings and the role of nativism in fomenting that crisis will be examined more extensively in Chapter 2.
32. Holman Hamilton, *Prologue to Conflict: The Crisis and Compromise of 1850* (Lexington: Univ. of Kentucky Press, 1964); Potter, *Impending Crisis*, 90–120.
33. Potter, *Impending Crisis*, 130–34; Stanley W. Campbell, *The Slave Catchers: Enforcement of the Fugitive Slave Laws, 1850–1860* (Chapel Hill: Univ. of North Carolina Press, 1968); Samuel J. May, *The Fugitive Slave Law and Its Victims*, rev. ed. (New York, 1861).

Passage of the Kansas-Nebraska Act confirmed for many Northerners that politicians had completely lost touch with the popular will. Illinois senator Stephen A. Douglas proposed this measure in order to organize the Kansas and Nebraska territories and thus speed construction of a trans-continental railroad through Chicago. In order to gain southern support for his bill, Douglas included a clause repealing the Missouri Compromise, which would have prohibited slavery in these territories. Instead, the inhabitants of each territory would vote on whether or not to allow slavery, a concept Michigan's Lewis Cass had labeled "popular sovereignty." Although Douglas predicted that Kansans would use popular sovereignty to prohibit slavery, Northerners vehemently opposed the bill. They held protest meetings throughout the North, calling the Missouri Compromise a "sacred agreement" and vowing to punish the Democratic party at the polls if it persisted in forcing the bill through Congress. Heeding the threats of their constituents, many northern Democrats refused to support the proposal, even when President Pierce declared it a test of party orthodoxy. But the many southern Whigs who voted in favor of the bill more than compensated for these Democratic defections, and on May 30, 1854, Pierce signed the Kansas-Nebraska bill into law.[39]

The Kansas-Nebraska Act has been aptly described as "the most monstrous and fatal of all political errors" ever committed by a party. Indeed, while the Democrats had dominated national politics for most of the previous twenty-five years, the Kansas-Nebraska Act initiated a chain of events that would eclipse them on the national stage for the succeeding quarter-century. Yet, ironically, the Whigs initially suffered most from passage of the Kansas-Nebraska Act. Northern Whigs were "very embarrassed . . . by the [favorable] vote of Southern Whigs upon the Nebraska bill," reported one correspondent to ex-President Fillmore. As a result, Senator Benjamin F. Wade of Ohio promised that he would have no "further political connection with the Whigs of the South," as did Senator Truman Smith of Connecticut. Although some Whigs vowed to retain their organization and transform it into an anti-slavery vehicle, many decided to abandon their party and start a new organization to oppose the extension of slavery.[40] With anti-slavery Whigs poised to leave the party in many areas, the Fillmore faction might have been expected to gain strength. But passage of the Kansas-Nebraska Act made their conservative position less tenable, because it discredited their argument that acceptance of the fugitive slave law would prevent further attempts by the South to spread slavery. Consequently, in states where anti-slavery Whigs controlled

39. Potter, *Impending Crisis*, 145–76; Gienapp, *Origins of the Republican Party*, 69–87; Gerald W. Wolff, *The Kansas-Nebraska Bill: Party, Section, and the Coming of the Civil War* (New York: Revisionist Press, 1977), 47–103, 148–82.

40. Alexander McClure, *Old Time Notes of Pennsylvania*, 2 vols. (Philadelphia, 1905), I, p. 210; Henry W. Williams to Fillmore, July 1, 1854, Fillmore Papers, SUNY-O; Gienapp, *Origins of the Republican Party*, 86–87 (quotation); Potter, *The Impending Crisis*, 235–41; Thomas Brown, *Politics and Statesmanship: Essays on the American Whig Party* (New York: Columbia Univ. Press, 1985), 225.

the party and seemed determined to remain in it (such as New York), most conservatives concluded that they would never regain party dominance. They began seeking a new conservative organization in which to base their political operations. Conversely, in states where conservative Whigs held sway (such as Massachusetts), anti-slavery Whigs began to search for a new base of political operations as well.[41]

By 1854, then, all the prerequisites for another outburst of American nativism were in place. Immigration had reached an all-time high, and the sheer number of newcomers, their religious affiliations, and their lack of skills made swift assimilation impossible. An existing cadre of die-hard nativists, organized in semi-secret fraternal organizations, waited to foment such an outburst. These groups had achieved political success in the past, particularly when religious animosity flared up in educational disputes, and almost invariably when the Whig party offered no resistance. The incipient collapse of the Whig party in the North, and anti-party sentiment pervading the country because of issues such as temperance and slavery extension that transcended conventional political divisions, offered nativist organizations the opportunity to steal disenchanted voters from their old parties. This political chaos, and a resurgence of religious controversies in 1853 and 1854, paved the way for the rise of the Know Nothing party.

41. Potter, *The Impending Crisis*, 246–47; Edward Everett to Millard Fillmore, Nov. 10, 1854, Fillmore Papers, SUNY-O.

2

The Rise of the Know Nothings

In about 1850, Charles B. Allen of New York City founded a new secret society similar to the other nativist fraternal organizations already in existence. Yet this new group, the Order of the Star Spangled Banner (OSSB),[1] differed from previous nativist groups in a number of ways. Organizations such as the Order of United Americans (OUA) and United Sons of America had been only "semi-secret." Meetings were closed to the public, but adherents could admit to membership, which became public anyway because they participated in parades and organized public lectures. Members of the OSSB, on the other hand, could not reveal anything about their organization, not even the fact that it existed. While the older nativist groups charged significant dues and required members to purchase expensive uniforms, it cost nothing to join the new group. The goals of the OSSB, however, were nearly identical to those of the existing nativist organizations. OSSB members pledged to use their votes and personal influence to reduce the political power of both immigrants and the politicians who purportedly pandered to them.[2]

By 1852 the OSSB could claim only forty-three members and seemed destined for obscurity. At about this time, however, the OUA discovered the OSSB's existence and OUA leaders instructed their members to join the new group. A year later they so outnumbered the OSSB's original members that they were able to oust Allen from control. Historians commonly ascribe the OUA's action to its desire to use the OSSB as its "political arm," but this does not seem likely.[3] As OUA founder Thomas R. Whitney noted, the OSSB's

1. Actually, no extant Know Nothing document calls the group the Order of the Star Spangled Banner. Instead, Know Nothings always referred to their organization simply as the "Order," the "Council," or (in their early days) the "Wigwam." It is possible that the group practiced such secrecy that even internal documents never used the real name. The only "document" I know of that uses this name is the apparently genuine exposé by the Philadelphia *Pennsylvanian*, reprinted in the New York *Herald*, Sept. 25, 1854.

2. Thomas R. Whitney, *A Defence of the American Policy* (New York, 1856), 280–81; Charles B. Allen to the Editor of the Newport *News*, in New York *Herald*, July 29, 1855.

3. Thomas J. Curran, "The Know Nothings of New York" (Ph.D. diss., Columbia University, 1963), 88–89; David H. Bennett, *The Party of Fear: From Nativist Movements to the New Right in American History* (Chapel Hill: Univ. of North Carolina Press, 1988), 111.

"plan of political action, like that of the Order of United Americans, contemplated the *control* rather than the *making* of nominations." In this regard, then, there was no significant difference between the two organizations, because neither sought to make independent nominations. On the other hand, Whitney had for some time been calling for the various nativist societies to merge under the auspices of the OUA, but had no success. Perhaps he and other OUA leaders felt that the OSSB would serve as a neutral organization in which all nativists could unite. The Know Nothings did eventually assume the independent political role that the OUA had opposed, but this, which occurred later, does not seem to have motivated the OUA takeover of the OSSB.[4]

When OUA infiltrators ousted Allen from the OSSB's presidency they replaced him with James W. Barker, a successful New York merchant who had been active in Whig politics. Allen and his supporters then seceded, though an *entente cordial* seems to have existed under which the Allen group continued to proselytize north and east of New York, while the OUA group concentrated on the south and west. Allen's group called its chapters "wigwams" or "lodges," while those under Barker's control were known as "councils." Recruitment continued in this bipartite manner until May of 1854, when an apparent reconciliation reunited the OSSB.[5]

At some point between May 1853 and May 1854 the OSSB became known as the "Know Nothings." The precise origin of this term is a mystery, but it apparently made its public debut in November 1853. At that time, the New York *Tribune* reported that the Whig candidate for New York district attorney had lost "through the instrumentality of a mongrel ticket termed the '*Know-Nothing.*' . . . This ticket," continued the *Tribune*, "is the work of the managers of a secret organization growing out of the Order of United Americans, but ostensibly disconnected therefrom." A few days later the *Tribune* again mentioned "the Know-Nothing organization," calling it "but a new dodge of protean nativism."[6] Neither reference mentions the now universal belief that the term "Know Nothing" derived from members' practice of feigning ignorance when queried about the organization. Nor does it appear that *Tribune* editor Horace Greeley coined the term. The *Tribune*'s use of the phrase suggests that rather than having concocted the term itself, the newspaper was simply reporting what had been relayed by some outside source.

If Greeley did not create the term, how did the OSSB become known as the Know Nothings? Perhaps the ticket mentioned by the *Tribune* had been

4. Whitney, *Defence of the American Policy*, 282–83; Charles B. Allen to the Editor of the Newport *News*, in New York *Herald*, July 29, 1855; Vivus Smith to William H. Seward, Sept. 4, 1854, Seward Papers, UR.

5. Charles Deshler to R. M. Guilford, Jan. 20, 1855, Deshler Papers, Rutgers University; Address of James W. Barker to the Know Nothing convention in Syracuse, Feb. 13, 1855, in New York *Times*, March 8, 1855; Anna Ella Carroll, *The Great American Battle* (New York, 1856), 269–70; "James W. Barker," *Dictionary of American Biography* (New York: Charles Scribner's Sons, 1943), I, p. 605.

6. New York *Tribune*, Nov. 10, 16, 1853.

nicknamed the "Know Nothing" ticket by its organizers. Local electoral tickets often assumed strange labels. Sometimes these names referred to the meeting which had formed the ticket (such as Bishop John Hughes's "Carroll Hall" ticket of 1841, created at an auditorium of that name). Other groups, such as the Whigs, adopted names used as slurs by their enemies. Perhaps poll watchers coined the term during the November 1853 New York City election, because they could not discover the source of the OSSB ballots. However the appellation originated, the influence of the *Tribune*, the most widely read newspaper in the nation, made it stick. From this point onward, the OSSB was referred to as the "Know Nothings," and the members initially did little to discourage the term's use.

Know Nothing lodges could be created in two ways. Occasionally, those interested in starting a lodge would venture to the residence of the head of the Order in their state and request a charter in person. If the state president agreed, a fee was paid, the applicant initiated, and a charter issued. The more common procedure, however, involved a traveling deputy of the state leader. In Canandaigua, New York, on June 15, 1854, for example, with eight prospective members present, a "Mr. Kennedy of New York administered the initiatory obligation" to create the Canandaigua "council." The group then chose officers, and "advanced to Mr. Kennedy the sum of $25, it being the amount understood to be requisite to secure a charter."[7] Thus, either personally or through deputies, the head of the Order in a given state exercised complete control over the creation of councils. In this way he could almost single-handedly determine who would run the lodges in his state.

Once a lodge had been formed, the new Know Nothings would begin the search for a secure meeting place. Finding one was vital, because members sought to hide both their identity and the subject of their meetings from the public. The Canandaigua Know Nothings made an agreement with the Odd Fellows (another nineteenth-century fraternal organization) to rent their hall. When Sub-Council 5 in East Boston was forced to leave its original meeting

7. Ethan Allen Council Minute Book, June 15, 1854, Ontario County Historical Society. This is the only extant minute book that describes the founding of a Know Nothing lodge. The creation of the organization discussed by Gerald G. Eggert, " 'Seeing Sam': The Know Nothing Episode in Harrisburg," *Pennsylvania Magazine of History and Biography* 111 (1987): 305–40, has not been considered here, because what Eggert describes was not a Know Nothing lodge, but that of a rival and less influential group known as the Guard of Liberty. Founded by a widely read novelist of the day known as Ned Buntline (a pseudonym for C. J. Z. Judson), the Guard of Liberty began in Maine and operated primarily in New England. Modeling itself on a military company (it used military names and terms in carrying out its business), the Guard of Liberty was apparently organized to counterbalance the growing number of immigrant militia units. Buntline, never a modest man, later claimed that he created the Know Nothings and invented their name, but real Know Nothings knew better. "Buntline had no more to do with its [the Know Nothings'] origins than the man in the moon," asserted one Massachusetts nativist. When the Know Nothings emerged as the most successful nativist fraternal order, the Guard of Liberty adapted itself to resemble their popular rivals. Boston *Know Nothing* in Harrisburg *Herald*, May 14, 1855 (quotation); Cleveland *Express*, July 1, 1854.

place, the members arranged to use the OUA's hall. Know Nothings found it especially difficult to maintain their secrecy in small towns, because townspeople became curious when too many citizens congregated for some unannounced reason. Know Nothing councils in Indiana solved this problem by meeting in cornfields, and delegates to an early Know Nothing convention deflected curiosity by pretending that they were gathering for a temperance convention.[8]

With a meeting place secured, the recruitment and initiation of new members could begin. Members of a council nominated prospective candidates for admission to the Order. In the Canandaigua lodge (the only one whose minutes record all the details of the selection process) a committee assigned at each meeting would investigate the proposed candidates. At the following meeting this committee would report whether the candidates qualified for membership and sympathized with the principles and objects of the Order. To qualify for membership, a candidate had to "be twenty-one years of age, . . . believe in the existence of a Supreme Being, as the Creator and Preserver of the universe; . . . be a native born citizen, a Protestant, born of Protestant parents, reared under Protestant influence, and not united in marriage with a Roman Catholic."[9] The candidates had to believe in resisting "the insidious policy of the Church of Rome, and all other foreign influences against the institutions of our country, by placing in all offices in the gift of the people, whether by election or appointment, none but native-born Protestant citizens."[10] The investigating committee had to determine whether the candidate met these criteria of birth and belief without letting him know that he was being considered for admission, and without any of the secrets of the Order or its very existence being revealed.[11] If the committee reported favorably on a candidate, the council as a whole would vote. In most places, five or more negative votes disqualified a candidate from membership. In many states, a

8. Ethan Allen Council Minute Book, June 17, 1854, Ontario County Historical Society; Sub-Council 5 Minute Book, April 25, 1855, Solomon B. Morse, Jr. Papers, MHS; Carl F. Brand, "The History of the Know Nothing Party in Indiana," *Indiana Magazine of History* 18 (1922): 74; R. S. Stanton to John G. Davis, Oct. 21, 1854, Davis Papers, IndHS; Ronald F. Matthias, "The Know Nothing Movement in Iowa" (Ph.D. diss., University of Chicago, 1965), 1–2.

9. *Constitution of the S[tate]. C[ouncil]. of the State of Connecticut. Adopted Sept. 7, 1854* (Hartford, 1854), Connecticut State Library. The requirements in some localities differed slightly. Lodges in New York and Massachusetts, for example, initially required not only that the candidate be native-born but that his parents and one set of grandparents also be American natives as well. An exception would be made if the candidate's parents or grandparents had fought against the British in the American Revolution. On the other hand, Indiana Know Nothings as of May 1855 were not even required to be native-born (although at least half of the members of each council had to be born in the United States), as long as they were Protestants.

10. *Constitution of the S.C. of the State of Connecticut. Adopted Sept. 7, 1854.*

11. Some lodges ignored these stringent guidelines for secrecy during recruitment. In Lancaster, Pennsylvania, lodge leaders made excursions to the countryside to round up perspective members, then brought them back to Lancaster to be initiated *en masse*. *Know-Nothingism in Lancaster County* (Lancaster, Penn., 1856), 11.

rejected candidate could not reapply for admission, even to a different council, for six months.[12]

If the candidate passed these tests, he was eligible for initiation. Not all
those elected actually joined (the proportion accepting membership in Canandaigua ranged from two-thirds when the lodge was first formed to one-third
by August 1854), but those who did took part in an elaborate ritual. First,
the initiate entered the anteroom of the council's meeting place, where he
would be asked if he believed in a "Supreme Being." If he answered affirma-
tively, the questioner then asked him to swear that he would never reveal
anything else that transpired in the lodge. Once this oath had been taken, he
would be asked if he was at least twenty-one years of age, if he and his
parents were Protestants, if he was married to a Roman Catholic, and if he
would use his influence and vote to place only native-born Americans in
office, "to the exclusion of all foreigners and aliens, and Roman Catholics in
particular, without regard to party predilections." If he answered all these
questions satisfactorily, he would then receive permission to enter the inner
sanctum of the council. Here he would swear to abide by the majority
decision of the council and other procedural matters, and would learn the
passwords, grips, signals, codes, and signs of the Order. This comprised
initiation into the "first degree" of the Order. After three weeks, a first-
degree member could apply for admission to the second degree, which was
voted upon by those already holding that status. Only second-degree members could hold leadership positions within the council, or be nominated by
the council for public office.[13]

Despite their fraternal innovations and elaborate initiation ritual, the Know
Nothings probably would have remained an obscure organization had not
several key events occurred at this point which increased the appeal of
nativism. The revival of educational controversies provided the initial impetus
for the resurgence of anti-Catholicism. The First Plenary Council of American
Catholic Bishops, which met in Baltimore in 1852, called American public
schools irreligious and decreed that Catholics should instead educate their
children in parochial schools.[14] This led Catholic leaders to renew their demand, first made in the 1840s, that the states finance Catholic schools.

The school controversies of the 1840s had been confined primarily to New
York and Philadelphia, but because immigration had increased so dramatically in the ensuing decade, the school funding debate affected dozens of
northern communities by 1854. In Cincinnati the school question elicited such

12. Although women could not join Know Nothing lodges, they established female auxilia-
ries to promote the nativist cause. See Jean Gould Hales, "Co-Laborers in the Cause: Women in
the Ante-Bellum Nativist Movement," *Civil War History* 25 (1979): 119–38; David H. Bennett,
"Women in the Nativist Movement," in Carol V. R. George, ed., *Remember the Ladies* (Syracuse: Syracuse Univ. Press, 1975), 71–89.

13. *Rituals of the First and Second Degree*, WHS.

14. *The Catholic Encyclopedia* (New York: Encyclopedia Press, 1907), II, pp. 235–36.

excitement that it became, in the words of one newspaper, the "all-absorbing topic" of the city's spring 1853 election. Three tickets, representing varying degrees of opposition to splitting the school fund to pay for Catholic schools, appeared by election day, including a "Free School" ticket headed by James D. Taylor, editor of the nativist Cincinnati *Times*. The existence of two additional tickets opposing a division of the school fund doomed Taylor's candidacy, but the Cincinnati election proved that the school issue could elicit as much excitement among voters as traditional political issues. When Detroit's bishop petitioned for a share of the school funds that same spring, opponents there united and succeeded in electing an independent ticket composed of Democrats and Whigs opposed to state funding for parochial education.[15] By 1854 nearly every northern state had experienced some sort of school funding controversy. "Are American Protestants to be taxed for the purpose of nourishing Romish vipers?" asked the Philadelphia *Sun* as the Pennsylvania legislature debated a Catholic petition on this issue. The Indiana legislature passed a bill prohibiting expenditures for parochial schools, while the New York legislature almost enacted a similar law. By the mid-1850s, even medium-size towns such as York, Pennsylvania, and Bordentown, New Jersey, contained enough immigrants to become embroiled in school controversies.[16]

As was the case in 1844, the school question involved not only the funding of parochial schools but the use of the Bible in the classroom. The most notorious Bible controversy occurred in Ellsworth, Maine. In the autumn of 1853 the new local priest, John Bapst, incurred the wrath of Protestants after telling Catholic children not to participate in school Bible readings. The burning of the school's Bibles by a group of Catholic vandals exacerbated Protestant outrage. Antipathy toward Bapst grew so intense that his superiors eventually transferred him to Bangor, and a town meeting celebrating his departure warned him never to return. When Bapst did visit a few months later, a mob tarred and feathered him, and then rode him out of town on a rail. Not all communities responded so violently to Bible controversies, but the situation in Ellsworth received national publicity even before the assault on Bapst. Such disputes convinced a growing number of Americans that Catholics were attempting "to overthrow and demolish our Common Schools," and increased the appeal of anti-Catholic organizations such as the Know Nothings.[17]

15. William E. Gienapp, *The Origins of the Republican Party, 1852–1856* (New York: Oxford Univ. Press, 1987), 63 (quotation); Ronald P. Formisano, *The Birth of Mass Political Parties: Michigan, 1827–1861* (Princeton: Princeton Univ. Press, 1971), 223–29.

16. Philadelphia *Sun*, Feb. 10, 1854; Pottsville *Miner's Journal*, April 22, May 14, 21, 1854; Cincinnati *Dollar Times*, Dec. 22, 1853, Jan. 11, 1855 (on Indiana); Harrisburg *Herald*, Aug. 18, 1854; J. Kelly and A. W. McClure, *The School Question; A Correspondence between Rev. J. Kelly . . . and Rev. A. W. McClure, Jersey City* (New York, 1853); James N. Sykes [a member of Boston Know Nothing lodge number 5], *Common vs. Catholic Schools. A Discourse Delivered . . . Nov. 24, 1853* (Boston, 1853); Ray A. Billington, *The Protestant Crusade, 1800–1860: A Study of the Origins of American Nativism* (Chicago: Quadrangle Books, 1938), 292–93.

17. H. S. Randall, *Decision . . . on the Right to Compel Catholic Children to Attend Prayers, and to Read or Commit Portions of the Bible, as School Exercises* (n.p., [1853]); George

The introduction of a third controversy, the debate over Catholic church property, further increased antipathy toward Catholics. In most Protestant denominations, a board of trustees elected by the congregation held the title to the church and the property on which it sat. The deed to Catholic church property, however, usually named the bishop as the owner. The only exceptions tended to occur among congregations composed of minority immigrant groups. For instance, French Catholic immigrants who objected to joining a primarily Irish Catholic congregation might buy their own plot of land and build their own church. "In particular, the emigrants . . . from Germany" tended to establish separate congregations, reported a Vatican official, because they "do not have a high regard for the Irish, whom they accuse of wishing to dominate them." The predominantly Irish-born bishops still assigned priests to these parishes, but if the congregation did not approve of the choice, the board of trustees might retaliate by refusing to pay him. While these disputes were usually settled amicably, two cases in which neither side would compromise gained widespread public attention in the 1850s.[18]

The first concerned the Church of the Holy Trinity in Philadelphia. A dispute dating back to the 1790s was revived in 1850 when the trustees refused to pay the salary of their priest. The trustees took their battle to the courts and initially won, but in March 1854 the Pennsylvania Supreme Court overturned the decision and awarded the church property to Bishop John N. Neumann.[19] The second and more publicized church property case involved St. Louis' Church in Buffalo. The trustees of this predominantly German church had been left to run their own affairs until 1847, when John Timon became the first bishop of Buffalo. From that point onward, Timon and the trustees of St. Louis' fought constantly, especially over the selection of their priest and the enlargement of the church. When Timon also began to have trouble with a German congregation in Rochester, Archbishop John Hughes arranged to have a bill introduced in the New York legislature that would give bishops title to all Catholic church property in the state.[20]

The proposal caused immediate outrage, especially among militantly Protestant New Yorkers. One could not believe the bill received serious consider-

---

B. Cheever, *The Right of the Bible in Our Public Schools* (New York, 1854); Richard H. Dana, Jr., *The Bible in Schools. Argument of Richard H. Dana, Jr.* (Boston, n.d.); Allan R. Whitmore, "Portrait of a Maine 'Know-Nothing': William H. Chaney," *Maine Historical Society Quarterly* 14 (1974): 31–42; Cincinnati *Dollar Times*, May 19 (quotation), Nov. 24, 1853; Boston *Know Nothing*, May 6, 1854; Cleveland *Leader*, Oct. 30, 1854; John W. Pratt, *Religion, Politics, and Diversity: The Church-State Theme in New York History* (Ithaca: Cornell Univ. Press, 1967), 192.

18. Sacred Congregation of Propaganda to Gaetano Bedini, April 5, 1853, quoted in James F. Connelly, *The Visit of Archbishop Gaetano Bedini to the United States of America (June 1853-February 1854)* (Rome, 1960), 14.

19. Connelly, *Bedini*, 24–25 n.; Patrick J. Dignan, *A History of the Legal Incorporation of Catholic Church Property in the United States (1784–1932)* (Washington: Catholic Univ. Press, 1933), 188–89, 199–200; Patrick W. Carey, *People, Priests, and Prelates: Ecclesiastical Democracy and the Tensions of Trusteeism* (Notre Dame: Notre Dame Univ. Press, 1987), 162, 170–71.

20. Dignan, *Catholic Church Property*, 180–88; Connelly, *Bedini*, 50–61.

ation at Albany, because it "would virtually establish Popery in this State." "I am afraid of the Roman Catholic influence," admitted another Protestant as the legislature debated the proposal in 1852, because "while the Episcopal Church is denied any relief from its burdens, . . . the Romanists are legislating all the church property into the hands of the bishops. I expect that we shall have to get up a party in politics composed of Evangelical Christians & others opposed to . . . the encroachments of the Romanists and their sympathisers." The bill failed to pass in 1852, but when re-introduced in 1853, it gained even more publicity and attention. One newspaper asserted that the proposed law represented "the first artful . . . advance on the part of the clergy" to attain despotic power. The bill again failed, but with church property, school funding, and Bible controversies erupting throughout the North, it seemed plausible to an increasing number of Protestants that Americans needed to take concrete steps to resist the new assertiveness of the Catholic Church.[21]

In an attempt to settle these trusteeship disputes, the Vatican sent Papal Nuncio Gaetano Bedini to visit the schismatic parishes. Bedini, however, could not have been more ill-equipped to handle the American situation. As commissary extraordinary at Bologna in 1849, Bedini had essentially functioned as military governor, and his role in suppressing the revolutionary uprisings in that part of the Papal States had earned him a reputation as a ruthless reactionary. Bedini had never dealt with Catholic issues in a predominantly Protestant country, and he lacked the tact necessary to strengthen American Catholicism without alarming sensitive Protestants. Nonetheless, Bedini initially attracted little attention when he arrived in America. He went first to Washington, where he delivered a note from the pope to President Franklin Pierce, and then on to Philadelphia and eventually Buffalo. Although he failed to settle either dispute, he continued to tour the country, officiating at Catholic ceremonies and visiting monasteries and seminaries throughout North America.[22]

Although the first few months of his tour proceeded without incident, Bedini met with increasing protest at each successive stop as his past caught up with him. These demonstrations were staged primarily by the "Exiles of '48," refugees who had come to America after the failed revolutions of 1848. Unlike native-born Americans, these immigrants knew of Bedini's reputation and still harbored resentment over the role that the Catholic Church had played in suppressing their short-lived republics. Newspapers published by these exiled revolutionaries, such as Friedrich Hassaurek's Cincinnati *Hochwächter* and G. F. Secchi de Casali's New York *Crusader*, printed vicious indictments of Bedini. These immigrants began taunting Bedini at each stop on his tour, and

21. Maunsell Van Rensselaer to James W. Beekman, Feb. 28, 1852, William H. Neilson to Beekman, March 9, 1852, Beekman Family Papers, NYHS; unidentified New York newspaper quoted in Cincinnati *Dollar Times*, July 14, 1853; George Babcock, *Remarks of Mr. Babcock, of Erie, on the Roman Catholic Church Property Bill: In the Senate, June 24, 1853, Upon the Motion to Strike Out the Enacting Clause of the Bill* (Albany, 1853).

22. Connelly, *Bedini*, 1–69.

Archbishop Hughes recognized that "the renegade Italians and the infidel Germans have made all the trouble."[23]

The lectures of Alessandro Gavazzi provided a second source from which Americans could learn the "truth" about Bedini. Gavazzi, a Barnabite friar from Bologna, had repudiated the pope when the pontiff refused to support the unification of Italy, and then became the chaplain of Giuseppe Garibaldi's revolutionary army. After the Roman republic collapsed, Gavazzi traveled to England, where he became a popular anti-Catholic lecturer, and in 1853 the American and Foreign Christian Union invited Gavazzi to undertake a speaking tour in America. Gavazzi's arrival, coinciding as it did with that of Bedini, proved ideal for nativists. Gavazzi reported that Bedini had been known in Italy as "The Butcher of Bologna" for his harsh treatment of the revolutionaries, and that his cruelest act had been to order the execution of Ugo Bassi, the beloved revolutionary priest who had preceded Gavazzi as Garibaldi's chaplain.[24]

Through Gavazzi and the immigrant press, Bedini's reputation eventually filtered into mainstream American newspapers. One reported that Bedini "is a known enemy of Republican principles," and a Boston paper called him one of the "bloodiest butchers of Italian patriots." By December 1853, native-born Americans joined with immigrants in the angry crowds that confronted Bedini at each stop on his tour. Violence marred Bedini's appearances in New York, Wheeling, Philadelphia, Boston, Baltimore, and Richmond, and a full-scale riot greeted the Nuncio in Cincinnati.[25]

Bedini's visit would have elicited far less excitement had he not lingered so long in America. Bedini completed his negotiations with the trustees in Philadelphia and Buffalo within weeks of his arrival, and he was scheduled to go to Brazil when he concluded these meetings. Yet the Nuncio stayed in the United States for more than half a year. Many Americans thought that there was a secret motive behind the extension of Bedini's visit. A New York newspaper suggested that Bedini's true objective had been to organize Catholics so that they could reverse their defeats in the recent school controversies. One Democrat, imagining equally sinister goals, believed that Bedini "intended to form amongst [Catholics] an organization so perfect that . . . the whole Catholic body" will "throw its weight into one scale in all our future

23. Hughes to Anthony Blanc, Feb. 3, 1854, Bedini to Purcell, Oct. 22, 1853, Blanc to Purcell, Jan. 12, 1854, University of Notre Dame Archives; Cincinnati *Hochwächter* in Connelly, *Bedini*, 98–100; New York *Crusader* in Harrisburg *Herald*, Sept. 12, 1854.

24. Alessandro Gavazzi, *The Lectures Complete of Father Gavazzi* (New York, 1854); Robert Sylvain, *Alessandro Gavazzi: Garibaldien, Clerc, Prédicant des Deux Mondes*, 2 vols. (Quebec: Le Centre Pédagogique, 1962), II, pp. 287–442; D. G. Paz, *The Priesthoods and Apostasies of Pierce Connelly: A Study of Victorian Conversion and Anticatholicism* (Lewiston, N.Y.: Edwin Mellen, 1986), 14–18; Billington, *Protestant Crusade*, 264–70.

25. Connelly, *Bedini*, 96–132 (quotation p. 132); Boston *Commonwealth* quoted in William G. Bean, "Party Transformation in Massachusetts with Special Reference to the Antecedents of Republicanism, 1848–1860" (Ph.D. diss., Harvard University, 1922), 226; Pottsville *Miner's Journal*, Jan. 28, 1854; Billington, *Protestant Crusade*, 302–3.

elections." Others would later state that Bedini's visit had been meant to pave the way for the pope's relocation to America.[26]

Even some Catholics thought Bedini possessed secret orders. Bishop Francis P. Kenrick, for example, concluded that Bedini had never intended to sail for Brazil. Kenrick believed that Bedini would stay in America as a tourist until the Pierce administration requested a papal representative in the United States, a position Bedini would then fill himself. Many Democrats had been pressing for stronger ties between the United States and the Papal States, a fact not unknown to Kenrick and Americans generally. Whatever the case, hostility to Bedini became so great that Catholic officials feared for his life, and in early February 1854 the Nuncio surreptitiously boarded a ship in New York harbor and sailed back to Europe. Bedini's visit, concluded Kenrick, had been "a blunder from every point of view."[27]

Among other things, Bedini's hostile reception demonstrated the extent to which apostate priests such as Gavazzi could influence Protestant audiences. After all, reasoned the American public, who would know more about the evils of Catholicism than a former prelate? "The horrors of the inquisition suddenly rushed into my mind," reported a Rhode Islander after having witnessed one of Gavazzi's detailed and convincing lectures on that subject. Even more skilled than Gavazzi at inflaming anti-Catholic sentiment was a street preacher named John Orr. Known to the public as "Angel Gabriel," Orr's exhortations to resist Romanism so affected a Chelsea, Massachusetts, crowd that at the conclusion of his harangue, Orr's audience smashed the windows of the neighborhood's Catholic church and tore down its cross.[28]

While reactions of this magnitude occurred infrequently, small-scale violence often broke out at these lectures, especially when Catholics heckled a speaker. To prevent this, many cities threatened street preachers with arrest if they incited violence, and others simply refused to license anti-Catholic lecturers. But such efforts only increased anti-Catholicism, by convincing many Protestants that Catholics held such sway over politicians that the public expression of Protestant values would soon be illegal. Two cases illustrate this point. Public protest in Pittsburgh over the arrest of anti-Catholic street preacher Joe Barker grew so intense that in 1850 voters elected Barker mayor while he was still in jail! Barker accomplished little in office, but his election demonstrated the lengths to which angered Protestants would go to defend critics of Catholicism. When New York City officials denied Daniel Parsons a

26. New York *Observer* in Pottsville *Miner's Journal*, March 18, 1854; C. Shaler to William Marcy, Jan. 7, 1854, Marcy Papers, LC; Albany *State Register*, June 26, 1855; Connelly, *Bedini*, 141–44; Marcellus Ells to Hamilton Fish, Feb. 14, 1854, Fish Papers, LC.

27. Kenrick cited in Connelly, *Bedini*, 21; Kenrick to Bishop John Purcell, Feb. 9, 1854 (quotation), University of Notre Dame Archives; Loretta Clare Feiertag, *American Public Opinion on the Diplomatic Relations between the United States and the Papal States (1847–1867)* (Washington: Catholic Univ. Press, 1933), 72–85.

28. Letter from Newport, Rhode Island, in Cincinnati *Dollar Times*, Oct. 6, 1853; Billington, *Protestant Crusade*, 305–6; Cleveland *Express*, Nov. 9, 1854.

license to speak in December 1853, he lectured anyway and was arrested. Angry New Yorkers held a protest rally in City Hall Park and chose none other than Know Nothing leader James Barker to preside over the meeting. Barker's participation demonstrates that the Know Nothings not only took advantage of the existing anti-Catholicism but actively helped inflame it as well.[29]

Political events exacerbated the anti-Catholicism fanned by these religious controversies. Referring to Winfield Scott's attempt to woo immigrant voters in the presidential campaign of 1852, a nativist newspaper promised that the Know Nothings would "teach American Demagogues that the time has come for them to cease their everlasting and stereotype prattle of 'the rich Irish brogue and sweet German accent.' " Native-born citizens deemed Scott's remark to be merely the most famous example of an all too common trend.[30]

President Pierce's appointment of James Campbell as postmaster general convinced even more Americans that politicians would stoop to any level to capture immigrant votes. Campbell, a Philadelphia Catholic, had been the only unsuccessful Democratic candidate in Pennsylvania's 1851 state-wide races, and Catholics blamed his defeat on nativism within the Democracy. Governor William Bigler sought to appease Catholics by appointing Campbell as his secretary of state, but Pennsylvania Protestants objected, claiming that Campbell had been offered the post solely because he was Catholic. When Pierce chose Campbell for his cabinet a year later, Protestant wrath increased. Campbell's rapid rise to power especially infuriated nativist Democrats, because they felt that Catholic gains in the party hierarchy came at the expense of Protestants. "This Irish influence must & will be put down," insisted one angry Democrat. Even other immigrant groups within the Democratic party were jealous of the preference given to the Irish. "If Pierce has sold himself to the Irish Catholics," commented a bitter German Democrat, "it is but proper that the German Protestants and Anti-Papists should show their hands and proclaim openly their hostility to Jesuitism in church and state."[31]

Campbell's appointment to any cabinet post would have upset nativists, but because the postmaster general controlled so much patronage, the decision to place him at the head of the Post Office Department aroused particularly bitter animosity. Political leaders dispensed post office patronage jobs to the party faithful, and these posts often represented a first step up the party ladder. When party leaders passed over native-born party members to give

29. Michael F. Holt, *Forging a Majority: The Formation of the Republican Party in Pittsburgh, 1848–1860* (New Haven: Yale Univ. Press, 1969), 110–12; Curran, "Know Nothings of New York," 95–96; Cincinnati *Dollar Times*, Dec. 22, 1853.

30. Sag Harbor *Corrector*, Nov. 4, 1854, quoted in Gienapp, *Origins of the Republican Party*, 98.

31. Alexander McClure, *Old Time Notes of Pennsylvania*, 2 vols. (Philadelphia, 1905), I, pp. 191–93; Peter Mager to William Bigler, June 17, 1853, Bigler Papers, HSP; Francis Grund to Edmund Burke, Aug. 17, 1853, Burke Papers, LC.

patronage positions to immigrants, natives lost not only a job but a chance for advancement within the party. A Pennsylvania newspaper that sympathized with the Know Nothings reflected this frustration, stating that the post office "should never have been given into the hands of a Jesuit who appoints his followers in every little country office." Referring to Campbell, an Ohioan admitted that he had always believed it to be "dangerous to proscribe men for religious opinion." But the "alarming" fact that so many Catholics "have been working themselves into our offices of government" had altered his views on this subject. He still found religious proscription dangerous, but believed it "more dangerous to permit our government to fall into the hands of romanists whose religion stands paramount to all other considerations & who make government and everything else subserve the interests of the [Catholic] church." Looking back years later, Pennsylvania politician Alexander Mc-Clure felt that the appointment of Campbell to a position "that controlled tens of thousands of appointments" contributed to the rise of the Know Nothings by sending disappointed office-seekers into their ranks. Many contemporaries agreed, stating that Campbell specifically—or the general feeling that immigrants received an unfair preponderance of the patronage—had aggravated American anti-Catholicism and aided Know Nothing recruiters.[32]

The visit of Archbishop Bedini, the appointment of Postmaster Campbell, and the emergence of controversies over school funding, school Bible reading, and Catholic church property all helped the Know Nothings attract members. But by May of 1854, after these controversies had been raging for months, the Know Nothings had recruited 50,000 members at most.[33] With this many devotees, the Order could boast that it had grown larger than any previous nativist organization, yet its membership was still limited to urban and suburban areas. When a state-wide convention of New York's fifty-four councils met in May, every officer elected was from New York City, indicating that

32. Wilkes Barre *Record of the Times*, July 5, 1854; Sidney Maxwell Diary, Sept. 24, 1854, Cincinnati Historical Society; McClure, *Old Time Notes*, I, p. 193; M. L. Rogers to Bigler, Aug. 21, 1854, E. A. Penniman to Bigler, June 18, 1854, Henry M. Phillips to Bigler, June 11, 1854, Charles Frailey to Bigler, June 14, 1854, Bigler Papers, HSP; Johnstown *Cambria Tribune*, June 17, 1854. A statistical analysis of customhouse appointments has revealed that while the Irish in no way dominated the patronage at this time, Pierce *had* appointed far more of them (about twice as many) to these highly prized patronage positions than had any previous administration. See Leonard Tabachnik, "Political Patronage and Ethnic Groups: Foreign-born in the United States Customhouse Service, 1821–1861," in Robert P. Swierenga, ed., *Beyond the Civil War Synthesis* (Westport, Conn.: Greenwood Press, 1975), 249, 252.

33. My membership figure is an estimate. Know Nothing president James Barker claimed that there were only 10,000 members in May but his figure must be low. Barker probably made this claim in order to take credit for the Order's growth after he became president of the reunited Order in May. Sub-Council 5 in Boston had 800 members by February 1854, and assuming that the other four councils had similar membership, that would make 4000 members in Massachusetts alone at this time. Because there were probably that many members in Philadelphia as well, and more in New York City, Barker's claim of fewer than 10,000 members in May 1854 cannot be true. New York *Times*, March 8 (Barker), 16 ("Vindex"), 1855.

most lodges were located there. A sympathetic Pennsylvania newspaper like-wise asserted at the end of May that there were enough Know Nothings "in all our major cities" to control municipal elections, but said nothing of their influence in the countryside. Private correspondence mentioning the Know Nothings at this time also emanated almost exclusively from city-dwellers. "The Native American feeling in the City is very strong," boasted a New York City Know Nothing about their growing influence. "I never knew it to be so strong before." A Bostonian agreed that anti-Catholicism had become the dominant topic there, stating that "this Catholic power is felt to be at the North a more dangerous power than the Slave Power and therefore absorbs all other considerations."[34]

It made sense that the initial Know Nothing converts were drawn from urban areas. Because most immigrants settled in large cities, the first protests against them naturally emanated from there. As impoverished newcomers filled American cities, they soon filled city poorhouses and jails as well, generating considerable resentment among natives. City-dwellers also blamed newcomers for increasing crime rates. Asked why her brother carried a gun, a New Yorker replied "why, for the same reason that my husband does—to protect himself against the Catholics." When the Catholic population in city neighborhoods became too numerous, many native-born Protestants moved away because, as one put it, "American citizens do not feel safe" in Catholic neighborhoods. While the foreign-born population of Boston increased 129 percent between 1845 and 1855, the native-born population *declined* by 2 percent, suggesting that some natives fled the city as immigrants arrived. The sheer magnitude of the immigrant influx and resentment over the many ways in which it transformed life in American cities combined to make early Know Nothingism a primarily urban phenomenon.[35]

The economic competition that immigrants posed to native-born workers may have also helped the Know Nothings gain urban adherents. Immigrants affected the urban workplace to an even greater degree than their numbers indicate because immigrant women and children worked more frequently than their native-born counterparts. Thus while immigrants made up less than one-half of the population of New York City, they comprised over two-thirds of its work force. Immigrants were willing to work for lower wages than native-born artisans and laborers, resulting in reduced wages for everyone. One Northerner saw no alternative for native mechanics except "to be borne down, crushed, or driven to western wilds." Former Secretary of State Edward Everett, though no mechanic himself, believed that the Know Nothings

34. Louis Dow Scisco, *Political Nativism in New York State* (New York: Columbia Univ. Press, 1901), 97–99; Johnstown *Cambria Tribune*, May 27, 1854; L. R. Shephard to William Marcy, Jan. 28, 1854, Marcy Papers, LC; E. Winslow to Charles Sumner, May 5, 1854, Sumner Papers, HU.

35. George E. Baker to Seward, April 19, 1855, Seward Papers, UR; E. Winslow to Charles Sumner, May 5, 1854, Sumner Papers, HU; *Abstract of the Census of the Commonwealth of Massachusetts for June 1, 1855* (Boston, 1857), 235.

originated as "a struggle of Native American *Labor* against the foreign rival article. This naturally brought in antagonism to Roman Catholics, the preponderating foreign element . . . being Irish." The economic downturn of 1854 may have convinced workingmen that the dire economic consequences of immigrant job competition had finally been realized and induced them to join the Know Nothings.[36]

It is probably a mistake, however, to ascribe too much importance to economic factors in explaining the rise of the Know Nothings. The recession of 1854 became noticeable at the end of the year, well after Know Nothing membership mushroomed. Furthermore, upswings in American nativism have rarely coincided with economic distress. The first outbreak of nativism in the nineteenth century occurred in 1835, during a period of economic prosperity; when the panic of 1837 struck, organized nativism was on the wane. This economic crisis had ended by 1844, when the next outbreak of political nativism occurred. The brief economic downturn of 1854 was followed by a severe depression in 1857, yet Know Nothingism did not revive. Some historians have attempted to explain these discrepancies by relating Know Nothingism to the general economic dislocations caused by industrialization.[37] But this seems unlikely as well, for while industrialization spread gradually across the country, Know Nothingism emerged almost overnight in mid-1854. Furthermore, while the independence of the Know Nothing councils made them particularly responsive to the concerns of their members, Know Nothing records rarely mention efforts to combat the economic competition of immigrants. A few lodges did make pledges to "buy American."[38] More frequently they made vague promises to "protect American labor," but this seems to be little more than a repetition of the Whig stance on the subject. Furthermore, "buying American" or raising the tariff, while providing protection against competition from abroad, offered no defense against immigrants already in the United States. While there can be no doubt that economic competition led

36. Robert Ernst, *Immigrant Life in New York City, 1825–1863* (New York: Columbia Univ. Press, 1949), 193, 214–17; George W. Morton to Fish, Feb. 27, 1854, Fish Papers, LC; Edward Everett to Mr. Trescot, Oct. 20, 1854, Everett Papers, MHS; Thurlow Weed to E. D. Morgan, July 8, 1854, Weed Papers, UR. The New York *Mirror* called 1854 "the year of punishment" because of the economic hardship. See issues of Nov. 27, 28, 1854, Feb. 22 (quotation) thru 26, 1855.

37. Robert W. Fogel, *Without Consent or Contract: The Rise and Fall of American Slavery* (New York: Norton, 1989), 314, 354–63; Michael F. Holt, "The Politics of Impatience: The Origins of Know Nothingism," *Journal of American History* 60 (1973): 325–30; John R. Mulkern, *The Know-Nothing Party in Massachusetts: The Rise and Fall of a People's Movement* (Boston: Northeastern Univ. Press, 1990), 5.

38. The only significant effort on the part of a Know Nothing lodge to press this issue that I know of is that of Massachusetts lodge 57, which issued a circular on the encouragement of American manufacturing. But this handbill was written by textile magnate Amos A. Lawrence, who undoubtedly had his own interests at heart. Lawrence wrote in January 1855 that he was trying "to inculcate the sentiment that we sh[oul]d give the preference to our own productions" into the Know Nothings, implying that this was not yet an important feature of the group. Circular, and Lawrence to J. N. S. Williams, Jan. 20, 1855, Amos A. Lawrence Papers, MHS.

workingmen to resent immigrants, this economic nativism remained relatively constant throughout the mid-nineteenth century. Economic nativism certainly existed, but it does not explain why Know Nothingism appeared with such suddenness in 1854.

The socio-economic background of Know Nothing lodge members also suggests that economic grievances were not at the heart of the Order's popularity. Historians have previously asserted that the Know Nothings shunned professionals (especially lawyers), and attracted a disproportionate number of young, relatively poor mechanics and artisans, those they claim were most affected by the economic competition of immigrants.[39] However, these conclusions were little more than speculation, either because they were based solely upon the impressionistic accounts of non–Know Nothings, or because the findings—when based on the analysis of lodge records— were not presented with a control group to enable the reader to determine the significance of the information. When occupational data concerning Know Nothing lodge members is compared with random samplings of those eligible for membership in the Order, one actually finds that the Know Nothings attracted an approximately average proportion of both artisans and professionals.

Occupations of East Boston Know Nothings[40]

	Know Nothings		Control Group	
	N		N	
Professionals	6	(1%)	8	(2%)
Merchants & Manufacturers	65	(11%)	38	(11%)
Lower-Status White Collar	54	(9%)	21	(6%)
Skilled Workers	401	(69%)	230	(69%)
Unskilled Laborers	53	(9%)	36	(11%)
TOTALS	579		333	

39. Holt, "The Politics of Impatience," 329; W. J. Rorabaugh, *The Craft Apprentice: From Franklin to the Machine Age in America* (New York: Oxford Univ. Press, 1986), 170; Amy Bridges, *A City in the Republic: Antebellum New York and the Origins of Machine Politics* (Ithaca: Cornell Univ. Press, 1984), 93–94; Gienapp, "Class, Economic Issues, and Northern Voting Behavior in the Realignment of the 1850s," Paper Delivered at Organization of American Historians Convention, St. Louis, April 1989; George H. Haynes, "A Chapter from the Local History of Know Nothingism," *New England Magazine* 21 (1896): 96; Seymour Martin Lipset and Earl Raab, *The Politics of Unreason: Right Wing Extremism in America* (New York: Harper and Row, 1970), 55–57.

40. There are 781 names listed in the East Boston minute book, of which 45 either lived out of town or were illegible. Of the remaining 736, 579 (79%) were located in the city directory, the

Occupations of Worcester (Council #49) Know Nothings[41]

	Know Nothings		Control Group	
	N		N	
Professionals	14	(4%)	17	(5%)
Merchants & Manufacturers	45	(13%)	30	(8%)
Lower-Status White Collar	35	(10%)	39	(11%)
Skilled Workers	212	(61%)	214	(58%)
Unskilled Laborers	26	(8%)	32	(9%)
Farmers	14	(4%)	38	(10%)
TOTALS	346		370	

Occupations of Portland (Lodge # Unknown) Know Nothings[42]

	Know Nothings		Control Group	
	N		N	
Professionals	5	(6%)	10	(2%)
Merchants & Manufacturers	28	(35%)	74	(18%)
Lower-Status White Collar	9	(11%)	36	(9%)
Skilled Workers	30	(38%)	247	(61%)
Unskilled Laborers	7	(9%)	32	(8%)
Farmers	1	(1%)	3	(1%)
TOTALS	80		402	

1855 state census, or the 1850 or 1860 federal census. The control group consists of a random sampling from the 1855 census of East Boston residents eligible for membership in the ward's lodge (male, at least 21 years of age, and born in the United States of native-born parents). The number of residents sampled is equal to about one-fifth of the ward's eligible citizens. See Appendix for a definition of the occupational categories.

41. Of the 433 Know Nothings in this lodge, 44 lived outside of Worcester, and consequently were not included in the sample, nor were the seven whose names were illegible. Of the remaining 382, 346 (91%) were found in either the city directory or the censuses of 1850, 1855, or 1860. The control group consists of a random sampling from the 1855 state census of those Worcester residents eligible for Know Nothing membership (male, at least 21 years of age, and born in the United States of native-born parents). The number of residents sampled is equal to about one-tenth of the city's eligible citizens.

42. Of the 86 Know Nothings in this lodge, 81 (94%) were found in either the city directory or the federal census of 1850. One Know Nothing listed as "retired" was not included on the chart. The control group consists of a random sampling from the 1850 census of those Portland residents eligible for Know Nothing membership (male, at least 21 years of age, and born in the United States). The number of residents sampled is equal to about one-tenth of the city's eligible citizens.

Occupations of Canandaigua, New York, Know Nothings[43]

	Know Nothings		Control Group	
	N		N	
Professionals	16	(7%)	11	(4%)
Merchants	29	(12%)	16	(7%)
Lower-Status White Collar	27	(12%)	20	(8%)
Skilled Workers	82	(35%)	68	(28%)
Unskilled Laborers	17	(7%)	33	(13%)
Farmers	61	(26%)	94	(38%)
Gentlemen	2	(1%)	3	(1%)
TOTALS	234		245	

These statistics contradict the widely held belief that the Know Nothings were an organization disproportionately dominated by workingmen. Working-men outnumbered other occupational groups within Know Nothing lodges, but they outnumbered other workers in the general population as well. In most cases, the Know Nothings also attracted an average proportion of profes-sionals. The Know Nothings did, however, attract a disproportionately high number of merchants and manufacturers (primarily the former). In addition, the proportion of manual workers (artisans, unskilled laborers, and farmers) in the Know Nothing lodges is in no instance greater than that in the general population. In fact, in three of four cases it is significantly *smaller*. Thus, it appears that the Know Nothings constituted no more of a workingman's party than the other political organizations.

However, the Know Nothings *did* consistently fail to attract an average proportion of farmers. This, according to some historians, indicates that the Order's nativist message held little appeal for country-dwellers whose jobs were not threatened by immigrants.[44] Such reasoning, however, does not withstand close scrutiny. For example, farmers *did* face immigrant competi-tion, as the tens of thousands of immigrant farmers streaming into the west produced grain that competed with that cultivated in the east. In addition, the Know Nothings often captured their largest electoral majorities in rural

43. Of the 379 Know Nothings in this lodge, at least 116 lived outside of Canandaigua. These outsiders were not included in the sample so that a reliable control group could be created. Of the remaining 263, 234 (89%) were found in either the census of 1850, 1855, or 1860, or had their occupation identified in the lodge minute book. Because the percentage of the population engaged in farming seems to have declined significantly between 1850 and 1860, I constructed a control group consisting of an equal proportion of residents from the 1850 and 1860 federal censuses, in order to approximate the town's occupational characteristics at mid-decade when the lodge was created. The samplings consisted of those residents eligible for Know Nothing member-ship (male, at least 21 years of age, and born in the United States of native-born parents). The number of residents sampled is equal to about one-fifth of the town's eligible citizens.

44. John R. Mulkern, "Western Massachusetts in the Know Nothing Years: An Analysis of Voting Patterns," *Historical Journal of Western Massachusetts* 8 (1980): 14–25.

farming counties, such as Cattaraugus and Chatauqua in New York, and Elk and Jefferson in Pennsylvania. Finally, the fact that the Know Nothings do not seem to have attracted disproportionate support from manual workers also implies that such factors do not account for the lack of farmers in Know Nothing lodges. It could be that geography explains the Know Nothings' lack of farmers. Farmers lived further from the center of town than the other members of Know Nothing lodges, and thus may have balked at the travel necessary to attend each meeting. Farmers' long hours, which undoubtedly differed from those of townspeople whose shops closed at a given hour, might also account for the deficit of farmers in Know Nothing lodges.[45] Whatever the case, the fact that the Know Nothings attracted a proportionate number of professionals, merchants, manufacturers, and clerks—whose jobs were not threatened by immigrants—indicates that a lack of job competition from immigrants did not account for the want of farmers in Know Nothing lodges.

As with occupational distribution, an investigation of Know Nothing wealth also contradicts the prevailing stereotype, because the Know Nothings were usually not poorer than other citizens.

Average Value of Property[46]

	Know Nothings	Control Group
East Boston	$3,326	$2,950
Worcester	$1,631	$3,136
Portland	$9,793	$1,162
Canandaigua	$5,175	$4,501

Averages, of course, can be misleading, but a breakdown of the data into wealth categories helps clarify the differences between the Know Nothings and an average group of native-born citizens.

45. The fact that skilled Know Nothing workers outnumber control-group skilled workers only in towns where there was a significant number of farmers suggests that the surplus of skilled workers in Know Nothing lodges may actually be caused by the lack of farmers. In other words, the presence of additional Know Nothing skilled workers (as well as merchants and manufacturers) in these places may be a proportional increase due to the lack of farmers.

46. Because the 1860 census—the first to list the value of both real and personal property—had not yet been indexed for Portland or Worcester at the time this study went to press, the figures for those cities compare real estate only, while those for East Boston and Canandaigua compare both real and personal property. I have used the 1860 census whenever feasible because the value of real estate alone does not reflect a person's living standards as reliably as real and personal estate combined. For the method used to compile these figures, and the reasons that those for Canandaigua may be less accurate than the others (especially for skilled workers), see the Appendix. I found property data from the 1860 census for 279 (38%) of the 736 East Boston Know Nothings, and 115 (43%) of the 263 Canandaigua Know Nothings. I found property data from the 1850 census for 152 (40%) of the 382 Worcester Know Nothings, and 58 (67%) of the 86 Portland Know Nothings.

Percentage of Know Nothings in Various Wealth Categories

| | | *Real and Personal Estate* | | |
| | | *East Boston* | | |
	$0–500	*$501–2500*	*$2501–5000*	*$5001–10,000*	*$10,001+*
Know Nothings	43%	24%	21%	8%	5%
Control Group	46%	18%	16%	16%	5%

| | | *Canandaigua* | | |
	$0–500	*$501–2500*	*$2501–5000*	*$5001–10,000*	*$10,001+*
Know Nothings	21%	30%	21%	16%	12%
Control Group	47%	18%	9%	15%	11%

| | | *Real Estate Only* | | |
| | | *Worcester* | | |
	$0	*$1–2500*	*$2501–5000*	*$5001–20,000*	*$20,001+*
Know Nothings	66%	17%	8%	7%	1%
Control Group	62%	14%	11%	10%	3%

| | | *Portland* | | |
	$0	*$1–2500*	*$2501–5000*	*$5001–20,000*	*$20,001+*
Know Nothings	63%	23%	5%	7%	2%
Control Group	79%	13%	3%	3%	1%

These figures indicate that even in Worcester, where the Know Nothings *were* on average less wealthy than other citizens, most of the difference between the Know Nothings and the control group resulted not from an overwhelming preponderance of poorer Know Nothings, but from the fact that few of the city's wealthiest residents joined the Order. In fact, nearly half the wealth in the Worcester control group was owned by just 3 percent of the citizens. This was also the case in Canandaigua, where one-third fewer citizens with property worth $20,000 or more appeared in the Know Nothing lodge than in the control group, and to some degree too in East Boston, where only one in eight Know Nothings owned property worth more than $5,000, compared with one in five in the control group. In those places, however, the preponderance of Know Nothings in the middle of the economic scale offset the lack of very wealthy citizens. Wealthy Americans joined Know Nothing lodges less frequently than others primarily because many of them considered it undignified to participate with the common rabble in the Order's activities. Upscale organizations such as the Masons catered to their fraternal inclinations. In fact, those wealthy citizens who did become Know Nothings often did so only if they could undergo initiation in their parlors.[47] The smaller proportion of

47. Fillmore to Dorothea Dix, Oct. 30, 1856, in Charles M. Snyder, ed., *The Lady and the President: The Letters of Dorothea Dix and Millard Fillmore* (Lexington: Univ. of Kentucky Press, 1975), 258; Robert C. Winthrop to Everett, Nov. 16, 1854, Everett Papers, MHS.

farmers who joined the Know Nothings also reduced the chances of finding very wealthy citizens in their lodges, because the large pieces of property owned by farmers were generally worth more than the small plots found in town.[48]

That the Know Nothings' surprising wealth was not an anomaly caused by the presence of a few wealthy members is substantiated when the wealth is broken down by occupational category.

Know Nothing Wealth by Occupational Category

| | **Real and Personal Estate** | | | | |
| | *East Boston Merchants and Manufacturers* | | | | |
	$0–500	*$501–2500*	*$2501–5000*	*$5,001–10,000*	*$10,001+*
Know Nothings	13%	18%	31%	15%	23%
Control Group	29%	0%	18%	29%	24%
	East Boston Skilled Workers				
	$0–500	*$501–2500*	*$2501–5000*	*$5001–10,000*	*$10,001+*
Know Nothings	44%	24%	21%	10%	2%
Control Group	45%	25%	16%	14%	0%
	East Boston Unskilled Laborers				
	$0–500	*$501–2500*	*$2501–5000*	*$5001–10,000*	*$10,001+*
Know Nothings	60%	28%	12%	0%	0%
Control Group	73%	18%	9%	0%	0%
	Canandaigua Merchants				
	$0–500	*$501–2500*	*$2501–5000*	*$5001–10,000*	*$10,001+*
Know Nothings	5%	30%	20%	25%	20%
Control Group	0%	33%	17%	22%	28%
	Canandaigua Skilled Workers				
	$0–500	*$501–2500*	*$2501–5000*	*$5001–10,000*	*$10,001+*
Know Nothings	33%	47%	17%	0%	3%
Control Group	61%	22%	9%	6%	2%

48. That the lack of farmers accounts in part for the dearth of very wealthy citizens in Know Nothing lodges is substantiated to some degree by the fact that in East Boston and Portland, with negligible farming populations, the Know Nothings attracted an average proportion of very wealthy citizens.

| | *Canandaigua Farmers* | | | | |
	$0–500	*$501–2500*	*$2501–5000*	*$5001–10,000*	*$10,001+*
Know Nothings	7%	14%	34%	30%	16%
Control Group	35%	16%	11%	25%	13%

| | *Worcester Merchants and Manufacturers*[49] | | | | |
	$0–500	*$501–2500*	*$2501–5000*	*$5001–10,000*	*$10,001+*
Know Nothings	5%	14%	14%	41%	27%
Control Group	7%	14%	10%	31%	38%

| | **Real Estate Only** | | | | |
| | *Worcester Skilled Workers* | | | | |
	$0	*$1–2500*	*$2501–5000*	*$5001–20,000*	*$20,001+*
Know Nothings	74%	20%	6%	1%	0%
Control Group	75%	13%	7%	4%	1%

| | *Portland Merchants and Manufacturers* | | | | |
	$0	*$1–2500*	*$2501–5000*	*$5001–20,000*	*$20,001+*
Know Nothings	47%	21%	11%	16%	5%
Control Group	61%	18%	8%	9%	4%

Thus, despite the prevailing stereotype, it seems that Know Nothings were not usually less wealthy than other citizens. While few of the wealthiest citizens joined their lodges, few of the poorest joined either. Instead, the Know Nothings primarily attracted those in the middle to upper-middle portions of their occupational groups' earnings categories. Know Nothings were not workers who "suffered most from the traumatic economic changes of the decade," but those whose lives were relatively prosperous and whose jobs were relatively secure.[50]

Perhaps the most indelible facet of the Know Nothing stereotype concerns their age. One historian has asserted that "virtually no Know-Nothing was past the age of thirty" and that "the party drew its greatest electoral support from among new voters just turned twenty-one."[51] Yet the four extant Know Nothing minute books suggest that this impression is also erroneous.

49. I have utilized figures from the 1860 census rather than that from 1850 for Worcester merchants and manufacturers because members of this occupational group were much less transient than manual workers, thus enabling me to find most of them even without a census index.

50. Holt, "Politics of Impatience," 329.

51. Rorabaugh, *The Craft Apprentice,* 170.

Average Age of Know Nothings[52]

	Know Nothings	*Control Group*
East Boston	35.5	35.3
Worcester	37.4	36.8
Portland	39.3	39.6
Canandaigua	34.8	38.5

Percentage of Know Nothings in Various Age Categories

	21–30	*31–40*	*41–50*	*51–60*	*61 & Older*
			East Boston		
Know Nothings	38%	33%	20%	7%	1%
Control Group	42%	28%	20%	8%	3%
			Worcester		
Know Nothings	28%	36%	20%	12%	3%
Control Group	38%	29%	17%	11%	5%
			Portland		
Know Nothings	17%	40%	29%	12%	2%
Control Group	32%	27%	20%	10%	11%
			Canandaigua		
Know Nothings	37%	33%	19%	8%	3%
Control Group	36%	24%	15%	11%	13%

In the only place where the Know Nothings are not of approximately average age, the difference between the Know Nothings and the control group is less the actual number of young people than the lack of very old people to inflate the average age. Historians have suggested that older people shunned the Know Nothings because they were more dedicated than younger men to their political parties. However, this assumes that when members first joined Know Nothing lodges, they knew it would develop into a third party. In fact, it was not until October 1854, after most Americans had joined Know Nothing lodges, that New York Know Nothings set the precedent of making independent nominations. Before then, most had believed that the Know Nothings

52. Age given for the Know Nothings is their age in 1854, when most Know Nothing lodges were formed. Control groups are the same as those used above for occupations. I was able to determine the age of 469 (64%) of the 736 East Boston Know Nothings, 227 (59%) of the 382 Worcester Know Nothings, 58 (67%) of the 86 Portland Know Nothings, and 182 (69%) of the 263 Canandaigua Know Nothings.

would emulate the Masons and other nativist organizations—acting not as a separate party, but as an influential force *within* existing organizations. Maybe very old men did not join the Know Nothings because the evening meetings were too tiring. Or perhaps older men tended to find the secret grips and signs childish. In any case, the belief that young men dominated the Order needs to be re-examined.

The statistics gathered for this study also call into doubt one final aspect of the Know Nothing stereotype. Scholars have characterized the Know Nothings as originating from America's "huge floating population—men who appeared one year in a town's directory and were gone the next, probably because they had left in search of a job."[53] Yet in both East Boston and Worcester, Know Nothings were significantly *less* likely to have left town over a five-year period than members of the control group. In East Boston, 59 percent of the Know Nothings found in the 1855 census were also found in East Boston in the 1860 census, while only 33 percent of the control group remained in the city at that time. In Worcester, too, significantly more Know Nothings (44 versus 35 percent) were found to have lived in the city five years earlier.

Admittedly, these findings reflect the composition of only four Know Nothing lodges. But to some degree these lodges do represent a cross-section of Know Nothing councils. The East Boston lodge provides insight into the Know Nothings in their earliest days, as this council, begun in 1853, was probably one of the first 50 of the 10,000 that would eventually be formed nationwide. The Worcester lodge was also created relatively early (April 1854), and unlike East Boston, Worcester was highly industrialized. In contrast, the Portland and Canandaigua lodges were started in June 1854, the month that Know Nothingism enjoyed its most phenomenal growth. The Canandaigua lodge offers the perspective of the small town where, in reality, most lodges were located, while Portland provides the perspective of a state where Know Nothingism did not flourish. In addition, the fact that the Portland Know Nothings differed so significantly in wealth and occupational distribution from the general population may indicate that this was a lodge created by the city's elite, who sought to avoid socializing with the workingmen who undoubtedly constituted a majority of members in Portland's other councils. Yet despite the variety of lodges represented, the data concerning occupational distribution, wealth, age, and geographic mobility is relatively consistent. The Know Nothings attracted an approximately average cross-section of workers, although they tended to draw fewer farmers and more merchants than one finds in a random sample of those eligible for membership. Few joining the lodges tended to possess extraordinary wealth, but in most cases members of the Order owned property more valuable than that held by the average member of their occupational group. Finally, despite the stereotype to the contrary, Know Nothings were of about average age, although signifi-

53. Holt, "Politics of Impatience," 329.

cantly fewer of the oldest members of the community joined their lodges. Obviously, we need much more data concerning the Know Nothing rank and file before definitive conclusions can be drawn. But on the basis of what little information exists, it seems clear that historians need to rethink their conception of who joined the Know Nothing party.

Until May 1854, the Know Nothings had enjoyed slow but steady growth. Beginning in June, however, Know Nothing membership soared, increasing from approximately fifty thousand to over one million by the end of October. No new religious controversy emerged in these months, and the economy did not suddenly collapse. Nonetheless, there was a mass exodus from the conventional political parties into Know Nothing lodges. While sympathy for the Know Nothings' nativist agenda motivated many of these new members to join the Order, the failure of the traditional parties to enact temperance legislation and prevent passage of the Kansas-Nebraska Act provided the main impetus to abandon the old organizations. The belief that the Know Nothings would provide an anti-liquor, anti-slavery alternative to the Whig and Democratic parties transformed the Know Nothings from a small fraternal organization to a political party of national importance.

In the early 1850s temperance became one of the most divisive issues in American politics. Although a significant temperance movement had existed in the United States for thirty years, its advocates had always preached voluntary abstinence. After the Maine legislature passed a law prohibiting the sale of liquor in 1851, however, the temperance crusade ceased to rely on moral suasion, and began to advocate legally enforced sobriety instead. Gaining momentum from enactment of the "Maine Law," temperance reformers convinced legislatures in many other states to pass such laws. But courts declared most of these acts unconstitutional, and New York's Democratic Governor Horatio Seymour vetoed another. When politicians and judges blocked the enactment of prohibition bills, many temperance advocates blamed the political influence of immigrants, especially within the Democratic party. After all, the stereotype in which the Irish swilled their whiskey and the Germans imbibed their lager beer had been well established in the minds of natives by this time. The New York *Tribune* reported that in New York City, "ninety per cent of the rum-holes in some of the Wards are kept by foreigners," and citizens in smaller towns also associated immigrants with intemperance. The fact that the newcomers drank and caroused on Sundays particularly offended American Protestants accustomed to a quiet observance of the Sabbath.[54]

The temperance crusade had previously employed nativist rhetoric, but the belief that immigrant political influence had helped defeat Maine Law

54. New York *Tribune*, Nov. 10, 1853; Pottsville *Miner's Journal*, July 8, 1854; Ian R. Tyrrell, *Sobering Up: From Temperance to Prohibition in Antebellum America, 1800–1860* (Westport: Greenwood Press, 1979), 298–302; Alice Felt Tyler, *Freedom's Ferment: Phases of American Social History from the Colonial Period to the Outbreak of the Civil War* (New York: Harper Brothers, 1944), 385.

proposals heightened nativism among temperance advocates. The Chicago *Tribune*, for example, confessed that the temperance movement had become a front for "the most virulent anti-Catholic bigotry." Inevitably, many temperance advocates came to believe that the Know Nothings, who promised to combat the political power of the newcomers, offered the best means of destroying the immigrant liquor interest. The *National Temperance Organ* predicted that if "the Know Nothings break down the demagogues who truckle for foreign votes and resist the officious intermeddling of the Germans and Irish, the power of the liquor traffic [will be] gone forever." Noting this veiled endorsement of their program, the Harrisburg Know Nothing organ promised that if the Know Nothings "succeed, the prohibition and outlawry of the liquor traffic is inevitable." A frustrated Democrat from rural Wayne County, Pennsylvania, apparently believed such pledges, writing that "we have been humbugged long enough by tavern keepers, and their groggeries, and naturalized citizens. . . . When I go home I think very likely I shall join the *Know Nothings*."[55] The fact that immigrants organized much of their political activity in their taverns meant that prohibition would strike not only at immigrants' drinking habits but at their political power as well. No doubt referring to this, the New York *Herald* asserted that "the Know Nothing Order is the sign of the first movement against these rum hole conventions and grog shop politicians."[56] It is not known how the Know Nothings acquired their anti-liquor reputation, because the Order had originally shunned "extraneous" issues such as temperance. Prohibition also tended to be unpopular in the cities where Know Nothingism originated. At some point, Know Nothing recruiters may have begun stressing the movement's potential for stamping out intemperance because they sensed that nativism did not sufficiently motivate rural voters. On the other hand, rural residents may have added temperance to the Order's platform after Know Nothing recruiters had departed. In any case, the belief that the Know Nothings would advance the cause of temperance won the Order many recruits who would not have otherwise joined a nativist organization.

Even more crucial, however, to the transformation of the Order from a small-scale urban movement into a national power was the belief that the Know Nothings represented an anti-slavery alternative to the existing parties. It is not surprising that most historians have failed to recognize this key component of the Know Nothings' appeal. The Know Nothings' first national platform called for adherence to the Kansas-Nebraska Act, and Know Nothing presidential candidate Millard Fillmore took the same position. But northern Know Nothings repudiated both the 1855 platform and the Fillmore candidacy, so neither provides an accurate picture of the northern Know Nothing position on slavery. In early 1855, when membership was at its peak, the vast

55. Chicago *Tribune* quoted in Bruce M. Cole, "The Chicago Press and the Know Nothings, 1850–1856" (M.A. thesis, University of Chicago, 1948), 55–56; Harrisburg *Herald*, Aug. 16, 1854; E. A. Penniman to Bigler, June 18, 1854, Bigler Papers, HSP.

56. New York *Herald*, Jan. 8, 1855.

majority of northern Know Nothings opposed the extension of slavery and
adamantly sought repeal of the Kansas-Nebraska Act.

As with temperance, it is not clear how the Order came to be identified
with the anti-slavery movement, because we know that early Know Nothing
leaders had wanted to ignore this issue. Perhaps the pro-slavery reputation of
the Catholic Church and its immigrant adherents led opponents of slavery
extension to join Know Nothing lodges. Know Nothings often argued that the
Catholic Church condoned slavery, pointing out that Archbishop Hughes had
recently praised slavery in Cuba, and that Catholic newspapers never condemned the institution. Know Nothings also reminded Northerners that not
one Catholic priest had signed the well-publicized anti-slavery petition submitted to Congress in 1854 and endorsed by thousands of New England ministers.
Massachusetts Congressman Anson Burlingame contended that the Catholic
church supported slavery because

> Slavery and Priestcraft . . . have a common purpose: they seek [to annex]
> Cuba and Hayti and the Mexican States together, because they will be Catho-
> lic and Slave. I say they are in alliance by the necessity of their nature,—for
> one denies the right of a man to his body, and the other the right of a man to
> his soul. The one denies his right to think for himself, the other the right to
> act for himself.

Know Nothings often echoed the words of Henry Wilson, who charged that
Catholicism "instinctively sympathizes with oppression in the Old World and
the New." Wilson's statement referred to the Catholic Church's support of
monarchy over republicanism in "Old World" Europe, and its refusal to condemn slavery in America. Burlingame even ascribed the origin of African
slavery to a papal bull promulgated by Pope Martin V. A Massachusetts lodge
summed up the feeling of most Know Nothings, insisting that "there can be no
real hostility to Roman Catholicism which does not embrace slavery, its natural co-worker in opposition to freedom and republican institutions."[57]

The Know Nothings also attracted anti-slavery advocates because native-
born Americans were convinced that nearly all Irish immigrants supported
slavery. Abolitionist William Lloyd Garrison had stated in the 1840s that "it is
a most deplorable circumstance that religiously and politically, almost the
entire body of the Irishmen in this country are disposed to go with the ac-
cursed South for every purpose and to any extent. They are a mighty obstacle
in the way of negro emancipation on our soil." Another Massachusetts abolitionist, Theodore Parker, lamented that "not an Irish newspaper is on the side

57. William G. Bean, "An Aspect of Know Nothingism—The Immigrant and Slavery,"
South Atlantic Quarterly 23 (1924): 321–22; Burlingame, *Oration by Hon. Anson Burlingame,
Delivered at Salem, July 4, 1854* (n.p., 1854), 22; Ernest A. McKay, *Henry Wilson: Practical
Radical* (Port Washington, N.Y.: Kennikat Press, 1971), 93; Spooner, *Report of the President . . .
June 5, 1855* (n.p., 1855), 8; resolution of a Norfolk, Massachusetts, Know Nothing meeting
quoted in Gerald P. Fogarty, "Public Patriotism and Private Politics: The Tradition of American
Catholicism," *U.S. Catholic Historian* 4 (1984): 11; Burlingame on Martin V in [Boston] *Libera-
tor*, Feb. 9, 1855; Billington, *Protestant Crusade*, 425.

of . . . freedom." A resident of Maine likewise stated that "I never saw one of the [Irish] race . . . who did not hate a negro," and asked "when has the voice of an Irishman—of an Irish Catholic—been heard on the anti-slavery platform?" Anti-slavery newspapers often quoted the sentiments of one of the most famous Irish immigrants in America, John Mitchel, who dreamed of owning "a good plantation well-stocked with healthy negroes in Alabama."[58]

Know Nothings argued that attacks on the South by anti-slavery politicians were pointless, because Southerners would always vote for pro-slavery candidates. The key to the Slave Power's dominance of Congress was the inexcusable fact that Northerners also sent pro-slavery politicians to Washington, and Know Nothings insisted that the influence of Catholicism and the votes of the Irish elected most of these northern traitors. "The foreign and Catholic influence have been for years on the side of slavery, and doing all in their power to sustain the South against the North," stated the Providence *Tribune*. Pro-slavery forces carried northern elections because "the foreign Catholic vote is almost unanimously cast for slavery," concurred a Pittsburgh newspaper, and the organ of the Cleveland Know Nothings insisted that "the Catholics and the slave holders are the Northern [and] Southern logs which support" the pro-slavery Democratic party. A New Hampshire journal attributed the victories of northern pro-slavery politicians to "the ignorance and superstition of a half a million semi-civilized Irish voters." Although it did not support the Know Nothings, a Pennsylvania newspaper agreed that "the Jesuit [i.e., Catholic] and Pro-Slavery politician are natural allies."[59]

These arguments were effective because Know Nothings convinced Northerners that anti-slavery sentiment was as characteristic of the Order as nativism. "Americanism [i.e., Know Nothingism] and Freedom are synonymous terms," asserted Ohio Know Nothing president Thomas Spooner. "Foreignism and Slavery are equally so, and the one is antipodes of the other." Hartford's Know Nothing organ agreed that "we contend for Freedom as well as Americanism. We oppose the extension of slavery as well as the spread of Romanism. We are as hostile to the march of the slave oligarchy as we are to the control of a foreign potentate over free America." Allow the Order to enact its agenda, Know Nothings argued, and the diminished influence of

58. Garrison quoted in Gilbert Osofsky, "Abolitionists, Irish Immigrants, and the Dilemmas of Romantic Nationalism," *AHR* 80 (1975): 906; William G. Bean, "Puritan versus Celt, 1850–1860," *New England Quarterly* 7 (1934): 71, 82; [Boston] *Liberator*, Aug. 4, 1854 (Maine quotation).

59. Providence *Tribune* quoted in Harrisburg *Herald*, Dec. 25, 1854; Pittsburgh *Dispatch* quoted in Holt, *Forging a Majority*, 164; Cleveland *Leader*, Oct. 4, 1854; Concord *Independent Democrat* quoted in Johnstown *Cambria Tribune*, April 14, 1855; Wilkes Barre *Record of the Times*, Aug. 19, 1854; Boston *Bee*, Aug. 11, 1855; Hartford *Courant*, June 9, 1856; Harrisburg *Herald*, July 11, 1854; *Know Nothing Platform: Containing an Account of the Encroachments of the Roman Catholic Hierarchy on the Civil and Religious Liberties of the People in Europe, Asia, Africa and America, Showing the Necessity of the Order of Know Nothings* (Philadelphia, n.d.), 7–8.

Irish immigrants would mortally weaken the political strength of the Slave Power.[60]

Once they discovered that the Know Nothings opposed the Kansas-Nebraska Act as vehemently as they opposed Catholicism, many rural residents who had little contact with immigrants, and city-dwellers who had been unmoved by their nativist rhetoric, rushed to join the Order. One such convert, a New Haven editor, explained that he "fell into the American movement with tens of thousands of others, who found it right on slavery and right on temperance. The end is the defeat of the rum and Nebraska forces." Edward Everett also recognized that the Know Nothing "mischief has been needlessly brought about by the introduction of the Kanzas & Nebraska bill." A letter to a Pennsylvania newspaper agreed that "this violation of a sacred promise" pushed Northerners into the Know Nothing ranks, because they considered "breaking down the old party distinctions" vital to prevent the enactment of similar abominations. According to the Order's Ohio president, both the Kansas-Nebraska Act and the "pandering" of politicians to foreigners "aroused the feelings and kindled the spirit so long pent up within the great American heart, and quickened into life and activity the American sentiment that gave birth to our Order." A resident of northern Pennsylvania likewise reported "that the feeling of opposition to Nebraska here helped give the Know Nothings strength. Those who were sour because of that were ready to jump into any organization. . . ."[61]

The Kansas-Nebraska Act also aggravated the anti-party sentiment that had been growing in the North during the 1850s, and this aided Know Nothing recruitment as well. Most scholars who have noted the existence of this revulsion toward the existing political parties concentrate on its origin in ethno-cultural controversies, and there can be no doubt that nativism contributed to its growth. One Northerner noted "a growing feeling that some [rebuke] should be given to the wily schemes of political demagogues who pander to the prejudices and passions of our foreign populations," and many believed that this "truckling" by politicians to Roman Catholic demands drew many adherents to Know Nothing lodges. The president of the Order in Pennsylvania asserted that the Know Nothings owed their success to the "corrupt combination between ambitious demagogues on the one hand and a political church, backed by hosts of ignorant foreigners, on the other." An Albany

60. Spooner, *Report of the President . . . June 5, 1855*, 8; Spooner, *To the State Council* [printed letter dated Jan. 3, 1856], Cincinnati Public Library (quotation); Hartford *Courant*, March 14, 1856. In Connecticut and Indiana, Know Nothings demonstrated their devotion to this issue by adding anti-slavery clauses to the Order's constitution. *Constitution and By-laws of the Order. Adopted, May, 1855* (Indianapolis, 1855), 3, IndSL; *Constitution of the [Connecticut] State Council*, Aug. 1855, CHS.

61. New Haven *Palladium*, April 4, 1855; Everett to Mr. Trescot, Oct. 20, 1854 (letterbook), Everett Papers, MHS; "Nihil Scio," in Johnstown *Cambria Tribune*, July 1, 1854; Spooner, *Report of the President of the State Council of Ohio, June 5, 1855*, 7–8; E. B. Chase to Bigler, Oct. 20, 1854, Bigler Papers, HSP; Jamestown [New York] *Journal*, Feb. 9, 1855; Providence *Tribune* quoted in Harrisburg *Herald*, Dec. 25, 1854.

helped the Know Nothings attract members outside of nativism's traditional urban strongholds.[66]

Finally, slavery and (to a lesser degree) temperance also drove many Northerners into the Order who had no intention of remaining in the organization permanently. Many Know Nothings, especially those in states where strong anti-slavery sentiment dominated the Order (such as Ohio, Indiana, and Maine), believed that the Order represented "simply a stepping-stone" for disenchanted Whigs and Democrats awaiting the organization of the Republican party. As one observer noted, Know Nothing secrecy "was wisely contrived to answer the purpose of getting men out of the old parties [and] into a new one without subjecting them to the ordeal of an open breach with former friends. It is a sort of covered way, or tunnel, through which men can burrow from one camp to another, without the risk of being shot on the way, or hanged as traitors." Joshua Giddings agreed that the Know Nothings functioned "as a screen—a dark wall—behind which members of old political organizations could escape unseen from party shackles, and take a position, according to the dictates of judgment and conscience." Many Northerners joined Know Nothing councils in the summer of 1854 for these reasons, and although they planned to leave the Order as soon as the Republican party was established, their presence in the lodges swelled Know Nothing membership immensely.[67]

In a little more than two years, the Know Nothings had grown from an organization of forty-three members to one that by the end of 1854 could boast more than one million adherents.[68] The takeover of the organization by the Order of United Americans provided the initial impetus for Know Nothing growth, by infusing it with a large number of experienced nativists who emphasized recruitment. The resurgence of American anti-Catholicism, motivated by school controversies, church property disputes, the visit of Papal

66. *Christian Advocate and Journal*, Sept. 14, 1854 (quotation); McClure, *Old Time Notes of Pennsylvania*, I, p. 240 (quotation); Joseph Wright to Matthew Simpson, Oct. 23, 1854 (quotation), Simpson Papers, LC; Edward Everett to Millard Fillmore, Dec. 16, 1854 (letterbook), Everett Papers, MHS; *Western Christian Advocate* in John B. Weaver, "Nativism and the Birth of the Republican Party in Ohio, 1854–1860" (Ph.D. diss., Ohio State University, 1982), 51; Cole, "The Chicago Press and the Know Nothings," 63; New York *Churchman* in Harrisburg *Herald*, July 25, 1854; *Presbyterial Critic* in Clearfield [Pennsylvania] *Raftsman's Journal*, May 30, 1855; John Law to William Marcy, Sept. 25, 1854, Marcy Papers, LC; H. B. Pickett to John G. Davis, Oct. 25, 1854, Davis Papers, IndHS; Indianapolis *Republican*, Sept. 21, 1855; Richard Carwardine, "The Know-Nothing Party, the Protestant Evangelical Community, and American National Identity," in *Religion and National Identity: Papers Read at the Nineteenth Summer Meeting and the Twentieth Winter Meeting of the Ecclesiastical History Society*, ed. Stuart Mews (Oxford: Blackwell, 1982), 449–63.

67. Roeliff Brinkerhoff, *Recollections of a Lifetime* (Cincinnati, 1900), 91–92; [Boston] *Liberator*, Nov. 10, 1854; Giddings quoted in Eugene H. Roseboom, "Salmon P. Chase and the Know Nothings," *MVHR* 25 (1938): 337; Youngstown *True American*, March 21, 1855.

68. Charles Deshler to James A. Henry, Jan. 26, 1855 (letterbook), Deshler Papers, Rutgers University. Deshler was corresponding secretary of the Know Nothings' National Committee.

Nuncio Gaetano Bedini, and the appointment of a Catholic postmaster general helped the organization expand further, because these events convinced many Americans that the political influence of immigrants and Catholics needed to be reduced. However, the identification of the Order with temperance and anti-slavery played the key role in the Order's expansion. The failure of prohibition laws, and especially the enactment of the Kansas-Nebraska bill, exacerbated an already existing anti-party sentiment, convincing Northerners to leave their old parties *en masse*. This brought the Know Nothing movement the broad-based support that previous nativist groups had failed to attract.

3

The Know Nothings Enter Politics

The growth of the Know Nothings captivated the nation during the summer of 1854. Newspapers vied to publish the first and most exhaustive exposés on the size and intentions of the organization. Sidewalk hucksters peddled pamphlets revealing codes, signs, and grips so that the uninitiated could eavesdrop on Know Nothing communications. Other entrepreneurs cashed in on the rage by offering consumers such items as "Know Nothing Candy," "Know Nothing Tea," "Know Nothing Toothpicks," "Know Nothing Cigars," and "Know Nothing Soap." When an Ohioan who had neglected his diary for a year attempted to summarize the important occurrences of 1854, he mentioned only two events: the death of his father and the rise of the Know Nothings.[1]

The Know Nothings had clearly captured the popular imagination, but the Order's members hoped that its success would earn them tangible rewards as well. Thus while hundreds of thousands of Americans flocked into Know Nothing lodges during the summer of 1854, leaders of the Order began parlaying those gains into political clout. The Know Nothings had always sought to influence American politics. The Order had been created, after all, to reduce the power of immigrants in the nation's political life. But the organization's modest size in its early years had limited its ability to exercise any noticeable influence. While Know Nothings had nominated tickets for local elections, their candidates were almost invariably non–Know Nothings chosen from amongst the nominees of the major parties. Aside from electing one of its leaders to the New York state senate in 1853 (by winning him the Whig nomination), the Order could claim few political triumphs. All that changed, however, with the Know Nothings' great expansion in mid-1854.

At this point, most Know Nothing lodges still drew up tickets composed of candidates selected by the established parties. If none of the candidates offered for a particular office met with Know Nothing approval, the Order

1. Ray A. Billington, *The Protestant Crusade, 1800–1860: A Study of the Origins of American Nativism* (Chicago: Quadrangle Books, 1938), 388; Thomas Horrocks, "The Know Nothings," *American History Illustrated* 17 (Jan. 1983): 22–29; Sidney Maxwell Diary, Jan. 1855, Cincinnati Historical Society (Maxwell does not appear to have been a Know Nothing himself).

chose its own candidate. Sometimes, this citizen would be unaware of his candidacy until the Know Nothings swept him to victory. In some places, however, the Know Nothings ignored the nominations of the major parties and chose an *entirely* independent slate. Occasionally, only lodge members would know of the existence of such a ticket, although most often, in an attempt to attract outside support, Know Nothings publicized it as an "Independent" or "Reform" slate.

Know Nothings utilized all of these strategies during the spring 1854 elections in Massachusetts and Pennsylvania. In eastern Massachusetts, where the Order had already grown quite large, Know Nothings elected mayors in Boston, Salem, and other towns. The influence of the Know Nothings in Pennsylvania became evident when in heavily Democratic Lancaster all the Democratic candidates except the three born abroad won re-election. "These 'Know nothings' act in perfect concert, it would seem," complained one Democrat to James Buchanan after witnessing the result, "but where they meet, or how they are organized, no one can tell." In Chambersburg, a town previously dominated by Whigs, that party expected to carry the election because the Democrats had not even bothered to field a ticket. Yet when the votes were tabulated, a Know Nothing slate—not publicly known to exist before the election—was victorious. Know Nothing tickets also triumphed in Schuylkill and York counties.[2]

The Philadelphia municipal election held in June 1854 was the most important Pennsylvania contest influenced by Know Nothings that spring. As early as March, one newspaper had reported that "there are certain persons who go about town whispering . . . that a 'surprise party' is to elect the city officials in June" and identified the Know Nothings as the subject of these rumors. However, few Democrats lent much credence to these reports. For the mayoralty, the top post being contested, they nominated Richard Vaux, who would later become the first modern political "boss" of Philadelphia. The Whigs countered with Robert T. Conrad, an attorney who had held a number of Philadelphia judicial positions, but had gained most of his fame as a dramatist and as editor of the Philadelphia *North American*.[3] It is not clear whether the Whigs who nominated Conrad realized that he was a Know Nothing, but once the campaign got under way his affiliation became apparent. Conrad promised to appoint only native-born Americans to office should he win the election. He also vowed to reduce the city's rapidly increasing crime rate, which

2. John R. Mulkern, *The Know-Nothing Party in Massachusetts: The Rise and Fall of a People's Movement* (Boston: Northeastern Univ. Press, 1990), 68–69; A. L. Hayes to Buchanan, May 8, 1854, Buchanan Papers, HSP; Alexander McClure, *Old Time Notes of Pennsylvania*, 2 vols. (Philadelphia, 1905), I, pp. 197–98; Harrisburg *Herald*, June 20, Aug. 29, 1854; Charles Frailey to William Bigler, June 14, 1854, Bigler Papers, HSP.

3. Philadelphia *Register* quoted in New York *Tribune*, March 25, 1854; Melvin G. Holli and Peter d'A. Jones, eds., *Biographical Directory of American Mayors* (Westport: Greenwood Press, 1981), 76; McClure, *Old Time Notes*, I, pp. 206–8; *Dictionary of American Biography* (New York: Charles Scribner's Sons, 1943), IV, pp. 355–56.

most native-born Philadelphians attributed to immigrants. His promise to close saloons on Sundays represented another thinly veiled attack on immigrants, because devout Protestants blamed immigrant drinkers for disturbing their quiet observance of the Sabbath. Conrad also denounced the recently signed Kansas-Nebraska Act during the campaign. As election day drew near, however, the temperance issue overshadowed all others, with one newspaper summarizing the voters' choice as "Lager Beer and Vaux" or "Temperance and Conrad."[4]

Although Whigs had dominated Philadelphia politics in the 1850s, the city's recent annexation of surrounding Democratic towns led Democrats to believe that Vaux would easily defeat Conrad. Pennsylvania Democrats planned to examine the results of the election closely, as they would provide the first major test of the party's strength since passage of the Kansas-Nebraska Act. To their dismay, Conrad out-polled Vaux by a nearly three-to-two margin. "I am completely astounded by the result of the Philadelphia election," confessed one Democrat. "If that is an index of what they will do in October," he continued, ". . . our party must go into a hopeless minority."[5]

While contemporaries disagreed as to the causes of Conrad's victory, most Democrats blamed nativism. "I take it for granted that hereafter, no foreigner or *Catholic* can be elected to any office in this city," concluded one Democratic observer. "At the bottom of this is a deep seated religious question—prejudice if you please, which nothing can withstand. Our party is made to bear the sin of *catholicism*." Most of these Democrats specifically ascribed the defeat to the party's identification with the unpopular postmaster general, Philadelphia Catholic James Campbell. "In my opinion, this is the direct result of Campbell-ism," insisted one Democrat. Many Americans, he explained, believed that "the Post Offices of the nation are filled with . . . Jesuits, for such stuff is talked of commonly as household words."[6]

It may have been psychologically soothing for Democrats to blame defeat on something out of their control, such as nativism, rather than on their own mistakes, such as the Kansas-Nebraska Act. Yet Conrad's supporters denied that nativism alone had provided his margin of victory. "It is [an] *anti-Nebraska, anti-Catholic triumph*," insisted the Harrisburg *Herald*. The Johnstown *Cambria Tribune* agreed that these two factors had combined with temperance to produce the Democratic defeat. Even one Democrat admitted to Pennsylvania governor William Bigler on the eve of the election that "the

4. Philadelphia *News* quoted in Henry R. Mueller, *The Whig Party in Pennsylvania* (New York: Columbia Univ. Press, 1922), 212.

5. E. B. Chase to Bigler, June 14, 1854 (quotation), Bigler Papers, HSP; Daniel T. Jenks to Buchanan, June 9, 1854, Buchanan Papers, HSP; John F. Coleman, *The Disruption of the Pennsylvania Democracy, 1848–1860* (Harrisburg: Pennsylvania Historical and Museum Commission, 1975), 67.

6. E. A. Penniman to Bigler, June 8, 1854 (quotation), Henry M. Phillips to Bigler, June 11, 1854 (quotation), Gabriel Wolf to Bigler, June 12, 1854, John Campbell to Bigler, June 26, 1854, Bigler Papers, HSP; Daniel T. Jenks to Buchanan, June 9, 1854, J. Glancy Jones to Buchanan, July 9, 1854, Buchanan Papers, HSP.

Nebraska bill is hurting us mightily. Vaux[,] who is really Anti-Nebraska[,] receives opposition from those who otherwise would have supported him simply because of their desire to have a democratic defeat." Another conceded that both "the Anti-Catholic feeling against a wing of the democracy, and the feeling against the new slave agitation raised by the Nebraska bill" had defeated Vaux. While Democrats were undoubtedly correct in pointing to the influence of nativism in the campaign, anti-Nebraska sentiment was equally important in bringing about the Know Nothing triumph.[7]

After the Philadelphia election, politicians paid greater attention to rumors and press reports concerning the Know Nothings' rapid growth. Still, nativist political organizations had found sympathizers in the Keystone State before, and the Know Nothings, like the American Republican party ten years earlier, might prove to be a fleeting movement confined to a few large cities. The true test of the Know Nothings' political strength would come in the fall, when nearly all the North held state elections.

The first of these contests took place in Iowa, Maine, and California. Although Democrats made claims to the contrary, Know Nothings did not form their first lodge in Iowa until July 26, just twelve days before the election, so the Order had little impact on the election there.[8] However, Know Nothings played a more significant role in September's Maine contest. Disagreement over the temperance issue led Maine Democrats to nominate one gubernatorial candidate who opposed liquor prohibition and another who favored the "Maine Law." Those hoping to take advantage of sentiment against the Kansas-Nebraska Act attempted to unite the Democrats' opponents behind Anson Morrill, the Free Soil nominee. Although many antislavery Whigs endorsed Morrill, the remainder of the party nominated their own candidate, creating a four-way race for the governorship.[9]

The emergence of the Know Nothings in Maine further complicated this already confusing situation. Because the percentage of immigrants in Maine's population actually decreased during the 1850s, Know Nothing recruiters could not hope to convince Maine's residents that immigrants threatened to overrun their state. On the other hand, the state's pervasive anti-Catholicism probably aided Know Nothing organizers. While no contemporary estimate exists of Know Nothing strength before the election, the Order in Maine probably contained 15,000 to 20,000 members (out of a voting population of

7. Harrisburg *Herald*, June 9, 1854; Johnstown *Cambria Tribune*, June 10, 1854; Henry Phillips to Bigler, May 28, 1854, E. K. P[rice] to Bigler, June 7, 1854, Bigler Papers, HSP; Charles D. Cleveland to Charles Sumner, June 7, 1854, Sumner Papers, HU. William E. Gienapp, *The Origins of the Republican Party, 1852–1856* (New York: Oxford Univ. Press, 1987), 100–101, emphasizes nativism as the driving force behind the election result.

8. Thomas R. Whitney, *A Defence of the American Policy* (New York, 1856), 284; Ronald F. Matthias, "The Know Nothing Movement in Iowa" (Ph.D. diss., University of Chicago, 1965), 9; Morton M. Rosenberg, *Iowa on the Eve of the Civil War: A Decade of Frontier Politics* (Norman: Univ. of Oklahoma Press, 1972), 93, 104–7.

9. Gienapp, *Origins of the Republican Party*, 129–31.

110,000) by September. The exact process by which Know Nothings selected their candidate for governor also remains a mystery, but rumor soon spread through the state that Morrill had received their endorsement. Although some nativists claimed that Free Soilers had disingenuously joined Know Nothing lodges at the last minute to aid Morrill's cause, many Free Soilers undoubtedly sympathized with the Order's anti-slavery, anti-liquor, anti-Catholic agenda.[10]

Whether the Know Nothings' endorsement played a significant role in Morrill's eventual victory is difficult to determine. The poor showing of the Whig candidate surprised observers, but Whig defections to Morrill may have been caused by factors other than Know Nothing support. In any case, because Morrill failed to poll a majority of the votes cast, the members of the Maine legislature were called upon to decide the election, and editor James G. Blaine believed that a majority of the legislators belonged to Know Nothing lodges. If so, then the Order undoubtedly aided Morrill's easy victory in the legislative balloting, although as with the popular voting, it is impossible to determine whether Know Nothing membership or free soil convictions influenced the legislators' votes to a greater extent. However, the New York *Herald*'s correspondent in Maine insisted that the answer to this question would not reveal the true significance of the election. Everyone had realized that the slavery and temperance issues would play a role in the contest, he wrote, but few had expected that "the mysterious and terrible Know Nothings" would scatter "confusion and dismay all around. . . . The movements of the Know Nothings," he therefore concluded, must "be regarded as the most significant result of the election."[11]

California also held its state election in September, and public attention centered on the two congressional races. The presence of two Democratic tickets in the field made Whigs think they might finally win a California election, but Democrats narrowly defeated Whigs in both contests. As in Iowa and Maine, Know Nothing influence on the California contest is difficult to gauge, for although Know Nothings had organized lodges in California as early as May, there is no evidence that the Order endorsed any candidates in the state-wide contests. One Californian complained to ex-President Millard Fillmore that "but for the Know Nothings, the whigs would have carried the State," but no corroborating evidence exists to support this assertion. In San Francisco, one of the few California cities containing a significant concentration of Know Nothings by September, the Order definitely influenced local contests. Dissatisfied with the Democratic and Whig choices for Mayor, San Francisco Know Nothings nominated their own candidate, Stephen P. Webb, while selecting nominees from the other parties to fill most of the remaining spots on their ticket. The Know Nothings advertised their slate of candidates

10. Gienapp, *Origins of the Republican Party*, 52, 131; Allan R. Whitmore, " 'A Guard of Faithful Sentinels': The Know Nothing Appeal in Maine, 1854–1855," *Maine Historical Society Quarterly* 20 (1981): 172.

11. Gienapp, *Origins of the Republican Party*, 133; New York *Herald*, Sept. 13, 1854.

as the Citizen's Reform Ticket in an attempt to gain votes from non–Know Nothings disgusted with San Francisco's notoriously corrupt politicians. Webb carried the election, polling 43 percent of the vote in the four-way race, compared with 38 percent for the Democratic candidate and only 11 percent for the Whig nominee. While few localities other than San Francisco reported significant Know Nothing activity during the September campaign, observers attributed this to the nascent state of the Order in California. Given the hostility that white Californians exhibited toward the state's Chinese and Mexican populations, eastern nativists predicted that the Know Nothings would soon replicate their San Francisco triumph throughout California.[12]

With these smaller contests out of the way, Americans turned their attention to the important elections scheduled for October. Because of the Order's recent success in Philadelphia, Know Nothings held especially high hopes for Pennsylvania. Conrad's victory there also convinced other politicians to treat the threat posed by the Order seriously as they prepared for the state contest. "This anti-Catholic movement looks more formidable by far than I expected," wrote one politician expressing the common sentiment. Using the term *American*, which Know Nothings used to identify their movement, a Philadelphian advised ex-President Millard Fillmore that "there is a deepseated *American* feeling in this state overriding everything else." Colleagues likewise reported to Buchanan that "politicians are dumbfounded. Editors are completely smashed into the middle of chaos, and the people stand amazed. It is the most remarkable revolution in politics since the formation of the government."[13] The Order continued its remarkable growth in Pennsylvania throughout the summer, and by October Know Nothings there claimed to have enrolled 80,000 members in 635 lodges.[14]

Democrats had expected Whigs to join the Know Nothings. Many of them believed the Order to be nothing more than a "Whig trick" designed to rally that disintegrating party by using anti-Catholic rhetoric to attract new support. But Democrats soon discovered that members of their own party were streaming into Know Nothing lodges as well. "A number of active Democrats have been led into it," reported one lieutenant of Democratic leader Simon Cameron. Another Democrat complained that "there are too many of

12. J. G. Baldwin to Millard Fillmore, Sept. 30, 1854, Fillmore Papers, SUNY-O; Peyton Hurt, "The Rise and Fall of the 'Know Nothings' in California," *California Historical Society Quarterly* 9 (1930): 24–33; Cincinnati *Dollar Times*, Dec. 21, 1854; Albany *State Register*, Oct. 24, 1854.

13. David Fullwood to Simon Cameron, Aug. 26, 1854 (quotation), C. A. Black to Cameron, Sept. 29, 1854, Cameron Papers, DCHS; Isaac Hazlehurst to Millard Fillmore, July 7, 1854, Fillmore Papers, SUNY-O; J. Franklin Reigart to Buchanan, July 28, 1854, Buchanan Papers, HSP.

14. Membership figures are taken from the proceedings of the October State Council meeting, reported by the Philadelphia *Pennsylvanian* and reprinted in the New York *Herald*, Oct. 7, 1854. While the *Pennsylvanian* seems to have fabricated some portions of its report, the membership figures seem plausible.

our young men in it. Sons of Democrats, that don't care, have no idea of the rong [sic] that they are doing to their country." Correspondence from nearly every portion of the state confirmed that the Know Nothings had gained many members from the Democratic ranks.[15]

The Democrats' preoccupation with the Know Nothings' expansion intensified as the October state election drew near. Candidates for the contest had been nominated in March, long before the Order's emergence. Democrats had re-nominated incumbent governor William Bigler and had chosen Jeremiah S. Black for justice of the Supreme Court and Henry S. Mott for canal commissioner. Although an intense debate over the Kansas-Nebraska Act had erupted at their convention, Bigler and his supporters pushed through a platform that ignored the Kansas issue altogether. In contrast, Pennsylvania Whigs hoped to use the fallout over the Kansas-Nebraska Act to revive their party, and their convention adopted a platform that denounced the Act's repeal of the Missouri Compromise. Yet their nominee for governor, lawyer and three-time congressman James Pollock, lacked strong anti-slavery credentials. In order to prevent free-soil Democrats from nominating a third candidate for governor, Pollock wrote "a stiff anti-slavery letter" which eventually earned him their support.[16]

While it took a concerted effort to win Pollock the support of the radical free-soilers, he was perfectly suited to the Know Nothings. Pollock was a devout Presbyterian of Scotch-Irish ancestry, and an acquaintance called him an "extreme Roundhead" in matters of religion. A biographer relates that Pollock was "extremely Puritanical in his attitude toward cards and liquor," and it was at Pollock's urging (as Director of the Mint) that "In God We Trust" was added to American currency during the Civil War. According to Philadelphia gossip, Mayor Conrad's Philadelphia lodge initiated Pollock into the Order in June, and a letter Pollock wrote after the election confirms his affiliation.[17]

Exactly how Pollock captured the Know Nothing endorsement is unclear. The Order held its own state-wide primary to determine which candidates it would support. Each lodge chose from the candidates nominated by the regular parties and forwarded the results to the State Council (the body that

15. Edward J. Fox to Cameron, July 29, 1854 (quotation), W. H. Butler to Cameron, Sept. 5, 1854, Cameron Papers, DCHS; Daniel T. Jenks to Buchanan, Oct. 3, 1854 (quotation), Buchanan Papers, HSP; H. Gross to Bigler, Aug. 23, 1854, S. A. Armour [?] to Bigler, Aug. 28, 1854, P. A. Jones to Bigler, Sept. 7, 1854, Bigler Papers, HSP; Philadelphia *American Banner* quoted in Pottsville *Miner's Journal*, May 27, 1854.

16. William Gienapp, "Nebraska, Nativism, and Rum: The Failure of Fusion in Pennsylvania, 1854," *Pennsylvania Magazine of History and Biography* 109 (1985): 429–35.

17. Robert Sobel and John Raimo, eds., *Biographical Directory of the Governors of the United States* (Westport: Meckler Books, 1978), III, p. 1308; McClure, *Old Time Notes*, I, p. 233; Frederic A. Godcharles, "Governor James Pollack," *Northumberland County Historical Society Proceedings* 8 (1936): 35–37; Tuscarora *Register* quoted in Warren F. Hewitt, "The Know-Nothing Party in Pennsylvania," *Pennsylvania History* 2 (1935): 76; James Pollock to John M. Clayton, Oct. 30, 1854, Clayton Papers, LC.

supervised the Order's operations in each state), which tallied the figures and announced the outcome at their convention held on October 3 in Philadelphia. At the convention, it was announced that Pollock had won an overwhelming 32,000-vote majority (out of approximately 80,000 cast) over the Native American candidate, Benjamin R. Bradford.[18] For canal commissioner, Know Nothings chose Democratic nominee Henry Mott, while they selected the Native American choice, Thomas H. Baird, for justice of the Supreme Court.[19] Yet Pennsylvania politician Alexander McClure implies in his memoirs that the Know Nothing leaders fabricated the primary results, awarding Pollock the Order's support only after extracting patronage concessions from Whig leaders. Historian Gerald Eggert has convincingly postulated that this deal resulted in the appointment of Know Nothing leader Stephen Miller to the lucrative post of flour inspector at Philadelphia.[20] The fact that one candidate from each of the three parties gained an endorsement, placating the various factions within the organization, also smacks of central coordination. However, the one Pennsylvania nativist group whose minutes are extant chose Pollock, Mott, and Baird, suggesting that the results announced at Philadelphia may have been genuine.[21] Jealous Whigs might have invented the story of a pre-election "deal," for Pollock would have been obliged to placate the Know Nothing portion of his constituency with patronage appointments even if no bargain had been struck. On the other hand, Know Nothing leaders might have elicited such a promise from Pollock even though they had no direct control over the results of the lodge elections. Thus, the question of how the Know Nothings chose their candidates for this contest remains an open one.

Meanwhile, the other parties confronted the threat posed by the Know Nothings. Some Whigs welcomed the advent of Know Nothingism, believing it could be used to re-invigorate their organization. Others undoubtedly agreed with the Philadelphian who called his party's relationship with the Order "an embarrassment, and the more so as no one likes to defy it."[22] The

18. The Native American party should not be confused with the Know Nothings. As mentioned in Chapter 1, the Native Americans were the surviving remnant of the Pennsylvania American Republican party of the 1840s. Unlike the Know Nothings, the Native Americans operated as an open political party and continued to nominate their own candidates for office even after the Know Nothings began doing so. Most Native Americans undoubtedly joined the Know Nothings, because their platforms were nearly identical. Native American leaders, however, refused to hand over control of their organization to the Know Nothing leaders and continued to operate separately in hopes that the Know Nothings would use the Native American party to carry out the Know Nothing political program. See Pottsville *Miner's Journal*, Aug. 26, 1854.

19. Philadelphia *Pennsylvanian* quoted in New York *Herald*, Oct. 7, 1854. The Know Nothings could not have endorsed George Darsie, the Whig nominee for canal commissioner, because he had been born in Scotland.

20. McClure, *Old Time Notes*, I, pp. 215–16, 221; Gerald G. Eggert, " 'Seeing Sam': The Know Nothing Episode in Harrisburg," *Pennsylvania Magazine of History and Biography* 111 (1987): 335–36.

21. Guard of Liberty Minute Book, [pp. 11–12], Pennsylvania State Archives.

22. W. B. Reed to Thurlow Weed, Aug. 10, 1854, Weed Papers, UR.

correspondence of Pennsylvania Democrats documents an increasingly pan-
icked attitude toward the Know Nothings as election day drew closer. In July,
one Democratic editor informed Bigler that he would begin scouring back
issues of nativist newspapers for old editorials that might embarrass the Know
Nothings. At the end of August, Postmaster Campbell insisted that the Democrats needed to take more decisive action. "Cannot we get by some means at
the number of Lodges & the extent of the organization of the Know Nothings
throughout the State," he asked. By election eve, an air of desperation had set
in, with one Democrat suggesting that "we must force our way into & buy up
some of the leaders in some of the K.N.L[odge]s" in order to carry the
election.[23]

Such alarm resulted in part from the clandestine manner in which the
Know Nothings conducted their campaign. Politicians usually sent spies to
their opponents' conventions, and commissioned informal polls to determine
their chances in upcoming elections. But Know Nothingism confounded party
leaders. Now no one could be trusted to tell how he would really vote, and any
spy might be a double agent. "They mix with us talk against themselves and
denounce the order," worried one Democrat. "We cannot trust our brothers
or friends." Another lamented that "we are without chart or compass" as far
as the Know Nothings were concerned.[24]

Know Nothingism was not the only factor affecting the course of the
election. Soon after the nominations, the nativist Philadelphia *Sun* predicted
that "the cause of Prohibition will override all party questions, and the candidate who does not fully pledge himself to that cause, must be defeated." With
a referendum scheduled to appear on the ballot asking if voters endorsed
outlawing liquor sales, temperance was sure to gain the attention of the electorate. To ensure that candidates would address this issue, the Pennsylvania
State Central Temperance Committee sent letters to both Bigler and Pollock,
asking if they believed that liquor prohibition was constitutional, and if they
would sign a prohibitory law if passed by the legislature. Both candidates
equivocated in their responses, but temperance advocates were especially
suspicious of Bigler, who had pocket-vetoed a bill that would have imposed
cumbersome licensing requirements on saloons. Consequently, the Temperance Committee endorsed Pollock. Know Nothing leader Stephen Miller
chaired the committee, demonstrating that the forces pushing for temperance
legislation were closely linked with the Order.[25]

Public outcry over the Kansas-Nebraska Act further complicated the elec-

23. J. Johnson to Bigler, July 14, 17, 1854, James Campbell to Bigler, Aug. 23, 1854, Bigler
Papers, HSP; J. P. Anderson to "Dear Sir," Oct. 4, 1854, Cameron Papers, DCHS.

24. R. M. DeFrance to Cameron, Oct. 12, 1854 (quotation), J. McClintock to Cameron,
Sept. 16, 1854 (quotation), Cameron Papers, DCHS; Jeremiah S. Black to Bigler, July 1, 1854,
Bigler Papers, HSP; Daniel T. Jenks to Buchanan, Oct. 3, 1854, Buchanan Papers, HSP.

25. Philadelphia *Sun*, March 22, 1854; Stephen Miller et al. to Bigler, May 18, 1854, Bigler
to Miller et al., June 6, 1854 (draft), H. G. Seisenring to Bigler, Aug. 8, 1854, Bigler Papers,
HSP; Coleman, *Disruption of the Pennsylvania Democracy*, 74; Daniel T. Jenks to Buchanan,
Aug. 18, 1854, Buchanan Papers, HSP.

tion forecast. "Nebraska makes many halt, who heretofore were first to sound the charge," warned a Pittsburgh Democrat. Another Democrat worried that defections would be numerous because of the belief that the act "*extends slavery* into all that territory. This is the general opinion and I find it has . . . taken a pretty deep hold." While some anti-Nebraska sentiment existed in every part of Pennsylvania, it was most evident in the northern and western portions of the state. Democrats especially worried that the slavery issue would hurt them in the "Northern Tier." This region traditionally polled reliable Democratic majorities, but it also contained the largest concentration of Free Soilers in the state. In contrast, the political debate in southern and eastern Pennsylvania seemed unaffected by the Kansas-Nebraska Act. Politicians reported that temperance and nativism overshadowed the slavery issue in those areas.[26]

The results of the October 1854 Pennsylvania election would have completely baffled anyone unaware of the Know Nothings' existence. Pollock beat Bigler by 37,000 votes, yet Bigler's running-mate, Henry Mott, defeated his opponent by more than 190,000 votes. The other Democratic candidate, Jeremiah Black, polled only as many votes as Bigler, yet Black won because the Whig and Native American candidates split the opposition vote for the judgeship. Although the Democrats had won two of the three state offices, their congressional candidates fared miserably, losing 18 of 25 races. In the final important contest—the temperance referendum—the forces opposing a Maine Law barely defeated those in favor.[27]

Political observers had expected Know Nothingism to produce some strange results, but nothing this extraordinary. A Pennsylvanian informed his brother:

> I am not yet sufficiently recovered from the surprise produced by the result of the election to write with any perspicuity on the subject. A Whig Governor has been elected by a large Majority in a Democratic State, and a whig Congressman defeated, in a county that had heretofore given an overwhelming whig majority. . . . I am still at a loss to see how it was done. Old party lines and issues have been entirely disregarded, and everything made subservient to a new organization. . . .

From all over the state came similar reports. "Democrats have been elected in some of the strongest Whig counties, and Whigs from Democratic counties," reported a Harrisburg newspaper. In something of an understatement, it concluded that "party nominations have been but little respected by the voters."[28]

26. J. Hastings to Bigler, May 26, 1854, D. Bull to Bigler, May 27, 1854, William Garvin to Bigler, June 14, 1854, C. A. Black to Bigler, June 21, 1854, John C. Dunn to Bigler, June 23, 1854 (quotation), A. Edwards to Bigler, June 27, 1854, John Nigley to Bigler, July 13, 1854 (quotation), Galusha A. Grow to Bigler, July 19, 1854, Henry Sherwood to Bigler, Aug. 12, 1854, W. S. Hirst to Bigler, Sept. 10, 1854, Bigler Papers, HSP.

27. *Whig Almanac* (1855): 43–44; Gienapp, "The Failure of Fusion in Pennsylvania," 451.

28. John Strohm to Isaac Strohm (copy), Nov. 7, 1854, Strohm Papers, OHS; Harrisburg *Keystone*, Oct. 12, 1854, quoted in Coleman, *Disruption of the Pennsylvania Democracy*, 75.

More surprising to most observers than the general chaos was the strength of the Know Nothings. A Democrat from the Northern Tier reported to Bigler that in his county he "confidently expected, up to the coming in of the returns, a larger majority than you had before [in 1851]. We did not dream that we had Know Nothings in our midst." From the west came similar news. A Democrat in Venango County notified Cameron that "we are whipt in everything . . . by the 'Know nothings.' I feel the worst I ever did in my life." And in central Huntingdon County a Democrat admitted that " 'know nothingism' has knocked the spots off us."[29]

An analysis of the vote for all three offices reveals the Know Nothings' strength:

Pennsylvania Election Results, October 1854[30]

	Governor	Canal Commissioner	Judge
Democrat	167,001	274,074*	167,010
Whig	204,008*	83,331	78,571
Native American	1,503	1,944	120,576*

*Supported by the Know Nothings

The Know Nothings controlled nearly 120,000 votes in Pennsylvania, approximately one-third of the total, and significantly more than the 80,000 that most observers had predicted. Even more pleasing to Know Nothings than the popularity of their state ticket was the success of their congressional candidates. Although it is difficult to know which candidates belonged to the Order, it seems likely that 17 of 25 congressmen-elect were Know Nothings. For a new and inexperienced political organization, electing two-thirds of Pennsylvania's congressmen represented no small accomplishment.[31] Because their candidate for governor was also elected, Know Nothings felt justified in calling the results "an AMERICAN TRIUMPH" and "a complete vindication of the principles of AMERICANISM and FREEDOM."[32]

29. E. B. Chase to Bigler, Oct. 20, 1854, Bigler Papers, HSP; R. M. DeFrance to Cameron, Oct. 12, 1854, J. P. Anderson to Cameron, Oct. 12, 1854, Cameron Papers, DCHS.

30. All Pennsylvania election figures, unless otherwise noted, are from *Whig Almanac* (1855): 43–44, and Gettysburg *Star and Banner*, Nov. 3, 1854.

31. Jacob Broom, James H. Campbell, John Covode, John R. Edie, Henry M. Fuller, John C. Kunkel, and Lemuel Todd attended Know Nothing conventions or signed Know Nothing proclamations, so their status in the Order is certain. Samuel C. Bradshaw, John Dick, Jonathan Knight, William Millward, John J. Pearce, Samuel A. Purviance, David Ritchie, Anthony E. Roberts, David Robison, and Job R. Tyson were probably Know Nothings, because they voted for Fuller (the Know Nothing candidate) for Speaker. Bradshaw and Purviance voted for Fuller on only the first few ballots, so their status is most difficult to determine. That all these men belonged to the Order is corroborated by Horace Greeley to Charles A. Dana, Feb. 6, 1856, in *Greeley on Lincoln, With Mr. Greeley's Letters to Charles A. Dana*, Joel Benton, ed. (New York, 1893), 116. I have not included in this list two congressmen who apparently joined the Order to aid their chances for election, and then abandoned the organization once elected.

32. Harrisburg *Herald*, Oct. 12, 1854.

The Know Nothing vote was not confined to any single region of Pennsylvania. Population density did not determine Know Nothing success either, nor did the presence of immigrants. Counties in which the Know Nothings did well tended to support the prohibition referendum, although several Know Nothing strongholds (York and Perry counties, for example) defeated the proposal by large margins. Nevertheless, some pronounced trends do emerge from an analysis of the Know Nothing vote. For example, Know Nothings fared relatively poorly in the counties southeast of the Appalachian Mountains (only 3 of their 17 strongest counties lay in this area). This region contained most of Pennsylvania's German-Americans. Michael Holt has found that many Protestant Germans in Pittsburgh voted the Know Nothing ticket, but reports from eastern Pennsylvania indicated that Germans who had previously been Whigs—fearing that Know Nothingism proscribed all immigrants, not just Catholics—voted Democratic.[33] As proof, these German-Americans pointed to the policies of Mayor Conrad, who appointed only native-born Americans to office. Conrad's strenuous efforts to close saloons on Sundays also piqued German-Americans, and the Order's identification with temperance may have contributed to the Know Nothings' poor showing in most southeast counties.[34] Trans-Appalachian Pennsylvania, on the other hand, populated primarily by Anglo-Saxons, provided more fertile ground for Know Nothing recruiters.

It might seem odd that the Order fared better in western Pennsylvania, where relatively few immigrants lived. However, the western counties, with few immigrants, contained a greater percentage of voters eligible for Know Nothing membership. Know Nothing success in this region also resulted to some extent from the belief that the Know Nothings would advance the temperance and anti-slavery movements. Bigler had predicted before the election that his party would fare poorly in Clinton, Centre, and Lycoming counties because this area of central Pennsylvania contained many "temperance democrats" who would desert the party over that issue. On election day, these proved to be among the strongest Know Nothing counties in the state, with the Order's ticket polling 48, 49, and 49 percent of the vote respectively.[35] As mentioned earlier, this was also the Pennsylvania region in which the Kansas-Nebraska Act had elicited the most protest. Thus, a large immigrant presence was not a prerequisite for Know Nothing electoral success.

An analysis of Pennsylvania voting also reveals that most of those casting Know Nothing ballots had voted for Whigs in the past. In Huntingdon and Berks counties, for example, comparison of the votes in the 1852 presidential

33. Michael F. Holt, *Forging a Majority: The Formation of the Republican Party in Pittsburgh, 1848–1860* (New Haven: Yale Univ. Press, 1969), 144; Daniel T. Jenks to Buchanan, Sept. 22, 1854, Buchanan Papers, HSP; Philadelphia *North American*, Oct. 19, 1854, quoted in Gienapp, *Origins of the Republican Party*, 145.

34. Daniel T. Jenks to Buchanan, Aug. 18, 1854, Buchanan Papers, HSP; G. G. Westcott to "Dear Sir," Sept. 7, 1854, James Campbell to W. S. Hirst, Oct. 2, 1854, Bigler Papers, HSP.

35. Bigler to Cameron, July 19, 1854, Cameron Papers, LC.

Know Nothing Vote for Supreme Court Judge
Pennsylvania, 1854

Less than 20%

20-29%

30-39%

40-49%

More than 49%

and 1854 Supreme Court races shows that Know Nothings gained most of
their adherents from the Whig ranks:

Huntingdon County Voting[36]

	Whig	Democrat	Know Nothing
1852	2,511 (55%)	2,041 (45%)	–
1854	585 (15%)	1,416 (36%)	1,977 (50%)

Berks County Voting

	Whig	Democrat	Know Nothing
1852	4,913 (34%)	9,503 (66%)	–
1854	2,474 (18%)	8,256 (61%)	2,794 (21%)

Even allowing for those German Whigs who voted Democratic in 1854 (there
were not many Germans in Huntingdon County) and for previous non-voters
who cast Know Nothing ballots in 1854, it seems evident that a large majority
of the Know Nothings had voted Whig in the past. As a Whig county in a
predominantly Democratic state, Huntingdon is in some ways exceptional.
However, even in traditionally Democratic strongholds such as Berks County,
Know Nothings seem to have recruited members primarily from Whig ranks.

A number of factors made Whigs desert their party more often than
Democrats. With their organization disintegrating nationally, Whigs had less
to lose in abandoning their party than their Democratic counterparts. Furthermore, because the Whig party had long been associated with mild nativism, its
members may have been more susceptible to Know Nothingism. Conversely,
Democrats were less likely to resent immigrant political power, as the newcomers often provided their margins of victory. Other Democrats were themselves immigrants or Catholics who could not become Know Nothings.

Although many Pennsylvanians abandoned their old parties and voted the
Know Nothing ticket, contemporaries disagreed about which issues had
prompted them to do so. Writing from the southern part of the state, one
Democrat reported that the "Douglas Nebraska bill disturbing the Compromise line of 1820 has been the cause of the mischief." An eastern newspaper
explained the outcome in the same way, declaring that the election demonstrated that "Pennsylvania has most emphatically rebuked the Nebraska iniquity."[37] Most Democrats, however, denied that anti-Nebraska sentiment had
caused their party's setback. The Democratic defeats "can only be explained
by the hostility to foreigners & Catholics, which seems to be deeply rooted in

36. The 1852 election figures are for President, while those for 1854 are for justice of the
Supreme Court. Percentages do not add up to one hundred because they have been rounded.
Whig Almanac (1855): 43–44; Gettysburg *Star and Banner*, Nov. 3, 1854.

37. D. Sheffer to Cameron, Oct. 14, 1854 (quotation), Cameron Papers, DCHS; West
Chester *Record*, Oct. 13, 1854 (quotation); E. B. Chase to Bigler, Oct. 10, 1854, Bigler Papers,
HSP; Pittsburgh *Gazette*, Oct. 17, 1854, quoted in Gienapp, *Origins of the Republican Party*, 146.

the minds of a large number of our people," explained one correspondent to Buchanan. "We owe our defeat more to the Protestant Ministry, and the professional religious *press*, than to any other cause," insisted another bitter Democrat.[38] Those searching for the specific cause for this outbreak of anti-Catholicism generally settled on resentment toward Campbell. "They have now got their revenge on Judge Campbell," concluded one of Buchanan's lieutenants, while a Democratic newspaper agreed that "the appointment of Judge Campbell . . . sealed [Bigler's] fate."[39] Yet the most perspicacious observers realized that both nativism *and* Nebraska had contributed to Pollock's victory. The leading Know Nothing newspaper in the state cited both the "Nebraska iniquity" and antipathy for "Political Roman Catholicism" as the causes of Bigler's defeat. An independent Philadelphia journal likewise called "*Campbellism* and *Nebraskaism* . . . the chief causes" of the Democratic losses.[40]

Realizing that nativism and anti-Nebraskaism were the decisive issues in the Pennsylvania election of 1854, historians have attempted to determine which of these factors *most* affected the election's outcome. A majority of those writing recently have settled on the former, and some of their arguments deserve individual attention. Frank Gerrity has asserted that anti-Catholicism must have been stronger than anti-Nebraskaism in Philadelphia, because a converted Catholic, Whig congressman Joseph Chandler, was denied renomination there even though he had voted against the Kansas-Nebraska Act. If slavery extension had dominated the campaign, says Gerrity, Chandler's stand against the Kansas-Nebraska Act would have earned him re-nomination. William Gienapp also argues that had anti-slavery been paramount, the Whigs, who stressed this issue during the campaign, would have carried the election. Because the Whigs were routed by the Know Nothings, Gienapp concludes that nativism was "the most powerful impulse in the election."[41]

Nativism, however, was not the only factor that motivated Know Nothing voters. As we have seen, the belief that the Order would oppose the extension of slavery drew many members to Know Nothing lodges. Thus, choosing a Know Nothing ballot did not necessarily imply that a voter considered nativism more important than the slavery extension issue. Instead, such a vote usually carried both anti-Catholic *and* anti-slavery connotations.[42] The temper-

38. James L. Reynolds to Buchanan, Oct. 23, 1854 (quotation), Buchanan Papers, HSP; George W. Bowman to Bigler, Oct. 23, 1854 (quotation), Bigler Papers, HSP; R. M. DeFrance to Cameron, Oct. 12, 1854, Cameron Papers, DCHS.

39. Daniel T. Jenks to Buchanan, Oct. 13, 1854, Buchanan Papers, HSP; Sunbury *American* quoted in Pottsville *Miner's Journal*, Oct. 21, 1854.

40. Harrisburg *Herald*, Oct. 12, 1854; Philadelphia *Evening Bulletin* quoted in Harrisburg *Herald*, Oct. 13, 1854; George Sanderson to Buchanan, Oct. 24, 1854, Buchanan Papers, HSP.

41. Frank Gerrity, "The Disruption of the Philadelphia Whigocracy: Joseph R. Chandler, Anti-Catholicism, and the Congressional Election of 1854," *Pennsylvania Magazine of History and Biography* 111 (1987): 161–94; Gienapp, *Origins of the Republican Party*, 147.

42. In exceptional instances, Pennsylvania Know Nothings did support pro-Nebraska candidates. In the sixth congressional district, Know Nothings seem to have divided over their choice for Congress, but enough supported the Democratic candidate, John Hickman, for him to win the

ance issue also drew many voters to the Know Nothing ticket, as did a general resentment toward the existing parties. Election coverage in Know Nothing journals reflected this last sentiment, revealing an almost childish glee at seeing the usual workings of the political system turned on their head. Professional politicians examining the results found nothing but "political insanity," yet this was precisely the impression Know Nothings hoped to create. One Democrat complained to Bigler that "the enormous vote polled for Baird, an old lump of irritability, whose very name is a laughing stock, shows that the organization which defeated you was deaf to the voice of reason." But by casting their ballots in some cases without regard for those whom their votes would elect, Know Nothings hoped to demonstrate that party leaders could no longer expect blind obedience from the rank and file. Politicians would now be beholden to the electorate. Thus, anti-Catholic, anti-Nebraska, anti-liquor, and anti-party sentiment—not merely nativism—contributed to the Know Nothings' popularity in 1854.[43]

These factors must be considered in determining whether nativism or anti-Nebraskaism had a greater influence on the election's outcome. Thus, the case Gerrity discusses does not prove that anti-Catholicism overshadowed the slavery issue, because Philadelphia voters did not choose an anti-Catholic candidate over an anti-slavery candidate. Instead, they selected a *Protestant* anti-slavery candidate over a *Catholic* anti-slavery candidate. Chandler's case demonstrates that *both* issues mattered to voters, and that many of them would not pursue one at the expense of the other. Gienapp's argument similarly implies that in choosing the Know Nothing ticket, voters were ignoring the slavery extension issue. However, the voters he analyzes did not choose anti-Catholic Know Nothings over anti-slavery Whigs. Rather, they supported an anti-Catholic, anti-slavery, anti-party, and anti-liquor Know Nothing ticket over a Whig slate emphasizing the slavery issue alone.

Historians have thus been misreading the options that faced voters in 1854, because a vote for the Know Nothings was much more than simply a vote for nativism. Furthermore, because it is impossible to determine which facet of the Know Nothing agenda motivated Pennsylvania voters to cast Know Nothing ballots, election returns alone cannot reveal whether nativism or anti-slavery brought about the Democratic defeat. However, it is possible to determine whether anti-slavery or *Know Nothingism* played the key role in the Democrats' defeat. If the question is posed in this manner, it is evident that Know Nothingism was the decisive factor in bringing about the

election. This district was situated in the southeast corner of the state, where anti-slavery sentiment was weakest. In the twenty-fourth congressional district, Know Nothings suspected that their candidate (Democrat David Barclay) did not endorse their anti-Nebraska views, but Know Nothings in this district were "kept in the dark" concerning his views on the slavery extension issue until it was "too late to do any good." On Hickman see McClure, *Old Time Notes*, I, p. 332; for Barclay see Clearfield [Pennsylvania] *Raftsman's Journal*, Dec. 26, 1855; *CG*, Thirty-fourth Congress, First Session, 337.

43. A. B. McCalmont to Bigler, Oct. 16, 1854, Bigler Papers, HSP.

Democratic setback in Pennsylvania. Outrage over the Kansas-Nebraska Act might have single-handedly overturned Democratic dominance in northern and much of western Pennsylvania. However, most Pennsylvanians lived in the southeast portion of the state, where the Nebraska bill elicited far less antipathy. Continued Democratic majorities in that region probably would have compensated for losses in the north and west, and enabled the Democrats to maintain control of the state if slavery extension had been the only issue. Know Nothingism, on the other hand, appealed to some voters in all portions of the state. In the Philadelphia area, Know Nothingism effectively capitalized upon anti-immigrant sentiment; in Harrisburg, the Order stressed anti-Catholicism, temperance, and anti-slavery; and in northern and western Pennsylvania, Know Nothingism focused on the anti-slavery and temperance issues. In this manner, the Know Nothings created a multifaceted coalition that broke the Democratic grip on Pennsylvania politics and elected both a governor and a majority of the state's congressmen.

In Ohio, which also held elections in October 1854, the early political activity of the Know Nothings is more difficult to trace than in Pennsylvania. With a relatively large immigrant population, and with the immigrant issue having received widespread attention in Cincinnati in the past, Ohio ought to have provided fertile ground for Know Nothingism. Furthermore, the temperance question had recently gained prominence in Ohio, and, as noted earlier, many native-born Americans believed that immigrants were largely responsible for blocking the enactment of liquor prohibition.[44]

Know Nothingism arrived in Ohio in the fall of 1853, and by the late summer of 1854 reports of the Order's increasing strength began appearing. In July a Whig noted that "the 'Know Nothings' are increasing rapidly." The Ohio correspondent of a Pennsylvania paper likewise reported that "the American feeling is very strong. The general opinion is that the state is to be purged of all foreign influences at the coming election."[45]

Yet while the Order had begun operations in Ohio well before the October election, it had not yet caught on to the extent that it had in Pennsylvania. The Order in Ohio could boast about 50,000 members by October, but that amounted to only 14 percent of the turnout in the state's 1852 election.[46]

44. Stephen E. Maizlish, *The Triumph of Sectionalism: The Transformation of Politics in Ohio, 1844–1856* (Kent: Kent State Univ. Press, 1983), 176–81, 202; Jed Dannenbaum, *Drink and Disorder: Temperance Reform in Cincinnati from the Washingtonian Revival to the WCTU* (Urbana: Univ. of Illinois Press, 1984), 122–48. Ohio's immigrants represented 14 percent of the state's population as of 1860.

45. William B. Fairchild to Isaac Strohm, July 2, 1854 (quotation), Strohm Papers, OHS; "W.A.G." in Cleveland *Express*, Sept. 26, 1854; A. Russell to Editor, Pottsville *Miner's Journal*, Oct. 7, 1854.

46. Columbus *Ohio Statesman*, March 18, 1855, quoted in Eugene H. Roseboom, "Salmon P. Chase and the Know Nothings," *MVHR* 25 (1938): 339. Ohio was the only northern state in which the Know Nothings would gain a significant number of recruits after the elections of 1854. See Chapter 7.

Furthermore, Ohio Know Nothings were not very active during the 1854 campaign. Future Know Nothing gubernatorial candidate Oren Follett recalled that "the Know Nothing organization was new and had manifested its power in local elections only; it was on this occasion left out of accounts. . . ." Salmon P. Chase agreed that the Know Nothings in 1854 had been numerous enough to form "a powerful auxiliary," but had lacked the strength to play a decisive role in the campaign.[47]

Know Nothingism played a secondary role in the election because although the slavery extension issue dominated the 1854 campaign in Ohio, the Order there was initially dominated by conservatives from the Cincinnati area who downplayed the slavery issue. Led by Chase in the Senate and Joshua R. Giddings in the House, Ohio boasted the most active and influential anti-slavery politicians of any midwestern state, and their popularity reflected a strong antipathy toward slavery among most Ohio voters. As a result, the Order would remain relatively weak in Ohio until it could shed this conservative image. Some Know Nothings did attend the state's anti-Nebraska convention, including future Ohio Know Nothing president Thomas Spooner and Cincinnati *Times* editor James D. "Pap" Taylor, Ohio's best-known nativist, but the Know Nothings in attendance did not attempt to divert attention from slavery to nativism. Instead, Ohio Know Nothing leaders followed existing Know Nothing policy, doing their best to influence nominations by participating in the operations of the regular parties.[48]

During the campaign, Know Nothingism did play a larger role in some parts of Ohio. Lewis D. Campbell and J. Scott Harrison (son of the former president), two Know Nothings running for congressional seats, predicted that the Order would influence the outcome in their districts.[49] In Cincinnati, Harrison's home, Know Nothings assumed an especially active role. The contest there focused on anti-Catholicism and political reform as well as slavery extension. Challenging the Democratic slate of candidates was the Know Nothing–controlled "American Reform" ticket whose candidates pledged to oppose both the extension of slavery into the territories and the influence of Catholics in American politics. While American Reform tickets had appeared in Cincinnati in the past, the 1854 ticket was significantly different. Earlier nativist tickets had expressed opposition to all immigrants (not merely Catholics) and had advocated temperance legislation. However, Cincinnati Know Nothings realized that they could not defeat the Democrats in 1854 without the support of Protestant Germans. These immigrants resented both the Catholic Church and the Kansas-Nebraska Act, but opposed liquor prohibition. Know Nothing supporters of the Cincinnati American Reform ticket of 1854 therefore limited their criticism of immigrants to Catholics, and toned

47. Maizlish, *Triumph of Sectionalism*, 206.
48. The presence of Spooner and Taylor at the fusion convention is noted by Gienapp, *Origins of the Republican Party*, 116.
49. Lewis D. Campbell to Isaac Strohm, Sept. 9, 1854, Strohm Papers, OHS; J. Scott Harrison to Benjamin Harrison, Sept. 30, 1854, Benjamin Harrison Papers, LC.

down their demands for a Maine Law, hoping that these concessions would convince Protestant Germans to support their candidates.[50]

In fact, the anti-Democratic candidates overwhelmed their opponents. While Democrats had won the state offices by 60,000 votes in 1853, in 1854 the People's candidates polled a 70,000-vote majority (out of 290,000 cast). Anti-Democratic candidates in the congressional races captured all 21 seats (having controlled only eight in 1852); none of the contests was even close. In Cincinnati, the American Reform ticket (including Spooner as candidate for city clerk) swept to victory by nearly a two-to-one margin.[51]

In analyzing the Ohio election results, most contemporaries stressed the impact of the Kansas-Nebraska Act. But discerning analysts pointed out that while opposition to the extension of slavery had provided the primary impetus for the Democratic defeat, Know Nothingism also contributed to the landslide. "The main element in effecting this wonderful change has been the *Nebraska bill*," wrote the Ohio correspondent of the New York *Times*, "though the Know-Nothing movement at the same time has had much to do with it." Nativism played the largest role in Cincinnati, where future president Rutherford B. Hayes found that "Anti-Nebraska, Know Nothings, and a general disgust with the powers that be, have carried this county" for the American Reform ticket. "How people do hate Catholics," Hayes noted, "and what a happiness it was to thousands to have a chance to show it in what seemed a lawful and patriotic manner."[52] Although it is impossible to determine the exact size of their contribution to the People's ticket's margin of victory, most contemporaries believed that by bringing in Democrats who would have otherwise remained loyal to their party, the Know Nothings were responsible for the unexpectedly large margin of victory.[53] The fact that many of the People's candidates for Congress were Know Nothings (the Cleveland *Express*, a Know Nothing journal, counted nine) also indicates that the Order exerted significant influence.[54]

The Know Nothings definitely drew many Protestant immigrants to the People's ticket. A German Democrat from Cincinnati complained that his countrymen had deserted the Democratic party "upon the false pretense of rebuking the pope of Rome." Another Cincinnati German explained that they had decided to "try the Know-Nothings this time for reform." Exclusion from membership in Know Nothing lodges did not deter these voters. As a

50. Dannenbaum, *Drink and Disorder*, 159–62.

51. *Whig Almanac* (1855): 46–47; New York *Times*, Oct. 20, 1854; Dannenbaum, *Drink and Disorder*, 161.

52. New York *Times*, Oct. 20, 1854; Hayes quoted in Dannenbaum, *Drink and Disorder*, 161.

53. New York *Times*, Oct. 20, 1854; Sidney Maxwell Diary, Jan. 10, Sept. 17, 1855, Cincinnati Historical Society.

54. Cleveland *Express*, Oct. 14, 1854. Congressmen Edward Ball, Lewis D. Campbell, Samuel Galloway, J. Scott Harrison, and Oscar F. Moore definitely joined the Know Nothings. Votes in Congress by Ball, Harrison, and Moore betrayed their membership in the Order, while participation by Campbell and Galloway in Know Nothing conventions proved their affiliation.

Scottish immigrant explained, "if we cannot belong to them, we know what we can do—*we can vote for their candidate*, if we can ascertain who he is; we can and will throw our influence with Protestantism against Popery."[55] That so many voters described their choice of candidates in these terms, not as a reaction to the Kansas-Nebraska Act, suggests that anti-Catholicism played a significant role in swelling the anti-Democratic majority in the Ohio election of 1854.

While Know Nothings played the role of junior partner in the Ohio anti-Nebraska coalition, Indiana Know Nothings dominated that state's anti-Democratic fusion ticket. Those favoring a fusion of the forces opposed to the Kansas-Nebraska Act had agreed to hold their nominating convention in Indianapolis on July 13, 1854. With that date in mind, Indiana Know Nothing leaders convened their first State Council meeting in the same city on July 11 and 12, nominating a slate of candidates for the state election. Because many of the delegates to the Know Nothing convention had also been chosen to represent their towns at the anti-Nebraska gathering, Indiana Know Nothing leaders hoped that the Order's candidates would win the nominations at the anti-Nebraska convention as well. The Know Nothing scheme worked perfectly. When the anti-Nebraska convention assembled (calling itself the "People's" convention), it nominated all the candidates endorsed by the Know Nothings on the previous day.[56]

The apparent ease with which the Know Nothings commandeered the People's movement in Indiana seems surprising at first, because Indiana possessed few immigrants and even fewer Catholics.[57] Nativism flourished there in part because the Indiana constitution permitted every resident to vote, including those who had not yet acquired American citizenship. Formulated to attract more settlers to the state, this proviso had become the focal point of resentment among Indiana nativists, who claimed that it gave the newcomers disproportionate political influence. Many Whigs also disliked the law, complaining that because most immigrants voted for Democrats, it gave that party an unfair advantage in elections.

Temperance also played a role in fomenting Know Nothingism in Indiana. Many of the state's residents felt that Indiana politicians (especially Democrats who controlled the legislature) had intentionally sidetracked the movement for liquor prohibition by enacting an unconstitutional local option law,

55. Henry Roedter to G. A. Neumann, quoted in Gienapp, *Origins of the Republican Party*, 121; Dannenbaum, *Drink and Disorder*, 162; Belmont [Ohio] *Independent Star* quoted in Harrisburg *Herald*, Sept. 21, 1854.

56. Gienapp, *Origins of the Republican Party*, 108–9; Carl F. Brand, "The History of the Know Nothing Party in Indiana," *Indiana Magazine of History* 18 (1922): 62–65.

57. In 1850, only 55,537 of Indiana's 977,154 white inhabitants had been born abroad. The census did not record the number of Catholics, but did note the number of Catholic churches in each county. In states east of Indiana, most counties contained at least one Catholic church. But in Indiana (and states to its west), counties with Catholic churches were the exception, not the rule.

and many of these disgruntled voters turned to the Know Nothings as a means to redress their grievances. Indiana Know Nothings also modified their membership requirements to help boost enrollment. In order to attract temperance advocates, Indiana Know Nothings required prospective members to pledge support for temperance legislation. To take advantage of the prevailing antipathy toward the Kansas-Nebraska Act, opposition to the extension of slavery was written into the ritual as well. Finally, by admitting Protestant immigrants, Indiana Know Nothings made the Order seem less proscriptive, attracting members who otherwise might not have joined a secret society. In Indiana, Know Nothingism clearly became the focal point for issues other than nativism.[58]

As a result, the Know Nothings enjoyed tremendous success in Indiana. "I never saw such a *ground swell* in Indiana as at the present time," reported an Indianan to Methodist leader Matthew Simpson. "The 'Know nothings,' " he continued, "are as thick as locusts in Egypt." Contemporaries estimated that 30,000 Indianans had joined the Know Nothings by May of 1854, 60,000 by July, and 80,000 by the eve of the October election (out of approximately 185,000 voters).[59]

As the campaign drew toward a close, it seemed possible that the People's coalition might succeed in ousting Indiana's entrenched Democratic party. Rejuvenated by the possibility of defeating their rivals for the first time in years, the state's Whigs appeared certain to turn out in large numbers. Many leading Whigs, however, had abandoned that party and joined Know Nothing lodges. Indiana's July Know Nothing convention elected Godlove S. Orth, a prominent Whig, president of the Indiana Order. Other well-known Whigs, ranging from devoted anti-slavery men such as Schuyler Colfax to conservatives such as Richard W. Thompson, also played leading roles in the organization. Although they did not contribute as many notable members, Democrats also joined Indiana Know Nothing lodges in large numbers. As election day approached, Know Nothings hoped that they had won enough converts from the Democracy to swing the contest to the People's candidates.[60]

When Indianans went to the polls on October 10, the ticket drawn up by the Know Nothings carried the election by nearly 13,000 votes.[61] In the congressional races, People's candidates won nine of the eleven seats, while Democrats had carried ten congressional districts only two years earlier. Of the nine victorious anti-Democratic candidates, at least two, Colfax and Will

58. *Constitution and By-laws of the Order* (Indianapolis, [1855]), IndSL.

59. Whitney, *Defence of the American Policy*, 284; Brand, "Know Nothing Party in Indiana," 61; Gienapp, *Origins of the Republican Party*, 109; E. R. Ames to Matthew Simpson, June 24, 1854, Simpson Papers, LC.

60. "D——" to John G. Davis, Aug. 24, 1854, A. W. Lowdermilk to Davis, Sept. 18, 1854, D. A. Farley to Davis, Sept. 24, 1854, Davis Papers, IndHS.

61. In the race for secretary of state, the top spot on the ticket, People's candidate Erasmus B. Collins won 99,636 votes (53%), while his Democratic opponent tallied 87,027 (47%). In comparison, Pierce had defeated Scott two years earlier in Indiana by more than 14,000 votes. *Whig Almanac* (1855): 48.

Cumback, were Know Nothings, while subsequent ballots cast in Washington by George C. Dunn and Harvey D. Scott suggest that they too belonged to the Order.[62] The ease with which the Order controlled the state fusion convention suggests that Know Nothings probably controlled other congressional nominating conventions as well.

The lack of a separate Know Nothing ticket makes it difficult to determine whether Know Nothingism or the slavery extension issue played the larger role in the Democratic defeat. Democrats within the state attributed their setback exclusively to the Know Nothings. "Our defeat was owing to the Secret Conclave & the Methodist church," complained one disheartened Democrat, blaming that denomination for spreading the moral fervor that attracted voters to Know Nothingism. Another insisted that "the KNs must have taken in hundreds the last 3 nights before the election" to swing the result in their favor. To aid their cause, Know Nothings "circulated the infamous falsehood that we had [illegally] imported 500 Irish to vote in this t[ownshi]p."[63] Democrats back east, on the other hand, believed that the Nebraska bill had cost Indiana Democrats the election. The Indianapolis *State Journal*, organ of the People's movement, correctly recognized that both these factors had contributed to the outcome, calling it a verdict against "slavery extension, and in favor of American Principles [and] Temperance," brought about by "the dishonesty of party leaders, and the imbecility of the [Pierce] Administration."[64] More explicitly than in any other state, Indiana Know Nothings added anti-slavery and temperance to the Order's standard anti-Catholicism. Consequently, Know Nothingism in Indiana enjoyed an appeal unmatched anywhere else in the Midwest. This allowed the Order to dominate the fusion movement, and to play the leading role in the defeat of the Democrats.

Know Nothings were ecstatic about the results of the elections held through October 1854. In every state where they had time to organize, they could claim some sort of victory. Their candidate captured the governorship in Maine, and members of the Order probably occupied a majority of the legislative seats. In California, they carried the election in the only city in which they were well organized. A Know Nothing would soon become governor of Pennsylvania, and most of the state's congressmen also belonged to the Order. Know Nothings won the election in Ohio's largest city, and dominated the process that created the victorious anti-Democratic ticket in Indiana. In all

62. Scott voted for Know Nothing Henry M. Fuller for Speaker, and Dunn also cast ballots for various Know Nothing candidates.

63. Indianapolis *Indiana State Journal*, Oct. 12, 1854; R. S. Stanton to John G. Davis, Oct. 21, 1854 (quotation), H. W. Daniels to Davis, Oct. 21, 1854 (quotation), H. B. Pickett to Davis, Oct. 25, 1854, Davis Papers, IndHS; John C. Sivey to Daniel R. Bearss, Oct. 19, 1854, Bearss Papers, IndHS.

64. Daniel T. Jenks to Buchanan, Oct. 17, 1854, George Sanderson to Buchanan, Oct. 24, 1854, Buchanan Papers, HSP; Indianapolis *State Journal*, Oct. 12, 1854.

these states except California, the Know Nothings utilized the same issues to optimize their appeal. Rather than positioning themselves merely as an anti-Catholic organization, Know Nothings also stressed their opposition to intemperance and the Kansas-Nebraska Act. This enabled the Order to attract more members and voters than they could have espousing nativism alone. While the Know Nothings established themselves as a major political force in these elections, their strategy of working in tandem with the other anti-Democratic elements makes it difficult to determine the relative importance of Know Nothingism and the Kansas-Nebraska Act in bringing about these Democratic defeats. However, the upcoming November elections seemed likely to resolve this uncertainty, for by the time the October ballots had been counted, anti-slavery forces in Massachusetts and New York had already nominated tickets that Know Nothing leaders seemed sure to reject. Know Nothing candidates would thus, for the first time, face competitors who could claim stronger anti-slavery credentials than their own. Only after these contests would it be possible to compare the relative appeal of Know Nothingism and anti-slavery sentiment and to determine the initial impact of Know Nothingism on the American political scene.

4

The Know Nothings and the Collapse
of the Second Party System

With the October contests behind them, many Know Nothings believed that the November elections in New York and Massachusetts would provide the true test of the Order's political potential. Although Know Nothings had dominated the anti-Democratic forces in Indiana and Pennsylvania, in most states the Order had functioned as a minority partner in anti-Nebraska coalitions. In the November elections, however, Know Nothing leaders decided to run independent tickets. This was a risky strategy, because many Know Nothings had not realized when they joined the Order that they would have to vote against all of their old party's candidates. Yet the Know Nothings' surprisingly strong showing in New York and landslide victory in Massachusetts proved that a significant proportion of Northerners had abandoned the conventional parties, and that the Whigs were destined for extinction. In light of these results, Northerners came to realize that the political order in which Whigs and Democrats vied for supremacy—what political scientists often call the second American party system—no longer defined American politics.

In New York, Know Nothings approached the upcoming contest with great confidence.[1] Whereas in other states the Order first organized just months or weeks before the 1854 elections, in New York the Know Nothings had been operating for years. While they had never conducted a state-wide campaign, New York Know Nothings had experience operating a communications network and working within a hierarchy of command. Furthermore, the Order had existed in New York long enough to allow Know Nothingism to spread through a large portion of the state by the eve of the election. "I find the Native American feeling very deep, very strong and very general," reported

---

1. The 1854 New York contest is the only one thoroughly documented in an extant Know Nothing manuscript collection. For this reason it will be described in some detail, in order to provide a case study of Know Nothing political operations in that critical year.

George E. Baker, Senator William H. Seward's most trusted political lieutenant. New York *Tribune* editor Horace Greeley likewise noted that "Know Nothingism is all the go this way, and it resolves to mess the deck."[2] Know Nothings hoped to use their strength to infiltrate the Whig convention and thus secure the Whig gubernatorial nomination for a member of the Order.

New York Know Nothings hoped to enlist as allies in this effort some of the state's conservative "Silver Gray" Whigs. The New York Whig party was controlled not by the Silver Grays (who, led by former President Millard Fillmore, actually preferred to be called National Whigs), but by Senator William H. Seward's anti-slavery faction. Under the day-to-day control of Seward's mentor Thurlow Weed, the Seward faction controlled the Whig nominations and patronage appointments. As the 1854 Whig nominating convention neared, however, some Silver Grays believed that they might use the secrecy of the Know Nothing organization to gain control of the proceedings. If they failed, Silver Grays believed they might convince the Know Nothings to nominate an independent slate of conservative candidates, providing Silver Grays with an alternative to the regular Whig nominees.[3]

Although many politicians had believed that nativism would dominate the campaign, it soon became clear that temperance was an equally potent issue. Earlier in the year, the New York legislature had passed a law prohibiting the sale of liquor, but Democratic Governor Horatio Seymour had vetoed it. Seymour's action outraged many New Yorkers, especially in the rural upstate region, where support for liquor prohibition was widespread. "The mean dastardly veto of Seymour has waked up the people," wrote one upstate Whig, "and no man can get much support . . . unless he is pledged in favor of the prohibitory law." Politicians had tried to sidestep this divisive issue, but after the public outcry over Seymour's veto, many concluded that "we've got to have that law & we may just as well face the music now as ever." Because Democrats seemed certain to re-nominate Seymour on an anti-prohibition ticket, Maine Law advocates looked to the Whig party to provide a candidate who endorsed their reform.[4]

2. George E. Baker to William H. Seward, Sept. 5, 1854, Seward Papers, UR; A. Calhoun to M. Ells, Aug. 9, 1854, Alexander Mann to Daniel Ullmann, July 13, 1854, Ullmann Papers, NYHS; Horace Greeley to Thurlow Weed, Aug. 10, 1854, J. J. Chambers to Weed, Oct. 31, 1854, Weed Papers, UR.

3. D. Perrin to Ullmann, Sept. 21, 1853, C. "B—man" to Benedict Lewis Jr., May 3, 1854, Alexander Mann to Ullmann, June 20, 1854, Ullmann Papers, NYHS; Thomas J. Curran, "The Know Nothings of New York" (Ph.D. diss., Columbia University, 1963), 100–105, 121, 124; Lee Warner, "The Silver Grays: New York State Conservative Whigs, 1846–1856" (Ph.D. diss., University of Wisconsin, 1971); Harry J. Carman and Reinhard H. Luthin, "The Seward-Fillmore Feud and the Disruption of the Whig Party," *NYH* 24 (1943): 335–57.

4. S. Potter Bradford to M. Ells, Aug. 24, 1854 (quotation), Samuel G. Mills to Robert Wetmore, Aug. 12, 1854, P. Smith to New York Central Whig Committee, Aug. 11, 1854, Ullmann Papers, NYHS; John M. Bradford to Thurlow Weed (quotation), June 24, 1854, Washington Hunt to Weed, Oct. 21, 1854, Weed Papers, UR; J. Austin to George E. Baker, April 18, 1854, William H. Seward Papers, UR; Washington Hunt to Hamilton Fish, April 8, 1854, Fish Papers, LC.

The attention of both temperance men and Know Nothings thus focused on controlling the Whig nominating convention that would meet in Syracuse on September 19. As a result, the local Whig meetings that chose delegates for the Syracuse gathering became the focal point of the struggle between Weed's forces and the Order. Know Nothings won enough convention seats to prevent Weed from dominating the proceedings, but neither Weed nor the Order controlled an outright majority. "I don't see how we are to get thru the convention safely," confessed Weed, yet he vowed to make no deals with the " 'Natives' and 'Silvers.' " Observers guessed that if Weed could not gain the nomination for his own gubernatorial choice, George W. Patterson, he would "go for the least exceptionable man of the order," the one he could best manage and control.[5]

Although it became clear when the convention assembled that Patterson could not win the nomination, the Know Nothings could not take advantage of Weed's weakness, primarily because they could not agree upon a candidate. New York Know Nothing president James Barker supported Joseph W. Savage, a long-time nativist who had served as secretary of the Native American Democratic Association of 1835. Savage enjoyed especially strong support among pro-temperance Know Nothings. Other nativists threw their weight behind William W. Campbell, then a judge of the Superior Court of New York. Campbell could also boast impressive nativist credentials, having served in Congress as a member of the American Republican party and having helped found the Order of United Americans. Still other Know Nothings supported Daniel Ullmann, a New York lawyer active in the Silver Gray faction. Taking advantage of Know Nothing indecisiveness, Weed eventually managed to secure the nomination for his second choice, state senator Myron H. Clark of Canandaigua. Clark's popularity derived primarily from the fact that he had sponsored the vetoed prohibition law of 1854. But many delegates, especially pro-temperance Know Nothings, only switched to Clark after they were assured that he was a member of the Order.[6]

After the convention, however, Know Nothing leaders denied that Clark belonged to the Order. They claimed that Weed, grooming Clark for the nomination, had hired renegade Know Nothings to establish a counterfeit lodge in Canandaigua so that Clark could join and gain Know Nothing support in Syracuse. Canandaigua's original Know Nothing council corroborated

5. Vivus W. Smith to Seward, Sept. 4, 1854, Seward Papers, UR; E. Pershine Smith to Henry C. Carey, Sept. 18, 1854, Henry C. Carey Papers, HSP; New York *Herald*, Sept. 13, 14, 17, 1854; Weed to George W. Patterson, Sept. 17, 1854 (copy), Weed Papers, UR; N. King to Ullmann, Sept. 8, 14 (quotation), 1854, D. L. Pettee to Ullmann, Sept. 18, 1854, Ullmann Papers, NYHS.

6. Nathan King to Ullmann, Sept. 8, 1854, A. Wolcott to Ullmann, Aug. 16, 1854, Stephen H. Hammond to Ullmann, Oct. 17, 1854, Ullmann Papers, NYHS; Curran, "Know Nothings of New York," 118–19; Mark L. Berger, *The Revolution in the New York Party Systems, 1840–1860* (Port Washington, N.Y.: Kennikat Press, 1973), 54; Henrdik Booraem V, *The Formation of the Republican Party in New York: Politics and Conscience in the Antebellum North* (New York: New York Univ. Press, 1983), 54–55; "Fideliter" in New York *Times*, May 22, 1855.

this story, and at least one letter to Weed confirms that his faction had created Clark's lodge specifically to win him Know Nothing support for the Whig nomination. Consequently, most Know Nothings concluded that Clark was not a member of the Order. Even one of Clark's most ardent supporters, New York *Tribune* editor Horace Greeley, derisively referred to the Whig nominee as "Myron H. Clark, the bogus Know Nothing."[7]

Know Nothing leaders had anticipated the possibility that none of their candidates would capture the Whig nomination. Even before the Syracuse convention met, Barker had sent a circular to New York lodges announcing a convention on October 4 in New York City to choose candidates for the election. Breaking from past Know Nothing practice, Barker's circular announced that the convention would not necessarily limit its choices to the candidates nominated by the other parties. Instead Barker offered delegates the option to "strike down the 'old politicians' " by nominating their own candidates, the alternative Barker hoped to follow if the Order failed to control the Whig convention.[8] Why did Barker suggest this unprecedented course? The leaders of the Order in New York were primarily conservative Whigs, understandably reluctant to endorse Clark or Seymour. Some believed that having failed to control the Whig nomination, the Know Nothings would support Greene C. Bronson, the nominee of the "Hard" Democrats.[9] However, Bronson's support for the Kansas-Nebraska Act and his opposition to the Maine Law made his chances for election—even with Know Nothing support—seem remote. With no candidate in the field who reflected their views, New York Know Nothing leaders probably saw no alternative but to make their own nominations, thereby establishing their independence from the "old politicians" while simultaneously promoting their political agenda.

The Know Nothing nominating convention gathered in New York on October 4. After dispensing with organizational questions, the convention considered whether to endorse candidates nominated by the regular parties or to select an independent slate. Many delegates urged the convention to endorse Clark, arguing that a split in the anti-Democratic forces would insure Seymour's victory. Barker, on the other hand, wanted the Order to make its

7. Nathan King to Ullmann, Sept. 16, 1854, Ullmann Papers, NYHS; "OK" in New York *Herald*, Sept. 27, 1854; E.G. Spaulding to Weed, Aug. 20, 1854, Weed Papers, UR; Greeley to Seward, Nov. 24, 1855, Seward Papers, UR.

8. Circular quoted in Vivus W. Smith to Seward, Sept. 4, 1854, Seward Papers, UR. That Barker preferred an independent nomination is suggested in the now lost Executive Records of the Order of United Americans which were available to Louis D. Scisco and cited in his *Political Nativism in New York State* (New York: Columbia Univ. Press, 1901), 117–18.

9. Democrats in New York had split into two factions. The division had developed over how to treat anti-slavery Democrats who had supported Martin Van Buren as the Free Soil candidate for President in 1848. The "Hards," who were generally more conservative on the slavery question, believed it unfair that the returning bolters were eligible for patronage, while their consistent loyalty to the party went unrewarded. The "Softs," containing a large majority of the party's members, believed that the anti-slavery Democrats should not be punished for their past digressions. Seymour was the Soft nominee. For the belief that the Know Nothings would support the Hard nominee, see L. A. Spalding to Weed, Aug. 3, 1853 [1854], Weed Papers, UR.

own nominations, and after a bitter debate, the Know Nothings sustained their president's wishes. The delegates who supported Clark then walked out of the meeting. Those remaining began selecting a candidate for governor, and on the first ballot they chose Ullmann. The convention quickly filled the rest of the ticket and then, without adopting a platform, adjourned.[10]

Why did Barker, who had supported Savage at the Whig convention, switch to Ullmann when the Know Nothings convened in New York? Ullmann operated a respected but far from prominent law practice in New York, and was active in Silver Gray affairs. Born in 1810, he had first gained public attention as the Whig candidate for New York attorney general in 1851. Although he lost, Ullmann re-surfaced in 1852 when Silver Grays at the Whig convention attempted unsuccessfully to nominate him for governor. One New York journal characterized Ullmann as an "inveterate and persevering office-seeker" who "ranks somewhere among the third or fourth rate members of the New York Bar," but for the most part his nomination was greeted with respect. Ullmann had tried to obtain the Whig nomination at Syracuse, but Weed and Barker had stymied his efforts.[11] Barker probably calculated that the Order possessed too few members in New York to carry the election without some outside support. With Savage as the Whig/Know Nothing nominee, Barker could have counted on the votes of many temperance advocates. With Clark in the field, however, the temperance vote seemed lost. Of all the New York factions, only the Silver Grays lacked a candidate, so Barker probably threw his weight behind Ullmann in the hope that Silver Gray support would make victory possible for the Know Nothing candidate.

Immediately after Ullmann's nomination, Know Nothings asked Silver Gray leaders to endorse Ullmann officially. With "the entire National Whig strength of the State, . . . Mr. Ullmann could certainly be elected," argued Know Nothing leader Stephen Sammons in a letter to Fillmore, while any other course would waste Silver Gray votes. Ullmann himself also urged leading Silver Grays to organize a meeting at which they could endorse his candidacy. But as word of this plan spread, others advised Ullmann to abort the effort. Official Silver Gray support, they argued, would cost Ullmann the votes of "a certain class in our order" as well as many outsiders.[12] Some Silver

10. New York *Herald*, Oct. 7, 1854; Know Nothing circular in New York *Times*, Oct. 26, 1854; Scisco, *Political Nativism in New York State*, 119–20. Ullmann received 256 votes, Savage tallied 114, and Order of United Americans founder Thomas Whitney garnered 45 out of the 514 votes cast. Before the walkout there were 953 delegates.

11. Rochester *American*, Oct. 28, 1854; Warner, "The Silver Grays," 237–38; New York *Mirror*, Oct. 6, 1854 (quotation); Ralph Basso, "Nationalism, Nativism, and the Black Soldier: Daniel Ullmann, A Biography of a Man Living in a Period of Transition, 1810–1892" (Ph.D. diss., St. John's University, 1986); Alexander Mann to Ullmann, July 13, 14, 24, 1854, Samuel Haight to Ullmann, July 22, 27, 1854, L. S. Parsons to Ullmann, Sept. 14, 1854, Ullmann Papers, NYHS; Curran, "Know Nothings of New York," 119–20, 123.

12. Stephen Sammons to Fillmore, Oct. 16, 1854, Fillmore Papers, SUNY-O; George F. Comstock to Ullmann, Oct. 6, 1854, E. F. Hovey to Ullmann, Oct. 17, 1854, George R. Babcock to Ullmann, Oct. 18, 1854, L. L. Pratt to Ullmann, Oct. 19, 1854, J. P. Faurot to Ullmann, Oct. 20, 1854 (quotation), Ullmann Papers, NYHS.

Grays also balked, fearing that such a course would lead to the "formal disbanding of the Silver Grays." In the end, the Silver Grays decided to give Ullmann unofficial backing. As one of Fillmore's lieutenants explained the arrangement, the endorsement "is not to be done by any formal address or open proclamation, but only recommended privately among friends."[13] This allowed the Silver Grays to maintain their independence while simultaneously aiding the candidate who most closely reflected their views. At the same time, the Know Nothings earned valuable backing for their ticket in a manner that would not drive off other supporters.

Even when only two parties contested an election in New York, the state's notoriously complex web of factions and cliques made predictions difficult. But with four slates of candidates in the field in 1854, observers concluded that the campaign would resemble "a sort of helter-skelter scrub race" that would be close right down to the wire.[14] Political insiders initially gave the Know Nothings little hope of winning the election, but soon word began to spread around the state that the Order had expanded tremendously since their convention. "I am amazed at the extent of the defections" to the Know Nothings, wrote one worried Whig to Thurlow Weed. Ex-governor Washington Hunt complained that the Order had "deranged half the towns" near his home in western New York. Most of these Know Nothing gains resulted from ambitious recruitment drives. Lodges started meeting nightly in order to expedite the initiation process, while Know Nothing leaders sent out deputies to establish lodges in areas neglected by previous recruiters.[15] Know Nothings established approximately one hundred new lodges during the month between their convention and election day, and membership in the Order increased by about one-third during that period.[16]

As the campaign progressed, the Know Nothing ticket also gained support from those who would not or could not join the Order. One non–Know Nothing supported Ullmann because he opposed "the influence of Popish priests" and "the elevation of foreigners to office," and because of Know

13. Francis Granger to Fillmore, Sept. 23, 1854, E. R. Jewett to [Fillmore], Oct. 24, [1854], Fillmore Papers, SUNY-O; New York *Times*, Nov. 1, 1854.

14. New York *Mirror*, Oct. 26, 1854.

15. H. A. Risley to Weed, Nov. 2, 1854, W. Hunt to Weed, Oct. 21, 1854, Weed Papers, UR; Ethan Allen Council [Canandaigua, New York] Minute Book, Oct. 31 to Nov. 6, 1854, Ontario County Historical Society; Charles G. Irish, Jr. to Ullmann, Oct. 11, 1854, H. Allen to S. Sammons, Oct. 30, 1854, Ullmann Papers, NYHS.

16. At the start of October, there were 515 New York Know Nothing lodges with approximately 75,000 members, a force equal to only one-sixth of the normal New York electoral turnout. Because a St. Lawrence County Know Nothing signed himself as treasurer of lodge 600 at the end of that month, I have inferred that approximately one hundred new lodges were formed before the election. The Canandaigua lodge increased its membership by 25 percent during October. This rate of increase in the old lodges, combined with the members added through the creation of new lodges, must have pushed membership to well over 100,000 by election day. Scisco, *Political Nativism in New York State*, 119; Nathan Crary to Ullmann, Oct. 31, 1854, Ullmann Papers, NYHS; Ethan Allen Council [Canandaigua, New York] Minute Book, Oct.–Nov. 6, 1854, Ontario County Historical Society.

Nothing efforts to expose "the corruption of Party leaders." Know Nothings across the state reported that many outsiders concerned with these issues would vote for the Order's candidates.[17] Among these outsiders planning to cast Know Nothing ballots were significant numbers of Protestant immigrants. Leaders of the American Protestant Association, an anti-Catholic organization made up primarily of naturalized citizens, promised Ullmann that even though its French and German Protestant members could not join the Order, many would nonetheless vote the Know Nothing ticket.[18]

However, accessions from outside the Order were eventually offset by defections from within over the temperance issue. After his nomination, Ullmann had followed the advice of a friend who warned, "*don't write any letters. Keep dark—'know nothing.' *" But Ullmann's silence on temperance worried upstate Know Nothings who supported prohibition. They deluged Ullmann with letters asking whether he would sign a Maine Law if elected. Ullmann had promised to sign a prohibition bill in a letter circulated at the Whig convention, but he now refused to issue a similar guarantee.[19] Ullmann may have personally opposed prohibition, or he may have feared alienating those urban nativists who opposed drinking restrictions. In any case, when the depth of this problem became clear, Ullmann embarked on a tour of upstate lodges in order to assure their members personally that he shared their views on temperance. Yet Ullmann's efforts paled beside Clark's outspoken pledges to sign any temperance legislation, prompting many upstate Know Nothings to support Clark rather than risk electing a candidate who might veto a prohibition law.[20]

While Know Nothing leaders scrambled to improve Ullmann's image among temperance advocates, another calamity beset his campaign. As a student at Yale, Ullmann had apparently fancied himself a man of the world, frequently appending "Calcutta" to his signature, even though he had been born and raised in Wilmington. Now this capricious whim came back to haunt him, as Whig opponents charged that Ullmann was a native of India. The belief that those born overseas were unfit for public office lay at the heart of

17. B. Slocum to Ullmann, Oct. 9, 1854 (quotation), E. F. Hovey to Ullmann, Oct. 17, 1854, J. T. Henry to Ullmann, Oct. 10, 1854, Ullmann Papers, NYHS.

18. Charles G. Irish, Jr. to Ullmann, Oct. 14, 16, 1854, G. F. Secchi de Casali to Ullmann, Oct. 16, 1854, G. Scroggs to Ullmann, Oct. 14, 1854, Ullmann Papers, NYHS; New York *Herald*, Oct. 29 (Albany correspondent), Dec. 26, 1854; New York *Express*, July 30, 1855 (on American Protestant Association). American Protestant Association President Charles Irish, Jr., was also president of a Know Nothing lodge.

19. Henry Sherman to Ullmann, Oct. 9, 1854 (quotation), Hiram Kling to Ullmann, Oct. 12, 1854, "O.L.S." to Ullmann, Oct. 10, 1854, H. C. Baker to Ullmann, Oct. 19, 1854, G. Searl to Ullmann, Oct. 23, 1854, E. Bickford to Ullmann, Oct. 23, 1854, G. N. Storn to Ullmann, Oct. 26, 1854, Nathan Crary to Ullmann, Oct. 31, 1854, Ullmann to D. Andrews, Sept. 16, 1854 (copy), Ullmann Papers, NYHS.

20. J. M. Coley to Ullmann, Oct. 15, 1854, S. H. Hammond to Ullmann, Oct. 17, 1854, Ullmann Papers, NYHS; Fillmore to John P. Kennedy, Nov. 1, 1854, Kennedy Papers, Enoch Pratt Library; New York *Mirror*, Oct. 25, 1854; Rochester *American*, Oct. 27, 1854.

Know Nothing ideology, and members therefore took the accusation very seriously. The report that Ullmann was born abroad "has gained considerable credence among the brothers of our order," reported one Know Nothing, and Sammons informed Ullmann that "this is *damaging* you to a certainty." Ullmann initially said nothing about the charge, but as such reports continued to stream in, advisors convinced him to answer the allegation. "If you were really born anywhere—for Heavens sake, say *where*," begged one Silver Gray.[21] Ullmann wrote letters to various councils attempting to convince lodge members of his American nativity. When these failed to quell the rumors, he sent a nativist editor to Wilmington to collect his birth records. New York Know Nothings wasted time and energy responding to this charge, and it pushed their campaign into a decidedly defensive posture.[22]

Whig newspapers also attracted wavering Know Nothings to Clark by subtly creating an anti-Catholic aura around their own candidates. Weed's Albany *Evening Journal* emphasized that the Whig ticket consisted of "American born, Protestant candidates," while the Troy *Family Journal* insisted that a vote for Clark was a vote against "Rum, Romanism, and Slavery."[23] As news of Know Nothing defections to Clark became widely known, some Know Nothings downstate, where Democrats dominated many councils, began switching to the Soft ticket. "Two thirds of this council will vote directly for Seymour," reported a Westchester County Know Nothing, and most of the Whigs in that lodge refused to "throw away" their votes on Ullmann if Democratic Know Nothings would not vote for him. Because Ullmann appeared to have no chance, and because the race between Clark and Seymour seemed so close, dozens of councils decided to "repudiate the State nominations, and . . . resolved to vote for . . . the Locofoco [Democratic] or Whig parties, as corresponds to their old party predilections." Although the disintegration of party ties had aided Know Nothing recruitment, the persistence of partisan prejudices convinced many members to abandon the Order's candidates.[24]

The fledgling Republican party would experience the same problems with inter-party rivalry based on past loyalties, but these difficulties were exacerbated for the Know Nothings by problems unique to their organization. Because they originated as a fraternal order, the Know Nothings possessed no

21. E. M. Holbrook to Ullmann, Oct. 12, 1854 (quotation), L. M. Crane to Ullmann, Oct. 14, 1854, D. Timberlake to Ullmann, Oct. 23, 1854, S. Sammons to Ullmann, Oct. 28, 1854, Charles Morris to Ullmann, Oct. 30, 1854, Charles Whitney to Sammons, Oct. 31, 1854, Francis Granger to Ullmann, Oct. 17, 1854 (quotation).

22. John A. Allderdice to Ullmann, Oct. 15, 1854, Charles G. Irish, Jr. to Ullmann, Oct. 16, 1854, G. F. Secchi de Casali to Ullmann, Oct. 30, 1854, Ullmann Papers, NYHS. Some newspapers embellished the Calcutta rumor to include the charge that Ullmann was the son of "Asiatic Jews." See Rochester *American*, Oct. 14, 1854; Ullmann to Rev. S. Cowles, Dec. 26, 1854 (draft), Cowles to Ullmann, Dec. 29, 1854, Ullmann Papers, NYHS.

23. Albany *Evening Journal* quoted in Rochester *American*, Oct. 17, 1854; Troy *Family Journal*, Oct. 13, 1854; George M. Grier to Seward, Nov. 18, 1854, Seward Papers, UR.

24. S. H. Wells to Ullmann, Oct. 30, 1854 (quotation), L. B. Dickinson to Ullmann, Oct. 25, 1854, Ullmann Papers, NYHS.

central committee to coordinate electioneering activities. Barker appointed "deputies" to run the campaign in each county, but their letters to Ullmann reflect their ignorance concerning many aspects of the canvass. The Know Nothings also lacked the funds to finance a state-wide campaign. Barker's pleas for donations from individual councils went largely unheeded, and candidates sometimes refused to pay expenses out of their own pockets.[25] However, lack of newspaper support may have hurt the Order most. While Whigs and Democrats could count on dozens of newspapers across the state to endorse their candidates and publish party propaganda, the Know Nothings could rely on no such organs. Many Silver Gray editors hinted that they preferred Ullmann, but they continued to run the regular Whig ticket on their mastheads, in some cases because they did not want to appear disloyal to their party, but mostly because they feared that advertising and subscriptions would decline if they identified themselves with the Order.[26] The refusal of the leading Silver Gray organ, the Albany *State Register*, to offer even a veiled endorsement may have dealt the decisive blow to Ullmann's campaign. Although its editor Samuel H. Hammond belonged to the Order, he believed that Ullmann could not win, and pleaded with the Know Nothing candidate to withdraw so that Clark could capture the election and "secure the triumph of the temperance cause." Know Nothing leaders had counted on the *Register*'s support, considering the paper's strong influence upstate essential to win over those Know Nothings who were wavering because of the temperance issue.[27] All these difficulties combined to create the impression in the public mind that Ullmann would finish a distant third behind Clark and Seymour.

Consequently, political prognosticators were amazed to discover Ullmann running neck-and-neck with Clark and Seymour as the first returns came in on election night. When the more remote counties reported in, however, Ullmann fell back into third place. The race for governor was so close that nearly two weeks elapsed before newspapers could safely proclaim Clark the winner. However, Ullmann's surprisingly strong showing was almost as newsworthy as Clark's victory. The Know Nothing ticket polled 122,282 votes (26%), compared with 156,804 (33%) for Clark, 156,495 (33%) for Seymour, and 33,850 (7%) for Bronson.[28] Know Nothings fared even better in congressional races,

25. William Avery to Ullmann, Oct. 10, 1854, G. Searl to Ullmann, Oct. 23, 1854, Louis B. Lott to Ullmann, Oct. 26, 1854, William W. Valk [Know Nothing congressional candidate from Long Island] to Sammons, Oct. 29, 1854, Ullmann Papers, NYHS; Barker circular printed in New York *Times*, Oct. 26, 1854.

26. A. Mann [Rochester *American*] to Ullmann, Oct. 9, 1854, J. T. Henry [Ellicottville *Union*] to Ullmann, Oct. 10, 1854, L. L. Pratt [Fredonia *Advertiser*] to Ullmann, Oct. 17, 1854, B. Slocum [Geneva *Clarion*] to Ullmann, Oct. 9, 1854, Ullmann Papers, NYHS; New York *Tribune*, Oct. 9, 1854.

27. S. H. Hammond to Ullmann, Oct. 17, 1854, S. Lathrop to Ullmann, Nov. 16, 1854, Ullmann Papers, NYHS; Francis Granger to Fillmore, Sept. 23, 1854, John Bush to Fillmore, Nov. 15, 1854, Fillmore Papers, SUNY-O; Albany *State Register*, Oct. 25, 1854.

28. *Whig Almanac* (1855): 41. All percentages in this chapter have been rounded and may not add up to one hundred.

electing four independent Know Nothing candidates (Bayard Clark, Francis S. Edwards, William W. Valk, and Order of United Americans founder Thomas R. Whitney). Seven victorious candidates originally nominated by other parties also definitely cooperated with the Order (Thomas Flagler, Amos P. Granger, Solomon G. Haven, Killian Miller, Russell Sage, Abram Wakeman, and John Wheeler).[29]

Ullmann's surprisingly large tally—and the success of so many Know Nothing congressional candidates—shocked most New Yorkers. "Who could have believed that K. N. fanaticism was so extensive and so well organized?" asked an intimate of Seward's, reflecting a view held both in and outside the Order. Diarist George Templeton Strong deduced from the New York result that the Know Nothings would elect the next president, and Ullmann's strong showing convinced a Silver Gray politician that the Know Nothings would soon control twenty-five states. Even newspapers that had opposed Ullmann admitted that "Americanism, on its first, and yet but half-disciplined rally, has achieved a glorious triumph."[30]

Despite Ullmann's loss, Know Nothings viewed the outcome as a "glorious" defeat. Know Nothings believed that their own secrecy had impeded them, because members could not communicate with each other and learn how popular Ullmann's candidacy had become. "Hundreds here say openly, 'Had we dreamed of your strength we should have voted your ticket,'" reported one lodge member. As a result, he concluded that "could the election be held over again tomorrow, we should carry *every thing, every where*." Even non–Know Nothings agreed that Ullmann would win a new election. One estimated that the Whigs had stolen 25,000 votes from the Order by convincing Know Nothings that Ullmann had no chance and by spreading false rumors about his nativity and temperance position.[31] In addition, Ullmann's promising showing had come even though a large portion of the state remained unorganized. Had lodges "been perfected in obscure and sparsely settled places we should have succeeded," asserted one of Ullmann's correspondents, because in "towns where the light of the [Know Nothing] Gospel had not shown you got a light vote."[32] Mapping the Know Nothing vote seems to substantiate this claim. Know Nothingism apparently spread out from New York and Buffalo, failing to reach the central and northern portions of the

29. The *Know Nothing Almanac* also listed Thomas Child, Jr., Jonas A. Hughston, William H. Kelsey, Rufus H. King, Orasmus B. Matteson, Andrew Z. McCarty, John M. Parker, Guy R. Pelton, and Benjamin Pringle as Know Nothings, but I have been unable to confirm their membership in the Order. *Know Nothing Almanac* (1855): 63.

30. George W. Patterson to Seward, Nov. 8, 1854, George E. Baker to Seward, Nov. 10, 1854 (quotation), Seward Papers, UR; *The Diary of George Templeton Strong*, Allan Nevins and Thomas H. Milton, eds. (New York: Macmillan, 1952), II, p. 196; Berger, *Revolution in the New York Party Systems*, 67; New York *Mirror*, Nov. 7, 1854 (quotation); Albany *State Register*, Nov. 9, 1854.

31. L. S. Parsons to Ullmann (quotation), endorsed Nov. 11, 1854, E. Holbrook to Ullmann, Nov. 20, 1854, Leslie Combs to Ullmann, Nov. 11, 1854, Ullmann Papers, NYHS; Jacob G. Sanders to James W. Beekman, Nov. 19, 1854, Feb. 17, 1855, Beekman Papers, NYHS.

32. S. Lathrop to Ullmann, Nov. 16, 1854, Ullmann Papers, NYHS.

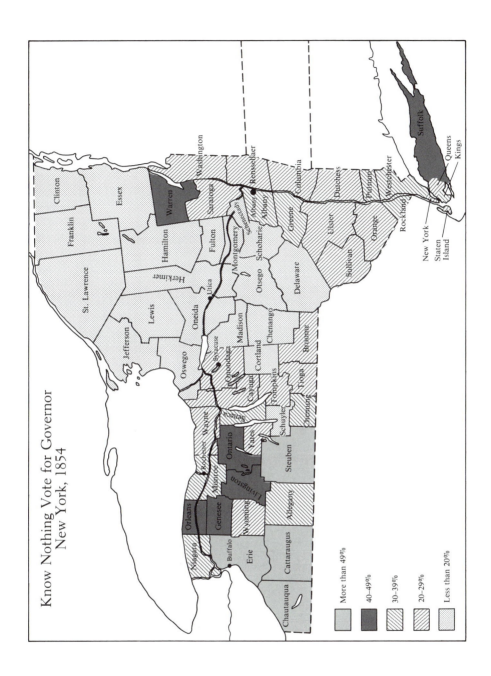

Know Nothing Vote for Governor
New York, 1854

More than 49%

40–49%

30–39%

20–29%

Less than 20%

state. Know Nothings reasoned that if they could organize lodges in these areas, while maintaining their strength in southern and western New York, the Order would inevitably dominate New York politics.

Analysis of the New York vote reveals other patterns. As in Pennsylvania, New York Know Nothings drew most of their support from former Whigs:

Erie County Voting[33]

	Whig	Soft Dem.	Hard Dem.	Know Nothing
1853	5,651 (49%)	3,409 (29%)	2,585 (22%)	–
1854	2,119 (14%)	5,252 (34%)	442 (3%)	7,712 (50%)

These figures also support the conclusion of contemporary observers that most Whigs casting Know Nothing votes came from the Silver Gray faction. Erie County, the home of ex-President Fillmore, was a Silver Gray stronghold. This helps to explain the extent to which Erie County Whigs abandoned their party's regular ticket. Where the Seward-Weed faction was strongest— in the Burned-Over District that stretched along the Erie Canal from Albany through the northern rim of western New York—Know Nothing candidates fared less well. While it was true, as one observer noted, that "the district which used to be called by the Albany Regency: the 'infected district,' is at this moment very badly infected with know-nothingism," most of this region's Know Nothings (especially those in the eastern half of the district) defected to Clark. However, other areas previously controlled by Seward's faction now yielded to Know Nothing domination. For example, results from Chautauqua County proved that "this heretofore Seward-and-Weed-ridden district" had fallen securely into Know Nothing hands.[34]

In Pennsylvania's 1854 election, Whig Know Nothings had outnumbered Democratic Know Nothings in virtually every county. In New York, however, Democrats supplied more converts than Whigs in many areas:

Putnam County Voting

	Whig	Soft Dem.	Hard Dem.	Know Nothing
1853	461 (33%)	237 (17%)	679 (49%)	–
1854	554 (29%)	617 (33%)	83 (4%)	638 (34%)

Putnam County was not exceptional, as at least a dozen other counties exhibited this same trend.[35] As the Erie and Putnam county figures demonstrate,

33. These statistics and those that follow are taken from *Whig Almanac*, 1854 and 1855.
34. John J. Bowen to "Sir," Oct. 30, 1854 (quotation), L. L. Pratt to Ullmann, Oct. 17, 1854 (quotation), Ullmann Papers, NYHS; Buffalo *Express* quoted in New York *Express*, Jan. 6, 1855.
35. They were Chanango, Herkimer, Orleans, Rockland, Suffolk, Allegany, Cayuga, Delaware, Montgomery, Niagara, Warren, and Chemung counties.

most of the Democratic converts to Know Nothingism came from the Hard faction. Some Hards may have joined the Know Nothings realizing that their faction was in a hopeless minority (like the Silver Grays) and hoping to rule the Know Nothings rather than play a subordinate role in the Democratic party. Hards may have also believed that a Democratic loss would force the Softs to make concessions to them. Nativism may have also drawn Hards to the Order. Many New York Democrats resented the increasing power of immigrants in their party, and even "Boss" William M. Tweed, famed for perfecting the immigrant-backed political machine, dabbled in nativism in the early 1850s. Although ex-Democrats would always remain a minority within the New York Know Nothing organization, their support helped swell Ullmann's totals.[36]

Know Nothingism in New York was unique. The Order stressed its anti-slavery stance in most northern states, but in the 1854 New York campaign the slavery issue played a minor role. Know Nothings drew strength from the temperance movement in the rest of the North, yet temperance apparently lost Ullmann more votes than it won for him. In other northern states, conservatives remained in the Whig party while anti-slavery men joined Know Nothing coalitions, but in New York, Silver Grays flocked to Know Nothing lodges. New York Know Nothings were also the first to transform the Order into an independent political party. Although Ullmann did not win the governorship, his strong showing gratified Know Nothing leaders, convincing them that they had not erred in nominating an independent ticket. They believed that in subsequent contests, the Order would triumph as an independent political party.

New York Know Nothings did not have to wait long to have their predictions of future triumphs confirmed: in Massachusetts, which held its election one week after New York's, the Order achieved a landslide victory. Local political conditions in Massachusetts created an ideal situation for Know Nothing recruiters. Whigs had long controlled Massachusetts politics, and both the Democratic and the Free Soil parties saw little hope of changing the situation. In 1850, though, Democrats and Free Soilers had devised a coalition in which the Free Soilers promised to support the Democratic candidate for governor if Democrats in the legislature would endorse the Free Soil choice, Charles Sumner, for the United States Senate. The plan succeeded, and the coalition managed to win the 1851 state election as well. But by 1852 the Whigs had recaptured control of the Massachusetts state government.[37]

The coalition sought to regain its lost power by proposing a new state

36. New York *Mirror*, Nov. 10, 1854; Berger, *Revolution in the New York Party Systems*, 68, 147 n. 32; *CG*, 34th Congress, First Session, Appendix, 597; Simeon Draper to Thurlow Weed, April 5, 1856, Weed Papers, UR; Ian Tyrrell, *Sobering Up: From Temperance to Prohibition in Antebellum America* (Westport, Conn.: Greenwood Press, 1979), 265 (Tweed).

37. Kevin Sweeney, "Rum, Romanism, Representation, and Reform: Coalition Politics in Massachusetts, 1847–1853," *Civil War History* 22 (1976): 116–37.

constitution, which would increase the representation of small towns that tended to vote Democratic. It would also outlaw the "block voting" system under which Bostonians voted for a slate of forty-four legislators, rather than allowing each district to elect its own candidate. This practice virtually guaranteed that Boston would send Whig representatives to the legislature, even though the large pockets of immigrants in the city would otherwise have elected Democrats. Other aspects of the proposed constitution were designed to give Democrats obvious advantages, such as the requirement of an Australian ballot only in large cities where Whigs predominated. While the existing constitution favored the Whigs, the new document represented such a blatant attempt to tip the scales the other way that many Democrats offered it only luke-warm support. Adoption of the new constitution required popular approval in a referendum, but Bay State voters defeated the measure.[38]

Although modern statistical analysis indicates that a majority of Irish immigrants voted in favor of the constitution, contemporaries blamed them for its defeat. The leading Catholic newspaper in Boston, the *Pilot*, had vehemently opposed the constitution, in part because one of its amendments (to be voted on separately) would have prohibited the financing of parochial schools with public tax money. The *Pilot* boasted that the Catholic vote had defeated the constitution, and Whig journals went out of their way to "thank" Catholics for opposing it. Supporters of the constitution therefore felt certain that Irish Catholics had voted against it, increasing anti-Catholicism in Massachusetts significantly, especially among the Free Soilers who had counted on approval of the constitution to improve their political position.[39] An early report of Know Nothing activity in Boston stated that "in this city and in many places it is controlled in great measure by the Free Soilers, who have been much outraged by the movement of the Catholics against the Constitution." A Know Nothing legislator asserted that "hundreds joined the new movement" because of the constitution's failure, and stated that "but for the defeat of the Constitution, I should not have joined" the Order. A Democratic leader calculated that "smarting under the defeat of the proposed constitution," 20,000 to 30,000 Coalitionists joined the Know Nothings. Even the *Pilot* admitted that "we can easily understand the reason why an anti-Popery epidemic rages just now" and cited the role of Catholic voters in the election of

38. *The Constitutional Propositions Adopted by the Convention of Delegates . . .* (Boston, 1853); Samuel Shapiro, "The Conservative Dilemma: The Massachusetts Constitutional Convention of 1853," *New England Quarterly* 33 (1960): 219–21; William G. Bean, "Party Transformation in Massachusetts with Special Reference to the Antecedents of Republicanism, 1848–1860" (Ph.D. diss., Harvard University, 1922), 147–66; Martin B. Duberman, "Friends Divided: Debate on the Massachusetts Constitution of 1853," *Mid-America* 45 (1963): 50–55; *Discussions of the Constitution Proposed to the People of Massachusetts by the Convention of 1853* (Boston: 1854).

39. Sweeney, "Rum, Romanism, Representation, and Reform," 136; Bean, "Party Transformation in Massachusetts," 174, 178–79; Bean, "Puritan versus Celt, 1850–1860," *New England Quarterly* 7 (1934): 74–75.

President Pierce and the defeat of the constitution for the rise of nativist groups such as the Know Nothings.[40]

A controversial fugitive slave case added to the anti-Irish sentiment stirred up by the constitution's defeat. Most Massachusetts residents were outraged in May 1854 when authorities captured runaway slave Anthony Burns in Boston and began preparing his return to the South. Opposition to enforcement of the fugitive slave law became so intense that officials, fearing a riot, called out the militia. Most militia units refused to assist in Burns's incarceration, but a number of Irish units consented to the call. The participation of the Irish militia units in the Burns case angered anti-slavery men and reinforced the already prevalent belief that the Irish supported slavery. Describing the Burns case, one of Sumner's correspondents complained that "the moment an Irishman lands upon these shores *he* identifies himself with slavery, upon the shallow pretext of upholding the laws." A letter in *The Liberator* likewise complained that "Irishmen, instead of shedding the tear of pity [for Burns], hardened their hearts, and did the business of the oppressor." Know Nothings throughout the North used the pro-slavery reputation of the Irish to attract members, but the Burns case made this a particularly potent weapon for the Order's Massachusetts recruiters.[41]

Massachusetts Know Nothings also benefited from factionalism among the state's anti-slavery politicians. With free soil sentiment so pervasive in Massachusetts, observers expected a strong Republican organization to form there in 1854. But many Whig leaders refused to abandon their party, and insisted that opponents of the Kansas-Nebraska Act join their organization. Free Soilers balked. Many Free Soil leaders (such as Henry Wilson and Nathaniel Banks) came from humble backgrounds, and resented both the aristocratic condescension of the Whig leaders and the role played by Whigs in defeating the proposed constitution. So when anti-slavery Whigs refused to abandon their organization for a Republican party, most Free Soilers, whose leaders had made overtures to the Know Nothings earlier in the year, joined the Order. Combined with the strong Puritan tradition of anti-Catholicism still prevalent in Massachusetts, these special circumstances contributed to the immense popularity of Know Nothingism there. By the eve of the November 1854 election, the Massachusetts Know Nothings could boast 410 councils with 73,000 members, corresponding to well over half the number of votes usually cast in state elections.[42]

40. "S" [James W. Stone] to Sumner, March 15, 1854, Sumner Papers, HU; Charles W. Slack and Whiting Griswold quoted in Bean, "Puritan versus Celt," 79; Boston *Pilot* quoted in Bean, "Party Transformation in Massachusetts," 237.

41. James Lodge to Sumner, [May 1854], Sumner Papers, HU; [Boston] *Liberator*, Sept. 29, 1854; Bean, "Party Transformation in Massachusetts," 187; Dedham *Gazette* quoted in John R. Mulkern, *The Know-Nothing Party in Massachusetts: The Rise and Fall of a People's Movement* Boston: Northeastern Univ. Press, 1990), 65–66.

42. Dale T. Baum, *The Civil War Party System: The Case of Massachusetts, 1848–1876* (Chapel Hill: Univ. of North Carolina Press, 1984), 133–35; Charles Francis Adams to Francis W. Bird, Oct. 16, 1854 (letterbook), Adams Papers, MHS; James W. Stone to Charles Sumner, March 15,

Massachusetts Whig leaders, not realizing that the Order had grown so large, believed that they could continue to dominate the state's politics. Whigs had controlled the Bay State (with only minor interruptions) for decades, and believed that the Democrats' role in passing the Kansas-Nebraska Act could only increase Whig popularity. Yet chinks had begun to appear in the Whigs' armor. In Boston—the stronghold of the party—refusal by Whig leaders to sanction a mass meeting to protest the Kansas-Nebraska Act had outraged much of the rank and file. Young Whigs increasingly resented the dominance of older members, exemplified when the party chose septuagenarian Edward Everett to fill a vacant United States Senate seat. Furthermore, having misinterpreted the defeat of the proposed constitution as an endorsement of the status quo, the 1854 Whig-controlled legislature ignored calls for reform of the Massachusetts political system. In fact, the perception that the proposed constitution represented a Democratic grab at power had more to do with its defeat than the reforms it included. Whig leaders therefore confidently renominated their incumbent officeholders. In an attempt to attract Know Nothing support, the Whig platform promised to "rescue" the government from foreigners "of questionable character and doubtful fidelity." Otherwise, Whigs betrayed little fear of the Know Nothing threat.[43]

Free Soilers, in contrast, hoped to use the Know Nothings as a springboard to power. To this end, they called together the state's first Republican convention in the first week of September and nominated Free Soiler Henry Wilson for governor. Many observers considered the proceedings a farce, because the Republican organization represented nothing more than the old Free Soilers under a new name. But unbeknownst to these critics, Wilson had joined the Know Nothings, undoubtedly hoping that the Order would follow its past practice of endorsing one of the candidates nominated by the regular parties. The Whig nominee was not a Know Nothing and the feeble Massachusetts Democrats were running an anti–Know Nothing campaign, so Wilson undoubtedly believed that he would receive the Order's nomination. Following the lead of their New York brethren, however, Massachusetts Know Nothings decided to make their own nominations. When their state convention gathered in Boston on October 18, the delegates spurned Wilson and instead gave the gubernatorial nomination to Whig Henry J. Gardner.[44]

1854, Seth Webb Jr. to Sumner, July 14, 1854, Sumner Papers, HU; Edward Everett to Mrs. Charles Eames, Aug. 31, 1854 (letterbook), Everett Papers, MHS; Everett to Fillmore, Nov. 10, 1854, Fillmore Papers, SUNY-O; New York *Herald*, Nov. 16, 1854 (Boston correspondent).

43. Gienapp, *Origins of the Republican Party*, 134; Bean, "Party Transformation in Massachusetts," 139, 188–89; Virginia C. Purdy, "Portrait of a Know Nothing Legislature: The Massachusetts General Court of 1855" (Ph.D. diss., George Washington University, 1970), 73–74 (quotation).

44. Gienapp, *Origins of the Republican Party*, 134–35; D. W. Alvord to Bird, Sept. 19, 1854, Bird Papers, HU; Ernest A. McKay, *Henry Wilson: Practical Radical* (Port Washington, N.Y.: Kennikat Press, 1971), 89–91; Elias Nason and Thomas Russell, *Henry Wilson* (Boston, 1876), 119; New York *Times*, Oct. 20, 1854.

In selecting Gardner, Massachusetts Know Nothings made a wise choice, for while opponents in most states called the Order a "Whig trick," choosing Wilson would have smacked of Free Soil dictation. According to Edward Everett, Gardner had been "a wild youth at college: was suspended—went home to his father & was rebuked—ran away & went to sea as a common sailor; & returned reformed and industrious." Gardner went back to school and earned his degree from Bowdoin College, and afterwards became a wool merchant. His "off-hand, sociable, free and easy" manner facilitated his entry into politics, and he served on the Boston Common Council from 1849 to 1853, the last two years as president. Gardner also held a seat in the Massachusetts legislature during the 1853 and 1854 sessions, and in the year before his gubernatorial nomination, he had served on the Whig State Central Committee. While known as a conservative of the Daniel Webster school, Gardner broke with that faction by participating in an anti-Nebraska meeting earlier in 1854. Know Nothing leaders in Massachusetts were primarily conservatives who could not stomach Wilson's radicalism on the slavery issue. They therefore turned to Gardner—a moderate, experienced politician not well known outside Boston—to head the Know Nothing ticket.[45]

Know Nothing leaders realized that they could not ignore the power of anti-slavery sentiment amongst rank-and-file Massachusetts Know Nothings, especially outside of Boston. Rather than risk large-scale defections such as those that had plagued the Order in New York, they made a deal with Wilson to insure the support of his followers. If Wilson agreed to drop out of the race, Know Nothing leaders promised to support him for the United States Senate. Realizing that he could not possibly win the election supported only by the Republicans, Wilson accepted the offer, declining the Republican nomination just before election day to insure that his party fielded no replacement candidate. Wilson's action on election eve forced politicians to revise their earlier assessments of the Know Nothings, for they realized that Wilson was "far too shrewd to allow himself to be made a catspaw" of a powerless organization.[46]

The Massachusetts campaign focused on Gardner. Opponents charged that it was not safe to vote for Gardner because neither he nor any other Know Nothing candidate had taken a public stand on the issues. Know Nothings replied that the Order in Massachusetts opposed the Kansas-Nebraska Act and supported temperance. Whigs then pointed out that Gardner had voted against a proposed Maine Law in the 1854 legislature and had supported enforcement of the fugitive slave law. Gardner responded that these actions had been taken on constitutional grounds. He claimed that the proposed Maine Law had been unconstitutional, and that even obnoxious

45. Edward Everett Diary, Nov. 15, 1854, Everett Papers, MHS; Benjamin B. French, *Witness to the Young Republic: A Yankee's Journal, 1828–1870*, Donald B. Cole and John J. McDonough, eds. (Hanover, N.H.: Univ. Press of New England, 1989), 265 (quotation).

46. Simeon Merritt to Francis Bird, Oct. 30, 1854, D. W. Alvord to Bird, Nov. 8, 1854, Bird Papers, HU; Charles Francis Adams Diary, Oct. 25, 1854, Adams Papers, MHS; McKay, *Wilson*, 89 (quotation).

laws such as that requiring the capture of fugitive slaves ought to be obeyed until repealed. To bolster his anti-slavery image, Gardner pointed out that he had proposed that Whigs support an anti-Nebraska fusion ticket, but that the Whig State Committee had rejected his proposal. Gardner attributed his abandonment of the Whig party to this defeat, and he called himself the most strongly anti-slavery candidate in the field.[47] For the most part, though, the campaign was an unusually quiet one. A correspondent of educational reformer Horace Mann believed that the Whigs and Democrats had canceled their usual campaign rallies because party leaders were afraid that their members, having secretly joined the Order, would not show up at the meetings. Others agreed that the quiet campaign boded well for the Know Nothings.[48]

Despite these hints that the Know Nothings would triumph in Massachusetts, their unprecedented margin of victory stunned observers. In the four-way governor's race, Gardner polled three times the vote of his closest rival, winning 63 percent.[49] Know Nothings triumphed in all eleven Massachusetts congressional contests, and captured all but three of the more than four hundred legislative seats up for grabs! Even seasoned political veterans were "stunned" at the "overwhelming completeness of the revolution."[50] William Lloyd Garrison's *Liberator* summed up the feeling best:

> Who was so wild, or so enthusiastic, as to dream that a party unheard of at the last election, with a self-chosen cognomen as ridiculous as satire itself could invent, . . . and burrowing in secret like a mole in the dark, would suddenly spring up, snap assunder the strongest ties of party, enlist under its banner the most incongruous elements, absorb the elective strength of the state, and carry everything before it, . . . leaving only the smallest fragments of the three parties which were struggling for supremacy? . . . Nothing like it can be found in the political history of the country. Even now, with the figures staring us in the face, it seems almost incredible.[51]

Analysts offered a variety of explanations for the Know Nothings' stunning victory. Some Massachusetts residents said that they had voted Know Nothing because the Order upheld their anti-slavery principles, and the obvious accession of Free Soilers into the Know Nothing ranks implied that many voters held this view. A minister, for example, explained somewhat apologetically to Charles Sumner that he had voted the Know Nothing ticket "because I

47. Boston *Atlas*, Oct. 25, 1854, quoted in Purdy, "Portrait of a Know Nothing Legislature," 77; Bean, "Party Transformation in Massachusetts," 250–53; Everett to Fillmore, Dec. 16, 1854 (letterbook), Everett Papers, MHS.

48. Samuel Downer to Horace Mann, Oct. 25, 1854, Mann Papers, MHS; Joshua Green to Amos A. Lawrence, Nov. 10, 1854, Lawrence Papers, MHS.

49. Gardner tallied 81,503 votes (63%), Washburn (Whig) 27,279 (21%), Bishop (Democrat) 13,742 (11%), and Wilson (Republican) 6,483 (5%). *Whig Almanac* (1855): 40.

50. Samuel Gridley Howe to Horace Mann, Nov. 14, 1854, Mann Papers, MHS; Everett to Mrs. Charles Eames, Nov. 16, 1854 (letterbook), Everett Papers, MHS; Charles T. Congdon, *Reminiscences of a Journalist* (Boston, 1880), 144 (not quoted).

51. *Liberator* quoted in Rochester *American*, Nov. 28, 1854.

thought it would help the Anti-Slavery cause." Yet others pointed out that "in Boston the new party is more pro-slavery than even the old Whig party, a majority of the party being either national Whigs or Yankee mechanics, who equally hate a nigger as they do an Irishman." Another analyst agreed that "two-thirds of those who voted the Know Nothing ticket in Massachusetts neither inquired nor knew what were the sentiments of their candidates on the Nebraska question."[52] Charles Francis Adams attributed the Know Nothing victory to a popular "zeal to *beat the Whigs.*" But this explanation is not fully satisfactory either, because, as Everett pointed out, "a majority of the Know-Nothings must be Whigs; a comparison of the votes of this year & last prove this to be the fact."[53] The Boston *Bee* and Springfield *Republican* believed that Massachusetts voters embraced the Know Nothings because they had tired of the same "old fogy" politicians and "were itching for something new." However, most of the legislators elected by the Know Nothings were old Free Soilers, and the Haverhill *Gazette* pointed out that one could not nominate an "old Fogy" like Gardner, "a member for years of the Boston Whig County Committee! a *Webster Whig*—and make him Governor, and call it putting down Whigism or Old Fogyism."[54]

Despite such contradictory assessments, each of these analyses contained some truth. The Order's overwhelming success resulted from the fact that Know Nothingism in Massachusetts represented entirely different things to different people. Some had voted for the Know Nothings because they had nominated the most strongly anti-slavery ticket. Others had hoped to strike a blow at the arrogant Whig organization, while still others had seen the Order as a fresh alternative to politics as usual. Many Free Soilers cast Know Nothing ballots because they thought they could wrest control of the Order from veteran nativists, and use it as the foundation for an anti-slavery party. Some

52. William C. Whitcomb to Charles Sumner, Jan. 16, 1855, Sumner Papers, HU; Samuel Downer to [Horace Mann], Jan. 7, 1855, Mann Papers, MHS; Rochester *American*, Nov. 22, 1854.

53. Adams to S. C. Phillips, Nov. 16, 1854 (letterbook), Adams Papers, MHS; Everett to Fillmore, Dec. 16, 1854 (letterbook), Everett Papers, MHS. Everett based his assertion on the following figures:

Massachusetts Voting for Governor

	Whig	Democrat	Free Soil	Know Nothing
1853	60,472 (46%)	35,254 (27%)	29,545 (22%)	–
1854	27,279 (21%)	13,742 (11%)	6,483 (5%)	81,503 (63%)

Source: Whig Almanac (1854–55).

Note: Figures for 1853 do not equal 100% because a renegade Democratic candidate received 6,195 votes (5%).

54. Springfield *Republican* quoted in Rochester *American*, Nov. 16, 1854; Haverhill *Gazette* quoted in [Boston] *Liberator*, Nov. 24, 1854; S. G. Howe to Horace Mann, Nov. 14, 1854, Mann Papers, MHS.

Know Nothing Vote for Governor
Massachusetts, 1854

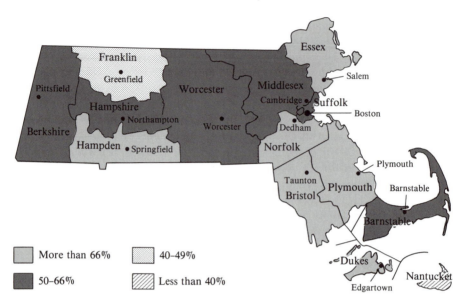

were simply taken in by the secrecy and ceremony of the Order, willing to follow the instructions of its leaders no matter what the political consequences. "They seemed altogether infatuated," noted one Free Soiler, "& ready to vote for any kind of cloven-foot provided he was the nominee of the 'Order.' "[55] Few analysts ascribed the Know Nothing victory to nativism, but the Order's anti-Catholicism certainly played a role in the landslide as well. Massachusetts's history of anti-Catholicism has already been noted, and Everett suggested privately that the Know Nothings' remarkable success resulted in part from the anti-Catholicism of the state's Protestant clergymen, which swelled the Know Nothing ranks because it led "our orthodox religionists generally to favor the organization." All these factors—anti-slavery, disgust with old politicians, resentment of the Whigs, and anti-Catholicism—worked in concert to bring about the Know Nothing landslide, unequaled before or since in Massachusetts history.[56]

In their first half-year in national politics, the Know Nothings had enjoyed greater electoral success than any previous nativist organization. A variety of circumstances accounted for their phenomenal popularity at the polls. First, religious controversies similar to those that had inspired previous nativist

55. D. A. Wasson to Samuel Johnson, quoted in Gienapp, *Origins of the Republican Party*, 138 n. 36.

56. Everett to Mrs. Charles Eames, Nov. 22, 1854, Everett to Fillmore (quotation), Dec. 16, 1854 (letterbook), Everett Papers, MHS.

movements revived in 1853 and 1854. As in the 1840s, many of these disputes concerned the role of the Bible in public schools and the use of tax money to finance parochial education. Previously, such issues had sparked controversy only in the large cities where significant numbers of immigrants lived, but because of the unprecedented influx of immigrants in the decade ending in 1854, these squabbles now elicited excitement in smaller towns as well. The development of a third controversy, concerning Catholic Church property, exacerbated the anti-Catholicism inspired by the school issues, especially after the disastrous American tour of Papal Nuncio Gaetano Bedini. The appointment of Pennsylvania Catholic James Campbell as postmaster general in 1853 also inspired significant anti-Catholicism, as did the failure of the Massachusetts constitution and the Burns case. These events provided the basis for a new outburst of nativism, which Americans vented through the Know Nothing party.

However, these controversies alone do not account for the breadth of the Know Nothings' popularity. Religious disputes had surfaced in the past, and would surface again in the future, but nativism would never attract nearly the political support that the Know Nothings enjoyed in 1854. The key to Know Nothing success in 1854 was the collapse of the second party system, brought about primarily by the demise of the Whig party. The Whig party, weakened for years by internal dissent and chronic factionalism, was nearly destroyed by the Kansas-Nebraska Act. Growing anti-party sentiment, fueled by anti-slavery as well as temperance and nativism, also contributed to the disintegration of the party system. The collapsing second party system gave the Know Nothings a much larger pool of potential converts than was available to previous nativist organizations, allowing the Order to succeed where older nativist groups had failed.

Until recently, few historians would have questioned the thrust of this evaluation.[57] Yet many scholars currently examining this period argue that the rise of the Know Nothings was not contingent upon the collapse of the Whig party and the second party system. Indeed, they insist that nativism *caused* their demise. These scholars argue that if the Kansas-Nebraska Act had played the decisive role, then the Whigs or Republicans would have swept the North in 1854. Yet because the Whigs fared so poorly in that year, and the Republicans in many states barely managed to organize, the revisionists argue that "nativism," exemplified by Know Nothingism, "represented the most powerful impulse in the 1854 northern elections" and was most responsible for the destruction of the Whig party. They insist that slavery became the dominant issue in northern politics only when the Republicans made concerted efforts to coopt Know Nothing voters by adding nativist planks to their platforms, and only after the caning of Senator Charles Sumner by Preston

57. The older view did not mention the role of temperance or anti-party sentiment, but its adherents would have agreed that the collapse of the party system contributed to the success of the Know Nothings. See, for example, Allan Nevins, *Ordeal of the Union* (New York: Scribner, 1947), II, p. 401.

Brooks and violence in Kansas proved to the North that the Kansas-Nebraska Act was not an aberration.[58]

In many ways, the revisionist argument makes perfect sense. Not one northern Whig voted for the Kansas-Nebraska Act, and Whigs attempted to capitalize on this fact during the 1854 campaign. Yet despite Whig efforts to exploit dissatisfaction with the Kansas-Nebraska Act in the party's platforms and speeches, the party's embarrassing showings in 1854 marked their finale as a significant political force. Furthermore, the defeats suffered by the Democratic candidates throughout the North in 1854 rarely resulted from purely Republican victories. In Pennsylvania, Ohio, Indiana, and Maine, the Democrats were defeated not by a unified Republican party but by loose coalitions that included Whigs, Free Soilers, and Know Nothings. In some key states—such as New York, Illinois, and (for all intents and purposes) Massachusetts—powerful Whig organizations blocked the formation of the Republican party altogether. The previous chapters have also confirmed the revisionists' claim that the Know Nothings represented a far more important factor in the 1854 elections than previous historians had realized. In the eyes of many observers, Know Nothingism emerged from the 1854 contests as the most potent rival to the Democratic party. The Know Nothings carried obvious momentum from the 1854 elections, while those who had believed that the Kansas-Nebraska Act would finally force the creation of a viable anti-slavery party were left depressed and discouraged. "This election has demonstrated that, by a majority, Roman Catholicism is feared more than American slavery," proclaimed one demoralized observer. Others complained that "when men were just beginning to see how slavery was mixed up with all their concerns, . . . there 'comes cranking in' this new Agitation, frightening honest people out of their wits with fears of the Pope." As a result, the revisionist interpretation has gained many adherents.[59]

Yet while the Know Nothings certainly surprised everyone with their strong performances in 1854, it cannot be said that they dominated the election more than any other component of the anti-Democratic coalition. The Know Nothings controlled the 1854 elections in only three states: Indiana, Pennsylvania, and Massachusetts. And only in the last of these did the Know Nothings achieve an independent victory. While each of the remaining

58. The most important pronouncements of this view can be found in Michael F. Holt, *The Political Crisis of the 1850s* (New York: Wiley, 1978), 139–81; Ronald P. Formisano, *The Birth of Mass Political Parties: Michigan, 1827–1861* (Princeton: Princeton Univ. Press, 1971), 217–18, 252–53; Gienapp, *Origins of the Republican Party*, 164–65 (quotation). On the wide acceptance of this view see Don E. Fehrenbacher, "The New Political History and the Coming of the Civil War," *Pacific Historical Review* 54 (1985): 132–33.

59. J. W. Taylor to Hamilton Fish, Nov. 11, 1854, Fish Papers, LC; [Boston] *Liberator*, Nov. 10, 1854. None of the major reviews of Gienapp's book questions his portrayal of the collapse of the second party system. See for example Michael Perman, *JAH* 75 (1988): 265–66; Johanna Nicol Shields, *AHR* 93 (1988): 1402–3; Richard L. McCormick, *Reviews in American History* 16 (1988): 396–402.

northern contests (except that in Illinois) produced a defeat for the Democratic party, Know Nothingism was not the most significant factor in any of them.

Furthermore, the argument that the Whigs should have benefited had slavery been the most important issue in the 1854 elections presumes that the Whigs were at that time a reasonably healthy political organization. In fact, they were not. The more radical wing, led by Seward, believed that the Whigs should utilize the antipathy toward the Kansas-Nebraska Act to shape the party into an anti-slavery vehicle. But the Fillmore Whigs felt that there had been enough slavery agitation and hoped that their party would pursue a moderate course. Had there been no such split, the Whigs might indeed have rallied around the Kansas issue and swept the North. The deeply divided Whigs, however, could not muster the unanimity necessary to take advantage of the opportunity offered by the Kansas-Nebraska Act.

Other factors prevented the northern Whigs from using the Kansas-Nebraska Act to revitalize their party. Anti-slavery Whigs magnanimously offered to make room in their organization for outsiders who objected to the Nebraska bill, yet most declined the invitation. Anti-slavery Democrats such as Gideon Welles of Connecticut and Free Soilers such as Henry Wilson vowed that they would never join the Whig party and would vote for the most pro-slavery Democrat rather than support a Whig. Charles Francis Adams recognized this problem, admitting that "to expect them . . . to go over to the Whigs is not consistent with a knowledge of what influences govern men."[60] Northern Whigs also failed to win new members after passage of the Kansas-Nebraska Act because their southern members made it impossible to portray the organization as anti-slavery. The most hated portion of the Nebraska bill—that which repealed the Missouri Compromise—had been appended to Stephen A. Douglas's original draft by Kentucky Whig Archibald Dixon. Northerners also knew that the pro-slavery rhetoric of Robert Toombs and other southern Whigs could match that of any fire-eating Democrat. Many anti-slavery Whigs therefore refused to remain in the Whig party after the Kansas-Nebraska bill passed Congress. "We certainly cannot have any further political connection with the Whigs of the South," proclaimed Ohio's Benjamin Wade. Connecticut senator Truman Smith concurred that "further cooperation with them will be impossible." Outsiders often cited this factor when explaining their refusal to join the Whigs, and anti-slavery Whigs pointed to it when explaining why they felt compelled to leave their party. As long as pro-slavery Southerners remained within the Whig fold, northern

60. Henry Wilson to Seward, May 28, 1854, Seward Papers, UR; Gideon Welles to James F. Babcock, March 14, 1855 (copy), Welles Papers, LC; Charles Francis Adams to John A. Andrew, July 23, 1854, Adams Papers (letterbook), MHS; Eric Foner, *Free Soil, Free Labor, Free Men: The Ideology of the Republican Party Before the Civil War* (New York: Oxford Univ. Press, 1970), 159–62.

Whigs would never succeed in recasting their organization as an anti-slavery party.[61]

Finally, the Whigs could not capitalize on the northern hostility toward the Kansas-Nebraska Act because the public had grown suspicious of *both* major parties. As previously mentioned, the failure of the major parties to deal effectively with local issues such as temperance and Bible reading in schools had created a popular distrust of both the Whigs and the Democrats. Whigs such as Seward who predicted that the Kansas-Nebraska Act would revive their party failed to consider adequately this anti-party sentiment. As Welles pointed out, "It has been one of the mistakes of Seward and his friends [in New York]—of the Whig leaders in Massachusetts—and in this state also—that the Whig party would gain what the [Democratic] administration lost. The truth is there is a general feeling to throw off both the old organizations and their intrigues and machinery." Northerners had grown tired of the promises of the two established parties, and this anti-party feeling represented yet another hindrance to the Whigs' efforts to take advantage of the popular antipathy for the Kansas-Nebraska Act.[62]

Conversely, the new Republican party did not dominate the elections of 1854 because Whigs blocked formation of the new organization. Although the Whigs could not capitalize on the fallout over the Kansas-Nebraska Act themselves, they retained enough strength in many states to hinder Republican organization. For example, many in New York favored the formation of a Republican party, but Whig leader Thurlow Weed resisted. Weed worried that conversion to a new organization in 1854 might jeopardize Seward's re-election to the Senate, which the legislature to be elected that fall would decide. Weed and his allies also believed that the Whigs might yet rid the party of conservatives, enabling them to reshape it into an anti-slavery organization. While the problems preventing such a metamorphosis have just been described, the severity of these obstacles had not yet become apparent to Weed and his supporters. Weed therefore used his influence amongst the delegates at New York's initial Republican convention to prevent them from making nominations. In other states where the Whigs remained powerful— such as Massachusetts and Illinois—Whig leaders also blocked Republican efforts to launch the new party.[63]

The newness of the Republican party also hurt their attempts to attract voters in 1854. Although the Know Nothings were also relatively new, the Order in 1854 was not a political party, but a fraternal organization. By November many Know Nothing lodges had been holding weekly meetings for half a year or longer, during which time the Order had created a sense of

61. Henry Wilson to Seward, May 28, 1854, Seward Papers, UR; B. Arnold to Benedict Lewis Jr., June 8, 1854, Ullmann Papers, NYHS; Wade and Trumbull quoted in Gienapp, *Origins of the Republican Party*, 86–87.

62. Welles quoted in Holt, *Political Crisis of the 1850s*, 165.

63. Jeter A. Isely, *Horace Greeley and the Republican Party, 1853–1861* (Princeton: Princeton Univ. Press, 1947), 86–97; Gienapp, *Origins of the Republican Party*, 122–24, 133–36, 150–53.

loyalty and comradery amongst its members. This fidelity had been strengthened by a sworn oath to follow the dictates of the lodge, so that when the Know Nothings entered the 1854 elections, most members for one reason or another felt obligated to vote for Know Nothing candidates. The Republican organizations, in contrast, were created in most cases immediately before the fall elections, and this left insufficient time to develop strong party loyalty among more than a handful of voters. These obstructions prevented the new Republican party from taking full advantage of the anti-slavery sentiment produced by the passage of the Kansas-Nebraska Act. Thus, the paralysis of the Whigs and the disorganization of the Republicans prevented these organizations from fully capitalizing on the Kansas-Nebraska Act. Their failures do not prove that nativism destroyed the Whigs or the second party system.

In fact, slavery played the key role in transforming the Know Nothings from a small nativist organization into a national political power. Many rural residents who had little contact with immigrants, and city-dwellers who had not been swayed by their original agenda, found the Know Nothing party irresistible once it gained its anti-slavery reputation. As the party's Rhode Island organ explained, "the American [i.e., Know Nothing] party had its origin, or at least the beginning of its triumphs, in the pro-slavery tendency of the old parties. The people of the North had got heartily sick of the old organizations, and chiefly because they had truckled to the South in every matter of great interest." The Harrisburg *Herald*, whose senior editor was a leading Know Nothing and whose junior editor became their Pennsylvania president in 1856, agreed that the Order had triumphed in the North in 1854 because "it was clearly and unqualifiedly identified with the anti-Nebraska sentiment . . . of the North." The chief Know Nothing newspaper in New Hampshire also thought it obvious that the Order's anti-slavery reputation had made it so popular. "If we eject from the principles of the party that issue," explained the Manchester *American*, "it at once becomes immeasurably weaker." A Know Nothing congressman-elect concurred that "the American party cannot stand an instant in New England after its anti-slavery principles are gone." The testimony of the Know Nothings' Ohio president, Thomas Spooner, accords with that of his eastern compatriots. According to Spooner, both the "pandering" of politicians to foreigners and the Kansas-Nebraska Act "aroused the feelings and kindled the spirit so long pent up within the great American heart, and quickened into life and activity the American sentiment that gave birth to our Order."[64]

Historians may have previously ignored the links between Know Nothingism and anti-slavery sentiment because of their perceptions of the two

64. Harrisburg *Herald*, Dec. 24, 1854 (quoting Providence *Tribune*), Feb. 29, 1856; Clearfield [Pennsylvania] *Raftsman's Journal*, March 5, 1856; Manchester *American*, May 5, 1855; Aaron H. Cragin to Weed, June 15, 1855, Weed Papers, UR; Spooner, *Report of the President of the State Council of Ohio, June 5, 1855*, 7–8; Jamestown [New York] *Journal*, Feb. 9, 1855; "Know Nothing" quoted in Thomas M. Keefe, "Chicago's Flirtation with Political Nativism, 1854–1856," *Records of the American Catholic Historical Society of Philadelphia* 82 (1971): 141.

movements. David Potter recognized that "it has been psychologically difficult, because of their predominantly liberal orientation, for [historians] to
cope with the fact that anti-slavery, which they tend to idealize, and nativism,
which they scorn, should have operated in partnership."[65] As a result, scholars have emphasized the manner in which the anti-slavery Republican party
eventually overpowered the nativist Know Nothing party, but have ignored
the fact that anti-Catholicism originally worked in concert with anti-slavery
sentiment. This aspect of the Know Nothings' appeal has also eluded detec-
tion because of the scarcity of sources available to historians. The correspondence of few Know Nothing leaders survives, and libraries have saved only a
handful of their short-lived newspapers. The tendency of historians to write
monographic state studies of the Know Nothings has also hindered recognition of this pattern, because the concentration on single states has obscured a
trend that becomes unmistakable in a wider survey.

Consequently, although temperance and anti-party sentiment contributed
to a certain extent, it was their anti-slavery reputation that provided the main
impetus for the Know Nothings' phenomenal success. This, combined with the
Know Nothings having determined the outcome in only three northern states in
the 1854 elections, suggests that slavery, not nativism, played the decisive role
in the destruction of the second party system. But one might well ask whether
slavery or *Know Nothingism* caused the party system's collapse. There can be
no doubt that in the west, the slavery issue killed the Whig party. New anti-
slavery coalitions formed in nearly all of these states before they felt the full
impact of Know Nothingism. In the east, on the other hand, the Whig party
might have struggled on for another year if Know Nothingism had not emerged
in 1854. Victories in New York and Massachusetts in 1854 might even have
enabled the Whigs to block the formation of the Republican party in that region
in 1855 and prevented the Republicans from mounting a creditable challenge to
the Democrats in the presidential election of 1856. Instead, the strong Know
Nothing showings in the east—fueled by both the large concentration of Catholic immigrants and increased preparation time—convinced most Whigs that
they could not revive their party, and caused its collapse. The slavery issue had
battered the Whig party since 1850, but only after the Know Nothings emerged
did that issue find the vehicle through which it could knock the staggering Whig
party out of the political ring.

Thus the second American party system, weakened to a degree by the
temperance and religious controversies, began to collapse with the passage of
the Kansas-Nebraska Act. The Democrats held themselves together remark-
ably well after they pushed the bill through Congress, thanks to the continuing
loyal support they received from immigrants and Southerners. The Whigs
were the immediate casualty of the Kansas-Nebraska Act, because ethno-
cultural issues such as temperance and anti-Catholicism had already weak-

65. David M. Potter, *The Impending Crisis, 1848–1861* (New York: Harper & Row, 1976),
252.

ened the party, and because passage of the bill convinced various factions within the Whig coalition to abandon the organization. During the 1854 elections, the impotence of the northern Whig party became evident. Instead of serving as a rallying point through which voters could show their contempt for the Democratic measure, the Whig party vanished in most of the west, supplanted either by the new Republican party or by anti-Nebraska coalitions comprised of Republicans, Whigs, Free Soil Democrats, and Know Nothings. In the east, where the Know Nothings had more members and more time to organize, the Order emerged with the greatest momentum from the 1854 contests. Know Nothings won a majority of the opposition votes in Pennsylvania, swamped their opponents in Massachusetts, and achieved a "glorious" defeat in New York. Subsequent Know Nothing victories in spring elections in Connecticut, New Hampshire, and Rhode Island would confirm the impression that Republicanism had made little progress in the Northeast. However, the Know Nothings did not win these elections merely on the strength of nativist sentiment. Instead their successes in 1854 resulted in large part from the belief that the Order also opposed the extension of slavery. Most Easterners who opposed the Democratic party preferred to cast anti-Catholic, anti-slavery, anti-party, and in most cases anti-liquor Know Nothing votes, rather than choose the simply anti-slavery ballots offered by the Whigs and Republicans. The Kansas-Nebraska Act dominated the campaigns in the west and played a significant role in strengthening the Know Nothings in the east, indicating that slavery extension was the most important issue of 1854. Nativism (primarily in the form of anti-Catholicism) also aroused many voters, as did temperance and a revulsion against the existing parties. The 1854 elections marked the last time that Whigs would seriously vie for office in the North, and their miserable showing in these contests brought about their party's demise. While factionalism caused by the slavery issue had severely weakened the Whigs, their collapse was finally brought about by the defection of hundreds of thousands of their members to the Know Nothing party.

Know Nothing leaders believed that the Order's performance in the 1854 elections boded well for the future. In a matter of months they had transformed a fraternal order with a few thousand members into the most feared political organization in the nation. They had controlled the outcome of the elections in Indiana, Pennsylvania, and Massachusetts, played a significant role in New York and Ohio, and created a strong core of membership upon which to build in every other populous northern state. At Governor-elect Gardner's victory banquet, Know Nothings displayed a banner depicting the White House, and its motto predicted that a Know Nothing would occupy the President's mansion in two years' time. Despite such lofty predictions, most Know Nothing leaders realized that hard work lay ahead if the Order wished to parlay its 1854 victories into real political power. Secrecy and mystery had attracted many to Know Nothing lodges, yet once such novelty wore off, the Order, like any other party, would have to attract voters with issues, candidates, and platforms. And while the 1854 results had been achieved by independent state organizations, nativists realized that no group, no matter how well drilled locally, could hope to win a presidential election without a national organization to coordinate the effort. An editorial in a newspaper that supported the Know Nothings reflected this combination of confidence and caution. "The 'Know Nothings' are a power," concluded the Rochester *American*, but "whether they are a *party* is not yet settled."[66]

66. New York *Herald,* Dec. 1, 1854; Rochester *American*, Nov. 21, 1854.

5

"Americans Must Rule America": The Ideology of the Know Nothing Party

While the aura of secrecy surrounding their organization helped the Know Nothings attract members, leaders of the Order recognized that their furtiveness also impeded the spread of their message. Since few newspapers had been willing to support the Know Nothings or their candidates overtly in 1854, nativists had been unable to circulate propaganda beyond the confines of the councils. Enemies had taken advantage of the Order's secrecy during these first campaigns, spreading false rumors about the organization that the Know Nothings could not publicly refute. Realizing that they could not allow their opponents' charges and criticisms to go unanswered, and hoping as well to make their organization appear more like a conventional political party, Know Nothings decided after the election of 1854 to break their code of secrecy and disseminate their ideology to the nation.

Any attempt to identify the ideology of the Know Nothings must take into account the fact that different Know Nothings interpreted the tenets of Know Nothingism differently.[1] Know Nothings in the North and South disagreed about even the most fundamental aspects of their movement. Northern Know Nothings, as we shall see, directed most of their animus at Catholic immigrants, while many southern councils allowed native-born Catholics to join Know Nothing lodges. Northern and southern Know Nothings also held divergent views on the issue of slavery. Even ignoring sectional distinctions, the decentralized structure of the Know Nothing organization led to the creation of councils that differed greatly from both state to state, and sometimes even

---

1. I utilize the term "ideology" here as defined by Lance Banning, who calls it "the more or less coherent body of assumptions, values, and ideas that bound [party members] together . . . [and] shaped their common understanding of society and politics. . . ." *The Jeffersonian Persuasion: Evolution of a Party Ideology* (Ithaca: Cornell Univ. Press, 1978), 15.

within a single state. Thus, it is impossible to identify a single Know Nothing outlook. However, there did exist a common core of beliefs shared by almost all northern Know Nothings which helps to explain their great appeal to antebellum Americans.

At the heart of the Know Nothing ideology lay six basic tenets. First, and most important, Know Nothings believed that Protestantism defined American society. Protestantism encouraged the individualism that flourished in America, said Know Nothings, because it allowed each Christian to interpret the Bible personally and to pray as he or she saw fit. Know Nothings also pointed with pride to the democratic aspects of Protestant Christianity. In most denominations, congregations chose their own ministers, and if church-goers disapproved of him, they could select a new one. Protestants also believed that their method of devotion was the most egalitarian. Even without attending church, the humblest person might attain saintly standing through study of the Bible and private prayer. Know Nothings insisted that American reverence for democracy and freedom evolved from these Protestant religious practices: "The freedom we enjoy, the liberty of conscience, the freedom of religious faith and worship, the sanctity of civil, religious, social, and personal rights, are but the normal results of the enlightened liberalism of the Protestant faith."[2]

Second, Know Nothings maintained that Catholicism was not compatible with the basic values Americans cherished most. While Protestantism was democratic, Know Nothings saw Catholicism as autocratic, because the pope directed all its adherents through his bishops and priests. As one Know Nothing newspaper described the hierarchy, "the Pope utters his wish to his Bishops, the Bishops bear it to their Priests, the Priest[s] direct the members of the church, and they all obey, because the Pope has a right to rule them, *they are his subjects. . . .*" Unlike Protestantism, Catholicism was also believed to restrain freedom of thought. Protestants contended that the notes in the annotated Douay Bible (the version Catholics read) and the fact that Catholics were discouraged from reading the Bible in private prevented them from freely interpreting the Scriptures. Catholicism also inhibited the individual autonomy that flourished under Protestantism, said Know Nothings, because priests interceded between the worshipper and God in almost every aspect of devotion. Catholicism also seemed to impose too many rituals, symbols, and images between God and the congregation:

> These vestments, and crossings, and genuflexions, . . . this swinging of censers and sprinkling of holy water, this tinkling of bells, this odour of incense, this glare of lighted candles at noonday . . . tend to divert the mind from the

2. Albany *State Register*, Oct. 4, 1854, Sept. 20, 1855 (quotation); Hartford *Courant*, Jan. 8, 1856; New York *Express*, March 26, 1855; Otis H. Tiffany [Methodist minister and president of the Pennsylvania Know Nothings], *Lecture on the Cultivation of the Christian Elements of Republicanism* (Carlisle, Penn., 1855), esp. 10–13.

essence of religion, to satisfy it with forms, to substitute frivolous and superstitious observances in the place of moral and religious duties.

The Catholic emphasis on miracles, the apparent worship of saints and the Virgin instead of God, absolution, and transubstantiation further persuaded Protestants that Catholicism was based on mysticism and ignorance, while Protestantism represented reason and progress. Because American institutions were rooted in Protestant values, Know Nothings concluded that "a Romanist is by necessity a foe to the very principles we embody in our laws, a foe to all we hold most dear."[3]

Third, Know Nothings insisted that although few "Papists" lived in the United States, Catholics had attained political power disproportionate to their numbers. According to nativists, priests usually determined how Catholics voted, which gave a few Catholic leaders the power to decide elections. When not following the instructions of their prelates, Catholics purportedly "sold" their votes to the highest bidder, usually in return for patronage. Know Nothings also believed that immigrants gained excessive political power through extensive fraudulent voting and through the instigation of election-day violence that discouraged native-born citizens from going to the polls. Know Nothings concluded that such practices would become the norm if America continued "to receive a class of voters who have no Sabbath, and no Bible; and who are not really Americans, but only residents in America." In fact, Know Nothings believed that Catholic immigrants threatened America's bold experiment in republicanism:

> The cornerstone of our Republic is political, mental and social liberty, and in direct antagonism with these principles, stands Romanism. It denies the liberty of free inquiry, the liberty of speech, and thus saps the fountain of freedom. . . . There can be no republicanism where Catholicism bears sway.

These conditions made it imperative that native-born citizens counteract the growing political influence exerted by Catholic immigrants.[4]

Antipathy for political parties and professional politicians formed the next facet of Know Nothing ideology. Nativists condemned politicians because they believed that conniving ones helped immigrants and Catholics acquire undue political power. Know Nothings charged that unscrupulous demagogues, concerned only with gaining office, sold their influence to immigrants in return for the newcomers' votes. But the Know Nothing critique of politicians went beyond their involvement with immigrants. Unlike the Founding

3. Hartford *American Dispatch*, July 14, 1855 (quotation); Civis [pseud.], *Romanism Incompatible with Republican Institutions* (1844; rpt., New York, 1854), 65–66 (quotation); unidentified exchange in Cleveland *Express*, Jan. 30, 1855 (quotation); Boston *Bee* quoted in Cleveland *Express*, Aug. 2, 1854; Harrisburg *Herald*, May 18, 1855.

4. Tiffany, *Christian Elements of Republicanism*, 19; J. S. Howard in Youngstown *True American*, March 28, 1855. See also Thomas Bayne, *Popery Subversive of American Institutions* (Pittsburgh, 1856).

Fathers, modern politicians lacked the commitment to "virtue" and "the public good" necessary for the operation of a successful republic. Elected officials placed party welfare before that of the nation, resulting in the passage of unpopular laws such as the Kansas-Nebraska Act. "The *national* interest is never considered by your real *'party man*,' " explained one Know Nothing leader. "His own success or that of his cabal, as a means for their own advancement in place or in fortune," motivated the new breed of politician. Only when voters removed professional politicians from office and reduced the influence of political parties would Americans manage to re-establish responsible government.[5]

Finally, most northern Know Nothings believed in legal limitations on both the extension of slavery and liquor consumption. Know Nothings did not display the unanimity of opinion on these issues that one finds amongst Know Nothings concerning the threats posed by Catholicism and corrupt politicians. Yet a vast majority of northern Know Nothings believed that the spread of slavery should be curbed and the sale of liquor curtailed. The Know Nothings' commitment to these issues derived from their devotion to Protestant values, as American ministers regularly condemned "rum, Romanism, and slavery" as the three evils cursing the nation. Most northern Know Nothings saw the increasing political power of liquor traffickers and slaveholders as a natural outgrowth of the declining influence of Protestantism in America and considered opposition to these evils to be an integral part of their agenda.[6]

Know Nothings proposed a number of remedies to combat the problems they identified. First, because the existing five-year probationary period before naturalization purportedly provided insufficient time for immigrants to assimilate, they suggested that the newcomers wait twenty-one years before attaining the privilege of voting. Second, Know Nothings urged voters to select only native-born citizens for office and to elect only those who would not appoint immigrants to patronage positions. Only those born and raised in America, they felt, understood the complexities of operating a republican government. While arguing that immigration laws also required modification to prevent the importation of paupers and criminals, Know Nothings never actually sought restrictions or quotas on the flow of immigration. Instead, they hoped to delay or mitigate the political influence of the newcomers. Only in this manner did Know Nothings believe that good government could be guaranteed and Protestant values preserved.

Know Nothings traced most of the problems facing their communities to the increasing number of immigrants arriving in the United States. While other

5. Charles D. Deshler, *"The Great American Middle Class": An Address Delivered Before the Order of United Americans* (New York, 1855), 14.

6. Because the place of anti-slavery and anti-liquor sentiment in the Know Nothing appeal has already been discussed at length in Chapter 2, these issues will not receive further consideration in this chapter.

Americans believed that the recent flood of newcomers would provide cheap labor and help populate the vast expanse of unsettled territory, Know Nothings saw only danger in the demographic trends. Most troubling to nativists was the belief that the immigrants of the "Great Migration" resisted assimilation. Whereas earlier immigrants had quickly adopted American customs, Know Nothings believed that those arriving in the 1850s were "determined that neither themselves nor their children shall ever conform to American manners, American sentiments, or the spirit of American Institutions." Because of the way "foreigners banded together" in resistance to assimilation, New York had become "much more a foreign than an American city," and Know Nothings believed that other American towns would soon suffer the same fate. In order to arrest this trend, Know Nothings wanted to mix immigrants "up in the American crucible and get them to adopt our ideas." New York Know Nothing Daniel Ullmann agreed that "where races dwell together on the same soil and do not assimilate, they can never form one great people—one great nationality." America, continued Ullmann, must "mold and absorb" the "castes, races, and nationalities" accumulating in the United States "into one great homogeneous American race," or else internal divisions would destroy the nation.[7]

Know Nothings also believed that immigrants threatened the nation's well-being because of their propensity to commit crime. A Massachusetts newspaper reported that forty of forty-one persons arrested in Charlestown in one week had been born abroad. Noting that immigrants were ten times more likely to be arrested than native-born citizens, a Know Nothing paper in Albany concluded that "immigration" represented "the chief source of crime in this country." Violent crime had reached epidemic proportions in all major cities, reported the Harrisburg *Herald*, and "if these disgraceful outrages are looked into . . . it will be found that [the perpetrators] are FOREIGNERS, in nine cases out of ten." Catholic immigrants were especially prone to commit crime because when they went to confessional, the priest absolved them of guilt. "They are thus duped and incited to the committal of new and perhaps worse crimes," explained the Cleveland *Express*, "because they know no matter what the deed, they will be forgiven." Know Nothings also felt that the patronage preference given by politicians to immigrants contributed to the increasing crime rates. In the nineteenth century, politicians appointed police officers to their posts, and Know Nothings believed that immigrants received an unfair share of these positions. Police departments, they claimed, were "corrupt in proportion to the number of foreigners of which they are composed." Statistics from nearly every major city indicated that immigrants perpetrated crimes far out of proportion to their numbers, and, according to

7. Cuba [New York] *American Banner* quoted in Youngstown *True American*, April 25, 1855; New York *Express* quoted in Russell McClain, "The New York *Express*: Voice of Opposition" (Ph.D. diss., Columbia University, 1955), 198; Daniel Ullmann, *The Course of Empire* (New York, 1856), 8, 20; Rochester *American*, March 2, 1855; Hartford *Courant*, March 19, 1856.

nativists, only when immigrants had been removed from police forces would American cities once again become safe.[8]

According to Know Nothings, increasing pauperism also resulted from immigration. Nativists pointed to statistics such as those from Buffalo—where 1,436 of 1,558 paupers had been born abroad—to show that America imported most of its almshouse residents. Know Nothings believed this resulted in part from the fact that "the character of our foreign immigration, and especially the Irish portion of it, has entirely changed." Earlier immigrants displayed industriousness and frugality, but many recent newcomers were simply "too lazy to work."[9] Know Nothings thought that most pauperism (and much crime as well) resulted from the European practice of "dumping" destitute citizens and convicts in America. "From the 'refuge of the oppressed,' we have come to be the great Botany Bay of the world," claimed one nativist journal. European governments deported paupers so that "the burden of their support might be placed on the American people," and Know Nothing newspapers printed dozens of circulars and letters purporting to document the frequency of the practice. Know Nothings particularly resented the number of Catholics who became public charges, for while "the fat sleek priests . . . build splendid cathedrals and churches, . . . we poor, good-natured Americans are taking care of their criminals and paupers."[10]

Until recently, historians had surmised that Know Nothings fabricated claims about pauper and convict dumping to suit their nativist agenda. But recent studies of immigration have found that European governments *did* commonly subsidize the emigration of paupers and, less frequently, convicts as well. The British government financed the emigration of 5,000 Irish paupers per year beginning in 1847, and Irish landlords sent an additional 50,000 destitute tenants to America during the decade ending in 1855. German towns also relieved budgetary strains by sending the inhabitants of their poorhouses to America. An official in Hanover, for example, admitted in a secret memorandum that the government had financed the emigration of "considerable numbers" of paupers and criminals to America. While these immigrants accounted for only a small portion of antebellum poverty, Know Nothings in-

8. Charlestown *Advertiser* in Ithaca *American Citizen*, Nov. 21, 1855; Albany *State Register*, Oct. 1, 6, 1855; Harrisburg *Herald*, June 6 (quotation), Nov. 12, 1854; Hartford *Courant*, Nov. 19, 1855; *Know Nothing Almanac* (1855): 25; Thomas R. Whitney, *A Defence of the American Policy* (New York, 1856), 366; Cleveland *Express*, Aug. 24, 1854 (quotation); Boston *Know Nothing*, May 13, 1854 (quotation).

9. Buffalo *American Rights* quoted in Harrisburg *Herald*, Nov. 11, 1854; Albany *State Register*, Sept. 21, 1855; Clearfield [Pennsylvania] *Raftsman's Journal*, May 9, 1855; Concord [New Hampshire] *Independent Democrat* quoted in Johnstown *Cambria Tribune*, April 14, 1855 (quotation); Cincinnati *Dollar Times*, Sept. 14, 1854 (quotation).

10. Youngstown *True American*, Feb. 21 (quotations), April 4, 1855; "Tom Muddie" to the editor of the Quincy *Patriot*, Nov. 11, 1854 (quotation), in James Tracy, "The Rise and Fall of the Know-Nothings in Quincy," *Historical Journal of Massachusetts* 16 (1988): 11; Harrisburg *Herald*, June 10, Sept. 11, 1854, July 16, 1855; *Know Nothing Almanac* (1855): 33; John P. Sanderson, *Republican Landmarks. The Views and Opinions of American Statesmen on Foreign Immigration* (Philadelphia, 1856), 48–80.

sisted that unless Americans protested, Europeans would expand the practice. The German states actually did suspend their pauper dumping because of Know Nothing complaints, a fact that undoubtedly would have pleased nativists had they known.[11]

Know Nothings also blamed immigrants for declines in the income and status of American workingmen. "Our native-born citizens hate to work by the side of an Irishman," reported a nativist journal, because they feel degraded "and dishonored by the contact. . . . It is the same feeling which makes it impossible for a respectable white man to labor by the side of slaves in the South." A Know Nothing council in Trenton likewise insisted that Americans should not have to work for the "foreign starvation wages" that immigrants accepted. Because immigrants had "been accustomed to live in poverty" in Europe, they continued to accept low pay when they got to America, and native-born workers realized that this drove down their wages. Even though many workers might not have yet noticed the effect of immigrant competition, Know Nothings insisted that "the enormous influx of foreigners will in the end prove ruinous to American workingmen, by REDUCING THE WAGES OF LABOR to a standard that will drive them from the farms and workshops altogether, or reduce them to a condition worse than that of Negro slavery."[12]

Know Nothings worried not only about America's economic prosperity, but about the country's military preparedness as well. They felt that if the United States fought a war against Germans or a Catholic nation, the presence of so many immigrants would threaten the nation's security. Nativists particularly condemned the frequency with which immigrants formed militia units composed entirely of those born abroad. Military companies served a primarily social function in antebellum America, and because immigrants tended to socialize amongst themselves, immigrant militia units became a popular form of recreation for the newcomers. But Know Nothings opposed the creation of these companies. "To organize these amongst us," asserted Ohio Know Nothing president Thomas Spooner, "with foreign names and foreign insignia, is an insult to the hospitality we have extended to those who compose them." The fact that many German militia companies displayed not the Stars and Stripes but the red "revolutionary flag of Europe, is a taunt too bold not to be REBUKED AND REFORMED." Military companies composed of Irish Catholic immigrants posed an even greater threat, warned

11. Benjamin J. Klebaner, "The Myth of Foreign Pauper Dumping in the United States," *Social Service Review* 35 (1961): 302–9; Kerby A. Miller, *Emigrants and Exiles: Ireland and the Irish Exodus to North America* (New York: Oxford Univ. Press, 1985), 295–96; Mack Walker, *Germany and the Emigration, 1816–1885* (Cambridge: Harvard Univ. Press, 1964), 75–76, 143–44, 169–70, 172–73; Wolfgang Kollmann and Peter Marschalck, "German Emigration to the United States," trans. Thomas C. Childers, *Perspectives in American History* 7 (1973): 517.

12. Concord [New Hampshire] *Independent Democrat* quoted in Johnstown *Cambria Tribune*, April 14, 1855 (quotation); Harrisburg *Herald*, May 26, 1855 (Trenton quotation), Sept. 5, 1856 (quotations); Albany *State Register*, Sept. 14, 1855; Cleveland *Express*, Oct. 30, 1854; Philadelphia *Sun*, Nov. 3, 1854.

Know Nothings. These groups would never respond to the needs of the United States, but instead "rally at the call of the Bishop and the Priest. They are the *soldiers of the Church of Rome*, bound to defend its interests at whatever peril, and *not* the citizens of Boston. . . ." Now that these immigrants lived in the United States, reasoned the New York *Express*, it was "their duty to amalgamate with, and become part of us,—in our American regiments."[13]

Although Know Nothings blamed some of the nation's problems on the overall increase in immigration, they concentrated their attacks on Catholic immigrants. "We are not now contending against foreigners, but against the principles of Roman Catholicism and its devotees," announced the Cleveland Know Nothing organ. As the Cincinnati *Times* explained it, "Romanism is the head and front" of Know Nothingism, while the proscription of all immigrants, known as "Native Americanism," was "secondary and contingent." Nativists justified this double standard on the grounds that "Protestant foreigners . . . appear to be open to reason, and act in accordance with their convictions," while Catholic immigrants were thought to be hostile to American values.[14]

Know Nothing emphasis on the differences between Catholic and Protestant immigrants varied from region to region. In the Midwest, where many Protestant German immigrants had settled, Know Nothings usually stressed that their movement sought only to counteract the influence of Catholics. They hoped that Protestant immigrants—who had demonstrated their fierce anti-Catholicism during Bedini's visit—would sympathize with the Know Nothing movement. In Indiana, Protestant immigrants were actually allowed to join Know Nothing lodges, while in the rest of the North, they served as what one German-American called "a sort of backstairs members of the Know-Nothing lodges." Most often Protestant immigrants accomplished this by joining anti-Catholic organizations such as the American Protestant Association, which catered to immigrants. A member boasted that this organization contained "a large number of foreigners . . . who work for and support the so-called 'Know Nothing' party, notwithstanding they are precluded from becoming members of that body." The head of this group corresponded frequently with Know Nothing leaders to insure that the actions of his organization harmonized with those of the Order.[15]

13. Thomas Spooner, *Report of the President of the State Council of Ohio, June 5, 1855* (n.p., n.d.), 13, OHS; Boston *Know Nothing*, May 6, 1854; New York *Express*, July 20, 1855; Pottsville *Miner's Journal*, June 18, 1855; *Know Nothing Almanac* (1855): 22.

14. Cleveland *Express*, Aug. 18, 1854; Cincinnati *Dollar Times* quoted in Eugene H. Roseboom, "Salmon P. Chase and the Know Nothings," *MVHR* 25 (1938): 336; Philadelphia *Sun*, Dec. 27, 1854 (quotation); Harrisburg *Herald*, Sept. 11, 1854; Boston *Bee* quoted in Cincinnati *Dollar Times*, July 27, 1854.

15. Charles Reemelin quoted in John B. Weaver, "Nativism and the Birth of the Republican Party in Ohio, 1854–1860" (Ph.D. diss., Ohio State University, 1982), 71; New York *Express*, July 30, 1855; Charles G. Irish Jr. to Daniel Ullmann, Oct. 14, 16, 1854, Ullmann Papers, NYHS. The American Protestant Association I refer to does not seem to have been connected with a group of

These immigrants acquired their anti-Catholic animus abroad, but native-born Americans could also draw upon a long domestic tradition of anti-Catholic sentiment. After all, the Puritans had left England because they believed that the Church of England too closely resembled the Roman Catholic Church. To prevent the trappings of Catholicism from encroaching upon their new congregations, many colonies banned Catholic churches and barred the immigration of Jesuits and priests. They also prohibited Catholics from holding political office or, to accomplish the same end, required anti-Catholic oaths for officeholders. In the eighteenth century, many believed that Catholics within the colonies would aid a French or Spanish invasion of English territory, a fear manifested in the anti-Catholic rhetoric of the French and Indian War. Most colonies consequently passed laws disarming Catholics, forbidding them to serve in the militia, and increasing their taxes. In order to monitor their movements, some colonies also passed laws mandating the registration of Catholics. New England, influenced by its Puritan heritage, harbored the strongest anti-Catholic sentiment, although even southern colonists were known to play a game called "Break the Pope's Neck." Of all the colonies, only Rhode Island allowed Catholics to settle without any legal restrictions. Passage in 1774 of the Quebec Act—which granted legal recognition to the Catholic Church in Quebec and extended the borders of that province south to the Ohio River—revived and strengthened anti-Catholicism. Outrage over the act helped make Pope Day (a New England tradition which featured parades and culminated in the burning of papal effigies) popular in all the colonies. Even the aid of Catholic France during the Revolutionary War did not fully assuage American anti-Catholicism. Seven of the thirteen new states initially allowed only Protestants to hold office, although most states had repealed these statutes by the early nineteenth century. However, the burning of convents, the lectures of itinerant ministers, and the publication of countless pamphlets during the first half of the nineteenth century proved that while it had lost its legal status, anti-Catholicism remained potent.[16]

Most Protestants living in nineteenth-century America carried this cultural baggage. Thus, when evidence of new Catholic "aggressions" began to appear in the early 1850s, many (especially those who could trace their ancestry to New England) were bound to succumb to Know Nothing rhetoric. Know Nothings were certainly religious bigots, but their insistence that the Catholic Church was making unprecedented efforts to influence American life in the 1850s was not entirely fabricated. The American Catholic hierarchy did

the same name founded in Philadelphia in 1844 and mentioned by Ray A. Billington in *The Protestant Crusade, 1800–1860: A Study of the Origins of American Nativism* (Chicago: Quadrangle Books, 1938), 183–84, 220–21, 235, 244, 438–39.

16. Thomas More Brown, "The Image of the Beast: Anti-Papal Rhetoric in Colonial America," in Richard O. Curry and Thomas M. Brown, eds., *Conspiracy: Fear of Subversion in American History* (New York: Rinehart and Winston, 1972), 1–20; Sister Mary Augustina Ray, *American Opinion of Roman Catholicism in the Eighteenth Century* (New York: Columbia Univ. Press, 1936); Billington, *Protestant Crusade*, 1–25.

begin to assert itself with unprecedented militancy around mid-century, which helps to explain increased Protestant animosity toward Catholics at this time. For instance, while in the past Catholic leaders had avoided proselytizing for fear of inciting retribution against the tiny Catholic population, in the mid-nineteenth century prelates began aggressively to seek converts. New York's Archbishop John Hughes publicly vowed that he would not rest until every American had been converted to Catholicism. Catholic leaders also increased their public criticisms of Protestantism in this period. Hughes called Protestants "infidels" and "heretics" and told American Protestants that if they did not like the fact that Catholic influence was increasing, they should "pack up as quickly as they can and go." The comments of Catholic convert and editor Orestes Brownson also disturbed Know Nothings. Brownson's claim that "Protestantism is effete, powerless, [and] dying out" did nothing to soothe Protestant fears. His assertion that Protestantism "has not and never can have any rights where Catholicism is triumphant" was equally appalling to Protestants. American Catholic leaders codified this new militancy at the First Plenary Council, held in 1852 in Baltimore. There they instituted many of the policies that would infuriate Know Nothings, such as the removal of Catholic students from public schools and the determination to unseat lay church trustees. Know Nothings believed that only by resisting the new Catholic militancy could Protestantism survive in America.[17]

Know Nothings believed that the new Catholic assertiveness carried grave implications for the future of American Protestantism. With Catholic immigrants pouring into the country, they would eventually outnumber Protestants. Once they gained hegemony, nativists reasoned, their purported intolerance would lead them to ban Protestantism altogether. According to Massachusetts Know Nothing Anson Burlingame, the Bishop of St. Louis had promised that " 'America will soon be Catholic, and then religious liberty will cease to exist.' " Other nativists agreed that Catholics "crushed out every feature and semblance of civil and religious liberty" in the countries they controlled. Such conditions existed in Catholic nations, concluded the Harrisburg *Herald*, because the "bigoted minions of the Pope know no toleration, nor will they allow any if they can help it."[18] Know Nothings also believed that if given the opportunity, Catholics would outlaw all Bibles, not just the Protestant version. They asserted that many Catholic nations banned Bibles, burned them if they were found, and imprisoned those who read

17. Hughes quoted in New York *Mirror*, Nov. 2, 1855; Hughes, *The Decline of Protestantism and Its Causes* (New York, 1850); Brownson quoted in *Know Nothing Almanac* (1856): 60; Hartford *Courant*, May 1, Nov. 5, 1855.

18. *Startling Facts for Native Americans Called "Know Nothings," or a Vivid Presentation of the Dangers to American Liberty, to Be Apprehended from Foreign Influence* (New York, 1855), 69–74; Anson Burlingame, *Oration by Hon. Anson Burlingame, Delivered at Salem, July 4, 1854* (Salem, 1854); Harrisburg *Herald*, Oct. 7 (quoting *Christian Advocate and Journal*), July 11, 1854; Cuba [New York] *American Banner* quoted in Youngstown *True American*, April 25, 1855.

them. "Give Popery sway," Know Nothings concluded from this evidence, "and there will be no Bible."[19]

Know Nothings claimed that if Catholics gained control of America, other liberties would suffer. "Romanism allows no freedom of thought," asserted the Hartford *Courant*, calling it "the most degrading despotism of which the world is cognizant." The Boston *Bee* agreed, stating that "Romanism . . . seeks to destroy all individual liberty, all private judgment, all power on the part of man to think or to act for himself. . . ." To prove the point, Know Nothing congressman Thomas R. Whitney quoted an encyclical written by the current pope, Pius IX, that called "liberty of conscience . . . absurd and dangerous" and "liberty of the press" a "great . . . horror." Efforts to suppress Protestant street preachers proved that Catholics had already begun "restraining the conscience, restraining thought, restraining all that makes up and characterizes and . . . gives beauty to the American name and nation."[20]

Know Nothings interpreted Catholic opposition to American public schools as proof that they resisted freedom of thought. As mentioned earlier, the First Plenary Council had directed Bishops to establish parochial schools rather than allow Catholic children to attend public ones, where students used the Protestant King James Bible and read textbooks tinged with anti-Catholicism. This followed the unsuccessful attempts of Hughes and others to have a portion of public school funds set aside for Catholic schools and to end the reading of the King James Bible in class. Know Nothings insisted that Catholic complaints were a mere subterfuge and that priests actually discouraged Catholics from receiving any education, because they "can have more influence over a degraded and ignorant population than over an enlightened and educated one." The Catholic hierarchy resisted sending its children to American public schools because "the practical equality taught in our schools, the liberality of sentiment, the self-control and independence inculcated there" weaken "the spiritual despotism claimed by the Romish Church over its devotees." Know Nothings also complained that Catholic refusal to send their children to public schools drove a wedge between Protestant and Catholic youngsters. If all children went to the same schools, they "would form similar associations, cultivate kindred political and social feelings, and in their manners and customs become peculiarly American." In addition, Know Nothings believed that Catholics' lack of respect for education would prove disastrous in a democratic nation, where voters had to weigh complex issues before choosing candidates for office. *"We cannot afford to have a single absolutely ignorant man among us,"* explained Know Nothing leader Charles Deshler.

19. Harrisburg *Herald*, June 8 (quotation), Oct. 28, 1854, May 11, 1855; *Know Nothing Almanac* (1855): 61; Whitney, *Defence of the American Policy*, 68; Albany *State Register*, Sept. 12, 1855; Tiffany, *Christian Elements of Republicanism*, 20.

20. Hartford *Courant*, Jan. 8, 1856; Boston *Bee* quoted in Cleveland *Express*, Aug. 2, 1854; Whitney, *Defence of the American Policy*, 96–97; *Christian Age* and Boston *Know Nothing* in Harrisburg *Herald*, Aug. 31, May 31 (quotation), 1854.

"Ignorance is the bane of a free government." In short, Catholic educational policies seemed certain to create both social friction and political chaos.[21]

According to the Know Nothings, Catholicism's discouragement of education, backward beliefs, and unswerving conservatism retarded human progress. For example, nativists traced the decline of Italy to the introduction of Catholicism. Italy, "once the teacher of the world, is now sunk in ignorance," and Catholicism "is the canker-worm that has eaten out her very vitals." Know Nothings also found Spain, Ireland, and Mexico to be "striking examples of the miserable condition to which both government and people are reduced, where Papacy controls Church and State." Because Catholic countries resisted progress, education, and science, they trailed Protestant nations in wealth and prosperity. Know Nothings concluded that "care should be taken lest Popery, which found [the United States] free, enlightened, and independent, should leave it enthralled, ignorant and debased."[22]

Know Nothings believed that Catholicism posed such a threat in part because of the power of the pope. While Protestants followed their own conscience, Catholics "march and countermarch with the precision of regular soldiers, at the tap of the Popish drum." The pope, said Know Nothings, determined the course of Catholic politicians and told Catholics how to vote as well as which American laws to obey. Revival of the doctrine of papal infallibility at this time convinced many Americans that the pontiff would stop at nothing until his control was absolute. Papal infallibility was both a theological and political issue. It meant that changes in ritual emanating from Rome must be instituted, even if they clashed with local customs. It also implied to many (including some of the Catholic leaders who opposed it) that the pontiff could claim jurisdiction over princes and states in non-religious matters. Pius IX's opposition to the European revolutions of 1848, combined with his effort to institutionalize papal infallibility, convinced many Protestants that the pope sought to suppress liberty everywhere. "The power of the Papacy is utterly incompatible with the liberties" Americans enjoy, argued one nativist journal, while a Know Nothing leader agreed that "a collision between the Papal Hierarchy and the Constitutions of this country is inevitable." The pope's thirst for power drove him to seek nothing less than the conversion of the United States "into a papal nation and government."[23]

21. Hartford *Courant*, July 25, 1855; Albany *State Register*, Sept. 12, 1855; Cuba [New York] *American Banner* quoted in Youngstown *True American*, April 25, 1855; Deshler, *"The Great American Middle Class,"* 26.

22. Youngstown *True American*, March 28, 1855 (quotation); New York *Express*, March 26, 1855 (quotation); Philadelphia *Times* in Harrisburg *Herald*, June 27, 1855; Whitney, *Defence of the American Policy*, 100–101; Cleveland *Express*, Aug. 7, 24, 1854; Hartford *Courant*, July 25, 1855 (quotation).

23. Harrisburg *Herald*, Aug. 4 (quotation), 31, 1854; Cleveland *Express*, Aug. 18, 1854; Hartford *American Dispatch*, July 14, 1855; New York *Express*, June 29, 1855; Boston *Bee* quoted in Philadelphia *Sun*, Feb. 6, 1854 (quotation); Daniel Ullmann, *Civil and Religious Liberty. An Address at Wilmington . . . July 4, 1855* (n.p., n.d), 33 (quotation); Whitney, *Defence of the American Policy*, 75, 79 (quotation).

Although the pope seemed a distant threat to many Americans, Know Nothings insisted that Catholic priests carried out the pontiff's subversive schemes in America. "It is the constant plotting of these Jesuitical craftsmen that we resist," argued nativists, especially "their endeavors to unite Church and State, and render both subservient to the nod of the Pope." Know Nothings believed that Catholics could never disobey their priests, because the priest might then reveal secrets divulged in the confessional or withhold absolution. This gave priests extraordinary power, which they used to enforce conformity amongst the laity. Furthermore, most American priests had been born abroad and had never taken oaths of citizenship. This reinforced the notion that their loyalties lay ultimately with Rome and convinced many natives that the power of priests ought to be curtailed.[24]

Following a traditional theme of anti-Catholicism, Know Nothings also accused priests of sexual licentiousness. Richard Hofstadter noted that "anti-Catholicism has always been the pornography of the Puritan," and the popularity of Maria Monk's convent "revelations" demonstrates that the Protestant obsession with sexual impropriety by the priesthood preceded the Know Nothings by many years. The notion that convents provided the setting for illicit sex was so prevalent that customers commonly referred to nineteenth-century brothels as "nunneries."[25]

While Know Nothing journals did not describe convent life in the sordid detail provided in convent exposés, their language left no doubt as to what they imagined went on within their walls. "Convents are the very hot-beds of lust and debauchery," reported one Know Nothing journal, while another described how they were "impregnated with vice and crime." Priests in convents exercised the most "shocking licentiousness and most unmitigated despotism over the hearts, minds, and persons of the nuns." Know Nothings asserted that the priests' authority allowed them to cover up their convent indiscretions by condemning their victims to a life of cloistered silence.[26]

Despite the array of evils that Know Nothings identified in the Catholic religion, Know Nothings claimed that their movement would not have been necessary had Catholics not attempted to gain control of American politics and thereby impose their views upon the rest of America. "Our opposition is not to the [Catholic] Church," insisted an Ohio Know Nothing leader, ". . . but to its grasping for political power." A New York newspaper agreed that "what Ameri-

24. Pottsville *Miner's Journal*, May 20, 1854 (quotation); *Christian Advocate and Journal* [a leading Methodist organ] in Harrisburg *Herald*, Sept. 1, Oct. 6 (quotation), 1854; Albany *State Register*, Sept. 15, 1855; Philadelphia *News* in Clearfield [Pennsylvania] *Raftsman's Journal*, Dec. 5, 1855; Hartford *Courant*, Nov. 26, 1855.

25. Richard Hofstadter, *The Paranoid Style in American Politics* (New York: Knopf, 1965), 21; Billington, *Protestant Crusade*, 68–76, 98–108.

26. Harrisburg *Herald*, Nov. 7, 1854 (quotation); Boston *Know Nothing*, May 6, 1854 (quotation); Clearfield [Pennsylvania] *Raftsman's Journal*, Dec. 12, 1855 (quotation); *Know Nothing Almanac* (1855): 50, (1856), 29, 49–52; Cleveland *Express*, July 27, 1854; Cincinnati *Dollar Times*, Aug. 3, 1854.

cans are battling in Catholicism is not the religion of Jesus, . . . but a political Roman Jesuitism, whose aim is, and ever has been, to grasp temporal with spiritual power. . . ." Know Nothings opposed Catholicism "as a political institution" and promised not to interfere with Catholic religious practices. They sought instead "to destroy their political influence."[27]

Catholics insisted that they sought no greater influence over American politics than any other religious group. But Know Nothings responded that "the systematic interference of the Church of Rome, *as an ecclesiastical organization*, . . . in the political controversies of this republic" set Catholicism apart from any other sect. Know Nothings asserted that ever since the time of Constantine, there had been "a *political* stripe along the whole length of Romanism." While Protestant ministers confined their activities to spiritual matters, Know Nothings found that "the Roman Hierarchy is the most gigantic political association on earth. . . . Its purpose [is] the government of mankind."[28]

According to Know Nothings, proof of the political designs of Catholicism could be found in the actions of the popes. Know Nothings reminded Americans that "the Pope himself has been an active agent in political quarrels, intrigues, and wars of Europe," attacking sovereign nations, ordering assassinations, and dethroning kings in order to carry out his political designs. "Roman Pontiffs ever since the institution of Popedom" had attempted not only "to subjugate civil rulers—and not only to connect church and state, but to invest the priesthood with the civil magistracy."[29] When Philadelphia congressman Joseph Chandler (a convert to Catholicism) responded that popes no longer exercised political power as they had in the past, Know Nothing newspapers reprinted articles from Catholic newspapers insisting that Chandler was wrong, and that the pope did still possess the power to depose sovereigns. Nativists pointed to recent events in Sardinia, for example, where the pope had declared null and void a law regulating Catholic Church property and threatened to put the island under interdict unless the statute was repealed. Know Nothings also listed recent incidents in Piedmont, Spain, England, France, Holland, Germany, and Ireland to prove that the pope had not lost his enthusiasm for interfering in political affairs.[30]

27. Thomas C. Ware, *Address of Thomas C. Ware, President of the State Council of Ohio. Delivered May 29th, 1856* (n.p., n.d.), 6, OHS; New York *Mirror,* Oct. 20, 1854; Harrisburg *Herald*, July 17 (quotation), Nov. 8, 1854; Cleveland *Express*, Sept. 16, 1854 (quotation).

28. Harrisburg *Pennsylvania Telegraph*, Nov. 28, 1855; Ullmann, *Civil and Religious Liberty*, quoted in Ralph Basso, "Nationalism, Nativism, and the Black Soldier: Daniel Ullmann, a Biography of a Man Living in a Period of Transition, 1810–1892" (Ph.D. diss., St. John's University, 1986), 156; Cincinnati *Dollar Times*, Aug. 3, 1854.

29. Harrisburg *Herald*, Oct. 7, 1854; Steubenville *True American*, Jan. 4, 1855.

30. Dublin [Ireland] *Tablet* quoted in Harrisburg *Herald*, April 7, 1855; Hartford *Courant*, Sept. 5, 1855; New York *Express*, June 9, 1856; Clearfield [Pennsylvania] *Raftsman's Journal*, March 14, 1855; Albany *State Register*, Sept. 3, 1855; Whitney, *Defence of the American Policy*, 71–77; John C. Pitrot, *Review of the Speech of Hon. J. R. Chandler of Pennsylvania on the Political Power of the Pope* (Boston, 1855); Frank Gerrity, "Joseph Ripley Chandler and the Temporal Power of the Pope," *Pennsylvania History* 49 (1982): 106–20.

   Many Americans could not imagine how the pope could influence American politics. But Know Nothings believed that the visit of Papal Nuncio Gaetano Bedini as well as Catholic attempts to remove the Bible from the public schools, split school funds, change church property laws, and create Catholic political tickets marked the beginning of Catholicism's political assault upon the United States. While Irish immigrants often insisted that a certain percentage of an electoral ticket be made up of Catholics, Know Nothings asserted that Presbyterians or Episcopalians never made such demands for their denominations. According to one Know Nothing, Bishop John Purcell of Cincinnati had bragged to Democratic leaders that he controlled the votes of 6,200 Catholics and had produced a list of names to prove it. It was this concentration of power in the hands of a few leaders (and ultimately the pope himself) that made Catholic influence in American politics so potentially dangerous.[31]

   In addition, while Protestant immigrants were divided between the Whig and Democratic parties, Know Nothings believed that Catholics always voted in an unbroken bloc for Democratic candidates. "There is no other denomination in the United States which moves in a solid body in elections," grumbled one Know Nothing journal. Another agreed that "their vote is almost always a unit." This uniformity at the polls proved to Know Nothings that Catholics did not choose their candidates, but rather "receive[d] their instructions and their tickets from the Priests, and vote[d] accordingly." Skeptics might argue that there were too few Catholics in America to alter election results, but Know Nothings contended that "in a government where the opposing parties are so nearly balanced as in this country, a slight addition to either side may determine the preponderance." Although the Catholic population was small, Know Nothings insisted that bloc voting gave them power to sway elections that exceeded their nominal strength.[32]

   According to Know Nothings, Irish-Catholic immigrants augmented the political power that bloc voting gave them by committing a preponderance of the voting fraud in America as well. Look at any American city, nativists said, and accounts of illegal immigrant voting could be found:

> At the Seventh Ward, Irishmen were seen after having voted, to fall into the ranks and work their way up to the window and vote again, while around the polls stood a wild, excited mob of a thousand Celts, threatening death to all who oppose them. Hundreds who were challenged and rejected at the wards on the South side, swarmed over to their countrymen on the north side, and there deposited their ballots. A great many swore in their votes who were unnaturalized, and when the Bible was held to them, grasping it, they kissed

   31. Hartford *Courant*, Sept. 27, 1855, June 9, 1856; Harrisburg *Herald*, Aug. 31, 1854; Whitney, *Defence of the American Policy*, 77; Albany *State Register*, June 26, 1855; Boston *Bee*, June 15, 1855.
   32. Fayetteville [North Carolina] *Observer* in Boston *Bee*, July 7, 1855; Cuba [New York] *American Banner* in Youngstown *True American*, April 25, 1855; Harrisburg *Herald*, July 19, 1854; Pottsville *Miner's Journal*, May 20, 1854; Hartford *Courant*, April 18, 1856.

their thumbs instead of the holy book, and by this dodge eased their tender
consciences.

The concluding sentence alludes to the fact that immigrants were not required to produce naturalization papers in order to vote. Voting laws required that they merely swear at the polls that they had been naturalized.
Know Nothings insisted that the ability to receive absolution at the confessional made all such oaths non-binding on Catholics and encouraged them to
continue their fraudulent voting. Nativists also asserted that the hiring of
immigrant "blacklegs and bullies" as poll watchers made it easier for newcomers to vote illegally, since immigrants were likely to ignore the crimes of
their countrymen.[33]

Know Nothings charged that in addition to casting too many ballots for
themselves, the newcomers created such riotous conditions at the polls that
many native-born citizens now abstained from voting. In the past, casting
one's ballot had been safe and easy. Only since ignorant immigrants had
begun pouring into the country, argued Know Nothings, had violence and
rioting at the polls become so frequent. "Government is a science," explained
the New York *Express*, "which an Irishman, who cannot read, or a German,
who knows not our language, and customs, and traditions, cannot learn in a
single day." Know Nothings believed that the fraud and violence immigrants
practiced at the polls threatened the very sanctity of the American electoral
process.[34]

The revival of the concept of republicanism formed an essential component of the Know Nothing indictment of immigrant political activity. The
catchwords of republicanism filled the political writings of eighteenth-century
Americans, and many scholars now believe that the colonists' devotion to it
united the otherwise diverse colonies and justified their attempt to wrest
independence from England. In its simplest form, republicanism referred to a
form of government controlled by "the people," through representatives selected either directly or indirectly by the preponderance of citizens. But
nineteenth-century Americans utilized the term primarily to denote the conditions necessary for the successful operation of a republican government.
Americans believed that without a citizenry committed to civic virtue, republican government could not survive. Vigilance against external sources of tyranny, combined with internal unity, were also necessary for the maintenance
of republicanism. The tenets of republicanism taught citizens that corruption

33. Chicago *Tribune* in Hartford *Courant*, March 28, 1856 (quotation); New York *Express*,
March 21, 1855 (quotation); Steubenville *True American*, Jan. 18, 1855; J. B. Baker (a Democrat
who boasts of his past service forging official signatures on fraudulent naturalization papers) to
James Buchanan, July 4, 1857, Buchanan Papers, HSP.

34. Youngstown *True American*, April 18, 1855; Dublin *Evening Mail* cited in New York
Crusader, Sept. 27, 1856; *Know Nothing Almanac* (1856): 46–47; Harrisburg *Herald*, Oct. 14,
1854 (excerpt from New York *Crusader*), March 15, Aug. 17 (excerpt from New York *Express*,
quotation), 1855.

often weakened governments surreptitiously from within, and only if a country's inhabitants valued the public good over personal gain could such malfeasance be prevented and their republic perpetuated.[35]

As one might expect, it was the threat posed to American political institutions by Catholicism that formed the core of the Know Nothing invocation of republicanism. Nativists argued that bloc voting, electoral frauds and violence, the despotism of Catholic authorities over the laity, and the Catholic disdain for education and assimilation all threatened to destroy America's republican form of government. Know Nothings believed that a number of factors made Catholicism and republicanism incompatible. First, they believed that Catholic leaders, preferring non-republican governments, had inculcated their followers with that predilection. "That the natural and constant tendencies of Romanism, are Monarchical, and of Protestantism, Republican, the history of both faiths abundantly proves," declared Spooner. His Pennsylvania counterpart, Otis H. Tiffany, agreed that the Catholic Church's consistent support of monarchy and repression proved that its "principles and practices are in direct hostility to our Republicanism."[36]

Know Nothings also argued that the despotism practiced by the Catholic Church in religious affairs and the despotic governments Catholic immigrants lived under in Europe made them unsuitable citizens for a republican government. "*Subjects* cannot become good citizens in a moment," explained Whitney. "The early republicans of the United States of America had more than a century of practical training in the theory of self-government, before they ventured on the bold experiment. . . ." A Pennsylvania journal likewise warned that the "utter submission and pliancy of their people in the hands of superiors" is totally inconsistent with "the essential doctrines of a *free* country." Know Nothings believed that without such freedom, voters could not make the independent decisions necessary for voting in a republic. Idiots and the insane were barred from voting because they were deemed incapable of independent action, and Know Nothings reasoned that Catholic immigrants

---

35. Bernard Bailyn, *The Ideological Origins of the American Revolution* (Cambridge, Mass.: Harvard Univ. Press, 1967); Gordon S. Wood, *The Creation of the American Republic, 1776–1787* (New York: W. W. Norton, 1969), 46–124; Robert E. Shalhope: "Toward a Republican Synthesis: The Emergence of an Understanding of Republicanism in American Historiography," *William and Mary Quarterly*, 3d Ser., 29 (1972): 49–80; Shalhope, "Republicanism and Early American Historiography," *William and Mary Quarterly*, 3d Ser., 39 (1982): 334–56. See also the fall 1985 issue of *American Quarterly*, devoted entirely to republicanism in American history, especially Jean H. Baker, "From Belief into Culture: Republicanism in the Antebellum North," 532–50.

36. Spooner, *Report of the President . . . June 5, 1855*, 11; Tiffany, *Christian Elements of Republicanism*, 19; Hartford *Courant*, Sept. 3, 1855; *Know Nothing Almanac* (1855): 27–29; Steubenville *True American*, Jan. 4, 1855; *Republican Quarterly Review* in Albany *State Register*, Sept. 4–7, 1855; Harrisburg *Herald*, July 17, Aug. 7, 1854; Pottsville *Miner's Journal*, May 20, 1854; Cleveland *Express*, Sept. 16, 1854, Jan. 30, 1855; Whitney, *Defence of the American Policy*, 94–103.

had so little experience with freedom of thought or action that they would be liable to the same improper influences.[37]

The importance of republicanism to the Know Nothings is reflected not only in their anti-Catholicism but in their treatment of American Jews as well. Contrary to what one might expect, and in stark contrast to future American nativists, Know Nothings did not condemn Jews or Judaism. To some extent, of course, this reflected the minute size of the antebellum Jewish-American population. But the Know Nothings also refused to denounce Jews because, unlike Catholics, Jews never allowed "their religious feelings to interfere with their political views." In fact, Know Nothings believed that Jews could make fine American citizens, because "however repugnant their religion may be, their religion is Republican. . . . Indeed, the Jews were the first Republican People in the world." Know Nothings contended that because of their republican propensities, evident in the democratic administration of their congregations, Jewish immigrants would never pose a threat commensurate to that of Catholicism.[38]

To a large extent, the version of republicanism expounded by the Know Nothings paralleled that of the Founding Fathers' generation. While the revolutionaries complained that the appointment of inferior colonial officials resulted from vice and corruption, Know Nothings blamed packed conventions, behind-the-scenes wire-pulling, intimidation at the polls, and immigrant support for demagogic candidates for bringing about the same result. Like the colonists, the Know Nothings believed that Americans no longer enjoyed good government because criteria other than merit determined which candidates gained office. Know Nothing and revolutionary propaganda also agreed that an external source of tyranny (the king and his ministers or the pope and his bishops) threatened American liberty. Yet the Know Nothings also modified the standard republicanism of the period to suit their unique agenda. For example, Know Nothings did not refer to the dangers of "luxury," a theme prominent in the revolutionary period. In addition, the republicanism of "sturdy independence," found by Sean Wilentz and Stephen Hahn to have inspired both urban trade unionists and rural upcountry yeomen seeking to maintain their distance from the dislocations of the market economy, is absent from Know Nothing rhetoric. Perhaps most important, the Know Nothings' republicanism bore a closer resemblance to classical rather than revolutionary-era republicanism in that it idealized the community of the like-minded, predicating the commonwealth on the existence of a relatively homogeneous body politic with shared interests. In this way they differed from Founding Fathers such as Madison, who dissented from classical republicanism by endorsing pluralism and the utility of a multiplicity of interests. Know Nothings believed that homogeneity,

37. Whitney, *Defence of the American Policy*, 29 (quotation), 33–41; Pottsville *Miner's Journal*, May 20, 1854 (quotation); Hartford *Courant*, Dec. 18, 1855; Harrisburg *Herald*, Feb. 1, 1855.

38. Rising Sun [Indiana] *Visitor*, Oct. 20, 1855; New York *Express*, Sept. 10, 1855.

not the competition between opposing interests, was the surest way to strengthen and preserve the republic.[39]

Know Nothings admitted that the country needed immigrants, and consequently they never proposed restricting the flow of newcomers as a means to preserve the homogeneity they valued. Instead, they sought to assimilate future immigrants more thoroughly and mitigate their political influence by modifying the naturalization laws that transformed immigrants into voting citizens. Naturalization laws required that in order to become American citizens, immigrants had to live in the United States for five years, and then swear before a judge that they disavowed all allegiance to their former home. Nativists found this naturalization procedure deficient for a number of reasons. Most important, they believed that immigrants could not be sufficiently "Americanized" in five years. "Foreigners are made . . . 'American citizens' altogether too rapidly," said the Boston *Know Nothing*. "Raw, verdant, outlandish fellows, fresh from the emigrant ship, with no more comprehension of the duties of a citizen; no more knowledge of our government; no more fitness to act the great character of a Republican than a Chinese automaton, are daily, by the thousands, metamorphosed into the stature and privileges of full American citizenship." Others complained that the naturalization process had become too perfunctory. An immigrant might spend his or her entire probationary period in a prison or poor-house, and still at the end of five years gain all the rights and privileges of "honest" natives. Know Nothings suggested that the waiting period before naturalization be increased to twenty-one years, since native Americans waited that long (from the day of their birth) before gaining the full rights of citizenship. Nativists argued that a twenty-one-year wait would allow immigrants to become fully assimilated and learn the responsibilities and rights "peculiar to our people, our country, and our republicanism." Massachusetts governor Henry J. Gardner summed up Know Nothing opinion on the subject best, asserting that Americans must "nationalize before we naturalize."[40]

While most Know Nothings pushed for a twenty-one-year waiting period before naturalization, more radical nativists contended that the naturalization laws should be completely repealed, so that only those born in America could exercise citizenship rights. These nativists believed that no amount of time could undo the bonds formed with the place of one's birth. Pursuing this line of reasoning, Whitney called the naturalization laws "a living statutory *lie*—a

39. Sean Wilentz, *Chants Democratic: New York City and the Rise of the American Working Class, 1788–1850* (New York: Oxford Univ. Press, 1984); Steven Hahn, *The Roots of Southern Populism: Yeoman Farmers and the Transformation of the Georgia Upcountry, 1850–1890* (New York: Oxford Univ. Press, 1983).

40. Boston *Know Nothing* quoted in Harrisburg *Herald*, June 14, 1854; Albany *State Register*, Sept. 19, 1855; Buffalo *Commercial Advertiser* in Rochester *American*, Dec. 21, 1854; Franklin [pseud.], *Know Nothingism; or, The American Party* (Boston, 1855), 9; Gardner quoted in William G. Bean, "Party Transformation in Massachusetts with Special Reference to the Antecedents of Republicanism, 1848–1860" (Ph.D. diss., Harvard University, 1922), 264.

theory which professes to perform impossibilities." Know Nothings noted that in England, only a special act of Parliament transformed an immigrant into a citizen. American naturalization laws were lax only because they had been created when the new nation desperately needed to lure inhabitants from Europe. Radical nativists argued that the United States could attract additional immigrants without the lure of citizenship, and that, consequently, Congress should repeal the nation's naturalization laws.[41]

Know Nothings also urged changes in the naturalization laws because they believed that politicians had transformed the naturalization process into a corrupt mechanism to manufacture votes. By the 1850s it had become common practice for the Democratic party to round up large groups of aliens and speed them through the naturalization process. Know Nothings charged that by cutting red tape, paying court fees, and finding judges who looked the other way if the immigrant could not prove five years' residence, Democrats were bribing immigrants to vote their ticket. Because these naturalization drives usually took place just weeks or days before elections and were usually conducted in private, Know Nothings concluded that the naturalization process had been corrupted into a systematic procedure to produce the votes necessary to keep unscrupulous demagogues in office.[42]

Until recently, most historians ignored the frequency with which Know Nothing propaganda censured native-born politicians and political parties. Yet Know Nothing abhorrence for them abounds in their writings and speeches. Nativists believed that the political corruption perpetrated by immigrants could never have grown so endemic but for the acquiescence of native-born politicians. The newcomers were actually encouraged by politicians to disrupt the political process, asserted Know Nothings, because by intimidating voters, fixing primaries, and casting illegal ballots, immigrants helped perpetuate the tenure of corrupt officeholders. Nativists also blamed immigrants for the rise of demagogism in American politics, insisting that only ignorant foreigners could be duped by the outrageous promises of this cunning new breed of politician.

The Know Nothings did not invent anti-partyism. In fact, until the Jacksonian era nearly all American politicians had condemned parties as factious and self-serving. Only by the 1820s did politicians such as Martin Van Buren convince voters that parties could serve beneficial functions. Van Buren argued that the pressures of party competition would prevent corruption. Par-

41. Thomas R. Whitney, *An Address on the Occasion of the Seventh Anniversary of the Alpha Chapter, Order of United Americans* (New York, 1852), 13 (quotation); Whitney, *Defence of the American Policy*, 135–50; Cleveland *Express*, Sept. 26, 1854; Pottsville *Miner's Journal*, July 1, 1854; Boston *Bee* in Cincinnati *Dollar Times*, Aug. 10, 1854 (quotation); Hartford *Courant*, April 23, 1855.

42. Rochester *American*, Dec. 19, 1854; Hartford *Courant*, March 16, 1856; Derby [Connecticut] *Journal* in Robert D. Parmet, "The Know Nothings in Connecticut" (Ph.D. diss., Columbia University, 1966), 120.

ties also fostered a truer democracy, said Van Buren, because conventions and primaries determined their nominations, while under the system of personal cliques that had previously prevailed, one or two leaders hand-picked the candidates for office. By focusing attention on the evils of antebellum political parties, Know Nothingism became the first national movement to repudiate Van Buren's assertion that parties were beneficial and desirable.[43]

Know Nothings promised that the Order would roll back the influence of demagogues and professional politicians. According to the Cincinnati *Times*, it was "the particular object of the American [i.e., Know Nothing] party to discourage these unprincipled persons who, without any qualifications save . . . that they are too lazy to work, turn politicians, and thus, by their demagogueism, afflict the country with one of the greatest curses it has ever known." Know Nothings promised to "cleanse the Augean Stable, and free our government from the . . . hordes of political leeches that are fattening their bloated carcasses in the people's money, robbing us of National honor, and sapping the very foundations of the citadel of freedom." Pennsylvania Know Nothing leader Jacob Broom asserted that "individual aspiration, and the blind zeal of *party*, have alike rendered our organization necessary" and promised that when his movement had triumphed, "the wild spirit of party" would "be signally rebuked by the matchless genius of American patriotism." Know Nothings insisted that unlike professional politicians, their members asked of proposed laws "not—will it aid the party? Will it help in another election? not even, will it be popular?—but always—Will it be RIGHT?" Know Nothings stressed that they chose "new men" for office, those not "surrounded by courtiers, or controlled by intriguants or cliques."[44]

A consistent undercurrent to the Know Nothing critique of political parties concerned the manner in which political conventions and primaries had become unresponsive to the public will. Nineteenth-century primaries were really nothing more than localized conventions, and these small gatherings of party members decided most nominations. But by the 1850s, especially in large cities, primaries had become mere formalities, as party leaders began hiring thugs and bullies to intimidate those attending the primaries into supporting the caucus candidates. According to the New York *Express*, " 'Tammany Hall' and 'Broadway House' [Tammany's Whig counterpart]—with their bruisers and boxers in the Primary Elections, had become so thoroughly rotten—that . . . foreigners of one or two years' residence" controlled Tammany nominations, while "it is notorious that a celebrated bruiser had more influence in Broadway House than General Winfield Scott." The Know Nothings offered an alternative to the

43. Richard Hofstadter, *The Idea of a Party System: The Rise of Legitimate Opposition in the United States, 1780–1840* (Berkeley: Univ. of California Press, 1969), esp. 1–73, 212–71.

44. Cincinnati *Dollar Times*, July 27, 1854; Youngstown *True American*, Feb. 21, 1855; Jacob Broom, *An Address Delivered at Castle Garden, February 22, 1854, Before the Order of United Americans* (New York, 1854), 18 [Broom was referring to the Order of United Americans, but his statement certainly applies to the Know Nothings as well]; Hartford *Courant*, July 18, 1855; Albany *State Register*, Dec. 12, 1855.

fixed primary, because the Order selected its candidates by vote of the entire council. The *Express* explained that the Know Nothings "have restored primary meetings to what they were originally, in both parties—meetings for consultation, deliberation, and fair counting."[45]

Although nearly every facet of the professional politicians' trade disgusted Know Nothings, they were especially appalled by the payments and attention conniving politicians showered upon immigrants. Demagogues induced Catholics to vote for them "because of the rewards bestowed by Mayors, Governors, and Presidents—because of the gold and silver that is poured into their coffers, and . . . by toadying to the priests, fawning to the Bishop, and deceitfully pandering to the ignorance and superstition of that people." The frequency with which immigrants received patronage appointments particularly piqued Know Nothings. "We have seen too many of our countrymen told to stand aside," complained a New York City paper, "while a foreigner, of far less ability, were conciliated by some position of emolument." Philadelphia nativist Lewis Levin likewise implored native-born citizens to "look at your Custom House and your Post Office. They are filled with foreigners." This was the fault of the politicians, who gave immigrants "far more than their fair share of the offices and honors" because newcomers could more reliably deliver huge blocs of votes to the spoilsmen.[46] Thus, Know Nothings insisted that political parties and professional politicians deserved blame for many of the problems apparently caused by immigrants.

Some Know Nothings sought to remedy such problems by modifying or completely abandoning the spoils system. The platform of a New York Know Nothing council condemned "as odious and un-American, the obvious abuse of Executive . . . patronage, which for many years past has more and more found favor in the Administrations of our Governments, both Federal and State." Inasmuch as the spoils system "proscribes the high minded and independent citizen, and puts the obedient tool of power in his place" and "often prefers the foreigner to the native citizen," Know Nothings deemed patronage detrimental to the cause of good government. Rhode Island Know Nothings also called for curtailment of "the present demoralizing system of rewards for political subserviency." One nativist newspaper even suggested that postmasters be elected rather than appointed to office. Only by such action could Americans hope to wrest control of the government from the "mere tools of unscrupulous partizans," and return it to those who had the best interests of the people at heart.[47]

45. Speech of Peter Cooper in New York *Herald*, Oct. 28, 1854; New York *Express*, Feb. 9, 1855; Albany *State Register* quoted in Rochester *American*, Nov. 11, 1854; "R" in Albany *State Register*, Sept. 10, 1855.

46. Cuba [New York] *American Banner* quoted in Youngstown *True American*, April 25, 1855; New York *National Democrat* and Levin quoted in Philadelphia *Sun*, March 17, 1854, Oct. 6, 1855; Hartford *Courant*, Jan. 4, 1855.

47. ["Council No. XII"], *Principles and Objects of the American Party* (New York, 1855), 33–35; Harrisburg *Herald*, March 17, 1855; Rhode Island State Council platform in Boston *Bee*, June 21, 1855; Pottsville *Miner's Journal*, March 24, Nov. 24, 1855.

Localized initiatives to outlaw the spoils never gained much national support within the Know Nothing organization. Instead, Know Nothings promised to bring honesty and integrity back to American politics through implementation of their favorite slogan: "Americans must rule America." With this demand, Know Nothings sought not only the election of native-born Americans but candidates who would keep foreigners out of appointive office as well. According to Gardner, the Founding Fathers had devised the Constitution for a nation that received 5,000 immigrants per year. Had they realized how many immigrants would come to America in the mid-nineteenth century, they would have banned all foreigners from government office. Know Nothings such as Gardner insisted that they were following the wishes of the revolutionary generation, merely codifying Washington's warning to beware of "foreign influence." When "governed EXCLUSIVELY BY AMERICANS— by those who have been born and reared upon its soil"—Americans could "confidently expect a return to the pure and thoroughly American Policy of our early Presidents."[48]

Know Nothings believed that the remedies they proposed for the corruption and unresponsiveness of the American political system should rank theirs as a great reform movement. "Its mission is one of *reform*, in every sense of the word," insisted the *Know Nothing Almanac*, "and only those who are personally interested in perpetuating the present corruptions in politics, are its opponents and defamers."[49] Other Know Nothings echoed this view, but historians have been reluctant to group Know Nothingism with other antebellum reform movements. One of the foremost scholars of American reform has asserted that Know Nothingism should not be classified as a "true reform movement" because its members "were fuzzy about what sort of social order they wanted. . . ."[50] Many nativists, it is true, would eventually clash over slavery and temperance. Nonetheless, Know Nothings could describe their ideal social order in great detail. They hoped to create an America in which Protestantism dominated Catholicism; immigrants heeded American customs and assimilated; children read the Bible in school; the immigration of paupers and convicts was discouraged; the ballot box was protected from fraud; and politicians heeded the will of their constituents. Historians are understandably reluctant to classify bigoted Know Nothings with admirable abolitionists in the ranks of American reform. Yet in spite of that bigotry, their anti-immigrant, anti-Catholic, anti-party ideology dis-

48. Gardner in Boston *Bee*, Jan. 4, 1856; Boston *Know Nothing* in Harrisburg *Herald*, May 31, 1854 (quotation); Fredonia [New York] *Advertiser* in Rochester *American*, Nov. 21, 1854 (quotation); "A.H." in Steubenville *True American*, Aug. 29, 1855; Youngstown *True American*, Feb. 14, 1855; Albany *State Register*, Sept. 20, 1855; "Know Nothing" in Harrisburg *Herald*, April 3, 1855; Hartford *Courant*, April 7, 1855; Pottsville *Miner's Journal*, May 6, 1854.

49. *Know Nothing Almanac* (1855): 16; Harrisburg *Herald*, Sept. 7, 1854; Clearfield [Pennsylvania] *Raftsman's Journal*, March 14, 1855.

50. Ronald G. Walters, *American Reformers, 1815–1860* (New York: Hill and Wang, 1978), 12.

played a precision and sophistication equal to that of other antebellum reform movements.

Know Nothings felt certain that with their ideology fully disseminated to the public, their movement could not fail to sweep the nation. In part, this confidence stemmed from their conviction that their world-view reflected fundamental American values, and this explains why Know Nothings began to call themselves the "American party" after the 1854 elections. At the center of this ideology was an unswerving belief that Protestantism defined American nationality. Protestantism accounted for the nation's political freedom, social stability, and economic prosperity. But the great surge of immigration at mid-century imperiled the social order that Protestantism had created. Although their concern encompassed all immigrants (except Anglo-Saxon Protestants), the Know Nothings felt most threatened by the preponderance of Catholics amongst the newcomers. Catholicism bred ignorance, despotism, and moral decay, and therefore any increase in Catholic immigration threatened American society. While admitting that the size of the Catholic population in America was still relatively small, Know Nothings insisted that through corruption and bloc-voting Catholics had already attained political power disproportionate to their numerical strength. Catholic attempts to divert public tax money to parochial schools and to ban the Bible from the classroom proved this and convinced Know Nothings that they must meet the Catholic threat while Protestants still held a numerical advantage. Finally, Know Nothing ideology also blamed unresponsive political parties and conniving politicians for the deterioration of Protestant values. Unlike the Founding Fathers, modern politicians pursued power and office instead of the public good. However, Know Nothings promised that when their movement succeeded, Americans would once again enjoy a virtuous, responsive government dedicated to the maintenance of Protestant values.

THE PROPAGATION SOCIETY.___ MORE FREE THAN WELCOME.

This 1855 print by Nathaniel Currier reflects the Know Nothings' belief that the Catholic church sought to dominate American religious and temporal life. Note that the prelate pulls the papal boat ashore by hooking a shamrock plant, symbolic of the nation's Irish immigrants. (Courtesy, Library of Congress)

Nativists blamed drunken immigrants for election-day violence. Here, a whiskey-drinking Irish immigrant and a beer-drinking German immigrant steal a ballot box while their compatriots riot at the polls.

This print recounts the saga of runaway slave Anthony Burns who, after escaping from the South, was eventually arrested in Boston in 1854 and returned to his owner. The fallout over Burns's capture helped convince Massachusetts voters to join the Know Nothings, and once in office, they used every means at their disposal to punish those responsible for Burns's rendition. (Courtesy, Library of Congress)

Once in office, Know Nothings used a variety of means to end purported fraud and corruption in naturalization proceedings. This portrait of naturalization hearings in New York, from Frank Leslie's Illustrated Weekly, *illustrates the type of scene Know Nothings hoped to eliminate.*

THE RIGHT MAN FOR THE RIGHT PLACE.

For Sale at N.º 2 Spruce St. N.Y.

The American party depicted their 1856 presidential nominee, Millard Fillmore, as the only candidate who could restore harmony between North and South. Fillmore is shown separating Republican candidate John C. Frémont (with the rifle) from Democratic nominee James Buchanan. (Courtesy, Library of Congress)

THE AMERICAN RIVER GANGES.

Animosity between Protestants and Catholics over the use of the Bible in the nation's public schools continued long after the demise of the Know Nothings, as this famous 1871 Harper's Weekly *cartoon by Thomas Nast demonstrates.*

6

The Know Nothings in Office

With more than 10,000 lodges and 1,000,000 members, the Know Nothings entered 1855 brimming with confidence.[1] In the first weeks of January, Know Nothing governors were inaugurated in Pennsylvania and Massachusetts, and the Order believed (correctly, as it turned out) that upcoming spring elections in New England would provide additional victories. But Know Nothings soon discovered that they could not automatically parlay their electoral successes into legislative accomplishments. In New York, Know Nothing leaders anticipated using their legislative strength to defeat the re-election bid of their archenemy, Senator William H. Seward. However, Know Nothing defections to the Seward camp enabled the senator to win a narrow victory. In Pennsylvania, too, the Order encountered difficulties. Factional divisions ran so deep within the Pennsylvania Order that although a majority of legislators were Know Nothings, they failed to elect anyone to the state's vacant United States Senate seat, and the resentment generated by this stalemate paralyzed the legislature for the remainder of the session. Even in Massachusetts, where their 400-seat majority assured easy approval of the Know Nothing legislative agenda, the session's achievements were partially overshadowed by the improprieties of one of their leaders. Nonetheless, when the legislative sessions of 1855 concluded, northern Know Nothings had enacted numerous laws addressing nativism, slavery, temperance, and political reform—the four major facets of the Know Nothing agenda.

Of course, the Know Nothings' activities in office were circumscribed by their numerical strength, and despite the impression created by their impressive showings in the elections of late 1854 and early 1855, Know Nothings actually controlled political affairs in only a handful of states. Besides capturing the governorship, Know Nothings in Massachusetts occupied every seat in the senate that convened in January 1855, and all but three of the 378 positions in the house. In Connecticut, Rhode Island, and New Hampshire, Know Nothings also controlled both the executive and legislative branches of government,

1. Charles Deshler to James A. Henry, Jan. 26, 1855 (letterbook), Deshler Papers, Rutgers University.

albeit with smaller legislative majorities.[2] In the rest of the North, the Know Nothings lacked the power that they wielded in these New England states. Know Nothings in Pennsylvania held the governorship and a majority in the house of representatives, yet because only a third of the senate seats in that state were contested each year, Know Nothings in that body were outnumbered two to one. A majority of Indiana legislators probably belonged to the Order (their participation in the state's anti-Nebraska coalition makes secure identification of all but a few impossible), but hostile Democrats controlled the governorship. The existence of anti-Nebraska coalitions also makes evaluation of Know Nothing strength in the Maine and Michigan legislatures difficult, but it seems likely that a majority in Maine and a minority in Michigan acted in concert with the Order. Finally, despite their impressive showing in the New York elections, Know Nothings occupied only about a third of the legislative seats in the nation's most populous state. In the rest of the North, the Order played an insignificant role in legislative politics. Thus, despite the great expectations confronting the Order, only in a few New England states could the Know Nothings realistically expect to achieve significant legislative success.[3]

A discussion of the Know Nothings' activities in office must first consider the officeholders themselves. As with the party's rank and file, a stereotype of the Know Nothing officeholder is well established in the historical literature. The Know Nothing politician was purportedly younger than average and a newcomer to politics. In addition, Know Nothings supposedly shunned lawyers and other professionals (with the exception of ministers) when choosing nominees for political office, with the result that their candidates tended to come disproportionately from working-class backgrounds. This conception of the Know Nothing officeholder was pervasive even in the 1850s. A Connecticut resident bemoaning her husband's electoral defeat complained that the Know Nothings who had displaced him were "an entire set of new men— . . . young men only four years from College—and others quite uneducated—and as it now appears unfitted for their places." A Massachusetts observer agreed that the recently elected Know Nothings were "young men . . . who usually take no interest in politics."[4]

2. Know Nothings had captured control of these three states in elections held during the spring of 1855. In New Hampshire and Rhode Island, the Order acted as a partner in anti-Democratic coalition tickets, while in Connecticut they ran an independent slate. See Robert D. Parmet, "The Know Nothings in Connecticut" (Ph.D. diss., Columbia University, 1966), 99–120; Thomas R. Bright, "The Anti-Nebraska Coalition and the Emergence of the Republican Party in New Hampshire, 1853–1857," *Historical New Hampshire* 27 (1972): 74–76; Richard H. Sewell, *John P. Hale and the Politics of Abolition* (Cambridge: Harvard Univ. Press, 1965), 158–60; John P. Hale to Thurlow Weed, Feb. 2, 1855, Weed Papers, UR; Larry A. Rand, "Know-Nothing Party in Rhode Island," *Rhode Island History* 23 (1964): 102–16.

3. The Know Nothings' role in the Thirty-fourth Congress, which did not convene until December 1855 when the political climate had changed dramatically, will be discussed in Chapter 8.

4. Emily Baldwin to Roger S. Baldwin Jr., April 3, 1855, Baldwin Papers, Yale University; John R. Mulkern, *The Know-Nothing Party in Massachusetts: The Rise and Fall of a People's Movement* (Boston: Northeastern Univ. Press, 1990), 88; Alexander McClure, *Old Time Notes of Pennsylvania*, 2 vols. (Philadelphia, 1905), I, p. 198.

Statistical evidence suggests that while some of these perceptions were accurate, others require reevaluation. For example, Know Nothing officeholders generally *were* younger than their counterparts from other parties.

Average Age of Know Nothing and Non–Know Nothing Legislators[5]

	Know Nothings	*Non–Know Nothings*	*Difference*
Massachusetts	42.3	45.9	3.6 yrs.
New York	40.4	43.3	2.9 yrs.
Connecticut	42.1	44.7	2.6 yrs.
Pennsylvania	41.3	42.7	1.4 yrs.
New Hampshire	45.2	46.3	1.1 yrs.
Indiana	38.4	38.3	−0.1 yrs.

Of the six states surveyed, only in Indiana were Know Nothing officeholders no younger than the politicians they displaced. However, the difference in age between the Know Nothings and non–Know Nothings was not as great as contemporaries suggested.[6]

Other facets of the Know Nothing officeholders' stereotype appear to be valid only in northern New England. For example, the impression that lawyers were underrepresented in the ranks of Know Nothing politicians is confirmed in Massachusetts, where Know Nothings in 1854 elected five times fewer attorneys than had voters in the previous year, and in New Hampshire, where they sent about 50 percent fewer attorneys to the legislature. But in Connecticut, Indiana, and Pennsylvania, Know Nothings elected an equal or greater proportion of lawyers to legislative office than did non–

5. Virginia C. Purdy, "Portrait of a Know Nothing Legislature: The Massachusetts General Court of 1855" (Ph.D. diss., George Washington University, 1970), 218–19; William Goodwin, *Goodwin's Annual Legislative Statistics of State Officers, Senate, and House of Representatives, of Connecticut* (New Haven, 1854–56); *Members and Officers of the Assembly of the State of New York for 1855*, broadside, New York State Library; Rebecca A. Shepherd et al., *A Biographical Directory of the Indiana General Assembly* (Indianapolis: Indiana Historical Bureau, 1980); Pennsylvania and New Hampshire figures based on information in the manuscript federal census. All the following statistics are based upon these sources unless otherwise noted. The Connecticut example compares house Know Nothings serving in 1855 to all house members from the previous session; the New York example compares 1855 Know Nothing assemblymen to 1855 non–Know Nothing assemblymen; the Pennsylvania, Indiana, and New Hampshire figures compare 1855 Know Nothing members of the lower legislative house with the officeholders elected from those districts in the previous year. The following comparisons use the same sources and control groups unless otherwise noted.

6. The Indiana and New Hampshire figures are less reliable than the rest because although the Know Nothings dominated the anti-Democratic coalition in both these states, and most officeholders probably had to join the Order to win nomination, it is impossible to know which of them did and did not become Know Nothings. For these states I have included as Know Nothings all non-Democrats, reasoning that because *most* were probably Know Nothings, the statistics concerning them should approximately reflect the composition of Know Nothing officeholders in those states.

Know Nothings in previous years.[7] The same pattern emerges concerning the election of ministers to office. In New Hampshire and Massachusetts, Know Nothings elected twice the proportion of clergymen as had served in previous legislatures. In Connecticut, Pennsylvania, Indiana, and New York, however, Know Nothings did not elect a disproportionate number of clergymen to office.[8]

A breakdown of the occupational background of Know Nothing legislators provides additional clues concerning the type of person Know Nothings elected to office. A few scholars gathered such data previously, but most failed to provide a valid control group with which to compare the Know Nothings. In addition, a majority of the data previously presented was compiled from newspapers in a haphazard manner that calls into doubt its statistical validity. More comprehensive samples are available, however, from which the socio-economic background of Know Nothing officeholders can be securely established.

Occupations of Know Nothing Legislators

| | Massachusetts Legislators | | | |
| | 1855 Know Nothings | | Control Group[9] | |
	N	(%)	N	(%)
Professionals	62	(15%)	94	(16%)
Manufacturers & Merchants	114	(28%)	188	(32%)
Lower-Status White Collar	32	(8%)	40	(7%)
Skilled Workers	118	(29%)	133	(22%)
Farmers	78	(19%)	141	(24%)
TOTALS	404		596	

Source: Adapted from Purdy, "Portrait of a Know Nothing Legislature," 262–65.

| | New Hampshire Representatives | | | |
| | 1855 Know Nothings | | Control Group | |
	N	(%)	N	(%)
Professionals	31	(16%)	28	(14%)
Manufacturers & Merchants	27	(14%)	28	(14%)
Lower-Status White Collar	13	(7%)	7	(3%)
Skilled Workers	38	(19%)	30	(15%)
Farmers	86	(44%)	111	(54%)
TOTALS	195		204	

7. Purdy, "Portrait of a Know Nothing Legislature," 262–63. The New York Know Nothing assembly delegation possessed fewer lawyers than did non–Know Nothings (three of 29 versus 17 of 99), but the tiny size of the Know Nothing delegation makes the comparison statistically insignificant.

8. Purdy, "Portrait of a Know Nothing Legislature," 166.

9. The control group consists of all legislators serving in the 1850 and 1860 Massachusetts legislatures.

	Connecticut Legislators			
	1855 Know Nothings		Control Group[10]	
	N	(%)	N	(%)
Professionals	16	(10%)	15	(9%)
Manufacturers & Merchants	41	(26%)	34	(21%)
Lower-Status White Collar	3	(2%)	3	(2%)
Skilled Workers	29	(18%)	17	(10%)
Farmers	71	(44%)	94	(58%)
TOTALS	160		163	

	New York Assemblymen			
	1855 Know Nothings		1855 Non– Know Nothings	
	N	(%)	N	(%)
Professionals	4	(14%)	22	(23%)
Manufacturers & Merchants	11	(39%)	21	(22%)
Lower-Status White Collar	4	(14%)	3	(3%)
Skilled Workers	1	(4%)	7	(7%)
Farmers	8	(29%)	42	(44%)
TOTALS	28		95	

	Pennsylvania Representatives			
	1855 Know Nothings		Control Group	
	N	(%)	N	(%)
Professionals	14	(25%)	13	(20%)
Manufacturers & Merchants	9	(16%)	13	(20%)
Lower-Status White Collar	7	(13%)	7	(11%)
Skilled Workers	2	(4%)	4	(6%)
Laborers	3	(5%)	1	(2%)
Farmers	20	(36%)	26	(41%)
TOTALS	55		64	

	Indiana Representatives			
	1855 Know Nothings		Control Group	
	N	(%)	N	(%)
Professionals	28	(54%)	16	(30%)
Manufacturers & Merchants	8	(15%)	7	(13%)
Lower-Status White Collar	2	(4%)	3	(6%)
Skilled Workers	4	(8%)	6	(11%)
Farmers	10	(19%)	21	(40%)
TOTALS	52		53	

10. The control group consists of 1854 legislators serving in districts that elected Know Nothings in 1855 or 1856.

A number of patterns emerge from these figures. First, Know Nothing office-holders were consistently less likely to be farmers than their predecessors. This resulted from the fact that farmers were less likely than other Americans to join Know Nothing lodges. Second, the Know Nothings did not in most cases elect a disproportionately small number of professionals, merchants, or manufacturers to office. Although they did elect fewer lawyers in Massachusetts and New Hampshire, Know Nothings in these states compensated by electing other professionals (primarily doctors and ministers) to office. Finally, while New England Know Nothings generally elected a few more artisans to legislative office than other parties, Know Nothings in the rest of the country chose only an average proportion of workingmen. In terms of occupational background, then, and with the exception of the consistent dearth of farmers, Know Nothing officeholders were not very different from other politicians.

While the occupations of Know Nothing officeholders may resemble those of other politicians more closely than one would have imagined considering the prevailing stereotype, the belief that Know Nothings were less wealthy than other politicians is borne out to some degree.

Average Real and Personal Estate of
Know Nothing and Non–Know Nothing Legislators[11]

	Know Nothings	Control Group
New Hampshire	$ 8,788	$ 9,697
Massachusetts	$ 2,532	$ 6,571
Connecticut	$ 7,884	$10,342
Pennsylvania	$23,931	$37,269

Real and Personal Estate of
Legislators Divided into Selected Categories[12]

	New Hampshire Representatives				
	$1–2500	*$2501–5000*	*$5001–10,000*	*$10,001–20,000*	*$20,001+*
Know Nothings	32%	22%	25%	17%	5%
Control Group	23%	26%	27%	14%	10%
	Connecticut Representatives				
	$1–2500	*$2501–5000*	*$5001–10,000*	*$10,001–20,000*	*$20,001+*
Know Nothings	17%	26%	38%	13%	6%
Control Group	13%	28%	37%	13%	9%

11. Based on 1860 manuscript census, except Massachusetts figures, which compare 1850 real estate holdings only, and are from Purdy, "Portrait of a Know Nothing Legislature," 121. The groups compared are the same as those for occupations above, except that the Connecticut group includes only representatives.

12. Massachusetts figures compare 1850 real estate holdings only, and are from Purdy, "Portrait of a Know Nothing Legislature," 118.

| | *Pennsylvania Representatives* | | | | |
	$1–2500	*$2501–5000*	*$5001–10,000*	*$10,001–20,000*	*$20,001+*
Know Nothings	24%	12%	19%	21%	24%
Control Group	22%	17%	24%	22%	15%

| | *Massachusetts Legislators* | | | | |
	$0	*$1–5000*	*$5001–10,000*	*$10,001–20,000*	*$20,001+*
Know Nothings	32%	55%	9%	2%	1%
Control Group	19%	52%	16%	9%	5%

Because the Know Nothings elected significantly fewer farmers (whose land holdings tend to make them wealthier than most city-dwellers) to office, these figures do not reveal whether Know Nothings within a given occupational category were less well-off than their non–Know Nothing counterparts.

Average Real and Personal Wealth of Know Nothing and Non–Know Nothing Legislators in Selected Occupational Categories[13]

	Know Nothings	*Control Group*
New Hampshire Professionals	$15,235	$14,150
New Hampshire Merchants & Manufacturers	$13,207	$23,490
New Hampshire Skilled Workers	$ 4,592	$ 7,438
New Hampshire Farmers	$ 7,286	$ 6,340
Massachusetts Farmers	$ 3,233	$ 3,763
Connecticut Merchants & Manufacturers	$11,022	$14,281
Connecticut Farmers	$ 8,384	$10,363
Connecticut Artisans	$ 3,851	$ 4,232
Connecticut Professionals	$ 4,220	$11,171
Pennsylvania Professionals	$61,562	$90,188
Pennsylvania Merchants & Manufacturers	$21,450	$60,715
Pennsylvania Farmers	$ 6,986	$13,144

Although this data appears to confirm that the Know Nothings were significantly less wealthy than their non-Know Nothing counterparts, the figures are deceiving. In almost every case in which the Know Nothings are found to be less wealthy, this results primarily from the presence of one or two *very* wealthy non–Know Nothing officeholders skewing the sample. In the New Hampshire merchants and manufacturers category, for instance, if we eliminate two very wealthy non–Know Nothings (whose combined wealth totaled $242,000), the Know Nothings are found to be no less wealthy than non–Know Nothings. The same is true in the case of Pennsylvania merchants and manufacturers, for if we eliminate the one manufacturer worth $450,000, the

13. Massachusetts figures compare 1850 real estate holdings only, and are from Purdy, "Portrait of a Know Nothing Legislature," 139.

Know Nothing officeholders become just as well-off as the non–Know Nothing politicians. This trend is evident when the officeholders' wealth is categorized in the following manner:

Real and Personal Estate of Legislators Divided into Selected Categories and Grouped by Occupational Category

	$1–2500	$2501–5000	$5001–10,000	$10,001–20,000	$20,001+
	New Hampshire Merchants and Manufacturers				
Know Nothings	17%	22%	28%	33%	0%
Control Group	0%	27%	27%	23%	23%
	Pennsylvania Merchants and Manufacturers				
Know Nothings	13%	13%	25%	13%	38%
Control Group	0%	9%	36%	36%	18%
	Pennsylvania Farmers				
Know Nothings	13%	25%	31%	31%	0%
Control Group	0%	18%	18%	36%	27%
	Connecticut Farmers				
Know Nothings	10%	31%	36%	19%	5%
Control Group	9%	30%	38%	13%	9%
	Connecticut Merchants and Manufacturers				
Know Nothings	10%	20%	40%	15%	15%
Control Group	6%	19%	44%	19%	13%

What is evident from these figures, however, is that less-wealthy citizens found it easier to gain office through the Know Nothing ranks than through the other parties. Nonetheless, despite the stereotype of Know Nothing politicians as middle- to lower-class, a comparison of these figures with those concerning the general population found in Chapter 2 demonstrates that in terms of wealth, Know Nothing officeholders usually came from the upper ranks of their occupational group. Thus, the main difference in terms of wealth between Know Nothing and non–Know Nothing politicians was that while both groups generally supported the well-to-do for office, Know Nothings elected a few more men of modest means, and fewer very wealthy citizens.

Unlike occupations and wealth, which are relatively easy to investigate, the political experience of antebellum politicians is extremely difficult to determine. Biographical information concerning local politicians is not easily uncovered, and census materials, the most valuable tool for investigating the lives of the nineteenth century's less prominent citizens, do not provide such information. One scholar has determined the extent to which Massachusetts Know Nothing legislators possessed previous *legislative* experience, but such information is not really revealing, inasmuch as many politicians gain experience in *local* government before moving on to state office.[14] A more thorough analysis of legislators in Indiana and Connecticut, however, indicates that the belief that Know Nothing politicians were less likely to have political experience than officeholders from other parties may be unfounded. Indiana legislators elected by the anti-Nebraska coalition dominated by the Know Nothings possessed previous experience in local or state politics to essentially the same extent (52%) as their predecessors (54%). In addition, a search through the *Connecticut Almanac*, which lists the political officers of every town in the state, reveals that Know Nothings were *much more* likely than their political opponents to have recent political experience. Fifty-six percent of Connecticut's 1855 and 1856 Know Nothing legislators either had previous legislative experience or had been elected to local office in the two years before the rise of the Know Nothings in mid-1854. In comparison, only 29 percent of non–Know Nothing legislators in 1855 and 1856 had such political experience. Of course, this type of survey is far from definitive. Non–Know Nothing legislators may have gained their political experience earlier than their Know Nothing counterparts, something that only a monumental search through decades of records would reveal. But this inquiry, considered in conjunction with the more definitive results from Indiana, suggest that the stereotype of Know Nothing officeholders as political neophytes may require reconsideration.

In sum, the Know Nothing legislator was slightly younger than his predecessor, somewhat less wealthy (albeit much wealthier than the average citizen), and significantly less likely to be a farmer. In New England in general, and in Massachusetts especially, the Know Nothing was less likely to be a lawyer and more likely to be a workingman, although this was not the case in the rest of the country. Overall, however, the same groups that had previously dominated the elective offices in these states—lawyers, merchants, manufacturers, and farmers—still constituted a majority (usually an overwhelming one) in the Know Nothing legislative delegations.

As one might expect with an organization created to decrease the political influence of immigrants and Catholics, Know Nothing officeholders devoted the bulk of their energies to the implementation of their nativist agenda. And because Know Nothings believed that the surest method for guaranteeing the supremacy of Protestant values in America lay in promoting Protestantism in the public schools, educational matters occupied a significant portion of their legislative agenda. Addressing Catholic attempts to end the use of the Protes-

14. Purdy, "Portrait of a Know Nothing Legislature," 149.

tant King James Bible in schools, Massachusetts Know Nothing lawmakers
enacted a law requiring students to read that version of the Scriptures every
day. That legislature also approved an amendment to the state constitution
(initiated at the previous session) that barred the use of state funds in sectarian
schools. This, Know Nothings hoped, would make parochial schools financially
unfeasible, forcing the children of Catholics to learn "American" customs in
the public schools.[15]

Not all educational legislation passed by the Massachusetts Know Nothings was proscriptive. One law required children working in factories to attend school at least eleven weeks each year until the age of fifteen (the
previous law had required eleven weeks' attendance for only one year). The
same legislature also desegregated Massachusetts's public schools, passing a
law that prohibited the exclusion of children for either racial or religious
reasons. The legislature might appear to have acted inconsistently, opening
Massachusetts schools to one minority group while proposing discriminatory
statutes against another. However, blacks were Protestants and native-born,
and posed no threat to the predominant Protestant curriculum that Know
Nothings found so important.[16]

Know Nothings also acted to reduce the military threat purportedly posed
by immigrants. In one of his first acts in office, Massachusetts Know Nothing
governor Henry J. Gardner exercised his authority as commander of the
state's militia to disband seven companies composed primarily of immigrants.
In Connecticut, Know Nothing governor William T. Minor disbanded the
state's six Irish militia units. Reflecting the prevailing prejudices, however, he
allowed a German unit to continue operations. Maine took a more moderate
approach to this supposed menace, limiting to one-third the proportion of
immigrants permitted in each militia company.[17]

Know Nothings believed that immigrants threatened not only the nation's
defenses but its finances as well due to the number of immigrants in American
poorhouses. The Rhode Island and New Hampshire legislatures sought to
address this issue by asking Congress to impose severe penalties upon those
who knowingly transported paupers or criminals to the United States. Massachusetts Know Nothings took more decisive action. Acting at the governor's
behest, officials evicted more than 1,000 residents from state almshouses in
1855, most of whom were immigrants, and of this number nearly a third were

15. Massachusetts, *Acts and Resolves* (1855): 810; Massachusetts, *House Journal* (1855):
564–70; Boston *Bee*, May 7, June 30, 1855.

16. William G. Bean, "Party Transformation in Massachusetts with Special Reference to the
Antecedents of Republicanism, 1848–1860" (Ph.D. diss., Harvard University, 1922), 287; Massa-
chusetts, *Acts and Resolves* (1855): 674–75; Carleton Mabee, "A Negro Boycott to Integrate
Boston Schools," *New England Quarterly* 41 (1968): 356–58.

17. New York *Express*, Jan. 15, 1855; Hartford *Times*, Feb. 7, 1855; Edward Everett to Mrs.
Charles Eames, Jan. 13, 1855, Everett Papers, MHS; Mulkern, *Know-Nothing Party in Massachu-
setts*, 102; Parmet, "Know Nothings in Connecticut," 133–36; Hartford *Courant*, Sept. 26, 1855;
Maine, *Acts and Resolves* (1855): 205.

deported to Europe. According to Gardner this policy saved the state more than one hundred thousand dollars.[18]

Sometimes the Know Nothings' zeal to promote "Americanism" and fight Catholicism drove them to absurd lengths, especially in Massachusetts. In their fervor to Americanize the state's public institutions, the Bay State Know Nothings replaced the Latin inscription above the house Speaker's podium with an English translation. The legislators also barred the teaching of foreign languages in Massachusetts public schools.[19] Their most outrageous act, however, involved the creation of a "nunnery committee." Believing that nunneries provided a secret setting for sexual misconduct by Catholic priests, Know Nothings in both Maryland and Massachusetts created committees to oversee the inspection of convents. The Maryland committee operated without incident, but controversy erupted in Massachusetts when a Whig newspaper accused committee members of indecently barging into convent rooms and intimidating nuns during their inspections. Nativists responded that because priests imprisoned young nuns in convents against their will, convent inspections required surprise visits and private interviews with the nuns and novices. Although the ensuing investigation indicated that the original charges were largely unfounded, the inquiry did reveal that the committee's chairman, veteran nativist Joseph Hiss, had lodged his mistress in the committee's hotel at the taxpayers' expense. Know Nothing legislators attempted to distance themselves from the controversy by expelling Hiss, but the scandal dominated the Massachusetts press for much of the session. This incident proved especially embarrassing because the Order had promoted itself as a virtuous alternative to the corruption of the established parties.[20]

Such frivolous pursuits did not preoccupy Know Nothing lawmakers. In fact, Know Nothings devoted most of their legislative energy not to immigrant social institutions but to their political power, because the belief that immigrants threatened the integrity of the American political process lay at the heart of Know Nothing ideology. Know Nothings espoused increasing the probation period before naturalization (modifying the wait from five to twenty-one years was the Order's usual proposal) as the optimal means of Americanizing the newcomers and protecting the nation's republican institutions. Only Congress could carry out this task, but, anxious to speed the process and perhaps fearing that gaining control of Congress might take some time, Know Nothing legisla-

18. Rhode Island, *Acts and Resolves* (Jan. 1855): 8; New Hampshire, *Laws* (1855): 1609–10; Mulkern, *Know-Nothing Party in Massachusetts*, 103.

19. Mulkern, *Know-Nothing Party in Massachusetts*, 102.

20. John R. Mulkern, "Scandal Behind the Convent Walls: The Know-Nothing Nunnery Committee of 1855," *Historical Journal of Massachusetts* 11 (1983): 22–34; Charles Hale, *"Our Houses Are Our Castles": A Review of the Proceedings of the Nunnery Committee of the Massachusetts Legislature* (Boston, 1855); Boston *Bee*, April 2, 4, 9–12, 14, 30, May 7, 9, 1855; *The Convent Committee, Better Known as the Smelling Committee, in the Exercise of Their Onerous and Arduous Duties at the Ladies Catholic Seminary, Roxbury* ([Boston, 1855]).

tors enacted laws that simulated stricter naturalization rules. One such law prohibited state judges from participating in any aspect of the naturalization process. Massachusetts, Connecticut, Rhode Island, and Maine all enacted such laws, and Know Nothings drastically restricted naturalization in New Hampshire courts as well. Such statutes were not designed to prevent naturalization completely, because that process would continue in federal courts. But Know Nothings reasoned that with fewer judges to choose from, corrupt politicians would find it more difficult to "manufacture" voters through fraudulent naturalization immediately before each election. This, in turn, would reduce the inordinate influence that immigrants peddled at the polls.[21] Know Nothings in Maine and Massachusetts attempted to achieve the same end by also enacting laws requiring immigrant voters to present their naturalization papers to town officials three months before election day. This would allow officials to prevent fraudulent voting, said nativists, because immigrants would no longer be able to use the chaos of the polling place to force their way to the ballot boxes, nor would a simple oath suffice for proof of eligibility.[22]

Eventually, of course, every immigrant would be able to gain naturalization legally, but nativists were prepared to obstruct their voting rights with a new obstacle: literacy tests. Because Know Nothings perceived the majority of immigrants to be ignorant and uneducated, they thought that literacy tests would significantly reduce immigrant voting and, by extension, immigrant political power. If literacy tests were implemented, explained a Know Nothing journal, "there will then be no dragging up to the polls of ignorant imbruted Irish, or besotted Dutch, to go through a process of which they know nothing further than that they are paid for it. . . ." Literacy tests also had the advantage of appearing to have no nativist underpinning, inasmuch as they might disenfranchise native-born voters as well. In fact, many Whigs had advocated literacy tests long before the advent of Know Nothingism. One such bill had been approved by the Whig-controlled Connecticut legislature in 1854. In 1855, Know Nothing lawmakers offered the measure almost unanimous support, and the addition of a few Whig votes in the house secured its approval. In Massachusetts, Know Nothings also initiated a literacy test amendment. When it gained final approval in 1857, however, Republicans—not Know Nothings—controlled Massachusetts politics, so its enactment owed nearly as much to the Republican party as to the Know Nothings.[23]

21. Massachusetts, *Acts and Resolves* (1855): 513–14; Connecticut, *Public Acts* (1855): 22; Parmet, "Know Nothings in Connecticut," 132–33; Hartford *Courant*, June 28, July 7, 1855; Rhode Island, *Acts and Resolves* (Jan. 1855): 11; Maine, *Acts and Resolves* (1855): 204; New Hampshire, *Public Acts* (1855): 1565–66. Because of the backlog of naturalization cases that developed, most states soon repealed these laws.

22. Maine, *Acts and Resolves* (1855): 222–23; Massachusetts, *Acts and Resolves* (1855): 815.

23. Connecticut voters ratified the amendment in October by a margin of 17,370 to 12,544. Connecticut, *Journal of the House* (1855): 367–68; Parmet, "Know Nothings in Connecticut," 137–41; Norwich *State Guard* in Hartford *Courant*, Sept. 20, 1855 (quotation); Hartford *Courant*, Aug. 31, Sept. 27, Oct. 18, 1855; *Debates and Proceedings in the Massachusetts Legislature* (1856): 152–53.

Know Nothings contended that the ballot box was not the only means by which immigrants gained excessive political power. The financial might of the Catholic Church, wielded—said nativists—through its vast property holdings, also contributed to the newcomers' disproportionate influence. Such concentrations of wealth, when put at the disposal of a single political party, threatened to tilt the nation's electoral balance permanently to one side. Consequently, Know Nothings made enactment of church property laws, which required lay boards of trustees to hold title to church real estate instead of bishops, one of their highest priorities. Know Nothings in Pennsylvania and New York were particularly anxious to address this issue, because church property disputes in Philadelphia and Buffalo had been festering for years. The bill proposed in Pennsylvania redressed nativist fears by ordering that "no Bishop, or other ecclesiastic in any church shall hereafter hold any real or personal estate . . . with a capacity to transmit the title thereof to his successor in office. . . ." Although Catholic leaders complained that the bill infringed upon purely religious functions, Know Nothings attracted enough support from Democrats and Whigs to enact it. In Connecticut, the legislature passed a particularly severe church property bill, mandating state confiscation of all church lands not transferred to the laity. Demonstrating that members of all parties could support such legislation, the Michigan legislature, in which the Know Nothings held only a minority of the seats, enacted a church property law with near unanimous support.[24]

The church property bill that elicited the most publicity was the one proposed in the New York legislature. A number of Know Nothings spoke in favor of the measure, but public attention soon focused on the remarks of one senator, Erastus Brooks, co-publisher with his brother James of the New York *Express*.[25] In a speech before the senate, Brooks claimed that New York Archbishop John Hughes controlled nearly five million dollars in real estate, and that passage of the church property bill would prevent the Catholic Church from increasing this dangerous concentration of wealth. Hughes, responding in a letter to the New York *Courier and Enquirer*, called Brooks's assertion preposterous and challenged him to prove it. Brooks promised to do so, and the resulting debate became a national sensation. The senator eventually uncovered forty-five property deeds worth $5,000,000 in Hughes's name, convincing the originally skeptical public that the Archbishop did control vast amounts of real estate. The senator won public approval even before he

24. Pennsylvania, *House Journal* (1855): 831–32; Pennsylvania, *Senate Journal* (1855): 656; Pennsylvania, *Laws* (1855): 328–33; Patrick J. Dignan, *A History of the Legal Incorporation of Catholic Church Property in the United States (1784–1932)* (Washington: Catholic Univ. Press, 1933), 198–200; Harrisburg *Herald*, Feb. 19, 1855; Connecticut, *Public Acts* (1855): 22; Parmet, "Know Nothings in Connecticut," 132–33; Hartford *Courant*, June 28, July 7, 1855; Michigan, *House Journal* (1855): 440–41; Michigan, *Senate Journal* (1855): 814; Michigan, *Laws* (1855): 313–21.

25. New York *Express*, Jan. 10, March 24, 1855; James O. Putnam, *Ecclesiastical Tenures* (Albany, 1855); Rochester *American*, Feb. 14, 1855.

documented the extent of Hughes's property, because the Archbishop's haughty, flippant letters angered Protestants who took the church property issue seriously. As a result, the controversy won sympathy for the Know Nothings from New Yorkers who had previously balked at voting for their candidates.[26]

Interest in the church property debate was not limited to Know Nothings and Catholics. The public became so enthralled with the controversy that each side published its own pamphlet edition of the correspondence, "copies of which," reported the *Courier and Enquirer*, "are now to be found in almost every house." In the end, non–Know Nothings and even many Catholics admitted that the church property controversy represented "a real triumph" for Brooks and the Order. As a result, by the time the legislature enacted the church property bill, the measure itself seemed inconsequential. More important, the dispute had created the Know Nothings' first public leader, an absolute necessity if the Order hoped to compete as a conventional political party.[27]

By reducing the number of illiterate and ineligible voters and reducing the financial clout of the Catholic Church, many Know Nothings believed that they had enacted laws that provided sufficient safeguards against the immigrant political menace. Devout nativists, however, contended that far more comprehensive restrictions on immigrant voting were necessary. As mentioned earlier, the consensus among Know Nothings called for increasing to twenty-one years the probation period before immigrants gained the rights of citizenship. In fact, Connecticut and Rhode Island Know Nothings gave initial approval to constitutional amendments that would have mandated such a waiting period before immigrants could vote.[28] In Massachusetts, however, the complete control that the Order held in state politics tempted some Know Nothings to strive for even more far-reaching restrictions on immigrant political power. Consequently, the 1855 Massachusetts legislature approved, with virtually no opposition, an amendment to the state constitution barring anyone owing allegiance to any "foreign prince, power, or potentate" (the Know Nothing catchwords for a Catholic) from holding government office in Massachusetts.[29] The Know Nothings also initiated an amendment permanently barring all immigrants from either voting or holding office. A supporter of this measure stated that such a law was necessary because the "opposition to

26. W. S. Tisdale, ed., *The Controversy between Senator Brooks, and "† John," Archbishop of New York, Over the Church Property Bill* (New York, 1855); John Hughes, *Brooksiana* (New York, 1855), 3–43; Boston *Bee*, May 15, 1855; Fort Wayne *Times*, May 31, 1855; Harrisburg *Herald*, April 5, 1855.

27. New York, *Assembly Journal* (1855): 990; New York, *Senate Journal* (1855): 814; Dignan, *Catholic Church Property*, 193–97; New York *Courier and Enquirer* in Albany *State Register*, Sept. 29, 1855; George R. Babcock to James W. Beekman, July 10, 1855, Beekman Papers, NYHS; Curran, "Know Nothings of New York," 164–65.

28. Connecticut, *Journal of the House* (1855): 412–14; Connecticut, *Public Acts* (1855): 137; Rhode Island, *Acts and Resolves* (Jan. 1856): 87.

29. Massachusetts, *House Journal* (1855): 1400–1404.

republicanism" inculcated abroad "could not be eradicated by a residence of ten years, twenty-one years, or even a lifetime." However, more moderate Know Nothings insisted that the proposed amendment was too harsh, because naturalized foreigners had never "been guilty of anything equal in enormity to the recent conduct of the Missourians." This reference to events in Kansas reflected the lines upon which Know Nothings split over the proposal. Veteran nativists supported it, while the many Massachusetts Know Nothings who had once been Free Soilers found it too proscriptive. "I am doing all I can to kill" the proposal, reported Henry Wilson, as he and other Free Soilers believed "its adoption will be disgraceful to the party and the state." The senate, dominated by veteran nativists, approved the lifetime ban, but the house, controlled by Free Soil Know Nothings, rejected it, although they did approve an amendment that reduced the exclusion to twenty-one years. Initially, it appeared that the refusal of both sides to compromise would prevent either version from receiving approval, but on the last day of the session a compromise was reached. The amendment was split into two portions, with the senate's permanent ban applying to holding office, while the twenty-one-year waiting period that the House preferred would apply to voting.[30]

Amending the Massachusetts constitution required a two-thirds' vote in two consecutive legislatures, and the Know Nothings did not dominate the legislature in 1856 as they had a year earlier. The Order controlled 173 of 329 legislative seats, but this left them far short of the number needed to approve constitutional amendments. Consequently, those banning Catholics and immigrants from holding office failed to win approval.[31] In addition, before the legislature convened in 1856, lawyers pointed out that as worded, the measure barring immigrants from voting for twenty-one years would have inadvertently prevented Americans born abroad, and those who had spent part of their youth outside the country, from voting once they turned twenty-one. A re-worded version of the amendment passed the senate in 1856, but in the house Republicans combined with a few dissident Know Nothings to amend the waiting period to a more moderate fourteen years. The senate reluctantly agreed to the house version, but these changes meant that the amendment would have to be approved again in 1857. By then, the Know Nothings had lost control of the Massachusetts legislature, so the eventual fate of Know Nothing attempts to impose waiting periods before immigrants could vote

30. Massachusetts, *House Journal* (1855): 1413, 1623–30, 1691–98, 1714–21, 1740–47; Bean, "Party Transformation in Massachusetts," 279–82; Henry Wilson to William Schouler, April 16, 1855, Schouler Papers, MHS; Boston *Bee*, May 1, 1855.

31. *Debates and Proceedings in the Massachusetts Legislature* (1856): 87, 165–66, 168, 177–84; Charles Hale, *All Men Are Born Equal. Speech of Charles Hale, in the House of Representatives of the Massachusetts Legislature, March 27, 1856, on a Proposition for Amending the Constitution to Deprive Persons of Foreign Birth of the Right to Hold Office in Massachusetts* (Boston, 1856). Although both the ban on immigrant office-holding and the twenty-one-year wait for voting had originally been part of the same amendment, the measure was divided in two in 1856.

would rest in Republican hands. Meanwhile, in Connecticut and Rhode Island, reduced Know Nothing representation in subsequent legislatures had also led to the defeat of their amendments restricting immigrant voting.[32]

Nonetheless, the failure to impose a twenty-one-year hiatus between naturalization and voting was the Know Nothings' lone dissappointment in the area of anti-immigrant legislation. By disbanding immigrant militia units, prohibiting state courts from conducting naturalization proceedings, passing church property laws, and imposing literacy tests, the Know Nothings had successfully enacted all but the most radical portion of their nativist legislative agenda.

As was the case with nativist legislation, the Know Nothings displayed remarkable unity in office when addressing the temperance issue. Although most urban nativists in the Northeast opposed drinking restrictions, Know Nothings enacted temperance legislation in every northern state in which they gained significant political power. In some states, such as Massachusetts, Rhode Island, and Maine, the Know Nothings passed or helped pass bills that strengthened already existing prohibition laws. In others, such as New Hampshire and Indiana, Know Nothing–controlled legislatures enacted the first prohibition statutes. New York Know Nothings, who held about a third of the legislative seats there, also lent near-unanimous support to that state's first prohibition law.[33]

Of all the Know Nothing legislatures, Pennsylvania's spent the most time debating temperance legislation. In fact, the Order probably drew greater strength from the temperance movement in Pennsylvania than in any other state. Most Pennsylvania Know Nothings probably favored the prohibition of alcohol. However, because the state's voters had narrowly defeated a prohibition referendum, the Order lacked a mandate to outlaw liquor. Instead, Know Nothing legislators decided to do everything short of prohibition to make liquor more expensive and difficult to obtain.

First the Pennsylvania Know Nothings passed a law banning the sale of liquor on Sundays, designed to redress complaints that immigrant drinking disturbed devout observance of the Sabbath.[34] Although that bill passed with little opposition, the stringent liquor license law that came before the legislators aroused greater debate. This proposal tripled the licensing fees required to sell liquor, directed liquor dealers to post a $1,000 bond, prohibited non-

32. Bean, "Party Transformation in Massachusetts," 330–31; *Debates and Proceedings in the Massachusetts Legislature* (1856): 91, 343–44, 348–49, 355; Connecticut, *Journal of the House* (1856): 231–33; Parmet, "Know Nothings in Connecticut," 140–41. For the eventual fate of the Massachusetts amendment, see Chapter 10.

33. Massachusetts, *Acts and Resolves* (1855): 623–43; Rhode Island, *Acts and Resolves* (Jan. 1856): 48–54; Maine, *Acts and Resolves* (1855): 166–92; New Hampshire, *Public Acts* (1855): 1527–38; Indiana, *Acts and Resolves* (1855): 209–23; Curran, "Know Nothings of New York," 163.

34. Pennsylvania, *Laws* (1855): 53; Harrisburg *Herald*, Feb. 20, 1855.

citizens from obtaining licenses, and, most important, forbade liquor sales in quantities less than a quart. Opponents of the proposal claimed that it discriminated against small, immigrant-run saloons that sold drinks for pennies a glass and could not afford the new licensing fees. Yet this was precisely the Know Nothings' intention, because nativists believed that crime and pauperism were incubated in immigrant saloons. The vote on the bill demonstrated, however, that Pennsylvania Know Nothings were far from united on the temperance issue. Although nearly three-quarters of all voting house Know Nothings supported the legislation, only 27 percent of ex-Democrats did so. Most of these dissenters represented southeastern counties such as Berks, Lancaster, and York, an area inhabited by large numbers of German-Americans who sympathized with Know Nothing anti-Catholicism but opposed drinking restrictions. Nonetheless, a vast majority of Pennsylvania Know Nothings, believing that the license bill represented the best solution to the liquor problem short of total prohibition, rejoiced when the bill became law. Its provisions seemed certain to strike "a death blow at our groggeries and drinking resorts," especially the whiskey dens and beer shops where Irish and German immigrants congregated.[35]

Despite the ease with which the Pennsylvania Know Nothings passed these laws, enforcing the new liquor legislation proved to be a problem. The Sunday closing law was ignored in many areas, particularly those heavily populated by Irish and German immigrants. The increased licensing fees likewise resulted in the closing of few saloons, because local officials often neglected to collect them. The fact that immigrants—who opposed liquor restrictions—dominated most urban police forces exacerbated the enforcement problem.

Philadelphia's Know Nothing mayor, Robert T. Conrad, tried to remedy this problem. Conrad had promised to close the city's saloons on Sundays and reduce crime when he entered office in 1854. Believing that a police force dominated by immigrants blocked implementation of these goals, Conrad fired all the foreign-born policemen and replaced them with native-born officers.[36] A year later, Know Nothings asserted that Conrad's "Americanization" of the police force had accomplished its goal:

> We can truly say that the reign of law and order is established and maintained among us. Our religious rights, our social rights, are secured and protected. The Sabbath day is remembered, and our people are allowed to keep it holy. Violence and outrage, once so familiar to our streets, are almost unknown.

35. Pennsylvania, *Laws* (1855): 225–28; Harrisburg *Herald*, April 12, 14 (quotation), 1855; *Pennsylvania, House Journal* (1855): 447; Harrisburg *Pennsylvania Telegraph*, Aug. 15, 1855 (for Senate vote); Clearfield [Pennsylvania] *Raftsman's Journal*, April 25, 1855; Pottsville *Miner's Journal*, April 21, 1855. Pennsylvania party affiliations described here and below are based on listing in Harrisburg *Herald*, Dec. 30, 1854.

36. Harrisburg *Herald*, June 15, 1854; James Campbell to Bigler, June 14, 1854, E. A. Penniman to Bigler, June 18, 1854, H. G. Seisenring to Bigler, Aug. 8, 1854, Bigler Papers, HSP.

Yet Conrad's appointment strategy elicited negative reactions as well. Because the mayor's appointment policy did not distinguish between Catholic and Protestant immigrants, it angered Philadelphia's Protestant newcomers, many of whom had voted for the Conrad in 1854. All observers agreed that Protestant immigrant resentment toward the Know Nothings, increased by the subsequent passage of the license law, brought about the dramatic drop in Know Nothing electoral strength when Conrad ran for re-election in 1855. Although he won a narrow victory, the Order lost its majority on the city council, and with it control of the city's government.[37]

Know Nothings experienced similar problems when they imposed drinking restrictions in Chicago. Know Nothing Levi D. Boone (grandnephew of the famous explorer) had won the Chicago mayoralty in 1855 with promises to curb or eliminate the liquor traffic. Under Boone's direction, the Common Council increased the liquor license fee from $50 to $300, mandated that saloon-keepers renew licenses every three months instead of once a year, and required that they post a $200 bond. As in Pennsylvania, the Chicago laws were designed to force small, immigrant saloon-keepers out of business, something Boone himself admitted. Boone also followed Conrad's lead by replacing foreign-born policemen with native-born officers.[38]

The Know Nothings' effort to curb drinking in Chicago resembled the Pennsylvania experience in one final respect. It was politically disastrous. Chicago's Protestant German immigrants were no more fond of drinking restrictions than their Pennsylvania counterparts, and they especially resented the strict manner in which Boone's police recruits enforced the city's previously ignored Sunday closing law. This hostility led to a violent riot, in which one citizen was killed and dozens injured. It also ended Protestant German support for Boone and his party. The Know Nothings would have had trouble maintaining the fragile coalition that had won them the city government even without the liquor fiasco, but displeasure with the Know Nothings' temperance activities resulted in their resounding defeat when they came up for re-election in 1856.[39]

Know Nothing efforts to close immigrant-run saloons reflected more than a petty desire to circumscribe the newcomers' social activities. On the most basic level, Know Nothings believed that curtailing drinking and carousing,

37. David R. Johnson, *Policing the Urban Underworld: The Impact of Crime on the Development of the American Police, 1800–1870* (Philadelphia: Temple Univ. Press, 1979), 38 (quotation); Pottsville *Miner's Journal*, Aug. 5, 1854; Daniel T. Jenks to James Buchanan, Aug. 18, 1854, Buchanan Papers, HSP; Edward Joy Morris to John M. Clayton, Feb. 21, 1855, Clayton Papers, LC; Harrisburg *Herald*, May 4, 17, 1855; *Message of Mayor Conrad, May 17, 1855* (Philadelphia, 1855), 10–17; Philadelphia *News*, May 31, 1855.

38. Levi Boone, *Inaugural Address* (Chicago, 1855); Thomas M. O'Keefe, "Chicago's Flirtation with Political Nativism, 1854-1856," *Records of the American Catholic Historical Society of Philadelphia* 82 (1971): 140–43; Richard W. Renner, "In a Perfect Ferment: Chicago, the Know-Nothings, and the Riot for Lager Beer," *Chicago History* 5 (1976): 163–65.

39. O'Keefe, "Chicago's Flirtation with Political Nativism," 143–51; Renner, "In a Perfect Ferment," 165–70.

especially on Sundays, would create a public atmosphere befitting a Protestant nation. In addition, nativists were convinced that reducing immigrant drinking would quickly lead to a decrease in crime and pauperism. But one must also realize that Know Nothings saw temperance legislation as a means to achieve their central goal: the reduction of immigrant political power. Much, perhaps even a majority, of immigrant political activity was organized around neighborhood saloons. Owning a tavern provided the aspiring immigrant politician with the name recognition and public respect necessary for a successful bid for office. Profits from the sale of alcohol also helped finance many immigrant political careers. It should therefore come as no surprise that many immigrant officeholders were saloon-keepers, and if one includes grocers (who also sold liquor), the correlation between liquor and immigrant politics becomes even greater. In addition, a vital facet of rough-and-tumble antebellum elections was control of the polling place. This often meant choosing a polling site that would encourage a large turnout of one's friends, while discouraging the opposition. The fact that saloons housed 89 percent of the polling places in New York's immigrant neighborhoods suggests that immigrants saw the saloon as the location most likely to bring about victories for their favorite candidates.[40] Even the new natives-only police forces established by the Know Nothings had a direct impact on immigrant political prospects. Politicians who catered to immigrant voters—such as New York mayor Fernando Wood—used policemen to electioneer, raise campaign funds (both through solicitation and by withholding a percentage of their pay), and intimidate the opposition with violence at the polls. Consequently, by removing immigrants from urban police forces, Know Nothings severely reduced the newcomers' chances for political success. Thus, through the temperance legislation they enacted, Know Nothings sought not only to impose their social mores upon the nation's adopted citizens but to destroy the liquor-related infrastructure through which immigrants gained political power.[41]

Although the number of laws passed by the Know Nothings dealing with temperance and nativism might imply that Know Nothing politicians were preoccupied with the purported threat posed by immigrants and liquor, the Order's selections for the United States Senate demonstrated that preventing the extension of slavery was of equal importance to them. In every state where Know Nothings elected senators, a successful candidate could boast strong anti-slavery credentials. And in Pennsylvania, the one state where Know Nothings failed to elect a senator, the belief that the Know Nothing candidate *lacked* a proven track record opposing the extension of the slavery played the

40. New York *Tribune*, Nov. 1, 1856; W. J. Rorabaugh, "Rising Democratic Spirits: Immigrants, Temperance, and Tammany Hall, 1854–1860," *Civil War History* 22 (1976): 154; Jon M. Kingsdale, " 'The Poor Man's Club': Social Functions of the Urban Working-Class Saloon," *American Quarterly* 25 (1973): 472–89.

41. New York *Herald*, Nov. 6, 1856; James F. Richardson, "Mayor Fernando Wood and the New York City Police Force, 1855–1857," *New-York Historical Society Quarterly* 50 (1966): 23.

key role in his defeat. When choosing candidates for the Senate, an established anti-slavery reputation mattered more to most northern Know Nothings than devotion to the Order's nativist agenda.

In Massachusetts, the first state in which Know Nothings selected a senator, the supporters of Free Soiler Henry Wilson anticipated the contest with
confidence. Gardner had promised to support Wilson for the Senate vacancy
in return for Wilson's withdrawal from the 1854 gubernatorial contest, giving
the popular ex-cobbler from Natick an apparently decided advantage over
other candidates. The surprisingly large vote cast for abolitionist Theodore
Parker for legislative chaplain also buoyed Wilson's prospects, indicating that
the new General Court was "far more anti-slavery than any legislature ever
elected" and thus more likely to support an anti-slavery radical such as Wilson. It therefore came as no surprise when Wilson secured the endorsement of
the house Know Nothing caucus.[42]

Election of a United States senator in Massachusetts required that both
the house and senate cast a majority of its ballots for the same candidate, and
although the results of the house Know Nothing caucus assured Wilson an
easy victory in that body, success in the senate would prove more difficult.
Whereas former Free Soilers dominated the Know Nothing contingent in the
house, veteran nativists, who held more conservative views on the slavery
issue, controlled the senate. Citing Wilson's past tendency to skip from party
to party, these Know Nothings insisted that Wilson "is more a Free Soiler than
a Know Nothing" and that he would inevitably sacrifice the tenets of Know
Nothingism in order to advance himself and the anti-slavery cause. Veteran
nativists also argued that electing an outspoken abolitionist such as Wilson
would drive Southerners from the Order. Many southern states held spring
elections, and devout nativists knew that if Wilson captured the Massachusetts Senate seat, it would taint the Order with abolitionism and hurt southern
Know Nothing candidates. As a result, the senate Know Nothing caucus
snubbed Wilson, voting instead to support Alfred B. Ely, a Boston lawyer and
veteran nativist.[43]

Gardner remained noticeably silent during the senatorial debate, which
some interpreted as a sign that he planned to double-cross Wilson. But political
prudence dictated Gardner's reticence. Wilson faced a tough battle in the senate, and if Gardner worked unsuccessfully for his election, it would prove that
the governor lacked power within the party and damage his influence. Unable
to count on Gardner for assistance, Wilson and his supporters initiated an intensive lobbying campaign to win over the senate. First they secured a postponement of the vote, which gave them time to convert recalcitrant senators. Realiz-

42. S. Downer to [Horace Mann], Jan. 7, 1855 (quotation), Mann Papers, MHS; S. G.
Howe to Sumner, Jan. 7, 1855, James W. Stone to Sumner, Jan. 13, 1855, Sumner Papers, HU;
Mulkern, *Know-Nothing Party in Massachusetts*, 131–32.

43. New York *Tribune*, Jan. 10, 1855 (quotation); Boston *Know Nothing* in Ernest A. McKay,
Henry Wilson: Practical Radical (Port Washington, N.Y.: Kennikat Press, 1971), 89; Boston *Bee* in
Bean, "Party Transformation in Massachusetts," 270; New York *Herald*, Jan. 20, 1855.

ing that doubts about his devotion to nativism hurt his candidacy most, Wilson composed a public letter extolling the Know Nothings' nativist agenda.[44] A few senators may have been swayed by this statement, but more switched to Wilson because they felt obligated to uphold Gardner's bargain. For senators who needed further prodding, Wilson's backers offered patronage in return for their votes. "The free soil politicians are super-human in managing for office," complained one veteran nativist as he watched Wilson gain support in this manner. As expected, Wilson won an easy victory in the house, but the senate tally proved that he needed every last vote his handlers had secured. Of the 40 senators, only 21 (the minimum necessary for election) cast their ballots for Wilson. Wilson's victory provided the first public indication that the anti-slavery crusade was just as important to most northern Know Nothings as nativism.[45]

The outcome of the Senate election in New York also demonstrated the importance to Know Nothings of resisting the Slave Power. One of the best-known foes of slavery in Congress, William H. Seward, occupied the seat in question, and political observers throughout the nation recognized that Seward's defeat would deal a devastating blow to the free soil movement. Anti-slavery Whigs consequently made winning the legislative seats necessary for Seward's re-election the priority of the 1854 campaign, but the Order's unexpected success in that election threw his prospects into doubt. With Whigs lacking a majority in the legislature, and Democrats certain to oppose the incumbent, the votes of Know Nothing legislators would determine Seward's fate.[46]

Initially, it seemed highly improbable that Know Nothings would vote for Seward, because no American politician was more fervently despised by devoted nativists than the New York senator. Although it had been more than a decade since then-Governor Seward had outraged devout Protestants by proposing the creation of state-financed parochial schools, nativist anger toward Seward had not abated. As one New Yorker noted, "a prejudice—rather a bigotry mainly Presbyterian—against him on this score has been the root of the opposition to him in this state for the past 13 years." Seward's insistence that the Whig party should actively court immigrant voters and his apparently amicable relationship with Catholic Archbishop John Hughes also damned the senator in nativist eyes.[47] In addition, southern Know Nothings anticipating

44. James W. Stone to Sumner, Jan. 20, 1855, Sumner Papers, HU; Richard H. Abbott, *Cobbler in Congress: The Life of Henry Wilson, 1812–1875* (Lexington, Ky.: Univ. of Kentucky Press, 1972), 60–62; William E. Gienapp, *The Origins of the Republican Party, 1852–1856* (New York: Oxford Univ. Press, 1987), 175–76.

45. Senator Daniel Warren quoted in Bean, "Party Transformation in Massachusetts," 269; Edward Everett to Mrs. Charles Eames, Feb. 18, 1855, Everett Papers, MHS; Amos A. Lawrence to Sally [Lawrence], Jan. 30, 1855, Amos A. Lawrence Papers, MHS; Mulkern, *Know-Nothing Party in Massachusetts*, 98.

46. Lyman A. Spaulding to Thurlow Weed, Aug. 3, 1854, Seward to Weed, Oct. 24, [1854], R. M. Blatchford to Weed, Dec. 7, 1854, Weed Papers, UR; New York *Herald*, Oct. 5, Dec. 18, 1854; John Bush to Millard Fillmore, Nov. 16, 1854, E. R. Jewett to Fillmore, Dec. 28, 1854, J. Ferndon to Fillmore, Jan. 10, 1855, Fillmore Papers, SUNY-O.

47. E. Pershine Smith to Henry C. Carey, June 14, 1854, Carey Papers, HSP.

upcoming elections in that region begged their New York brethren to block Seward's re-election and thus prevent Democrats from associating the Order with abolitionism. "It will hurt us greatly in this part of the country if he should be elected by 'Know-Nothing' votes," reported North Carolina Know Nothing leader Kenneth Rayner. "For God's sake, have him defeated, if possible." Finally, many New York Know Nothings believed that Seward's ouster would greatly enhance the prospects of their choice for President, Millard Fillmore, because Southerners would be indebted to New York Know Nothings for the defeat of their arch-enemy. Thus, it seemed before the legislature convened that "if Seward relies for election upon old friends, no matter how steadfast, who are now know-nothings, he leans upon a broken reed."[48]

When the legislative session began, however, it became apparent that Seward's past and the demands of southern Know Nothings mattered little to most Know Nothing legislators. Know Nothing votes enabled a Seward supporter to capture the speakership of the assembly, a result that doubly embarrassed Know Nothing leaders because the winner—an admitted Know Nothing—had repudiated the Order before the speakership election and vowed to support Seward.[49] Fearing that similar defections would result in Seward's re-election, anti-Seward Know Nothings sprang into action. They pointed to the victories of two anti-Seward Know Nothings in recent special legislative elections as proof that New Yorkers did not want Seward re-elected. Councils sent letters to Know Nothing legislators, reminding the lawmakers that their initiation oath had included a vow never to oppose a lodge member in any election and promising to expel the legislators and boycott their businesses if they voted for Seward. Know Nothing leaders also sent lobbyists to Albany to reinforce these threats in person.[50] But these efforts at intimidation backfired. "The oaths taken by their members shock everyone," one Whig reported, and others pointed out that Know Nothing tactics resembled those of the Catholic hierarchy.[51] Seward's

48. Joseph Segar to Ullmann, Jan. 5, 1855, Francis S. Edwards to Ullmann, Jan. 14, 1855, Kenneth Rayner to Ullmann, Jan. 22, 1855, Daniel Ullmann Papers, NYHS; Solomon Haven to Fillmore, Dec. 22, 1854, Fillmore Papers, SUNY-O; Albany *State Register* quoted in Rochester *American*, Nov. 20, 1854; Curran, "Know Nothings of New York," 153; Elmira *Advertiser* in Albany *State Register*, Nov. 16, 1854 (quotation).

49. Albany *State Register* quoted in Rochester *American*, Jan. 6, 1855; New York *Express*, Jan. 13, 1855 (Albany correspondent); E. P. Smith to Henry C. Carey, Jan. 12, 1855, Carey Papers, HSP; S. Haven to Fillmore, Jan. 29, 1855, Fillmore Papers, SUNY-O; J. D. Colver to Ullmann, Nov. 21, 1854, F. Edwards to Ullmann, Jan. 14, 1855, Ullmann Papers, NYHS; J. G. Sanders to James W. Beekman, Feb. 6, 1855, Beekman Papers, NYHS.

50. New York *Express*, Jan. 5, 1855; Alex Mann to Fillmore, Jan. 31, 1855, Fillmore Papers, SUNY-O; E. P. Smith to Henry C. Carey, Feb. 10, 14, 1855, Carey Papers, HSP; speeches of L. S. May and C. C. Leigh in *United States Senatorial Question* (Albany, 1855), 25–28; Roswell Hart to Ullmann, Jan. 25, 1855, Ullmann Papers, NYHS; S. A. Andrews to Weed, Dec. 28, 1854, T. Cary to Weed, Feb. 18, 1855, Weed Papers, UR.

51. Henry Morgan to Weed, Feb. 8, 1855 (quotation), Weed Papers, UR; George Curtis to Seward, Feb. 15, 1855, D. M. Nagle to Seward, Feb. 24, 1855, Seward Papers, UR; *Senatorial Question*, 19, 23.

mentor, Whig boss Thurlow Weed, intensively lobbied the Know Nothing legislators, postponing all patronage appointments until after the senatorial vote.
He then dangled these "loaves and fishes" before wavering Know Nothing
legislators and promised to deliver them in exchange for Seward votes. Weed
also offered to supply Whig votes for two Know Nothing priorities—liquor
prohibition and a church property law—if Know Nothings would support Seward. Seward's opponents predicted that Weed would break these promises once
Seward won re-election, but such charges changed few votes. Seward won re-
election by a comfortable margin, with more than half the legislature's Know
Nothings supporting him.[52]

Know Nothing leaders attributed Seward's victory to a variety of circumstances. Most cited patronage as the key to Seward's success, and in fact a few
Know Nothings did emerge with the promised appointments.[53] Some blamed
reluctance to sever previous party ties for Seward's triumph, noting that of the
30 Know Nothings who supported Seward, 29 had been Whigs. Conversely, of
the Know Nothings who voted against Seward, Democrats outnumbered
Whigs 12 to 7, and nearly all these Whigs had belonged to the Silver Gray
faction that had traditionally opposed Seward.[54] Yet while few of Seward's
Know Nothing opponents cared to admit it, the slavery extension issue, and
its place in the Order's agenda, motivated most of the Know Nothings who
supported Seward. One stated that although Seward had made mistakes as
governor fourteen years earlier, he was now "recognized throughout the
whole country as the uncompromising opponent of slavery extension." Therefore, "a refusal to return *him* would be a concession to the slave power that
could not be countervailed by the election of any other individual." Another
Know Nothing lawmaker voted for Seward because "there are none who
would rejoice so heartily in his defeat as the upholders and defenders of
slavery." These Know Nothings considered their support for Seward perfectly
consistent with the party's agenda. As one explained it, "true Americanism
must . . . oppose tyranny, and every tendency towards slavery in every form
in which it can be presented. It can no more love or tolerate slavery in the
negro than in the white, under the southern planter than under the Pope."[55]

52. Daniel D. Barnard to Hamilton Fish, Jan. 30, 1855, Fish Papers, LC; Roswell Hart to
Ullmann, Jan. 25, 1855, Ullmann Papers, NYHS; E. R. Jewett to Fillmore, Feb. 4, 1855, Fillmore
Papers, SUNY-O; "M" [O. B. Matteson] to Weed, Jan. 25, 1855, A. Johnson to L. Fairchild, Feb.
6, 1855, Weed Papers, UR; *Senatorial Question*, 13; New York *Herald*, Jan. 24, Feb. 6, 7, 1855;
Curran, "Know Nothings of New York," 161–62; New York *Express*, Feb. 1, 1855; Rochester
American, Feb. 10, 1855; Jamestown [New York] *Journal*, Feb. 16, 23, 1855.
53. John Sanders to James W. Beekman, Feb. 17, 1855, J. Watts Depeyster to Beekman,
Feb. 18, 1855, George R. Babcock to Beekman, July 10, 1855, Beekman Papers, NYHS; Albany
State Register, Feb. 8, 1855; Rochester *American*, Feb. 15, 1855; Curran, "Know Nothings of New
York," 160.
54. Curran, "Know Nothings of New York," 161–62; S. Haven to Fillmore, Jan. 10, 1855,
Fillmore Papers, SUNY-O. To Curran's breakdown of the vote I have added Know Nothing (and
non–Silver Gray Whig) Francis Palmer, who voted against Seward.
55. *Senatorial Question*, 6–7, 9, 11, 22–23 (quotations); Charles C. Leigh to Seward, Feb.
20, 1855, Seward Papers, UR.

Most northern Know Nothings saw opposition to slavery extension as an integral part of their platform, and this explains why so many New York Know Nothings ignored their leaders and helped re-elect Seward.

The results of senatorial elections in other states confirm that most northern Know Nothings made the candidates' stance on slavery a priority when making their choices for the Senate. In 1856, Connecticut Know Nothings elected James Dixon, a forty-one-year-old lawyer with strong anti-slavery credentials. Know Nothings apparently chose Dixon, who had served two terms as a Whig congressman during the 1840s, because he was not commonly associated with the Order. Whigs and especially Republicans had begun to resent the Order by 1856, and Know Nothings hoped that Dixon—with no overt links to the Order—would gain sufficient outside support to win the election. Initially, Republicans spurned Dixon and it appeared that a deadlock would ensue. But Know Nothings held firm to their candidate, and eventually the offer of a judgeship, plus the fear that no one would be elected, secured enough Republican and Whig support to give Dixon the election. Although Dixon later denied that he had ever been a Know Nothing, his friend Gideon Welles confided to his diary in late 1855 that "Dixon . . . is inclined to join the K.N's," and Dixon almost certainly had to join the Order to gain its nomination.[56] In New Hampshire, another state controlled by the Order, Know Nothing lawmakers elected James Bell and John P. Hale to the Senate. The election of Hale, who like Wilson and Seward was considered a "radical" on the slavery issue, again demonstrated the devotion of northern Know Nothings to the anti-slavery cause.[57]

Only in Pennsylvania did Know Nothings fail to elect an anti-slavery candidate to the Senate. In fact, divisions within the Pennsylvania Know Nothing party ran so deep that *no one* secured the vacant Senate seat. Yet the *lack* of strong anti-slavery credentials played a decisive factor in the defeat of the leading candidate. It had been clear from the start that Pennsylvania Know Nothings would have difficulty choosing a senator. Know Nothings from western Pennsylvania insisted that the candidate come from that portion of the state, but few eastern legislators thought highly of the western choices. In addition, many Democratic Know Nothings vowed that they would vote only for an ex-Democrat, while ex-Whigs insisted that no Democratic Know Nothing was worthy of the post. Nonetheless, Democrats vowed to remain firm. As a correspondent of Senate hopeful Simon Cameron explained, "democratic [Know Nothings] . . . will not consent *to Whigify* so strongly

56. Nelson R. Burr, "United States Senator James Dixon: 1814–1873, Episcopalian Anti-Slavery Statesman," *Historical Magazine of the Protestant Episcopal Church* 50 (1981): 29–72; Gideon Welles Diary, Nov. 14, 1855, LC; Connecticut, *Journal of the House* (1856): 103–4, 111–12, 135–37, 181; Charles L. English to Gideon Welles, May 23, 24, 30, 1856, James Bunce to Welles, May 30, 1856, Welles Papers, LC.

57. Richard H. Sewell, *John P. Hale and the Politics of Abolition* (Cambridge, Mass.: Harvard Univ. Press, 1965), 158–62; Albert G. Browne to Sumner, Jan. 3, 1855, Sumner Papers, HU; George Bradburn to Salmon P. Chase, May 10, 1855, Chase Papers, LC.

their party after having *so* secretly elected a Whig Governor."[58] Among these Democratic Know Nothings, Cameron was clearly the favorite. He had served in the Senate in the 1840s, and had carefully avoided making a public endorsement of the Kansas-Nebraska Act in order to keep alive his hopes for a return to Washington. Cameron's well-known "prejudices against the Irish" and his consistent opposition to the Democratic faction that had supported Catholic James Campbell for postmaster general also aided his cause. Over the years, however, Cameron's factional intrigues had earned him a reputation as a schemer. He had also amassed a small fortune by taking full advantage of the investment opportunities offered to the politically well connected, and this wealth reinforced his image as a man on the make.[59] Nonetheless, those who opposed Cameron could not agree upon an alternate. Among the names most frequently mentioned were ex-Whigs Andrew G. Curtin, whom Governor Pollock had just appointed secretary of state, and William F. Johnston, a popular former governor.[60]

As the date for the Know Nothing senatorial caucus approached, Cameron's supporters felt confident. Because ex-Whigs had recently received two important appointments—state treasurer and Philadelphia flour inspector—ex-Democrats believed that they could not be denied the Senate seat. Pollock had also hinted that he would support Cameron.[61] In an attempt to assuage the animosity that ex-Whigs harbored toward him, Cameron composed a letter for his backers to circulate at the Know Nothing caucus. In it he promised to work for restoration of the Missouri Compromise and repeal of the fugitive slave law. He also recognized the right of Congress to ban slavery in the territories, pledged to support a protective tariff and internal improvements, and called for lengthening the probationary period before naturalization to twenty-one years.[62] The letter focused on slavery because Cameron realized that anti-slavery Whigs who had become Know Nothings opposed his candidacy most vehemently. Directing this faction was a non-legislator, Thaddeus Stevens. Like Cameron, Stevens had acquired a reputation as a political opportunist. He apparently joined the Know Nothings less out of a devotion

58. Harrisburg *Herald*, Nov. 18, 1854; W. F. Coplan to Cameron, Nov. 24, 1854 (quotation), J. P. A[nderson] to Cameron, Dec. 29, 1854, J. B. Amwake to Cameron, Jan. 5, 1855, H. P. Laird to Cameron, Feb. 8, 1855, Cameron Papers, DCHS.

59. T. Koss to Cameron, June 15, 1854, Francis Grund to Cameron, Nov. 20, 1854 (quotation), Edward Fox to Cameron, Nov. 21, 1854, Cameron Papers, DCHS; E. B. Chase to Cameron, Nov. 7, 1854, Cameron Papers, LC; Lee F. Crippen, *Simon Cameron: The Ante-bellum Years* (Oxford, Ohio: Mississippi Valley Press, 1942); Gienapp, *Origins of the Republican Party*, 172–73.

60. J. P. LeClerc to Cameron, Dec. 24, 1854, Cameron Papers, LC; John C. Dunn to Cameron, Nov. 24, 1854, John Keatley to Cameron, Dec. 12, 1854, William S. Garvin to Cameron, Jan. 15, 1855, William Quail to Cameron, Jan. 23, 1855, J. Glancy Jones to Cameron, Jan. 29, 1855, Cameron Papers, DCHS.

61. J. W. Killinger to Cameron, Nov. 18, 1854, J. P. A[nderson] to Cameron, Dec. 29, 1854, J. J. Pearce to Cameron, Jan. 31, 1855, Cameron Papers, DCHS.

62. John M. Kirkpatrick to Cameron, Cameron to Kirkpatrick, Feb. 9, 1855, Cameron Papers, LC.

to nativism than a desire to free himself from the conservative Whig organization that ruled his hometown of Lancaster. Stevens did not desire a Senate seat tainted with Know Nothingism, but he was determined to prevent Cameron from obtaining it. Although those opposing Cameron could not agree on an alternative candidate, they preferred to leave the seat unfilled rather than allow Cameron to hold it for the full six year term.[63]

This division revealed itself on February 9 when the Know Nothing legislative caucus met to decide the senatorial question. Cameron's opponents cried foul as soon as the meeting began. They pointed out that ninety-one legislators were present, more than had attended the Order's previous caucuses. Admitting that these newcomers did belong to the Order, Cameron's opponents nonetheless insisted that because these pro-Cameron legislators had refused to follow caucus dictates previously, they should be excluded. After debating the issue, the caucus voted to seat the newcomers, but their opponents seethed because the newcomers' ballots contributed to their own margin of victory. The hostility between the two camps increased when the caucus voted to choose its senatorial nominee with secret ballots. Rumors describing bribes paid for Cameron votes had circulated through the hotels, saloons, and oyster bars frequented by the legislators, and Cameron's enemies had counted on an open ballot to ferret out the traitors. With a secret ballot, Know Nothings who opposed Cameron contended that his supporters would have every illicit method at their disposal.[64]

When the caucus balloting began, Cameron led all candidates, but stood far short of a majority. Cameron's tally grew on subsequent ballots, but his lead diminished as his opponents began to unite behind Curtin. On the sixth ballot, Cameron appeared to win the nomination with forty-six votes. However, when it was discovered that one vote too many had been cast, Cameron's opponents charged that his supporters had planted the extra vote in order to win him the nomination fraudulently. When the chairman ruled their call for an adjournment out of order, twenty-nine legislators stormed out of the meeting in protest. Those remaining proceeded to vote for a seventh time, and with many of his opponents gone, Cameron easily won the nomination.[65]

Those who bolted from the caucus issued a circular to defend their action. The seceders insisted that they could no longer take part in the caucus because the corruption involved had become "too palpable." Cameron had too recently been a loyal Democrat, they asserted, to merit their trust as a foe of slavery. The bolters also pointed out that the Know Nothings had succeeded in 1854 because of their promise to "rebuke corruption," and asked how the Order could in good conscience nominate the infamously corrupt Cameron

63. The Stevens biography that best analyzes his Know Nothing involvement is Richard N. Current, *Old Thad Stevens: A Story of Ambition* (Madison: Univ. of Wisconsin Press, 1942).
64. The best newspaper account of the caucus was filed by the Harrisburg correspondent of the Gettysburg *Star and Banner*, Feb. 16, 1855.
65. Gettysburg *Star and Banner*, Feb. 16, 1855.

"and thus hold him up to the world as the exponent, embodiment, and personi-fication of Americanism!"[66] Despite these claims, the prior party affiliations of the bolters suggested that partisan prejudice, rather than ethical standards, motivated their walkout. Of the twenty-five seceders whose previous party affiliation could be ascertained, twenty-one had been Whigs, and the remain-der were Free Soil Democrats. In fact, Cameron's opponents—not his backers—may have planted the extra vote to create a justification for leaving the caucus. They needed an excuse to free themselves from the obligation to support the caucus nominee, and it seems strangely coincidental that the extra ballot appeared just when Cameron was poised to win the nomination.

When the legislature convened in joint session on February 13 to begin the balloting for senator, the Know Nothings had not repaired the split within their delegation. With more than 90 of the 133 legislators belonging to the Order, Know Nothings should have faced little trouble imposing their senato-rial choice upon the legislature. But when the voting began, the legislature was deadlocked. On ballot after ballot, the vote for Cameron hovered around fifty-nine, eight short of the number necessary for election. Meanwhile, dissi-dent Know Nothings scattered more than thirty votes among nearly a dozen hopeless candidates.[67] The legislators agreed to postpone further balloting for two weeks, and during this interim Cameron's forces attempted to capture the handful of votes that separated them from victory. To this end they issued their own circular to refute the charges contained in the bolters' broadside. In addition, many lodges attempted to force their representatives to vote for Cameron, threatening those who resisted with expulsion. Cameron also tried to win over wavering legislators by reiterating his devotion to the anti-slavery cause and pledging his admiration for the temperance movement as well.[68]

But Cameron's opponents resisted every appeal. They continued to play upon geographic prejudices, insisted that only "political traders" supported Cameron, and predicted that his election would "kill Americanism's good name in Pennsylvania, stone-dead." Balloting resumed on February 27, but the two-week interval had not added any supporters to Cameron's column. The legislators voted to consider the matter again in October, but unless some state emergency occurred, the session would be concluded by then. On March

66. Bolters' Circular, Feb. 12, 1854 [1855], filed under Feb. 1854, Cameron Papers, LC; J. S. Black to James Buchanan, Feb. 17, 1855, Buchanan Papers, HSP; Alexander McClure, *Old Time Notes of Pennsylvania*, 2 vols. (Philadelphia, 1905), I, p. 270.

67. *Pennsylvania Legislative Documents* (1855): no. 55, pp. 564–84. Of those voting for Cameron, 17 had been Democrats, 26 Whigs, and five Native Americans. Of the Know Nothings voting against Cameron, 27 had been Whigs and four had been Free Soil Democrats. The previous affiliation of 11 Know Nothing Cameron voters and four Know Nothings who opposed him could not be determined.

68. Know Nothing caucus circular, [c. Feb. 14, 1855], Cameron to Powell (draft), Feb. 20, 1855, Circular of Council 48, Uniontown, Feb. 22, 1855, circular of Hollidaysburg meeting, Feb. 23, 1855, George Lear to Cameron, Feb. 24, 1855, Cameron Papers, LC; L. G. Levin to Cam-eron, Feb. 13, 1855, S. Fuller to Cameron, Feb. 17, 1855, Robert Williams to Cameron, Feb. 20, 1855, Frederick A. Van Cleve to Cameron, Feb. 21, 1855, Cameron Papers, DCHS.

4, Pennsylvania would forfeit half its representation in the United States Senate, and blame rested squarely with the Know Nothings.[69]

The Know Nothings' inability to elect a senator in Pennsylvania resulted in part from the structure of the Order there. Two separate organizations had vied for supremacy in the state from the time Know Nothingism had arrived. One, led by veteran nativist Jacob Broom, was centered in Philadelphia, and tried to exclude all issues except nativism from the purview of the Order. The other faction, eventually led by Methodist minister Otis H. Tiffany, believed that the Order should fight slavery and intemperance as well, and by the end of 1854 Tiffany's forces had gained control of the state's Know Nothing hierarchy. Even after Tiffany had become state Know Nothing president, the leaders of these factions constantly fought to regain or retain their power, and this internal division often prevented Pennsylvania Know Nothings from acting with even a semblance of unity. In addition, the Know Nothing legislative delegation lacked a leader who could inspire party unity at crucial moments. Ideally, Governor Pollock would have filled this role, but ever since his inaugural message, which had barely addressed nativism, the governor had maintained his distance from the Order. Tiffany attempted to fill this void, but although he commanded great respect both inside and outside the Order, he lacked the political experience and patronage power necessary to rally Know Nothing legislators for important votes.[70]

In the end, however, distrust of Cameron's anti-slavery credentials was the primary reason that Pennsylvania failed to elect a senator in 1855. Stevens, the leader of the anti-Cameron forces, later explained that he had opposed Cameron because "I did not think him true to freedom." Many Pennsylvania Know Nothings shared Stevens's concern, and although it caused the Order great embarrassment, they refused to elect a senator who was not known to oppose firmly slavery's extension.[71]

The Know Nothings' commitment to the anti-slavery cause was not limited to senatorial elections. "Never did we have such an opportunity as this," insisted James W. Stone—the legislative leader of the Massachusetts Know Nothings' Free Soil faction—upon discovering Wilson's popularity among the Order's legislators. This unexpectedly strong anti-slavery sentiment in the Massachusetts legislature convinced Stone and other former Free Soilers to push for enactment of a wide-ranging anti-slavery program. First the legislators addressed the slavery question by passing a series of resolves calling for restoration of the Missouri Compromise, the prevention of illegal voting by Missourians in Kansas, and the repeal of the fugitive slave law. The adoption

69. John C. Dunn to Cameron, Feb. 20, 1855, Cameron Papers, DCHS; Untitled Circular, Cameron folder, Society Collection, HSP; Pottsville *Miner's Journal*, Feb. 17, 24 (quotation), 1855; K. Pritchette to Cameron, Feb. 22, 1855, George Lawrence to Cameron, Feb. 23, 1855, Cameron Papers, LC; Harrisburg *Herald*, Feb. 28, 1855; New York *Herald*, Feb. 28, 1855.

70. *History of the Rise, Progress & Downfall of Know-Nothingism in Lancaster County*, 11–12; Philadelphia *News*, June 22, 1855; McClure, *Old Time Notes*, I, pp. 239–43.

71. Stevens to Dr. E. D. Gazzam, Dec. 4, 1856 (copy), Edward McPherson Papers, LC.

of such resolutions may seem insignificant, but they elated anti-slavery forces in Massachusetts, who since 1851 had failed to win approval for even the most perfunctory anti-slavery resolutions.[72]

The Massachusetts Know Nothing legislators also took more concrete steps to fight the Slave Power, passing a "personal liberty law," one of a number enacted by northern legislatures to thwart enforcement of the fugitive slave law. The Massachusetts bill addressed the most unpopular aspects of the federal statute, by forbidding authorities to detain runaway slaves without the right to habeas corpus, and by requiring that each detainee receive a jury trial. Although Gardner had recommended a law with these provisions in his inaugural message, the legislators went even further. They prohibited state courts from participating in fugitive slave cases, forbade state jails to house runaways, barred all Massachusetts officials from participating in such cases, disqualified from state office any federal official who certified the return of a fugitive slave, and banned from the state courts any Massachusetts lawyer who represented a claimant in a fugitive slave case. Calling these clauses patently unconstitutional, Gardner vetoed the bill, but the desire to repudiate the fugitive slave law ran so deep amongst the Know Nothing legislators that they easily overrode the governor.[73]

Not satisfied with these blows against the fugitive slave law, the Massachusetts Know Nothings also set out to punish the official who personified the state's past acquiescence to the statute. In his capacity as federal commissioner, Judge Edward G. Loring had presided over the rendition of runaway slave Anthony Burns in early 1854. While the legislators could not remove Loring from his federal office, they did hope to oust him from his state judgeship. To accomplish this they made use of an obscure clause in the state constitution that allowed the governor to remove a judge upon the address of both houses of the legislature. When Gardner refused to act upon their recommendation, the legislators passed a bill that prohibited a federal official from also holding state office. Gardner vetoed this measure as well, arguing that the legislators' actions unfairly singled out Loring for punishment, when it was Congress that had imposed the fugitive slave law on Massachusetts. Gardner insisted that until public protest convinced Congress to repeal the act, Massachusetts politicians should reluctantly uphold it.[74] Some believed

72. James W. Stone to Sumner, Jan. 13, 1855, Sumner Papers, HU; U.S. House of Representatives, *Miscellaneous Documents*, 34th Congress, 1st Session, Documents 41, 42, 81; Bean, "Party Transformation in Massachusetts," 278.

73. Massachusetts, *Acts and Resolves* (1855): 924–29; Thomas D. Morris, *Free Men All: The Personal Liberty Laws of the North, 1780–1861* (Baltimore: Johns Hopkins Univ. Press, 1974), 168–73; Mulkern, *Know-Nothing Party in Massachusetts*, 104–5.

74. [Boston] *Liberator*, March 2, May 18, 1855; James W. Stone, *Removal of Judge Loring. Remarks of James W. Stone in the Massachusetts House of Representatives, April 13, 1855* (Boston, 1855); Massachusetts House *Documents* (1855): nos. 63, 93, 205; Boston *Bee*, May 11, 1855 (Gardner's veto message); John L. Swift, *Speech of John L. Swift, Esq., on the Removal of Edward G. Loring . . . Delivered in the Massachusetts House of Representatives, Tuesday, April 10, 1855* (Boston, 1855).

that Gardner blocked Loring's removal in the hope that a moderate course would improve his chances for the Know Nothing vice presidential nomination. Yet while Gardner undoubtedly coveted higher office, he had never subscribed to the "higher law" school of anti-slavery politics that condoned defying the constitution as a means to combat slavery. Consequently, he probably would have vetoed such legislation even had he not sought national office.[75]

Although the Know Nothings went to great lengths to neutralize the fugitive slave law, they, like most Northerners, hesitated to grant blacks equal rights in their own communities. Connecticut's anti-slavery vanguard, for example, had long condemned the state constitution's prohibition of black suffrage. A constitutional amendment deleting the discriminatory clause had won the simple majority necessary for approval during the 1854 legislative session, meaning that the Know Nothing–controlled legislature of 1855 would determine whether the proposal would go to the voters for final approval. The senate endorsed the amendment overwhelmingly, but the house twice failed to concur (the 135 to 74 tally on the second vote fell 17 votes short of the two-thirds' majority necessary for approval in the second year). An analysis of the second House ballot indicates that the Know Nothings' tendency to vote with their old party on non-nativist issues was most responsible for the defeat of the amendment. Almost 40 percent of ex-Democrats refused to support the measure which, combined with near unanimous Democratic opposition, insured the proposal's defeat.[76]

Despite this setback, the Know Nothings' record on the slavery issue was overwhelmingly positive. Through the passage of anti-slavery resolutions and personal liberty laws and the election of senators renowned for their hostility to the Slave Power, the Know Nothings demonstrated to the nation their

75. Edward Everett to Mrs. Charles Eames, June 4, 1855, Everett Papers, MHS; Edmund Quincy in Mulkern, *Know-Nothing Party in Massachusetts*, 105; S. P. Hanscom, *To His Excellency Henry J. Gardner, Governor of the Commonwealth of Massachusetts* (n.p., [1855]), 7.

76. Parmet, "Know Nothings in Connecticut," 138; Hartford *Courant*, June 1, 2, 1855. Because a "no" vote hurt the amendment's chances more than voting "absent" or not voting at all, I have broken down Know Nothing opposition to the amendment:

House Opposition to Black Suffrage among Know Nothings

	Total	Voting No	Absent	Total Opposed
Ex-Democrats	45	12	5	17 (38%)
Ex-Whigs	56	6	0	6 (11%)
Ex-Free Soilers	9	0	1	1 (11%)
Unknown	38	2	3	5 (13%)

Political antecedents have been determined from legislator's own responses to the survey compiled by William Goodwin in *Goodwin's Annual Legislative Statistics* (1855). "Absent" category includes both those voting "absent" and those who cast no ballot.

conviction that opposition to the extension of slavery was just as important, and sometimes more important, than nativism.

The final facet of the Know Nothing ideology, after nativism, anti-slavery, and temperance, concerned political reform, and during their short tenure in office the Know Nothings enacted laws that addressed this problem as well. In Massachusetts, several significant constitutional amendments initiated before the rise of the Know Nothings were approved. Three of these made government officials more accountable to the public by making their positions elective rather than appointive. The Know Nothings also approved amendments that streamlined the political process by scheduling state and federal elections on the same day and allowing pluralities to decide contests with more than two candidates. In addition, the Know Nothings instituted stiffer penalties for corrupt government officeholders and amended legislative rules to bar senators from voting on bills in which they held a direct financial interest.[77]

Pennsylvania Know Nothings also acted to curb malfeasance. Referring to the state-run canal system as a "running sore of corruption" because of the high costs and favoritism that characterized its operation, reformers had tried to force its sale for years. Know Nothings were especially anxious to dispose of the canals because they believed that "the thousands of foreigners that swarm our public works" in patronage jobs "control our elections, and over ride native Pennsylvanians." Consequently, the Know Nothing legislature set up a procedure for selling the canals, although many were disappointed that the lawmakers declined to abolish the patronage-ridden Canal Board as well. Still, the Know Nothing action demonstrated a sincere desire to battle government waste and corruption.[78]

Unfortunately, the Know Nothings' attempts at political reform were only partially successful. Concerned that a prospective canal purchaser might negotiate a sweetheart deal or buy all the canals and create a monopoly, the Pennsylvania Know Nothings created such strict conditions for the sale and operation of each canal that no one bid at the auction. And despite their supposed hostility to the patronage system, once in office Know Nothings eagerly utilized the "loaves and fishes" to consolidate their political base. Sometimes the Know Nothings were guilty of corruption themselves. As described earlier, one of the Know Nothings' Massachusetts leaders was expelled from the legislature for lodging his mistress in a hotel at the taxpayers' expense. Although nothing was ever proven, charges of bribery also surfaced in Pennsylvania in connection with the senatorial election. A Know Nothing member of the Ohio Board of Public Works, Jacob Blickensderfer, was in-

77. Boston *Bee*, May 7, 1855; Massachusetts, *Acts and Resolves* (1855): 923; Purdy, "Portrait of a Know Nothing Legislature," 97.

78. Pottsville *Miner's Journal*, July 30, 1853; McClure, *Old Time Notes*, I, pp. 223–25 (quotation); Harrisburg *Herald*, April 25, 1855 (quotation); Pennsylvania, *House Journal* (1855): 802.

volved in a scandal that cost the state thousands of dollars. Finally, Know Nothing congressmen Francis E. Edwards and William Welch were implicated in influence-peddling scandals. Recent scholarship has demonstrated that corruption was rampant in the 1850s, and it may well be that the Know Nothings were guilty of fewer improprieties than their Whig and Democratic counterparts. But these isolated transgressions severely tarnished the Know Nothings' image, convincing the public that Know Nothings were no more virtuous than the "old fogy" politicians they had replaced.[79]

Know Nothings argued that they could institute political reforms more easily than conventional political parties because the Order was more responsive to the will of its members and less likely to knuckle under to lobbyists and special interest groups. That this was a valid assertion is suggested by the number of laws passed by the Know Nothings that augmented the legal rights of workingmen. The Know Nothing legislatures in Massachusetts and Connecticut both enacted mechanics' lien laws that allowed artisans to place a lien on the property of customers who refused to pay them for services provided. The New Haven *Palladium* predicted that such statutes "will save hundreds of honest working men and traders from bankruptcy." Connecticut Know Nothings also restructured the state's judiciary system with a measure that made the state's legal process more equitable for those of meager means. According to the *Palladium*, this law abolished the system by which "a man of wealth . . . [could] keep a poor man out of his just dues for several years, by a postponement of his trial, till he was nearly ruined with costs, and was therefore willing to compromise with his debtor on almost any terms."[80]

Know Nothings also created additional protection for workingmen who could not pay their *own* bills. One Massachusetts law helped give bankrupt artisans the means to repay their debts by increasing to $800 the value of tools they could exempt from seizure, while Connecticut Know Nothings also enacted legislation increasing the rights of debtors. In addition, Massachusetts Know Nothings passed a married woman's property law that forbade forfeiture of a wife's property to pay her husband's debts. As with most such laws passed in the nineteenth century, this statute had nothing to do with women's rights. Instead it sought to protect male debtors by allowing them to hide property from creditors by placing it in their wives' names. Know Nothings in

79. S. Sammons to Ullmann, Dec. 4, 1855, James Thompson to Ullmann, Jan. 27, 1856, Ullmann Papers, NYHS; Charles W. Beach to Weed, Feb. 6, 1856, C. Gardinier to Weed, Feb. 13, 1856, Weed Papers, UR; "Reports of the Joint Committee Appointed to Investigate the Charges of Improper Influences in the Election of U.S. Senator," *Pennsylvania Legislative Documents* (1855): no. 64, pp. 612–77; Mark W. Summers, *The Plundering Generation: Corruption and the Crisis of the Union, 1849–1861* (New York: Oxford Univ. Press, 1987), 261–62.

80. Massachusetts, *Acts and Resolves* (1855): 826–28; Connecticut, *Public Acts* (1855): 24–35, 96–99; Hartford *Courant*, July 26 (excerpt from New Haven *Journal*), Sept. 17 (quotations from New Haven *Palladium*), 1855.

Massachusetts also ended imprisonment for debt, and came close to enacting a law limiting the work day to ten hours.[81]

It should be noted that the Know Nothings did not initiate the movement for these reforms. Most had been proposed at previous legislative sessions. Nevertheless, the Know Nothings' willingness to pass such legislation, which had failed time and again in legislative bodies controlled by the old political parties, is significant. To some degree, the Know Nothings' receptiveness to such legislation may have resulted from the greater-than-normal representation of workingmen in the Connecticut and Massachusetts Know Nothing legislatures. Yet while this difference was substantial in Massachusetts, tradesmen still held a small minority of the legislative seats there. In Connecticut, too, artisans held fewer than a dozen more seats than in the past. Representational changes alone, then, fail to account for the legislation passed in these states. Furthermore, the evidence presented in Chapter 2 indicating that workingmen were not disproportionately represented in Know Nothing lodges suggests that the socio-economic makeup of the Know Nothing party does not explain the success of such legislation either. Instead, it seems that the Know Nothings' unique responsiveness to the wishes of the rank and file created an atmosphere conducive to the success of such legislation. While workingmen made up essentially as large a proportion of the Democratic and Whig parties as they did in the Know Nothing organization, wealthy elites monopolized the leadership positions of the older organizations. In the Know Nothing ranks, however, artisans held many of the key positions occupied almost exclusively in the other parties by lawyers, manufacturers, and merchants. Thus, legislation designed to relieve workingmen, which artisans of all parties undoubtedly favored, was more likely to receive support from Know Nothing leaders than from the leadership hierarchy of the old parties, which were controlled by elites who frowned upon such reforms. Consequently, although the Know Nothings' record on political reform was mixed at best, their accomplishments in the area of workingmen's rights were quite impressive, and one of their longest lasting legacies.

The Know Nothings' tenure in office revealed a great deal about the Order and its prospects for the future. Their successful efforts to enact church property laws, restrict naturalization, and disband immigrant militia units confirmed their dedication to nativism, putting to rest Democratic charges that Know Nothingism was merely a "Whig trick" designed to revive that defunct party. In addition, the Know Nothings' ability to enact popular legislation that had consistently failed to win approval in the past pleasantly surprised many observers. William Lloyd Garrison's *Liberator*, for example, had ridiculed the Massachusetts Know Nothings before they entered office, but by the end of the 1855 legislative session it praised them warmly:

81. Massachusetts, *Acts and Resolves* (1855): 682–83, 710–11, 853–58; Connecticut, *Public Acts* (1855): 83–90; Manchester [New Hampshire] *American*, April 10, 12, 13, 16, 1855; Norman Ware, *The Industrial Worker* (1924; rpt., Chicago: Quadrangle Books, 1964), 161–62.

... embodying an unusual amount of moral worth and honesty of purpose, controlled by the progressive spirit of the age, self-guided to the prostration of all ambitious leadership, and indicating no lack of speaking or working talent . . . , [the Know Nothing legislature] turned a deaf ear to the evil prognostications of Hunkerism, trampled in the dust the temptations of pro-slavery Nationalism, foiled alike the wealth and the graft of State street, and used with great moderation the power committed to its hand, with reference to foreign immigrants to these shores. This is simple historical justice. . . . [82]

Others took a far different view. A Pennsylvanian, reviewing the record of that state's Know Nothing legislature, labeled it "a blot on the annals of the Commonwealth."[83]

In truth, the Know Nothings' tenure in office was neither as good nor as bad as these comments suggest. On the positive side, the Know Nothings' ability to enact legislation concerning every aspect of their agenda demonstrated that they could function effectively not only as a fraternal organization but as a political party as well. The church property controversy in New York proved that Know Nothings could wage a skillful public relations battle, and the Connecticut senate fight indicated that the Order could artfully wield patronage and maintain party unity in order to win crucial votes. Finally, their willingness to legislate for the workingman provided a refreshing alternative at a time when corruption and special-interest legislation were becoming increasingly common. All in all, the Know Nothings proved themselves to be just as competent as other politicians.

Nonetheless, the Know Nothings' performance in office elicited more cause for concern than optimism. The embarrassing expulsion of Hiss in Massachusetts and the factional bickering that paralyzed the party in Pennsylvania proved to the public that the Know Nothings were not significantly different than the old parties. This was not a liability for most new political organizations, but in the case of the Know Nothings, who had portrayed themselves as an alternative to "politics as usual" and had promised to revive the virtue, integrity, and concern for the public good that had supposedly once characterized American politics, their accomplishments in office were a profound disappointment. Because many Northerners had initially voted for the Know Nothings for the sake of novelty or to rebuke unresponsive party leaders, only a stellar performance in office or some evidence that the Know Nothings could become a viable permanent party would have convinced these citizens to vote the Know Nothing ticket a second time. Yet the Know Nothings' tendency when casting key ballots to vote according to the dictates of their old parties, rather than the decision of the Know Nothing caucus, convinced many of these voters that the party had no future. The most disturbing of these divisions amongst Know Nothing officeholders concerned slavery, because in key states such as New York, Pennsylvania, and Massachusetts,

82. [Boston] *Liberator*, June 1, 1855.
83. McClure, *Old Time Notes*, I, p. 223.

hostile factions had developed pitting those who believed that the party should stress anti-slavery *and* nativism against those wanted to exclude slavery from the party's agenda. In addition, although the party could do little more concerning temperance or nativism, the slavery controversy would resurface every time violence broke out in Kansas, Congress convened, or a Senate seat became vacant. Consequently, a showdown loomed in the aftermath of the legislative sessions of 1855, as both Know Nothing factions plotted strategies that would establish their position on the slavery issue as the party's national policy.

7

"Our Order Must Be Nationalized": Slavery Divides the Know Nothing Party

Many Know Nothing leaders attributed the Order's early electoral success to the party's ability to adapt to local political situations.[1] But by early 1855 it became apparent that the loose coalition of councils that had sufficed for state and local contests could not elect a President. To win the White House in 1856 the Order would need to present a single agenda that appealed to voters in all sections of the Union and disseminate that agenda through a coordinated national organization. Consequently, many Know Nothings began calling for "A NATIONAL AMERICAN PARTY . . . , the heart of which will throb from Maine to Texas, from the east to the far west. . . . To carry out our glorious destiny," these nativists insisted, "we must be shaped into a national form."[2]

The Order had held several conventions that leaders hoped would create a sense of national cohesion. Their first national meeting, which assembled in New York City in June 1854, had done little to foster Know Nothing unity. This gathering selected national officers for the Order, but these officials did little more than sanction state organizations and distribute copies of the initiation ritual.[3] A more significant step toward "nationalizing" the party took place at its Cincinnati convention in November 1854. Woefully little is known about this gathering, except that the Know Nothings voted to add a third degree to their ritual. This third level in the Know Nothing hierarchy became known as the "Union degree" because to achieve it, a Know Nothing pledged

1. Thomas Spooner, *Report of the President of the State Council of Ohio, June 5, 1855* (n.p., [1855]), 9, OHS; Otis H. Tiffany in Philadelphia *Sun*, Aug. 27, 1855.
2. Boston *Know Nothing* quoted in Harrisburg *Herald*, Nov. 8, 1854.
3. Virtually nothing is known about this initial Know Nothing convention, although a list of delegates can be found in the Charles Deshler Papers, Rutgers University. Also see Louis D. Scisco, *Political Nativism in New York State* (New York: Columbia Univ. Press, 1901), 97–98; Ray A. Billington, *The Protestant Crusade, 1800–1860: A Study of the Origins of American Nativism* (Chicago: Quadrangle Books, 1938), 382–84.

to "discourage and denounce any and every attempt . . . designed or calculated to destroy or subvert [the Union] or weaken its bonds." Veteran nativists
hoped that the third degree would diminish sectional hostility. As the degree's
author (North Carolinian Kenneth Rayner) put it, "it seems to me that when 2
millions of men in this country have taken that third degree that the Union
must be safe." However, most northern Know Nothings interpreted the new
degree not as a patriotic gesture, but as a thinly veiled attempt by Southerners
and veteran nativists to eliminate anti-slavery sentiment from the Order.
Northern councils accepted the third degree because they knew its vague
wording could not prevent them from addressing sectional issues, yet they
vowed to make no more concessions to the southern slaveholders and northern "doughfaces" who had created it.[4]

The first months of 1855 proved that the third degree had by no means
eliminated debate concerning the slavery issue within Know Nothing ranks.
Ignoring the pleas of national leaders, northern Know Nothings elected radical anti-slavery men such as Henry Wilson and John P. Hale to the United
States Senate. The Massachusetts and New Hampshire state council meetings
also angered southern Know Nothings by passing strong anti-slavery resolutions.[5] "Even if we desired to 'ignore' that great issue," contended Indiana
Know Nothing Schuyler Colfax in response to pleas for moderation from
southern nativists, "how could we do it with their monstrous outrages in
Kansas that they call 'elections.' . . . They have been driving us to the wall for
10 years past," Colfax insisted, "and we can't cry Peace when there really is no
peace."[6]

Occasionally, outsiders reinforced this determination to stand firm on the
slavery issue. Joseph Medill, a non–Know Nothing who edited the Cleveland
Leader, sympathized with the anti-Catholicism of the Order, but asserted that
"an order that degrades the Protestant citizen who happened to be born in
Europe or Canada to the level of the negro is unworthy of a Freeman's
support." Medill, believing that Southerners would inevitably control the
Order once it assumed a national form, decided to create an alternative
organization, the Independent Order of the Friends of Equal Rights, which
became known as the Know Somethings. Medill had two goals for the new
group. By placing greater emphasis on the slavery issue and allowing Protestant immigrants into the new order, Medill sought to lure men out of the
Know Nothing party and eventually deliver them to the Republicans. In addition, Medill hoped that members of his new group would infiltrate the Know
Nothing Order and destroy it from within. "It works as a *wheel within a*

4. Scisco, *Political Nativism in New York State*, 134–38 (quotation); New York *Herald*, Nov.
16, Dec. 20, 28, 1854; Rayner to Daniel Ullmann, Jan. 22, 1855, Ullmann Papers, NYHS; Mason
W. Tappan to John P. Hale, May 2, 1855, Hale Papers, New Hampshire Historical Society.

5. Manchester *American*, May 3, 1855; New York *Herald*, May 5, 1855; Rayner to Ullmann,
Feb. 17, May 8, 1855, V. Ellis to Ullmann, May 13, 1855, Ullmann Papers, NYHS; E. Pershine
Smith to Henry C. Carey, Feb. 1, 1855, Carey Papers, HSP.

6. Colfax to Will Cumback, April 16, 1855, Cumback Papers, Indiana University.

wheel," said Medill in explaining this second function. He believed that the Know Somethings would "keep K. N'ism from doing mischief until the fever for secret societies is past."[7]

The Know Somethings began serious recruiting in January of 1855 with Medill's assistant editor, John Vaughn, installed as president. Yet the Know Somethings attracted a significant number of converts only in areas where the Know Nothings were considered too conservative on the slavery issue. In Massachusetts, where the Know Somethings were apparently most popular, Free Soil Know Nothings dominated the new order, and Charles Francis Adams believed that the Know Somethings would prevent formation of a united anti-slavery party there.[8] The Know Somethings also enjoyed some success in New York, where dissident Know Nothings had already organized a separate organization.[9] In the rest of the North, however, the Know Somethings made little headway. They attracted some support in northern Ohio and Illinois, but at their peak they totaled no more than 10,000 or 20,000 members nationally, putting hardly a dent in the Know Nothing ranks. Despite Know Something claims that Southerners and northern "doughfaces" would soon control the Order, most northern Know Nothings were content with the party's stance on slavery.

Although anti-slavery sentiment pervaded the Order in most northern states, Southerners insisted that Know Nothingism would fail in their region unless northern Know Nothings curtailed their free soil pronouncements. These calls to "nationalize" the Order increased after the Virginia gubernatorial election of May 1855. Know Nothings, flushed from their northern victories in late 1854 and early 1855, confidently predicted that they would unseat incumbent Democrat Henry Wise, one of the Order's most vociferous critics. A veteran politician exaggerated only slightly when he commented that "no state election was ever anticipated with more interest all through the Union." Observers reasoned that if the Order could win in Virginia—which Democrats had controlled for years—then perhaps the Know Nothings truly did possess the strength to win the presidency. During the campaign, Wise portrayed the Know Nothings as an abolitionist party, pointing to the Massachusetts personal liberty law and the elections of Wilson, Hale, and William H.

7. Cleveland *Leader* in Fort Wayne *Times*, Oct. 26, 1855; Joseph Medill to Oran Follett, Jan. 27, April 18 (quotation), 1855, in Belle L. Hamlin, ed., "Selections from the Follett Papers, V," *Quarterly Publication of the Historical and Philosophical Society of Ohio* 13 (1918): 71–72; Joseph P. Smith to R. B. Pullan, Feb. 9, 1897, in Pullan, *Origins of the Republican Party* (n.p., n.d.), 3, pamphlet collection, OHS; C. Bratz to Joel H. Wilson, Dec. 14, 1854, Wilson Papers, Huntington Library.

8. Ichabod Codding to Marie Codding, April 14, 1855, Codding Papers, IISHL; Ohio correspondence, New York *Tribune*, Jan. 17 (probably written by Medill or Vaughn), March 7, 1855; James W. Stone to Sumner, Feb. 3, 1855, Sumner Papers, HU; Samuel Gridley Howe to Sumner, Feb. 9, 1855, Howe Papers, HU; Charles Francis Adams to G. Bailey, April 15, 1855, Adams Papers, MHS; William G. Bean, "Party Transformation in Massachusetts with Special Reference to the Antecedents of Republicanism, 1848–1860" (Ph.D. diss., Harvard University, 1922), 310–14.

9. New York *Herald*, Nov. 4, 1854, Jan. 10, 1855; New York *Tribune*, Nov. 3, 1854.

Seward in New York as proof. The fact that Wise easily defeated his Know Nothing opponent in heavily Democratic Virginia should not have been surprising. Yet southern and conservative Know Nothings were convinced that "the influence of Massachusetts ultraisms" as well as anti-slavery statements made by other northern Know Nothings had caused the Order's Virginia defeat.[10]

The Virginia election convinced conservative and southern Know Nothings that the Order could fulfill its national potential only if it pursued a course on the slavery question acceptable to voters in both sections of the Union. "Our order must and will be nationalized," insisted Kentuckian Garrett Davis, and with the third national Know Nothing convention scheduled to begin at Philadelphia soon after the Virginia canvass, these nativists looked to achieve their goal at that meeting. Yet most northern Know Nothings had decided to resist such demands. "I want to preserve the nationality of our order," explained Indiana Know Nothing president Godlove Orth, but only *"if it can be done without a sacrifice of principle."* Orth's views reflected those of most northern Know Nothings. They wanted Know Nothingism to spread across the nation, but felt that Northerners had too often capitulated to the South at national political gatherings. Colfax thus hoped that "we can have such men there as Hale, Wilson, [Massachusetts Free Soiler Anson] Burlingame, [Maine Free Soiler Anson?] Morrill, . . . & others so that we can make a *demand* that the antislavery sentiment of the North shall be respected. . . ." Even the Harrisburg *Herald*, which had led the call to "nationalize" the Order months earlier, now agreed that "if the [southern Know Nothings] expect the North to tolerate further encroachments of slavery and to allow territory now free to be blighted by this desolating curse, they ask too much. . . ." Northern Know Nothings, insisted the *Herald*, "will be among the last to consent to such an arrangement." Because each state would send an equal number of delegates to the convention, most observers expected a solid South to combine with conservatives from the North to push through a platform unsatisfactory to anti-slavery Know Nothings. But most northern Know Nothings were determined not to repeat the mistakes of other parties, and decided that if the convention "undertakes to make a *National* [pro-slavery] *Platform*," the "K.N. of the Free States will *Bolt*."[11]

The entire nation turned its attention in early June to the Know Nothings' Philadelphia convention. Even non–Know Nothing politicians, convinced

10. Benjamin B. French, *Witness to the Young Republic: A Yankee's Journal, 1828–1870*, Donald B. Cole and John J. McDonough, eds. (Hanover, N.H.: Univ. Press of New England, 1989), 256 (quotation); D. Timberlake to Ullmann, May 8, 24, 30, 1855, Ullmann Papers, NYHS; William Hodge to Fillmore, June 25, 1855, John P. Kennedy to Fillmore, Nov. 18, 1855 (quotation), Fillmore Papers, SUNY-O; George R. Babcock to James W. Beekman, July 10, 1855, Beekman Papers, NYHS.

11. Garrett Davis to Lewis Campbell, June 5, 1855, Campbell Papers, OHS; Godlove Orth to Will Cumback, April 14, 1855, Colfax to Cumback, April 16, 1855, Cumback Papers, Indiana University; Colfax to Rev. E. M. Jackson, March 15, 1855 (quotation), Colfax Papers, Indiana University; Harrisburg *Herald*, May 11, 1855; Steubenville *True American*, March 1, 1855; Aurora [Indiana] *Standard* quoted in Indianapolis *Journal*, June 6, 1855; N. Darling to Thurlow Weed, May 30, 1855 (quotation), Weed Papers, UR.

that the outcome would affect all parties, planned to monitor its proceedings closely. Republicans were particularly concerned because the persistence of Know Nothingism had prevented them from replacing the Whigs as the primary challenger to the Democratic party. Yet Republicans disagreed about how to combat the Know Nothing threat. Most radical anti-slavery men, such as Seward, New York *Tribune* editor Horace Greeley, and Ohio Free Soiler Joshua Giddings, wanted to destroy the Know Nothing movement as quickly as possible. Other Republicans, however, thought that their organization would eventually need the support of Know Nothings if it hoped to gain ascendancy in the North. Believing that "*combined*, K.Nism & Anti-Slavery can sweep the country—divided Slavery must triumph," these Republicans rarely attacked the Know Nothing party, preferring to let it die on its own. Prominent proponents of this approach included Ohio Free Soiler Salmon P. Chase, New York lieutenant governor (and New York *Times* editor) Henry J. Raymond, and Cincinnati *Gazette* editor William Schouler.[12]

As the Republicans debated what stance to take toward the Order, Know Nothings argued over what course to follow at the convention. Southerners and northern conservatives, wanting the Order to function as a party of sectional conciliation, hoped that the platform adopted at Philadelphia would declare the slavery issue settled.[13] Veteran nativists claimed that only nativism came under the purview of their organization, and hoped that the Order would completely ignore the slavery issue. Many moderates (such as Massachusetts governor Henry J. Gardner and Ohio congressman Lewis D. Campbell) and even some conservatives (including Erastus Brooks) supported this strategy, fearing that with the Kansas-Nebraska Act still in place, northern voters would refuse to call the slavery issue settled. They believed that the convention "will have to 'agree to disagree' on the Slavery question—or else be ground to powder" by northern resentment.[14] The remaining northern Know Nothings would not consent to participate in a party that did not openly condemn the Kansas-Nebraska Act. Of this group, some sought restoration of the Missouri Compromise, while others planned to press for a platform demanding no more slave states. Members of this latter, radical faction had no desire to nationalize the Know Nothing party and sought instead to fashion an anti-slavery, anti-Catholic, anti-liquor party that would replace the Whigs as the main northern challenger to the Democrats. Some radicals, however, such as Henry Wilson and the New Hampshire delegates, espoused this course

12. Thurlow Weed to Seward, Feb. 27, 1855, George E. Baker (describing views of New York *Tribune* assistant editor James S. Pike) to Seward, April 19, 1855 (quotation), Seward Papers, UR.

13. The only southern leaders who dissented from this view were the few such as Kenneth Rayner and Washington *American Organ* editor Vespasian Ellis who were intensely devoted to nativism.

14. S. W. Parker to Samuel Galloway, May 16, 1855 (quotation), Galloway Papers, OHS; New York *Express*, June 12, 13, 1855; Lewis D. Campbell to Edward L. Pierce, June 4, [1855], Pierce Papers, LC; Garrett Davis to Campbell, June 5, 1855, Campbell Papers, OHS.

disingenuously, hoping that their extreme demands would split the Order and force anti-slavery nativists into the Republican party.[15]

These divisions became apparent when the delegates convened in Philadelphia on Friday, June 8, 1855. In order to dramatize southern resolve, delegates from that section made a perfunctory attempt to contest the seats of Wilson and his Massachusetts "Abolition" colleagues. Wilson responded by challenging the credentials of the District of Columbia's delegates. Although these moves were aimed solely at impressing the voters back home, a serious debate did develop concerning the Louisiana delegation. Citing the traditional hostility of French Catholics to Rome, Louisiana Know Nothings allowed powerful Creole Catholics to join their organization. A second Louisiana Know Nothing organization which banned Catholic members had also sent delegates to Philadelphia, but it represented a much smaller number of lodges than the organization that admitted Catholics. A few other southern states permitted Catholics to join their lodges, but only the Louisiana organization flouted the ban on Catholics so flagrantly. Consequently, after spending the entire first day debating the issue, the convention voted to seat Louisiana's anti-Catholic delegation.[16]

On Saturday, while the convention selected new national officers, the platform committee began its work, and after a weekend of furious debate, the committee presented the fruits of its labor to the full convention on Monday afternoon. The delegates began considering the proposed planks in numerical order, but were so anxious to decide the slavery issue that they soon skipped to that section, the twelfth of the fourteen before them. Divisions ran so deep on this plank that the committee found it necessary to submit both majority and minority versions. Blaming the slavery controversy on the old parties, the majority's Section Twelve (written by Virginia delegate William M. Burwell) decreed that "the National Council has deemed it the best guarantee of common justice and of future peace, to abide by and maintain the existing laws upon the subject of Slavery, as a final and conclusive settlement of that subject, in spirit and in substance." The majority proposal also stated that Congress could not deny a state admission to the Union because it did or did not permit slavery; that Congress could not prohibit slavery from a territory; and that Congress should not abolish slavery in the District of Columbia. The minority report, signed by all the northern committee members except those from New York, California, and Iowa, condemned the majority's tacit

15. Aaron Cragin to Weed, June 15, 1855, Seward Papers, UR. Outsiders aided Wilson as well, most importantly Samuel Bowles, editor of the Springfield *Republican*. Gienapp, *Origins of the Republican Party*, 182–87, describes Bowles's efforts in great detail, but overestimates their impact on the convention's outcome.

16. Henry Wilson, *History of the Rise and Fall of the Slave Power in America* (Boston, 1876), II, pp. 423–24; New York *Express*, June 8, 1855; New York *Herald*, June 9, 10, 1855; Charles Gayarre, *Address on the Religious Test to the Convention of the American Party Assembled in Philadelphia on the 5th of June, 1855* (New Orleans, 1855); Leon C. Soule, *The Know Nothing Party in New Orleans* (New Orleans: Louisiana Historical Association, 1961), 65–70.

acceptance of the Kansas-Nebraska Act. It called the repeal of the Missouri Compromise "an infraction of the plighted faith of the nation" and insisted that Congress should either restore it or refuse to admit as a slave state any territory in which slavery had been banned under that agreement.[17]

Debate on Section Twelve began Tuesday afternoon and continued until Wednesday evening. Most northern delegates could not understand why the South would not accept restoration of the Missouri Compromise as the basis for the slavery plank. With "the restoration of the Missouri Compromise as our rally cry," insisted Massachusetts Know Nothing president John W. Foster, the party could "carry every free State from the Atlantic to the Mississippi." Ohio delegate Thomas H. Ford argued that if southern Know Nothings did not consent to the moderate slavery plank advocated by the northern delegates, radical anti-slavery men in the North would gain the upper hand. "Sewardism, gentlemen, at this moment has its heel on 'Sam's' [Know Nothingism's] neck in Ohio," asserted Ford, "and unless you give us a liberty-loving, justice-like looking platform, the Ides of October next will find Sewardism standing with both feet on the political grave of every 'Sam' in this land."[18]

Nevertheless, southern delegates insisted that they would not accept a platform that did not include the majority version of Section Twelve. In a speech that dramatized the difference between northern and southern Know Nothingism, Burwell stated that southern Know Nothings cared little about nativism. Southerners had joined the Order merely as a means to protect the Union, argued Burwell, but were willing to accept northern demands for the proscription of immigrants in order to maintain party harmony. Southerners believed that in return, the North ought to accept their slavery plank, which took a completely neutral position on the slavery issue. Southern delegates also argued that their Section Twelve would neutralize the Order's abolitionist reputation in time for the South's summer elections. "Before your elections come round again," the Southerners told their northern colleagues, "the Kansas question will be settled."[19]

Voting on the various slavery proposals commenced late Wednesday evening, June 13. First the convention considered the minority version of Section Twelve. If every northern delegate in attendance had supported it, the measure would have passed, but enough conservative Northerners joined with a

17. V. Ellis to Fillmore, Sept. 17, 1856, Fillmore Papers, SUNY-O; New York *Herald*, June 13, 1855. The best record of the convention's proceedings is the extracts from the official minutes in New York *Express*, July 13, 1855.

18. "Sam," the nephew of Uncle Sam, was the personification of Know Nothingism, and members often used the term to refer to the Order. John R. Mulkern, *The Know-Nothing Party in Massachusetts: The Rise and Fall of a People's Movement* (Boston: Northeastern Univ. Press, 1990), 120 (quotation); Youngstown *True American*, July 11, 1855 (quotation); Boston *Bee*, June 25, 1855.

19. New York *Herald*, June 14, 1855; Hartford *Courant*, June 30, 1855 (quotation); Rayner to Ullmann, Aug. 21, 1855, Ullmann Papers, NYHS; Troy [New York] *Family Journal*, Sept. 8, 1855.

unanimous South to reject the proposal by a vote of 52 to 91.[20] Next the convention took up a compromise measure proposed by Rayner, but it lost by an even larger margin. Recognizing that other compromise proposals stood little chance, the delegates next considered the majority version of Section Twelve, which, with the help of eleven conservative Northerners, won approval by a vote of 78 to 63. The convention then adjourned for the evening.[21]

The next morning, most northern delegates gathered at the Girard House to formulate a response to Section Twelve. Wilson and his allies, who had hoped that adoption of a pro-slavery platform would drive northern nativists into the Republican party, demanded that the group announce their separation from the Order and call for a fusion of all anti-slavery forces in the North. Gardner angrily responded that he "would be d——d if he would be abolitionized," and a majority of those present agreed that such a party would be too radical. These Know Nothings believed that the Order might still win northern elections if it continued to combine nativism with a moderate anti-slavery policy based on restoration of the Missouri Compromise.[22] As a result, Know Nothings at the Girard House meeting did not formally secede from the Order. Instead they simply boycotted that morning's session, issuing a statement (signed by fifty-three delegates representing twelve states) that re-affirmed their commitment to 1) restore the Missouri Compromise line, 2) protect settlers in Kansas, 3) modify the naturalization laws, and 4) stop the immigration of paupers and convicts. While the protest declared that "we cannot conscientiously act with those who will not aid us in the correction of these National wrongs," it did not explicitly rule out cooperation with the National Council at a later date.[23] However, those at the Girard House meeting created a corresponding committee to facilitate communication among northern Know Nothings, implying that a separate organization might yet develop. The issuance of a second northern protest added to the uncertain status of these dissenters. This circular, signed by fifteen delegates and apparently written by Pennsylvanian William F. Johnston, condemned the introduction of the slavery question into the convention and stated that "we cannot consistently act . . . with any Na-

20. Of the northern delegates voting against the minority version, seven were from Pennsylvania, six from New York, four from California, two from New Jersey, and one from Minnesota. My figures for this and subsequent votes are based on the extracts from the official minutes printed in the New York *Express*, July 13, 1855.

21. With the exception of two delegates from Delaware, every Southerner voted for the majority version. The Northerners supporting it included four from New York and California, two from Pennsylvania, and one from New Jersey.

22. Gardner quoted in New York *Tribune*, Oct. 31, 1855. This description of the Girard House meeting—written by Samuel Bowles—must be used with great caution because it was published in an attempt to defeat Gardner's re-election bid in 1855.

23. The Indiana delegates, however, in a separate statement issued that same morning, declared that "the order in the State of Indiana will cease to acknowledge the authority of this National Council" upon publication of Section Twelve. New York *Express*, July 13, 1855; New York *Times*, June 15, 1855; Carl F. Brand, "The History of the Know Nothing Party in Indiana," *Indiana Magazine of History* 18 (1922): 191–92.

tional organization" that refuses to sanction restoration of the Missouri Compromise.[24] Thus, although the northern delegates did not formally walk out of the convention, 63 of the approximately 75 Northerners in attendance indicated their intention to repudiate its platform.[25]

With most northern delegates absent, the convention proceeded to consider the remaining planks in the proposed platform, and nearly all of them met with unanimous approval. As far as other sectional issues were concerned, the platform declared Know Nothing opposition to all attempts to weaken the Union and, without mentioning either by name, called for enforcement of the fugitive slave law while condemning the repeal of the Missouri Compromise. On the subject of immigration, the document called for "a radical revision" of the immigration laws to prevent convicts and paupers from emigrating to the United States, a repeal of all state laws that allowed unnaturalized foreigners to vote, and a rescinding of all acts of Congress making grants of land in the territories available to aliens.[26] One plank targeted Catholics by promising continued resistance to the "aggressive policies and corrupting tendencies" of the Roman Catholic Church through enforcement of the Know Nothing credo "Americans only shall rule America." Another criticized Catholicism indirectly by condemning all attempts to exclude the Bible from school curricula. A number of planks reiterated Know Nothing hostility to political corruption, insisting that officeholders emulate the conduct of politicians who served "during the purer days of the Republic" and calling for the reduction of executive patronage as well. Although the Know Nothings rarely addressed issues of foreign policy, one section of the platform did so by attacking filibustering. Lastly, the final plank called for the Order to drop much of its secrecy, by allowing Know Nothings to admit membership in lodges, openly avow their principles, and publicly announce the location of meetings.[27] The next afternoon (Friday, June 15), after a tumultuous eight days in Philadelphia, the convention adjourned.

"With the lessons of the past before us, why could we not avoid the dangerous rock of slavery?" asked a dejected Kenneth Rayner after the

24. It is unclear why Johnston insisted on issuing a separate circular, since in substance his differed little from the Girard House document. By presenting his protest personally in the convention, Johnston may have wished to leave open the possibility of returning if Section Twelve was repealed. See James A. Dean to Simon Cameron, June 22, 1855, Cameron Papers, LC. For the circular see New York *Express*, July 13, 1855.

25. The number of protesters totaled 63 because five men signed both protests.

26. Significantly, this section had originally stated that Know Nothings would modify the naturalization laws so that future immigrants could neither vote nor hold political office, but Southerners modified this once the northern delegates had left the convention. New York *Express*, July 13, 1855.

27. The committee's version of this plank had included a clause mandating that the Order keep the proceedings of all councils secret, but the Southerners, who preferred to run the Order more like a conventional political party than a fraternal organization, eliminated this proviso after the Northerners withdrew. New York *Express*, July 13, 1855.

Philadelphia convention. Northern Know Nothings immediately recognized that Section Twelve would damage the Order, and most would later attribute the Order's eventual downfall to its adoption. Why then did the Philadelphia convention endorse this controversial measure? Most northern Know Nothings blamed the New York delegates, who, according to one Know Nothing leader, "were corrupt, in the main," and had voted disingenuously for Section Twelve to elicit southern support for a New York presidential nominee. Even many New York Know Nothings agreed that "our delegates to that convention entirely mistook and misrepresented" New York opinion on the slavery issue.[28] Others pointed to the intrigues of Wilson and those Know Nothings who had gone to Philadelphia hoping for a split. Just when Rayner's compromise seemed certain to pass, insisted these conservatives, "Wilson . . . sprang to his feet, and denounced the south with so much bitterness, and with such intemperance of language, that even most of the moderate men from the South were alarmed, and under the feelings of resentment and disgust produced by Wilson's harangue, they all voted against Rayner's proposition."[29]

Yet neither of these factors explains why the convention accepted Section Twelve. Only four New York delegates voted for the controversial plank, so it would have passed even without their support. Furthermore, while it is true that Wilson hoped for a split at the convention, his efforts did not cause that result. The Girard House meeting demonstrated that Wilson wielded little influence among the seceding delegates. Rather, it was the unanimity of the Southerners that was in the last analysis most responsible for the adoption of Section Twelve. The northern delegation consisted of relatively radical anti-slavery men who opposed the creation of new slave states, moderates willing to accept restoration of the Missouri Compromise, and conservatives who wanted slavery agitation to end. In contrast, a relatively homogeneous set of ex-Whigs represented the South at Philadelphia. Furthermore, the Virginia election had convinced southern Know Nothings that in order to win the South's summer elections, they needed a platform that would dissociate them from anti-slavery nativists. "The taunts of our enemies drove us to the attempt to harmonize the conflicting views of the two sections of the Union on this distracting subject," noted Rayner, "and the same enemies are now laughing and cajoling over our troubles." Southerners determined to leave Philadelphia with a platform that would satisfy their constituents combined with a small number of northern conservatives

28. Rayner to Ullmann, Aug. 21, 1855, (quotation), V. Ellis to Ullmann, Oct. 22, 1855 (quotation), J. D. Colver to Ullmann, July 21, 1855, (quotation), Ullmann Papers, NYHS; speeches at Massachusetts State Council meeting in Boston *Bee*, June 29, 1855; speech of Otis H. Tiffany in Philadelphia *Sun*, Aug. 27, 1855.

29. Buffalo *Commercial Advertiser* in New York *Express*, June 23, 1855 (quotation); speech of Alfred B. Ely in Boston *Bee*, Feb. 8, 1856. Gienapp, *Origins of the Republican Party*, 183–87, emphasizes this explanation.

who wished to end debate on the slavery issue to bring about the adoption of Section Twelve.[30]

Outsiders believed that northern outrage over Section Twelve would quickly destroy the Order. "The Know-nothings, thank God, are in their graves," commented New York *Tribune* managing editor Charles A. Dana in a statement that reflected the prevailing view.[31] Observers such as Dana were correct in one respect, because most northern Know Nothings did despise their new slavery plank. The Philadelphia platform will be " 'spit upon' with disdain," predicted one nativist journal. "It is, in fact, a virtual endorsement of the Nebraska bill," complained Pennsylvania Know Nothing president Otis Tiffany, and as such it "stultifies and degrades us before the people." Some Know Nothings admitted that "for the purpose of harmonizing the party, we could have submitted to a little pro slavery, but . . . now, . . . nothing short of a restoration of the Missouri Compromise will satisfy the northern sentiment."[32]

Although nearly all northern Know Nothings rejected Section Twelve, they did not believe that it would bring the ruinous results predicted by outsiders. Democrats had often split over the tariff and internal improvements, yet their party still dominated national politics. Furthermore, these Know Nothings argued, the platform "as a whole, is a noble structure. . . . That it is not absolutely perfect, we admit," said the Albany *State Register*, but "what human code of principles . . . is?" Others asserted that the platform was "not a '*finality*' " and that it would be changed at the next national convention when each state would be proportionately represented. Some nativists even insisted that "there was no 'split' in that Convention at any time; nothing but an honest difference of opinion," and that "at our next convention a different course will be pursued, and harmony will be restored." Such Know Nothings believed that "by the disagreement, the Order in both sections remains substantially intact. . . . Slavery remains an open question."[33] Some of these optimists were anti-slavery advocates who thought that

30. Manchester *American*, June 16, 1855; Gardner quoted in Boston *Bee*, June 29, 1855; James P. Thompson to Ullmann, June 28, 1855, Rayner to Ullmann, Aug. 21, 1855, Ullmann Papers, NYHS.

31. Dana quoted in Jeter A. Isely, *Horace Greeley and the Republican Party, 1853–1861* (Princeton: Princeton Univ. Press, 1947), 125; New York *Courier and Enquirer* quoted in New York *Express*, June 16, 1855; Trumbull Cary to Seward, June 19, 1855, Seward Papers, UR; C. K. Watson to Salmon P. Chase, June 25, 1855, Chase Papers, LC; Boston *Pilot* quoted in Billington, *Protestant Crusade*, 427.

32. Norwich *State Guard* in Hartford *Courant*, June 25, 1855 (quotation); Philadelphia *Sun*, Aug. 1, 27 (quotation), 1855; Francis S. Edwards to Ullmann, June 15, 19, 1855, H. Pultz to Ullmann, June 22, 1855 (quotation), Ullmann Papers, NYHS; Philadelphia *Times* and *Juniata Sentinel* quoted in Philadelphia *News*, June 22, 1855; Boston *Bee*, June 19, 1855; Gardner to William Schouler, June 15, 1855, Schouler Papers, MHS; Cleveland *Express*, June 18, 1855.

33. Boston *Bee*, June 22, 27, 1855; Albany *State Register*, June 21, 1855 (quotation); Harrisburg *Herald*, June 22, 1855 (quotation); New York *Express*, June 20, 1855; Johnstown *Cambria Tribune*, June 23, 1855 (quotation); Chicago *Literary Budget*, July 7, 1855 (quotation); New York *Herald* quoted in Philadelphia *News*, June 21, 1855 (quotation).

the Know Nothing party still represented the best means of restoring the Missouri Compromise. Most, however, were conservatives who hoped that the Philadelphia split would finally rid the Order of abolition radicals. They proclaimed that with the radicals gone, "the American Party is the only Union, National, Conservative Party in the land." In this form, they believed that the Know Nothings would eventually dominate American politics.[34]

Even adamantly anti-slavery Know Nothings found reasons to express optimism for the Order's future. In fact, they argued that the secession of the northern delegates represented the boldest attack on the Slave Power ever undertaken. "Whoever before saw delegates from the North, manfully and firmly, resist Southern encroachments"? asked the Hartford *Courant*. "What other national party has ever dared to take such a decisive step?" The Boston *Bee* likewise asserted that the northern bolt was "the boldest expression of Northern sentiments ever uttered in this country." Their resolve to follow an anti-southern course in the wake of the Philadelphia convention was redoubled by the fact that Section Twelve did not produce the election victories southern Know Nothings had promised. Even the Philadelphia *Sun*, which had originally urged acceptance of Section Twelve, now admitted that it had been foolish to allow the South to foist the plank upon the convention:

> Having forced the North . . . to sacrifice to a great extent its honor and its principles, the party in the South were bound to testify their appreciation of such a course by triumphant successes in every State. That . . . they did not, shows us the folly of yielding a jot of our principle. . . . The entire history of this matter affords another instance of Southern Aggression upon the rights of the North. . . .

Northern Know Nothings believed that the Order could rebound from Section Twelve and resolved to use the North's near unanimous rejection of the Philadelphia platform as evidence of the Order's anti-slavery sentiment.[35]

Know Nothings hoping to pursue this strategy realized that they would have to act quickly, because Republicans were already citing Section Twelve to prove that pro-slavery forces controlled the Order. "We must have a special meeting of our state Grand Council and set our state right—and that before long, or we are done—for that platform will crush any party," asserted an Iowa Know Nothing leader. "That 12th article introduced into the platform at Phila must come out forthwith in this state," agreed a New York nativist, "or we are lost!"[36] Just days after the Philadelphia convention ended, the Rhode Island

34. Evansville *Journal*, June 16, 1855; New York *Herald*, July 7, 1855; Albany *State Register*, June 21, 25, 29 (quotation), 1855; J. Van Deusen to Ullmann, July 9, 1855, James Thompson to Ullmann, July 11, 1855, Ullmann Papers, NYHS.

35. Hartford *Courant*, June 18, 1855; Boston *Bee*, June 16, 1855; Philadelphia *Sun*, Aug. 27, 1855; Rayner to Ullmann, Aug. 21, 1855, Ullmann Papers, NYHS; Fort Wayne *Times*, June 21, 1855; Cleveland *Express*, June 18, 1855.

36. William Loughbridge [Iowa delegate to Philadelphia] to William Penn Clarke, June 20, 1855, quoted in Ronald F. Matthias, "The Know Nothing Movement in Iowa" (Ph.D. diss., University of Chicago, 1965), 97–98; J. D. Colver to Ullmann, July 21, 1855, Ullmann Papers, NYHS.

State Council repudiated Section Twelve and seceded from the national organization. Other northern states quickly followed suit. Yet conservatives objected
to this response. "What right had they to absolve the party from all connections
with the national council?" asked an indignant Indiana newspaper. "What is to
become of our pledges to stand by the Union?" But in most cases these protests
were ignored as Northerners hastened to distance themselves from the Philadelphia platform. Had they acquiesced to Section Twelve, "the American party
would have been blown to atoms in every Northern State," insisted Connecticut
governor William T. Minor. New York congressman-elect Killian Miller concurred that repudiation was necessary, because "with the slavery clause in the
platform I very much doubt whether a single County in the State can be carried. . . ." Most states did not dissolve ties with the national organization, but
by the end of the summer Know Nothing conventions in every northern state
had rejected Section Twelve.[37] Four nativist strongholds—Ohio, Pennsylvania,
New York, and Massachusetts—were to hold elections that fall, and Know
Nothings realized that these contests would represent the first opportunities to
gauge the impact of Section Twelve and its repudiation.

The Order in Ohio had changed dramatically since the 1854 election. While
Know Nothing membership had peaked in most states in the fall of 1854, in
Ohio the Know Nothings continued to grow rapidly into the winter. "Know-
Nothingism . . . has become an epidemic," reported a newspaper correspon-
dent from Cincinnati, and official membership figures corroborated his impres-
sion. The Ohio Know Nothings grew from 783 councils and 50,000 members in
October 1854 to 1,195 councils and 130,000 members by June of the following
year. The Order in Ohio expanded during the winter of 1854–55 primarily
because it shed its image as a conservative group dominated by southern
Ohioans and became known instead as a stronghold of anti-slavery sentiment.
The key in this transformation was the November 1854 election of Thomas
Spooner to the presidency of the Ohio Order.[38] Spooner had been active in

37. Greencastle *Banner* in Brand, "Know Nothing Party in Indiana," 199; William T. Minor
to Ullmann, July 14, 1855, Killian Miller to Ullmann, June 24, 1855, Ullmann Papers, NYHS. In
Illinois, New York, and Iowa, the State Councils did not specifically renounce Section Twelve, but
essentially did so by passing resolutions calling for restoration of the Missouri Compromise line.
For the various state conventions, see Hartford *Courant*, June 23 (Rhode Island), 29 (Connecticut), July 21 (Vermont), 1855; Brand, "Know Nothing Party in Indiana," 198; Fort Wayne *Times*,
July 19 (Illinois), 24 (Indiana), 1855; Boston *Bee*, June 29 (Massachusetts), July 23 (New Jersey),
1855; Harrisburg *Herald*, July 7, 1855 (Pennsylvania); Youngstown *True American*, Aug. 15, 1855
(Ohio); New York *Times*, Aug. 31, 1855 (New York); Matthias, "Know Nothings in Iowa," 98–
99, 113.
38. Rochester *American*, Dec. 12, 1854 (quotation); M. H. Nichols to Chase, April 14,
1855, Chase Papers, LC; Columbus *Ohio Statesman*, March 18, 1855, cited in Eugene H.
Roseboom, "Salmon P. Chase and the Know Nothings," *MVHR* 25 (1938): 339; proceedings of
the October 1854 State Council meeting, Columbus *Ohio Statesman*, March 1–28, 1855; Spooner
to the Executive Council, June 2, 1855, in Cincinnati *Commercial*, June 8, 1855; "Digest of
Proceedings" of the June 1855 Ohio State Council meeting, Western Reserve Historical Society.

the Liberty party before the rise of Know Nothingism. His uncle Samuel Lewis—who worked closely with Ohio abolitionist politicians Salmon P. Chase and Gamaliel Bailey—had twice run as the Liberty party candidate for governor. In addition, Spooner had represented Cincinnati at the anti-Nebraska People's convention of 1854. Aided by Spooner's free soil credentials, the Ohio Know Nothings enlisted a majority of the state's anti-slavery voters.[39]

Know Nothing success at recruiting anti-slavery Ohioans posed a dilemma for politicians who sought to organize the Republican party there. Some advised taking a conciliatory stance toward the Order. Most of these politicians believed that Republicans and Know Nothings should fuse to create a single party to oppose the Democrats. Other Ohio Republicans wanted to run a campaign completely independent of the Order, either because they opposed the Know Nothings' proscription or because they believed that cooperation with nativists would prevent anti-slavery immigrants from joining the Republican movement. Led by Joshua Giddings, these politicians vowed that if Know Nothings gained control of a Republican convention, Republicans would run a separate ticket, even if it insured that the Democrats would win the election.[40]

Salmon P. Chase, Ohio's best-known anti-slavery politician and a leading contender for the 1855 gubernatorial nomination, sought to carve out a middle ground between these conflicting strategies. Having already served in the United States Senate, Chase hoped that election to the Ohio governorship would make him the leading Republican presidential contender. Chase had originally believed that the rise of the Know Nothings would spoil his strategy. However, as it became clear in early 1855 that anti-slavery sentiment dominated the Order in Ohio, Chase embarked on a plan to win Know Nothing support for the gubernatorial nomination. First he advised E. S. Hamlin, editor of the Columbus *Ohio Columbian* (perceived by most Ohioans to be Chase's organ), to stop criticizing the Order. "It would be better if you admitted that there was some ground for the uprising of the people against papal influences & organized foreignism," suggested Chase, "while you might condemn the secret organization & indiscriminate proscription on account of origin or creed." Chase also attempted to flatter the Know Nothings directly, telling a leading nativist that in the actions of some priests and immigrants

---

39. R. B. Pullan, *Origins of the Republican Party* (n.p., n.d. [c. 1898]), 7–8, pamphlet collection, OHS; Stephen E. Maizlish, *Triumph of Sectionalism: The Transformation of Politics in Ohio, 1844–1856* (Kent: Kent State Univ. Press, 1983), 100, 171, 185; Cincinnati correspondent in Rochester *American*, Dec. 12, 1855; Wilmington [Ohio] *Herald of Freedom* in [Boston] *Liberator*, Nov. 24, 1855.

40. R. Mott to Joshua Giddings, June 2, 1855, Giddings Papers, OHS; Aaron Pardee to Chase, May 11, 1855, Chase Papers, LC; Giddings to Chase, April 10, May 1, 1855, Chase Papers, HSP; John B. Weaver, "Ohio Republican Attitudes Towards Nativism, 1854–1855," *Old Northwest* 9 (1983–84): 289–305.

"there has been something justly censurable & calculated to provoke the hostility which has embodied itself in the Know Nothing organization."[41]

Chase's strategy seemed to produce the desired result, as reports from throughout Ohio indicated that many Know Nothings supported Chase for governor. However, some Know Nothings feared that nominating an outsider such as Chase would jeopardize the independence of the Order and speed the absorption of its members into the Republican party. Most of these nativists supported the gubernatorial candidacy of Jacob Brinkerhoff, like Chase a Free Soil Democrat but also a Know Nothing. Brinkerhoff had helped introduce the Wilmot Proviso (which he may have written) in Congress, and could thus boast anti-slavery credentials nearly as strong as Chase's.[42] Ohio Know Nothing leaders had decided to make their nominations by polling lodge members, the results to be announced at the Ohio Know Nothing convention in early June. But while the form sent to each lodge listed several choices for each of the minor positions on the ticket, only one name—Brinkerhoff's—appeared for governor. Furthermore, at a secret meeting in Cincinnati, Know Nothing leaders had decided upon the ticket they would push for in local lodge meetings, and Brinkerhoff's name headed this slate. Lodge members were free to vote for other candidates, but Know Nothing leaders obviously supported Brinkerhoff.[43]

Republicans believed that the only way to block Brinkerhoff's selection as the Know Nothing candidate was to prevent the Order from making any nominations. To this end they threatened to run Chase as a third candidate if the Know Nothings nominated Brinkerhoff at their convention in Cleveland. "The peculiar friends of Mr. C[hase] have about made up their minds to 'rule or ruin,' " complained Brinkerhoff as he sensed this strategy taking effect.[44] The fact that many Know Nothings also opposed making nominations at the June meeting helped the Republican effort. One reported that "we are about to ask Spooner and the officers of the S. C. [State Council] to countermand the order for nominations," and many other nativists advocated this strategy. They realized that if the Order made nominations, outsiders would view the move as an attempt to dictate the anti-Democratic ticket and would use this as

41. Chase to Oran Follett, Jan. 1, Feb. 14, 1855, "Follett Papers," 62, 64; Chase to E. S. Hamlin, Nov. 21, Jan. 22 (quotation), Feb. 9, 1855, Chase to "Dear Sir," Jan. 12, 1855, Follett to Chase, Jan. 7, 1855, Chase Papers, LC; Chase to John Paul, quoted in Gienapp, *Origins of the Republican Party*, 194 n. 17; Eugene H. Roseboom, "Chase and the Know Nothings," 335–49.

42. Edward Wade to Chase, April 14, 1855, Chase Papers, HSP; C. K. Watson to Chase, June 25, 1855, Chase Papers, LC; Campbell to Isaac Strohm, April 21, 1855, W. B. Thrall to Strohm, July 8, 1855, Strohm Papers, OHS; Eric Foner, "The Wilmot Proviso Revisited," *JAH* 56 (1969): 262–64.

43. "Alpha" in Columbus *Ohio Columbian*, May 2, 1855; Medill to Follett, April 18, 1855, Chase to Follett, May 4, 1855, "Follett Papers," 71, 73–74. Cincinnati *Commercial*, May 12, 1855, contains the proposed ticket.

44. Brinkerhoff to Follett, May 21, 1855, "Follett Papers," 74–76; Chase to Campbell, June 2, 1855, Samuel Galloway to Campbell, June 23, 1855, Campbell Papers, OHS; R. Mott to Giddings, June 2, 1855, Giddings Papers, OHS; Maizlish, *Triumph of Sectionalism*, 213–14.

an excuse to run Chase as a third candidate. Spooner adopted this view, explaining to the Know Nothing Executive Committee that cooperation with outsiders was essential because "even by the union of our entire membership, we have not the numbers to secure the election." Most Know Nothings attending the Cleveland convention agreed, and voted by 283 to 81 to seal the lodge ballots and participate instead in the public anti-Democratic convention that had been called for July 13 in Columbus.[45]

Although it might seem strange that the Know Nothings would squander the opportunity to make independent nominations, they did so because they felt confident that they could easily impose their choice upon the Columbus meeting. "Why, gentleman, you can't select enough prominent 'Republicans' in Ohio, to act as delegates to the convention without having in it a majority of Know Nothings," boasted the Know Nothing Cleveland *Express*. "The KNs have a perfect organization & a full treasury while we have nothing," complained a Republican as he explained why Know Nothings controlled the delegate selection process. Furthermore, nativists believed that if the nominations came from the open convention, instead of from a secret Know Nothing gathering, then Republicans would be forced to accept its verdict.[46]

When the Columbus convention got under way, Know Nothings did control a majority of the delegates. Yet with the Republicans persisting in their threats to secede, it was not clear how the gubernatorial nomination would be resolved. Before the expected confrontation materialized, however, Brinkerhoff agreed to withdraw from contention. Considering how smoothly the convention ran from that point, it seems likely that the delegates followed a pre-arranged script. While Republicans were mollified with the nomination of Chase and a platform that ignored nativism, all the remaining nominations went to Know Nothings. Brinkerhoff received the nomination for Supreme Court judge, while Thomas Ford's stirring speech at Philadelphia against Section Twelve earned him the nod for lieutenant governor. Although many Know Nothings described the coalition as a temporary arrangement that would end when the Kansas controversy was settled, outsiders believed that the convention marked the creation of the Ohio Republican party.[47]

Historians usually cite Chase's nomination as a Republican victory over Know Nothingism. This argument has its merits, inasmuch as the fusion ticket weakened the Know Nothings' distinctive identity and paved the way for the Order's absorption into the Republican party in Ohio. But such reasoning fails

45. "G" [William G. Gibson] to [Galloway], April 23, 1855 (quotation), Galloway Papers, OHS; Spooner to Chase, Feb. 5, 1856, Chase Papers, LC; Spooner to Executive Committee, June 2, 1855, in Cincinnati *Commercial*, June 8, 1855; Digest of the Proceedings of the June 1855 Ohio State Council, Western Reserve Historical Society; Youngstown *True American*, June 13, 1855.

46. Cleveland *Express* quoted in Roseboom, "Chase and the Know Nothings," 339; N. S. Townshend to Chase, June 9, 1855, Chase Papers, HSP; P. Bliss to Chase, June 6, 1855 (quotation), Chase Papers, LC.

47. Cleveland *Leader*, July 16, 1855; Roeliff Brinkerhoff, *Recollections of a Lifetime* (Cincinnati, 1900), 92; Pullan, *Origins of the Republican Party*, 16, 20–22, pamphlet collection, OHS.

to consider the fact that most Know Nothings had advocated Chase's nomination. Reports from all over Ohio indicated that rank-and-file Know Nothings preferred Chase. As one Know Nothing newspaper put it, "in no [better] way can the people so sternly rebuke iniquity in high places," especially among politicians beholden to the Slave Power, "as to elect him Governor."[48] Before the Philadelphia convention, Ohio Know Nothings might have nominated Brinkerhoff despite the Republicans' threats. After Section Twelve's adoption, however, Ohio nativists believed that only the election of a nationally prominent radical such as Chase would send the proper signal to the South. Furthermore, we have seen that many Northerners joined the Order simply as a halfway house until the Republican party was formed, and such Know Nothings were especially prevalent in Ohio. This lack of determination to perpetuate the Order played just as important a role as Free Soil intimidation in convincing Know Nothings to support Chase's candidacy.

Not all Ohio Know Nothings accepted Chase's victory at Columbus. Some were veteran nativists who had expected the Know Nothing party to become an independent political organization; others were residents of southern Ohio whose geographic proximity and economic ties to the South made them hesitant to support a radical such as Chase; and the remaining dissidents were conservative Whigs who wanted the Know Nothings to become a pro-Union organization. Cincinnati *Times* editor James "Pap" Taylor fell into all three categories. Insisting that "SAM is a freesoiler in Ohio, but he is not a rampant abolitionist," Taylor helped to organize a new convention on August 9 in Columbus, where "true" Know Nothings could undo "the trickery and treachery" of Spooner and his accomplices.[49] Their septuagenarian nominee, ex-governor Oren Trimble, was not a Know Nothing, but, then again, neither were half the delegates, who like Trimble were conservative Whigs. The convention made no other nominations, in part because all the other fusion nominees were Know Nothings, but primarily because their goal was to defeat Chase.[50]

"Never was there a more fierce canvass," wrote one political veteran about the Ohio election of 1855. Politicians across the nation followed the Ohio contest, knowing that a fusionist defeat in the most adamantly antislavery state in the Midwest "would no doubt kill the Republican movement most effectually everywhere." The Trimble Know Nothings adopted a campaign strategy similar to that of the Democrats, whose ticket was headed by incumbent governor William Medill. Both claimed that slavery was a "false issue" in the campaign, because a governor could do nothing about slavery in

48. Youngstown *True American*, May 9, 1855 (quotation); James N. Taylor to Chase, May 10, 1855, James Walker to Chase, June 20, 1855, M. H. Nichols to Chase, July 7, 1855, Spooner to Chase, Feb. 5, 1856, Chase Papers, LC.

49. Cincinnati *Dollar Times*, July 19 (quotation), 26 (quotation), 1855; Maizlish, *Triumph of Sectionalism*, 218.

50. J. Scott Harrison to Benjamin Harrison, July 28, Aug. 20, 1855, Benjamin Harrison Papers, LC; Cincinnati *Dollar Times*, July 26, Aug. 16, 23, 1855.

either the South or the territories. Trimble Know Nothings also argued that Ohio had sufficiently demonstrated its anti-slavery resolve in the congressional elections of 1854, and they criticized the fusionists for ignoring issues such as taxation. They called Chase a "DISUNIONIST AND AN ULTRA ABOLITIONIST," predicting that he would institute black suffrage and force white children to attend school with blacks. They also asserted that Chase's election would cost Ohio merchants their southern business. Trimble's advocates insisted that by supporting the ex-governor, Ohioans could demonstrate that an alternative existed to the sectionalism espoused by the other parties.[51]

Fearing that Know Nothing votes for Trimble might help elect Medill, pro-fusion Know Nothings worked diligently for the Chase ticket. They insisted that "Trimble is not the candidate of the American party of Ohio" but only of "a few disaffected pro-slavery men," and called it a "personal injustice to the old gentleman, thus to bring him before the people in the last half hour of his life." They also denied that the Order had abandoned nativism by supporting Chase, stating that "the balance of the ticket is sufficiently K N. to . . . [satisfy] the most ultra Anti Catholic Native American that can be found." Stressing the slavery issue, pro-Chase Know Nothings charged that Trimble's supporters had "niggerized and sold out to the South." In a final appeal to wavering Know Nothings, Spooner called the Trimble candidacy "a cunningly devised . . . [Democratic] trick to catch gullible Know Nothings," charging that Southerners would interpret a vote for Trimble or Medill as "an endorsement . . . of the Kansas-Nebraska swindle." With Protestant German immigrants vowing to oppose Chase due to his collaboration with the Know Nothings, Spooner realized that limiting Know Nothing defections might mean the difference between victory and defeat.[52]

On election day, Chase out-polled Medill by 16,000 votes, while Ford and the other Know Nothings enjoyed a 36,000-vote majority. Trimble won only 8 percent of the vote, carrying just two southern counties.[53] Pro-fusion Know Nothings claimed responsibility for the victory, stating that it was engineered by "the American party with the Anti-Slavery element taken into its composition." Others interpreted the result differently. One observer believed that the Order had "been swallowed up in the name of 'the Republicans,' " inas-

51. Benjamin Wade to Israel Washburne, Oct. 13, 1855 (quotation), Israel Washburne Papers, LC; H. Kreisman to Charles Sumner, Sept. 18, 1855 (quotation), Sumner Papers, HU; "Address of the American Central Committee to the People of the State of Ohio," in Cincinnati *Dollar Weekly Times Extra*, [c. Sept. 1855] (quotations).

52. Steubenville *True American*, Aug. 22, 1855 (quotation); R. H. Folger to Galloway, July 18, 1855 (quotation), Galloway Papers, OHS; J.M. Clements to the Editor, Cincinnati *Dollar Times*, Oct. 4, 1855 (quotation); Spooner to the Editor of the Cincinnati *Times*, in Columbus *Ohio State Journal*, July 12, 1855; Spooner to the Members of the American Order in Ohio, July 23, 1855, in Cincinnati *Commercial*, July 24, 1855; Spooner to Ohio Know Nothings in Cleveland *Herald*, Oct. 4, 1855 (quotation).

53. Chase won 146,641 votes (49%), Medill 131,091 (43%), and Trimble 24,310 (8%). In the race for lieutenant governor, 169,439 voters (56%) chose Ford, while 133,485 (44%) cast their ballots for the Democratic nominee. *Tribune Almanac* (1856): 44.

much as many Know Nothings had referred to their ticket by that name. Others saw the result as a blow to the Order because the campaign had proven nativism to be a liability. "The Nebraska question was the real rock of danger here," reported one Democrat, "and if we had not had Know nothingism to fight, [we] would have been beaten badly." Giddings agreed that in the wake of the Ohio contest, "the prestige of the K Ns is gone I think forever." As a result, Republicans believed that Know Nothing leaders would soon abandon the Order for "a Republican organization" and that "their Americanism was subservient to that end."[54]

Although the independence of the anti-slavery Know Nothings in Ohio *was* crumbling, Ohio Republicans spoke too soon when they eulogized the Order. Two months after the election, Ford angered Republicans by presiding at a Know Nothing meeting, and Spooner rebuffed Republican requests that he resign his Know Nothing presidency and disband the Order. The Trimble group likewise showed no signs of dissolving, and its leaders began forging ties to the national Know Nothing organization. So while Republicanism was definitely eclipsing Know Nothingism in Ohio, it was not clear how or when the Ohio Republicans would manage to destroy the Know Nothing party.[55]

Pennsylvania's Know Nothing organization had seemed hopelessly divided after the legislative session of 1855. Despite their success in many of the state's spring municipal elections and reports that many conservatives Whigs were joining the party,[56] the factionalism that had prevented the election of a United States senator had not abated. But ironically, Section Twelve instilled Pennsylvania Know Nothings with new confidence, because they anticipated that opposition to the Philadelphia platform would help unify the state's factionalized nativists and make Pennsylvanians forget the Order's recent legislative troubles.

When the State Council met in Reading on July 3, Pennsylvania Know Nothings moved to initiate their revival by voting 143 to 30 to repudiate Section Twelve. Although many delegates advocated a platform that rejected the admission of any more slave states, the Pennsylvanians instead approved a document calling for a restoration of the Missouri Compromise. This reflected the Know Nothings' belief that a moderate position on slavery would earn them the most broad-based support in Pennsylvania. The delegates next entertained a resolution calling for a convention of northern Know Nothings to

54. Steubenville *True American*, Oct. 10, 1855; O. F. Fishback to L. Campbell, Oct. 30, 1855, Campbell Papers, OHS; J. M. Cornell to William Medill, Nov. 28, 1855, Medill Papers, LC; Giddings to Chase, Oct. 16, 1855, Chase Papers, HSP; M. H. Nichols to Chase, Dec. 11, 1855, Chase Papers, LC.

55. G. Bailey to Chase, Nov. 27, 1855, Chase Papers, HSP; James M. Ashley to Chase, Oct. 21, 1855, T. M. Tweed to Chase, Oct. 25, 1855, M. H. Nichols to Chase, Dec. 11, 1855, Chase Papers, LC.

56. Harrisburg *Herald*, March 20, 1855; Edward Joy Morris to John M. Clayton, Feb. 21, 1855, Clayton Papers, LC.

meet in Cincinnati in January. Proponents hoped that such a meeting would promote unity amongst Northerners attending the Know Nothings' February presidential nominating convention, furthering the candidacy of a nativist who supported restoration of the Missouri Compromise. Ten delegates from the Philadelphia area, asserting that it was treasonous even to contemplate such a meeting, walked out in protest. Meanwhile, the remainder of the Reading delegates approved the resolution calling for the Cincinnati convention, and adjourned confident that most Pennsylvania Know Nothings would ratify their action.[57]

After the Reading convention, Pennsylvania Know Nothings continued to emphasize their anti-slavery credentials, in part to forestall the launching of the Republican party in their state. In a widely reprinted address, Pennsylvania Know Nothing president Otis H. Tiffany called slavery "the greatest and most pressing issue . . . now before the people" and promised that the Order would fight its extension. Know Nothings asserted that only "old 'party hacks' " want "a *new party*" and that the Order alone possessed the strength necessary to defeat the Democrats. If "hostility to slavery . . . [is] to triumph in Pennsylvania," argued Know Nothings, "it must be through the agency . . . of the American party."[58]

Despite these efforts, Pennsylvania Republicans did nominate a candidate for canal commissioner, the single state office voters would fill that fall. In fact, the moribund Whigs (whose convention one delegate called "an assembly of leaders without rank and file") and the old Native American party also made nominations. Know Nothing nominee Peter Martin brought to four the number of anti-Democratic candidates. Neither the Whig nor Native American candidate could possibly win the election. Even the Republicans had no chance, having nominated Passmore Williamson, a radical abolitionist then serving a prison sentence for obstructing the rendition of a fugitive slave. Reminding them of their hopeless position, Know Nothings urged the anti-Democratic forces to unite behind their candidate. "Those anti-Slavery men who are disposed to act separately and distinctly from the American party, are but repeating the mistake other anti-Slavery parties have committed," insisted the Harrisburg *Herald*, and "are but dividing the North, and making it an easier victim to Southern tactics."[59]

Whig and Republican leaders agreed just days before the election to discuss creation of a coalition ticket with the Know Nothings. Representatives of the three parties gathered in Harrisburg on September 27, and the breakthrough came when Tiffany suggested Thomas Nicholson (long-time chief

57. Harrisburg *Herald*, July 6, 7, 10, 1855; New York *Herald*, July 6, 7, 9, 1855.

58. Tiffany speech in Harrisburg *Herald*, Aug. 29, 1855; Pittsburgh *Commercial Journal* in Youngstown *True American*, Aug. 15, 1855 (quotations); Pittsburgh *Times* quoted in Harrisburg *Pennsylvania Telegraph*, Aug. 22, 1855.

59. Gienapp, *Origins of the Republican Party*, 209–11; Alexander McClure, *Old Time Notes of Pennsylvania*, 2 vols. (Philadelphia, 1905), I, pp. 235–36 (quotation); New York *Herald*, June 12, 1855; Harrisburg *Herald*, Sept. 8 (excerpt from Pittsburgh *Times*), 10 (quotation), 1855.

clerk in the state treasurer's office) as the compromise candidate.[60] Meanwhile, Democrats had focused throughout the campaign on the liquor license law passed by the 1855 legislature, hoping to win the support of the state's Protestant German-Americans. Although their virulent anti-Catholicism had driven many of these immigrants to support the Know Nothings in 1854, German-Americans generally opposed liquor restrictions. Despite coalition efforts to deflect debate toward slavery and anti-Catholicism, the temperance issue dominated the campaign.[61]

Nicholson lost by fewer than 12,000 votes, but because the percentage of votes cast for the anti-Democratic ticket had fallen so dramatically from 1854, Know Nothings considered the result "a Waterloo defeat."[62] Anti-temperance Know Nothings blamed the setback on the license law, with the Philadelphia *Times* calling Know Nothing support of temperance "the supremest insanity." The Philadelphia *News* concurred, stating that the Know Nothing effort "to re-establish the old blue law *regime* of New England" had diminished the Order's popularity. Even some Know Nothings who supported temperance legislation concluded that the license law had injured the fusion ticket. Other nativists ascribed their defeat to the defections of Protestant immigrants who resented the Order's continuing refusal to admit them.[63] Although less willing to admit it publicly, Pennsylvania nativists realized that factionalism—such as that displayed during the senatorial election—had also contributed to their defeat. "The people expected [that] we would elect [a senator]," noted one Know Nothing, "and . . . failing to do so, . . . we lost popular confidence, and so lost our election."[64]

Pennsylvania Know Nothings were divided as to how the 1855 result would affect the Order's future prospects. Some boldly predicted that if "the officers of every Council . . . call regular stated meetings, and compel general attendance," enthusiasm for the Order would revive. Others asserted that the Pennsylvania Know Nothings would never again defeat the Democrats, and urged a "Union with the Republican sentiment of Pennsylvania."[65] Events outside of Pennsylvania's borders would help to determine the future relation-

60. Harrisburg *Pennsylvania Telegraph*, Oct. 3, 1855; McClure, *Old Time Notes*, I, p. 240; Harrisburg *Herald*, Oct. 1, 4, 1855.

61. Philadelphia *Sun*, Aug. 4, Sept. 13, 1855; James A. Dean to Cameron, Sept. 18, 1855, J. S. Craft to Cameron, Sept. 18, 1855, Stephen Miller to Cameron, Sept. 20, 1855, C. S. Eyster to Cameron, Sept. 22, 1855, Cameron Papers, LC.

62. J. M. Kirkpatrick to Cameron, Oct. 31, 1855, Cameron Papers, LC. Democratic candidate Arnold Plumer received 161,281 votes (50%), Nicholson 149,745 (46%), and Native American candidate Kimber Cleaver 4,056 (1%). In comparison, Pollock had captured 55% of the vote a year earlier. The withdrawn candidates received the remaining votes. *Tribune Almanac* (1855): 42.

63. Philadelphia *Times* quoted in Philadelphia *Sun*, Oct. 13, 1855; Philadelphia *News*, Oct. 11, 13 (quotation), 17, 1855; Johnstown *Cambria Tribune*, Oct. 20, 1855; Pottsville *Miner's Journal*, Oct. 13, 1855; Charles Dunning to Chase, Nov. 4, 1855, Chase Papers, LC.

64. J. M. Kirkpatrick to Cameron, Oct. 31, 1855 (quotation), Cameron Papers, LC; Philadelphia *News*, Oct. 18, 1855.

65. Clearfield [Pennsylvania] *Raftsman's Journal*, Nov. 14, 1855; Harrisburg *Pennsylvania Telegraph*, Nov. 21, 1855.

ship between these two organizations. If the Order suffered November defeats in New York and Massachusetts, those favoring fusion would be in a better position to press their case. If the Know Nothings triumphed, however, Republicans might find it more difficult to convince nativists to abandon their organization.

"The division of parties in the State of New York is one of the most inextricable puzzles that was ever presented to the political mathematician to solve," commented the Hartford *Courant* in 1855. "It is worse than a sight at 'fluxions' to a raw Sophomore."[66] The tangle of cliques that divided the old parties in New York even afflicted the Know Nothings, with a number of factions vying for control as the Order turned its attention toward the autumn election of 1855. Despite these divisions, New York Know Nothings looked forward to the 1855 contest with great confidence. With 1,050 councils and 178,000 members as of May 1855, the Order controlled only one-third of the state's voters, but because they expected four different parties to enter the race, Know Nothings felt certain that they could carry the election. Know Nothing leaders also believed that the church property debate between state senator Erastus Brooks and Archbishop John Hughes would win the Order additional support. Consequently, Know Nothings confidently predicted that in 1855 "we shall carry the state beyond a doubt."[67]

New York Know Nothings realized that their prospects depended to a great extent on how their State Council dealt with Section Twelve. Of all the northern states, New York's reaction to the national platform was most difficult to predict, because a majority of its Philadelphia delegates had favored the unpopular plank. Although they preferred to ignore the slavery issue, New York leaders realized that unless they repudiated Section Twelve, the Order would lose the support of anti-slavery voters, especially those in the "Burned Over District" stretching from Albany to Buffalo. Even conservatives admitted that Section Twelve "should be thrown out," although they cautioned that this should be done "as quietly & with as little noise as possible."[68] At their State Council meeting in Binghamton, western delegates proposed a vigorous denunciation of the Philadelphia platform, but conservatives won approval of a mild statement that did not specifically mention Section Twelve. However, the resolutions approved by the convention implicitly rejected the hated plank, condemning the repeal of the Missouri Compromise, demanding that slavery "should derive no extension from such repeal," and

66. Hartford *Courant*, Oct. 25, 1855.

67. James Barker to the State Council of New York, May 8, 1855, Order of United Americans Scrapbook, New York Public Library; New York *Herald*, July 29, 1855; Scisco, *Political Nativism in New York*, 127–28; Daniel Ullmann to John M. Clayton, July 18, 1855 (quotation), Clayton Papers, LC; J. G. Sanders to James W. Beekman, Feb. 6, 1855, Beekman Papers, NYHS; James Thompson to Ullmann, March 24, 1855, Ullmann Papers, NYHS.

68. Killian Miller to Ullmann, June 24, 1855, J. D. Colver to Ullmann, July 21, 1855, Jerome Fuller to Ullmann, July 24, 1855 (quotation), Ullmann Papers, NYHS.

asserting that the slavery issue "has no rightful place in the platform of the National American Party."[69]

New York Know Nothings interpreted the Binghamton platform in accordance with their views of the slavery issue. Deeming Section Twelve "repudiated," a journal from the Burned Over District applauded the new document because it allowed Know Nothings to be "true to their Northern instincts." On the other hand, Erastus Brooks's New York *Express* asserted that "no attempt was made to act on" Section Twelve. "It was neither repudiated nor endorsed, but left to itself." This was precisely the dual reaction Know Nothings had hoped for, because it proved that the Order could construct a platform that satisfied both conservatives and anti-slavery men.[70]

Know Nothings made their nominations one month later, choosing a relative political novice, author Joel T. Headley, for secretary of state, the top spot on the ticket. After failing as a minister in Massachusetts, Headley had moved to New York to launch a literary career, and immediately became a popular success. "His works are marked by a peculiar energy and vivacity of diction, and a graphic power of description, possessed by few contemporary authors," commented one literary journal. With virtually no past political record to haunt him (he had served just one term in the state senate), Headley seemed the ideal candidate, and Know Nothings predicted certain victory.[71]

Only the newly formed New York Republican party appeared capable of challenging the Know Nothings in the 1855 election. Although their platform included a plank condemning the Order, Republican leader Thurlow Weed realized that his organization could not carry the election unless it gained support from anti-slavery Know Nothings. Reports from upstate indicated that many Know Nothings, especially those in the Burned Over District and western New York, *were* becoming Republicans.[72] But Know Nothings compensated for these losses by making conversions from other parties. Many conservative Whigs who had abstained from voting in 1854, particularly those in and around New York City, joined the American party in 1855. One newspaper asserted that "the young Whigs and the old Whigs of the city are going over, by wholesale, to 'Sam.' In all the uptown wards especially, hundreds are being initiated at every meeting of the councils. . . ."[73] Reports also indicated that most Democrats belonging to the "Hard" faction "are with us heart & hand" and would "be found [voting] with the American party in November."

69. New York *Times*, Aug. 29–31, 1855.

70. Albany *State Register*, Sept. 3 (quoting Auburn *American*), 11, 1855; New York *Express*, Sept. 1, 1855.

71. New York *Times*, Sept. 26, 27, 1855; New York *Express*, Sept. 26, 1855; Thomas J. Curran, "The Know Nothings of New York" (Ph.D. diss., Columbia University, 1963), 190–94; New York *Mirror*, Nov. 16, 1855 (quotation).

72. Gienapp, *Origins of the Republican Party*, 223–28; E. P. Smith to Henry C. Carey, June 8, 1855, Carey Papers, HSP; George W. Patterson to Weed, Oct. 13, 1855, Weed Papers, UR.

73. New York *Sun* in Boston *Bee*, Sept. 8, 1855 (quotation); D. Littlejohn to Weed, Oct. 15, 1855, Weed Papers, UR; New York *Mirror*, Oct. 24, 1855.

By replacing anti-slavery radicals with new converts from the Whig and Democratic ranks, Know Nothings believed they could maintain their size and increase ideological unity within the party.[74]

Whereas temperance and nativism had overshadowed all other issues during New York's 1854 campaign, slavery dominated the canvass in 1855. In order to reduce the Republicans' appeal, the Know Nothings argued that their party was sufficiently anti-slavery to fight southern aggression. "The American party in New York is Anti-Nebraska to the back bone," insisted one Know Nothing newspaper. "It would be difficult to find a dozen members of the Order in any one Council who are not." Republicans, in contrast, were portrayed as irresponsible radicals bent upon "sowing the seeds of discord—breeding discontent, and aggravating sectional animosities already too strong."[75] Republicans tried to deflect these attacks by importing speakers such as Henry Wilson to appeal to anti-slavery Know Nothings. Wilson argued "that the American party was ruined at Philadelphia" and that New York Know Nothings had demonstrated their pro-slavery orientation by supporting Section Twelve at the national convention. Know Nothings responded by pointing out that Preston King (who headed the Republican ticket) had himself cast pro-slavery votes as a Democrat in Congress, and insisted that the moderate stance of the Binghamton platform represented New Yorkers' true position on the slavery issue.[76]

While emphasizing the slavery issue, the Know Nothings did not abandon nativism. Instead, they tried to portray themselves as a more flexible party than the Republicans, one that mixed anti-slavery and anti-Catholicism in the proper proportions. For example, Know Nothings charged that it made no sense for Republicans to agitate the slavery issue during the 1855 campaign, because "there is not a single . . . officer to be elected this fall who will have a voice, directly or indirectly, in the [slavery extension] matter." By concentrating solely on the slavery issue, Republicans were attempting "to make us forget our own households and homes, and . . . wrestle with shadows elsewhere," while the incursions of the Irish and Catholicism occurred "very near us, right at our own doors and all around us." Know Nothings believed that their combination of anti-Catholicism and moderate anti-slavery created a multi-faceted appeal that neither the single-issue Republicans nor the discredited Democrats could match.[77] On election day, the Order's confidence in

74. J. Van Deusen to Ullmann, July 9, 1855 (quotation), J. Thompson to Ullmann, Sept. 12, 1855, Ullmann Papers, NYHS; New York *Herald*, July 7, 29 (quotation), 1855; Albany *State Register*, July 2, 9, 10, 1855; N. Darling to Alexander H. Schultz, Sept. 12, 1855, Weed Papers, UR; Gienapp, *Origins of the Republican Party*, 228.

75. Elmira *Republican* in New York *Mirror*, Oct. 4, 1855 (quotation); Albany *State Register*, June 27, 1855 (quotation); [Greene] *Chenango American*, Oct. 11, 1855.

76. Wilson speech in New York *Mirror*, Oct. 10, 1855; Albany *State Register*, Oct. 3, 1855; George E. Baker to Seward, Oct. 5, 1855, Seward Papers, UR.

77. Albany *State Register*, June 30 (first quotation), July 2 (third quotation), Oct. 1, 1855, Kingston *People's Press*, Oct. 5, 1855 (second quotation); George E. Baker to Seward, Aug. 3, Oct. 13, 1855, Seward Papers, UR; Ullmann speech in New York *Express*, Oct. 16, 1855; James Thompson to Ullmann, Sept. 1, 1855, Ullmann Papers, NYHS.

their strategy was apparently vindicated, as Headley and the Know Nothing ticket out-polled the Republicans by a 12,000-vote margin.[78]

Observers were astounded that the New York Know Nothings had managed to rebound from their Philadelphia debacle. "It's a resurrection from the dead," exclaimed a surprised diarist. "People thought 'Sam' defunct or disorganized," but the result indicated that "our antipathy to the Pope and to Paddy is a pretty deep-seated feeling." One of Seward's correspondents, having thought that "the *honest* ones who had been duped to examine the mysteries of Know Nothingism . . . had left them," now glumly admitted that the Order possessed more appeal than he had realized. Know Nothings were ecstatic, with the wife of one council president aptly summarizing the result as "a great American triumph, . . . a clear Protestant victory."[79]

The Order's ability to offset the loss of anti-slavery members with an unexpectedly large accession of Democrats and conservative Whigs played a major role in the Know Nothing victory. Republicans also ascribed their defeat to insufficient preparation time. The Know Nothing "organization is magnificent because it reaches every little nook, marshalling & drilling its forces in every school district almost," noted one envious Republican. "We on the other hand, formed the Republican party so late, that Whigs & Democrats had not finished looking at each others faces & wondering what company they had got into, when they were called to the polls."[80]

However, the key to the Know Nothings' triumph lay in their ability to retain their anti-slavery image despite Section Twelve. "It was only by professing to be free soil," reported one Whig, "that the Know-Nothing organization in the country[side] kept enough of the former Whigs from the support of the Republican ticket to defeat it at the recent election." A Republican similarly discovered in Essex County that "*all* the Whigs were & *are* Seward men [i.e., strongly anti-slavery], but are in the lodges & voted the Hindoo ticket. . . ." Even "the impracticable abolitionists for whom Seward did not go far enough, are also with lodges." Republicans had assumed that most anti-slavery Know Nothings would quit the Order over Section Twelve. Yet the Binghamton platform and "strong anti-slavery resolutions by the local councils" kept many of them in the Know Nothing camp.[81] Republican disorganization, the church property dispute, and the conversion of conservative Whigs and Hard Democrats all contributed to New York Know Nothing strength in 1855. Nonethe-

78. The official results read: Headley 148,557 (34%), King 136,698 (31%), Hatcher ("Soft" Democrat) 91,336 (21%), Ward ("Hard" Democrat) 59,353 (14%). *Tribune Almanac* (1956): 41.

79. Allan Nevins and Milton H. Thomas, eds., *The Diary of George Templeton Strong* (New York: Macmillan, 1952), II, p. 241; Aaron Delano to Seward, Dec. 10, 1855, Seward Papers, UR; Jane Sanders to James W. Beekman, Nov. 19, 1855, Beekman Papers, NYHS.

80. E. P. Smith to H. C. Carey, Nov. 13, 1855 (quotation), Carey Papers, HSP; J. Sanders to James W. Beekman, Nov. 19, 1855, Beekman Papers, NYHS; O. B. Pierce to Weed, Nov. 26, 1855, Weed Papers, UR.

81. William Cornwell to Hamilton Fish, Dec. 15, 1855, Fish Papers, LC; E. P. Smith to H. C. Carey, Nov. 13, 1855, Carey Papers, HSP.

less, it was their success at distancing themselves from Section Twelve that made victory possible.

Impressive though it was, close inspection of the 1855 election returns indicated that the Order's triumph rested upon a shaky foundation. First, the number of votes cast for the Know Nothing ticket fell far short of their publicly reported membership totals, indicating that many members had abandoned the Order. The distribution of the Know Nothing vote distressed nativists even more. Know Nothings had expected that by organizing eastern upstate New York (an area neglected during the 1854 campaign), they would add victories in this region to complement their western strongholds. However, while the Order did sweep the eastern portion of the state in 1855, it lost control of western New York. Know Nothings attributed this shift to the concentration of anti-slavery radicals (who joined the Republican party) in western New York. Eastern New York, they said, contained the level-headed moderates whom the Know Nothings now sought. But Republicans interpreted the results differently. They pointed out that wherever the Know Nothings had done well in 1854, they fared poorly in 1855, and vice-versa. Consequently, Republicans concluded that the novelty of Know Nothingism and the popular desire to strike a one-time blow at conventional political parties motivated most Know Nothing voters, and that the Order, having now succeeded once in every part of the state, would quickly decline hereafter. Thus, despite the Know Nothings' New York victory, Republicans felt certain that the Order would soon begin to fade from the political scene.[82]

Those Republicans envisioning a quick collapse of the Know Nothing party assumed that their Massachusetts brethren would defeat the Know Nothings in that state's 1855 election. The struggle for control of the Order between veteran nativists and Free Soilers, they believed, had left the Massachusetts Know Nothings "hopelessly divided." Furthermore, the influx of conservative Whigs that the Order had enjoyed in the rest of the North by early 1855 had not occurred in Massachusetts. These conservatives believed that under the control of Henry Wilson and his ally, Massachusetts Know Nothing president John W. Foster, the Order would remain "a nest of pestilent abolitionists." The knowledge that Wilson and Foster would attempt to steer Know Nothings into the Republican movement also contributed to over-confidence in the anti-slavery party. Wilson had declared after the Philadelphia convention that he would do "all that can be done" to draw Know Nothings into the Republican party. Foster agreed that "the recent *events* at Phila affords the true anti-slavery men of Massachusetts an opportunity of laying the foundation of a great republican party." With Wilson and Foster working inside the Know Nothing party to advance the Republican cause, Massachusetts Republicans

82. John M. Bradford to Fish, Nov. 8, 1855, Fish Papers, LC; E. P. Smith to H. C. Carey, Nov. 13, 1855, Carey Papers, HSP; Batavia *Republican Advocate*, Feb. 12, 1856; Gienapp, *Origins of the Republican Party*, 234.

felt certain that defections from the Know Nothing ranks would enable them to carry Massachusetts in 1855.[83]

However, Republicans underestimated the tenacity with which many anti-slavery nativists adhered to the Know Nothing organization. Led by Gardner, these Know Nothings asserted that the Order could dominate northern politics with the dual platform of anti-slavery and anti-Catholicism. Thus, at the State Council meeting held immediately after the Philadelphia convention, the delegates rejected calls for fusion with the Republicans, adopting instead a set of resolutions written by Gardner that repudiated Section Twelve, dissolved ties with the national organization, and ordered that the secret Know Nothing Order begin operating as the open "American party."[84] Six weeks later, at a State Council meeting held in Springfield, Wilson and those favoring fusion made a second attempt to draw the Massachusetts Know Nothings into the Republican movement. Although most delegates agreed that restoration of the Missouri Compromise line should be the cornerstone of the new party platform under discussion, sharp debate ensued over the fusion question. Veteran nativist Alfred B. Ely insisted that outsiders should join the American party if they wanted to create a united anti-slavery organization. Wilson responded that because the Know Nothings' national organization had been "broken and shivered to atoms" by Section Twelve, it could never serve as the basis for an anti-slavery party. "By fusion alone can the people of the Free States baffle the darling schemes of the Chiefs of the Black Power . . . ," the senator insisted. "The people want union, and *will have it*, *through* your organization or *over* your organization." Wilson also called for Know Nothings to drop their demand for a twenty-one-year wait before immigrants could vote, because "this intense Nativeism . . . is killing us" by making fusion more difficult. The delegates refused to delete the twenty-one-year proposal from their platform, but deadlocked on the fusion issue. Finally, a compromise was proposed allowing Know Nothings to unite with outsiders as long as those outsiders supported the Know Nothing platform, and it passed by a two-to-one margin. The result represented a partial victory for both sides. Wilson and Foster could begin negotiations with those wishing to form a Republican organization, while Ely and the conservatives could justify backing out of the arrangement if the Republicans failed to support the Know Nothing agenda.[85]

Know Nothings spent the rest of August wrangling with Republicans over the terms under which Know Nothings would participate in a fusion conven-

83. Ezra Lincoln to Schouler, May 24, 1855, Schouler Papers, MHS; John P. Kennedy to Robert C. Winthrop quoted in Bean, "Party Transformation in Massachusetts," 301; Wilson to Samuel Bowles, June 23, 1855, Bowles Papers, Yale University; Foster to Julius Rockwell, June 16, 1855, quoted in Gienapp, *Origins of the Republican Party*, 214.

84. Boston *Bee*, June 29, 1855; Mulkern, *Know-Nothing Party in Massachusetts*, 123.

85. Boston *Bee*, Aug. 8, 9, 16 (quotations), 1855; Mulkern, *Know-Nothing Party in Massachusetts*, 124. The platform included calls for a twenty-one-year wait before naturalization; laws to allow the deportation of immigrant criminals and paupers; a ban on immigrants in important political and diplomatic positions; retention of the Bible as a school textbook; and restoration of the Missouri Compromise.

tion.[86] The various parties eventually agreed to hold a Republican convention in Worcester on September 20, although both Know Nothings and their opponents were careful to leave avenues of escape should their foes control the gathering. Non–Know Nothings thus insisted that a mass meeting convene in addition to the delegate convention. Worcester was a stronghold of anti-slavery sentiment, and Republicans knew that if Know Nothings controlled the delegate convention, the mass meeting of Worcester's citizens would reject the results. Know Nothings made similar arrangements. The vague announcement for a "Native American Convention" to meet on October 3 in Boston was obviously intended to leave Gardner an alternative should the Worcester delegates reject him.[87]

The Worcester convention began harmoniously, with the delegates unanimously adopting a platform that ignored nativism while demanding in essence that no more slave states be admitted to the Union. On the first ballot for governor, Gardner came tantalizingly close to winning the nomination. In the debate that ensued, however, Gardner's opponents called for the nomination of Julius Rockwell (who had placed second on the initial ballot), claiming that while Gardner had not publicly pledged to support the convention's nominee, Rockwell had given up all other allegiances when he joined the Republican movement. Gardner's supporters attempted to counter this argument by reading a letter in which the governor supposedly demonstrated his devotion to fusion. But the vacillating tone of the letter, combined with the publicly announced "Native American" convention, convinced enough delegates that Gardner's dedication to Republicanism was contingent upon his nomination. On the subsequent ballot, Rockwell edged out Gardner for the nomination. The convention then nominated incumbent Know Nothings for three of the remaining five positions on its ticket and adjourned.[88]

Know Nothing councils from around the state denounced the convention's decision, repudiated its nominations, and called for an independent Know Nothing convention to renominate Gardner. The State Council had agreed to participate in the fusion movement on the condition that the new organization endorse the Springfield platform, and inasmuch as the Worcester platform dealt only with slavery, Know Nothings considered themselves free to ignore its action. Furthermore, despite their pledge that Gardner would be eligible for the gubernatorial nomination, the fusionists at Worcester "repeatedly declared, both out of the Convention and in it, that under no circumstances would they support Gov. Gardner should he be the nominee." Know

86. Boston *Bee*, Aug. 16, 17, 23, 30, 1855; Charles Francis Adams to G. Bailey, Sept. 2, 1855 (copy), Adams Papers, MHS; Gienapp, *Origins of the Republican Party*, 216–17; letters from "One Who Was Present," E. C. Baker [secretary of the Massachusetts Know Nothing organization], and Alfred B. Ely in Boston *Bee*, Oct. 2, 9, 12, 1855; Gardner to Samuel Bowles, "Tues Morn Early" [Aug. 1855], Bowles Papers, Yale University.

87. Boston *Bee*, Sept. 11, 15, 1855; Lowell *American Citizen*, Aug. 25, 1855; Gardner to Bowles, Sept. 17, 1855, Bowles Papers, Yale University; Bowles to Richard Henry Dana Jr., Sept. 15, 1855, Dana Papers, MHS; Gienapp, *Origins of the Republican Party*, 218.

88. Boston *Bee*, Sept. 21, 1855.

Nothings felt that the "treachery and broken pledges of the leaders in the new movement" totally absolved them "from all obligations to stand by and support their ticket."[89]

Because historians admire the Republican agenda and scorn that of the Know Nothings, this struggle has ordinarily been portrayed as one pitting Wilson, the selfless foe of the Slave Power, versus the scheming Gardner, who allowed his personal ambition to jeopardize the anti-slavery cause. But Gardner's insistence that his renomination be a condition for participation in the fusion movement was not unreasonable. After all, Chase's use of the same tactic in Ohio had been considered courageous, not selfish. Having demonstrated his devotion to the anti-slavery cause by convincing northern moderates to bolt at Philadelphia (and sacrificing a possible Know Nothing vice presidential nomination in the process), Gardner felt it only fair that he retain the governorship in a new Republican party. He therefore allowed the Know Nothings who repudiated the Worcester results to cooperate with the veteran nativists who had spurned fusion from the start. These two groups joined forces at the American party convention on October 3, which denounced the Republican ticket and unanimously renominated Gardner for governor.[90]

"Slavery governs everything," reported one Massachusetts newspaper in identifying the issue that dominated the 1855 campaign. In order to prevent defections to the Republican party, Know Nothings reminded voters of their anti-slavery record, insisting that "a more thorough anti-Nebraska party than ours has no existence." Besides, said Know Nothings, the Republicans "are too ultra for a majority of our people to accept." Know Nothings also attempted to revive the anti-immigrant spirit that aided the Order in 1854, suggesting that a Republican victory would bring a return to the very immigrant abuses that had caused the rise of Know Nothingism in the first place. With both parties offering similar anti-slavery credentials, Know Nothings argued that the only question facing the voters was whether Massachusetts "shall be controlled by *American* or *Foreign* votes."[91]

Realizing that their success depended upon converting anti-slavery Know Nothings, Republicans aimed their campaign at the nativists instead of the Slave Power. Echoing Wilson's assertion that Massachusetts needed to "get in line" with the anti-slavery movement in other states, Foster noted that the rest of the North had chosen the Republican party to rebuff Southern aggressions. Thus, "by refusing to go into this movement, we isolate ourselves from all sympathy with our sister States of the North . . . , and imperil the cause of freedom itself." As for nativism, Republicans maintained that "the American

89. Boston *Bee*, Sept. 22, 24 (excerpts from Gloucester *Telegram*), 25 (quotations), 26, 27 ("A True American"), 28, 29, Oct. 1, 2 ("One Who Was There"), 1855.

90. Gardner to Bowles, Aug. 17, 1855, Bowles Papers, Yale University; Boston *Bee*, Oct. 4, 1855.

91. Worcester *Transcript*, Oct. 30, 1855 (quotation); Boston *Bee*, Aug. 7 (quotation), 29, Oct. 1 (quotation), 6 (letter of E. C. Baker to Wilson), 1855; Bean, "Party Transformation in Massachusetts," 324–25; campaign circular dated November 5, 1855, Boston Public Library (quotation).

party has aroused the public mind" to such an extent "that there is at present no imminent danger from foreign influences, and public opinion is thus left free to grapple with another adversary of our institutions—slavery."[92]

The Republican strategy succeeded to some extent. Several Know Nothing lodges, for example, dramatized their transition to Republicanism by publicly dissolving their councils. Nevertheless, Republicans found it more difficult than they had expected to convert Know Nothings. Republican editor Samuel Bowles reported that "Gardner's partizans are spending money, traversing the state, waking up the council fires, poisoning the public mind, misrepresenting the Worcester Convention, & playing the deuce generally." However, the real difficulty lay in convincing voters that they would better aid the anti-slavery movement by becoming Republicans. "There is great sympathy for G[ardner] among good honest anti-slavery men," noted Bowles dejectedly, and a belief that the "Springfield platform is just as good republicanism as ours."[93]

Most Republican leaders expected their party to triumph despite these difficulties, and were surprised at the Know Nothings' 15,000-vote victory.[94] John G. Palfrey, a leading Massachusetts Free Soiler, was amazed that so many voters still clung to the Know Nothing organization, and Senator Charles Sumner found the result "humiliating." Yet as in New York, not all signs boded well for the Know Nothings. The percentage of voters casting Know Nothing ballots had fallen by more than one-third since 1854, with defections particularly great among Free Soilers, Democrats, and those living in western Massachusetts. Some decline in Know Nothing support was inevitable, for as the Hartford *Courant* noted, many Massachusetts voters had cast Know Nothing ballots in 1854 primarily to register their disdain for the existing parties.[95] Furthermore, the radical conduct of the legislature had scared off many conservatives who had previously supported the Order's candidates. With most of the party's elected leaders having defected to the enemy, however, Gardner considered a victory of any size satisfying. Even Republicans agreed that the Order's ability to retain voters was more surprising than the losses it suffered:

> When the Worcester convention adjourned Gardner . . . [and other promi-
> nent Know Nothings] were apparently flat on their backs, deserted and over-

92. Wilson to E. C. Baker, Sept. 29, 1855, Foster to Baker, Sept. 25, 1855, both in *Republican Campaign Documents for the People to Read* (Boston, 1855), 4–9; Simon Brown to Charles A. Perry, Aug. 23, 1855, in Boston *Bee*, Aug. 30, 1855 (quotation); S. P. Hanscom, *To His Excellency Henry J. Gardner, Governor of the Commonwealth of Massachusetts* (n.p., [1855]).

93. Hartford *Courant*, Sept. 8, 1855; Boston *Bee*, Sept. 27, Oct. 2, 1855; Bowles to Richard H. Dana Jr., Oct. 15, 1855, Dana Papers, MHS; Seth Webb Jr. to Bowles, Oct. 9, 1855, Henry L. Dawes Papers, LC.

94. Gardner polled 51,674 votes (38%), Rockwell 36,521 (27%), Democrat Edward Beach 34,920 (25%), and Whig Samuel Walley 14,454 (11%). *Tribune Almanac* (1856): 40.

95. J. G. Palfrey to Joshua Giddings, Dec. 2, 1855, Giddings Papers, OHS; David Donald, *Charles Sumner and the Coming of the Civil War* (New York: Knopf, 1961), 275; Bean, "Party Transformation in Massachusetts," 326; Dale Baum, *The Civil War Party System: The Case of Massachusetts, 1848–1876* (Chapel Hill: Univ. of North Carolina Press, 1984), 36; Hartford *Courant*, Nov. 6, 1855.

thrown by their own trusted associates and leaders. Nearly every man whom they had placed in high office, State or national, abandoned them, and with the prominent men went tens of thousands of others. Their lodges were broken up in many parts of the State, and where not finally broken up, were deserted, while the very president of the order himself went over to the enemy. To rally under such circumstances, and to carry the State so completely, shows not only a commendable courage, but the possession of both some political skill, and a powerful *ad captandum* argument for the people.

As in New York, observers believed that the Know Nothings had "risen from the dead" to capture the Massachusetts election.[96]

An effective joining of anti-slavery and anti-Catholicism allowed the Massachusetts Know Nothings to overcome their losses to the Republicans and win the 1855 election. By leading the bolt at Philadelphia, severing ties with the national organization, and adopting the Springfield platform, Know Nothings demonstrated their dedication to free soil principles. They also succeeded in portraying Republicanism as a radical movement, with the Boston *Bee* calling the result "an emphatic protest by Massachusetts against having her heartfelt anti-slavery sentiment carried out to sedition."[97] Know Nothings also continued to take advantage of the anti-Catholicism that permeated Massachusetts. "The people will not confront the issue we present," complained one Republican, referring to slavery. "They want a Paddy hunt & on a Paddy hunt they will go." The New York *Tribune*'s Boston correspondent agreed. He noted that "the Know-Nothings command and use two of the strongest prejudices of the Yankee nature—hatred of Paddies and hatred of Popery. Combining these with enough Anti-Slavery principle to make it difficult to attack them from the Anti-Slavery side, and also with the Maine law principle, they have been victorious over parties which offered only a single issue or unpopular issues." Wilson believed that Republicans had "overestimated the power of the Anti Slavery sentiment." In fact, they had *underestimated* the extent to which voters identified the Order with anti-slavery sentiment, and this was the key to the Know Nothings' Massachusetts victory.[98]

After the Philadelphia Know Nothing convention split over the slavery question, most contemporary analysts predicted that Know Nothingism would quickly fade from the political scene. With its southern members determined to leave the Kansas-Nebraska Act intact, and most of its northern adherents insistent on its repeal, the Order had seemed destined for collapse. The

96. Gardner to Ullmann, Nov. 12, 1855, Ullmann Papers, NYHS; Gardner to George R. Morton, Nov. 17, 1855, quoted in Gienapp, *Origins of the Republican Party*, 222; New York *Tribune* (Boston correspondence), Nov. 9, 1855.

97. J. P. Gould to Nathaniel P. Banks, Dec. 4, 1855, Banks Papers, LC; Sumner to Seward, Nov. 11, 1855, Seward Papers, UR; Boston *Bee*, Nov. 13, 1855; Gloucester *Telegraph and News*, Nov. 10, 1855; W. L. G. Greene to Robert Carter, Oct. 18, 1855, Carter Papers, HU.

98. Edward L. Pierce to Chase, Nov. 9, 1855, Chase Papers, LC; New York *Tribune*, Nov. 9, 1855; Wilson to Chase, Dec. 17, 1855, Chase Papers, HSP; Artemus Carter to Sumner, Nov. 16, 1855, Sumner Papers, HU.

October election results in Ohio and Pennsylvania had apparently confirmed such predictions. After all, the Republican party had essentially swallowed up the Ohio Know Nothings, despite the Order's dramatic growth there in early 1855. In Pennsylvania, one of the states that seemed best suited to Know Nothingism, the Order's popularity had declined substantially. However, Know Nothing victories in New York and Massachusetts demonstrated that the Order could still attract significant electoral support. Know Nothing triumphs in these states resulted in part from the difficulties faced by Republicans in organizing campaigns for the first time. But the Know Nothings' ability to distance themselves from Section Twelve and portray the Order in the North as an anti-slavery party played an equally important role in their victories.

"The American organization has received a new lease on life, by virtue of its victories in Massachusetts and New York," noted a Democratic newspaper in the wake of the nativists' November triumphs. Demoralized Republicans agreed that "Know nothingism has received a new impulse and will work mischief everywhere." Republicans were especially dejected, because they had thought that the Philadelphia split would leave their organization as the only anti-slavery party in the North. Now Republicans feared that "their victory in New York & Massachusetts will induce them to retain their organization and so divide the Anti Slavery force" during the 1856 presidential campaign.[99] The Know Nothings' impact in 1856 would depend upon a number of developments. The convention of northern Know Nothings proposed at Reading was scheduled to meet at Cincinnati in late November. Republicans had hoped that Know Nothings would use this meeting to announce their switch to the Republican ranks, but after the November elections that seemed unlikely. Nevertheless, the Cincinnati convention would determine whether moderates such as Johnston and Gardner, or more radical Know Nothings such as Spooner and Colfax, controlled the Order in the North. Whatever the outcome at Cincinnati, Republicans planned to attack Know Nothing cohesion when Congress convened in Washington in December. Republicans believed that the sight of southern Know Nothings casting votes for pro-slavery candidates for Speaker would embarrass northern Know Nothings and force them into the Republican camp. In contrast, Know Nothings hoped to use the congressional session to reunite their northern and southern factions and believed that the election of the House Speaker would provide such an opportunity. Thus, the outcome of the speakership contest would have a tremendous impact in determining whether the Republicans or the Know Nothings would ultimately establish themselves as the leading opponents of the Democratic party.

99. Boston *Atlas* quoted in Boston *Bee*, Nov. 10, 1855; H. Kreisman to Sumner, Nov. 13, 1855, Sumner Papers, HU; Kingsley S. Bingham to Chase, Nov. 16, 1855, Chase Papers, LC.

8

"*Slavery* Is at the Bottom of All Our Troubles": The Decline of the Know Nothing Party

The confidence with which the Know Nothings had originally anticipated the 1856 presidential election had ebbed by the end of 1855, because Section Twelve had disillusioned most northern nativists. Still, many members of the American party remained optimistic in late 1855. Know Nothings had won the most recent state-wide elections in New York, California, Massachusetts, Connecticut, New Hampshire, Rhode Island, Maryland, Delaware, Kentucky, and Louisiana, and they had proven in the past that they could carry Pennsylvania and Indiana as well. The Republicans, who like the Know Nothings were trying to establish themselves as the principal challenger to the Democratic party, seemed in much worse shape. The only important state Republicans had carried in 1855 was Ohio, and that victory had required Know Nothing assistance. The Know Nothing victories in New York and Massachusetts had been especially important in reviving optimism within the Order. According to the Philadelphia *Times*, the November results showed "how firmly, how strongly, how inextricably the great principle of Americanism— that Americans should rule America—is rooted in the minds of the American people." On the other hand, continued the *Times*, northern voters had demonstrated that "the insidious, artful, and dangerous treachery of 'republicanism,' (which was but another name for disunion)" did not interest them. Know Nothing editor Vespasian Ellis agreed that in the wake of the November contests, "*we are safe*—the American party will triumph—& the Union is perpetuated!"[1] Yet perceptive Know Nothings recognized that Republicanism had broader appeal than the 1855 election results indicated. In New York, for example, where the Order had just carried the election, a nativist newspaper

1. Philadelphia *Times* in Boston *Bee*, Nov. 10, 1855; V. Ellis to Daniel Ullmann, Nov. 8, 1855, Ullmann Papers, NYHS.

admitted that outside New York City "the Republicans are the leading party." After surveying the situation at Albany, Know Nothing leader Stephen Sammons likewise concluded that "the central influence" at the capital "*is fusion* [i.e., Republicanism]. There is no mistake about this."[2]

In addition, factionalism continued to plague the American party. Of the three distinct sub-groups within the northern Know Nothing ranks, two believed that the Order could still carry the presidential election in 1856. One of these, best described as "moderates," contended that the Order could revive its popularity if it replaced Section Twelve with a pledge to restore the Missouri Compromise. Because Northerners would control a larger proportion of delegates at future Know Nothing conventions, these nativists felt certain that they could repeal the hated plank. With this revised platform, said moderates, the American party would easily out-poll the one-issue Republicans and establish themselves as the most viable competitor to the Democratic party. Among the most prominent moderates were Massachusetts governor Henry J. Gardner and ex-governor William F. Johnston of Pennsylvania.

Vying for control with this moderate group was a more conservative faction, made up primarily of conservative ex-Whigs. With radical antislavery and temperance advocates having left for the Republican ranks, conservatives believed that the Know Nothings would attract an entirely new constituency, one that placed perpetuation of the Union above all other issues. This strategy particularly pleased veteran nativists, who had envisioned just such an agenda when they established the Order. Although vastly outnumbered by moderates in the North as a whole, conservatives held a numerical advantage in the "lower North," the region encompassing New Jersey as well as the southern portions of New York, Pennsylvania, Ohio, Indiana, and Illinois. Furthermore, conservatives believed that unanimous support from southern Know Nothings would counter-balance their minority status above the Mason-Dixon line. Because this faction stressed safeguarding the Union and had insisted upon "nationalizing" the Order at Philadelphia, its adherents (such as New York's Erastus Brooks and Indiana's Richard W. Thompson) called themselves "National Americans."

Members of the third Know Nothing faction were usually referred to as "fusionists." These nativists realized that the Order's strength was irreversibly declining, and that most Know Nothings would eventually join the Republican party. Some, such as Ohio Know Nothing president Thomas Spooner and Indiana congressman Schuyler Colfax, remained Know Nothings in hopes of forcing the Order to aid the Republican cause. Others, recognizing that they wielded a great deal of power as *potential* converts, hoped to gain concessions from the Republicans as their price for switching parties. Some of these Know Nothings sought patronage from the Republicans in return for their support. Others wanted the Republicans to endorse nativist proposals. Of the three

2. New York *Mirror*, Nov. 9, 1855; Sammons to Ullmann, Nov. 24, 1855, Ullmann Papers, NYHS.

Know Nothing factions, the moderates held the key to the Order's future. If they forged a coalition with the National Americans, then the Order's hopes of winning the presidency in 1856 would remain viable. If the moderates joined forces with the fusionists, however, then the Order would lose most of its northern members, destroying all hope of reviving the American party.[3]

The meeting of northern Know Nothings that convened in Cincinnati on November 21, 1855, provided the first indication of the moderates' intentions. National Americans had feared that fusionists would use this "North American convention" to formalize their separation from the national organization, and injure the Order's prospects for 1856 "by acting in too sectional a manner."[4] But conservative fears were unwarranted, as most of the nativists attending the convention sought conciliation with their southern colleagues. The delegates dramatized this by inviting Know Nothing president E. B. Bartlett (who lived just across the Ohio River in Covington, Kentucky) to attend their sessions and by rejecting a platform proposed by fusionist Thomas Spooner. Although Spooner's proposal stressed the party's devotion to the Union and included a promise not to interfere with slavery where it already existed, it also called slavery the issue "of paramount importance" and suggested that Know Nothings "cheerfully and cordially cooperate with all their fellow citizens who are ready to unite with them" to fight its extension. Moderates steadfastly opposed such a course, believing that it would hasten the Know Nothings' absorption into the Republican party and prevent implementation of their nativist agenda. Instead, the convention adopted a platform that specifically condemned "coalescing with any Party which demands the postponement or abandonment of American principles, or the disorganization of the American Party." The resolutions also called for the Order to replace Section Twelve with a pledge to restore the Missouri Compromise, and proposed a special meeting so that the National Council might effect such a change before the Know Nothings made their presidential nomination in February.[5] Some North Americans denounced the convention's conservative stance on the slavery issue, but most applauded its action as enhancing the prospect that northern and southern nativists might reunite. With Congress about to convene, Know Nothings also hoped that the progress made in Cincinnati would help strengthen Know Nothing unity in Washington.[6]

"Much, we might say almost everything, depends upon *Americanizing* Congress," asserted a nativist newspaper in 1854. "[O]ur cause . . . depends very

3. Estimating the size of each faction is difficult, because their strength changed over time and from state to state. As of January 1855, the northern Know Nothings probably consisted of about 20% conservatives, 40% moderates, and 40% fusionists. A year later, with most fusionists having joined the Republicans, and many conservative Whigs having entered the Know Nothing ranks, the breakdown probably approximated 35% conservatives, 50% moderates, and 15% fusionists.

4. F. W. Prescott to Amos A. Lawrence, Nov. 15, 1855, Amos A. Lawrence Papers, MHS.

5. New York *Times*, Nov. 27, 1855 (quotation); Cincinnati *Times* reports in Fort Wayne *Times*, Nov. 26–28, 1855; Cincinnati *Commercial*, Nov. 22–24, 1855. Approximately 51 delegates from nine states (Ohio, Indiana, Illinois, Pennsylvania, Rhode Island, Massachusetts, Michigan, Vermont, Wisconsin) attended this convention.

6. Steubenville *True American*, Jan. 3, 1856; *Address of the Plymouth Rock Council, December 12, 1855*, broadside, Cincinnati Historical Society.

much upon it." Know Nothings made control of Congress their top priority because only that body could implement the most fundamental tenet of Know Nothingism: revision of the naturalization laws. By December 1855, however, the impending session had taken on added significance, because the meeting would mark the first encounter between northern and southern Know Nothings since the contentious Philadelphia convention. Furthermore, observers believed that with no party holding a clear majority in the House of Representatives, the speakership election would help determine whether Republicans or Know Nothings became the chief rival to the Democrats, who controlled the Senate and the presidency. If the American party could put aside sectional differences and elect a Speaker, it might convince voters that the Order had overcome its previous factionalism and would henceforth function as a viable party. But conservatives realized that if Know Nothing divisions recurred, it would invigorate the Republicans and "break up what little nationality we have left."[7]

The speakership election which commenced when the Thirty-fourth Congress convened on December 3, 1855, was as unpredictable as any Washington had ever witnessed. In part this resulted from the drastic changes in the political situation since 1854, when most voters had chosen their representatives. Many New England congressmen elected as Know Nothings had become Republicans. Other Northerners who had won office as Whigs had since joined the Know Nothing ranks. Most difficult to assess was the allegiance of the many congressmen elected as members of nebulous "anti-Nebraska" coalitions, supported by both Republicans and Know Nothings. Some of these politicians had already publicly announced their devotion to either the Republican or Know Nothing cause, but many others, hoping to test the political wind at the last possible moment, waited until Congress convened to make their decision. Their uncertain status heightened the suspense as Congress commenced its session.

Despite these uncertainties, Know Nothings approached the speakership contest with optimism. Neither Republicans nor Democrats could elect a Speaker on their own, and a majority of the representatives had belonged to Know Nothing lodges when elected.[8] National Americans therefore reasoned that moderates from the North and South would eventually have no alternative but to support a National American candidate such as Buffalo congressman Solomon G. Haven, Millard Fillmore's former law partner. Fusionist

7. Cleveland *Express*, Sept. 25, 1854 (quotation); Edward Everett to James Hamilton, Dec. 3, 1855 (quotation), Everett Papers, MHS; Joshua Giddings to Gamaliel Bailey, Nov. 11, 1855, Giddings Papers, LC.

8. Determining the exact number of Know Nothings in the House is difficult, but if we take the 106 listed in the *Know Nothing Almanac*, add the six Americans elected after the *Almanac* went to press, and then add Know Nothings the *Almanac* did not know about (Thorington of Iowa; Edie, Knight, Purviance, Ritchie, and Tyson of Pennsylvania; Miller of New York; Evans of Texas; Kennett, Porter, and Lindley of Missouri), then 123 of the 234 representatives House had been affiliated at some point with the Order. However, the list in the *Almanac* probably overestimates slightly the number of congressmen affiliated with the Order. For a listing of Know Nothing congressmen from the major northern states, see Chapters 3 and 4.

Know Nothings, on the other hand, planned to support an anti-Nebraska nativist in hopes of attracting Republican votes. Fusionists thus hoped to score a victory for both the anti-slavery and anti-Catholic movements. Midwesterners and ex-Whigs within this camp sought to elect Ohio congressman Lewis D. Campbell, while Easterners and ex-Democrats generally supported Massachusetts representative Nathaniel P. Banks, Jr.[9]

National Americans immediately discovered the futility of their effort when voting on the speakership began. Instead of concentrating their votes upon a single candidate, most southern Know Nothings (dubbed "South Americans" by the press) supported Southerners for the office, while most northern nativists (labeled "North Americans") voted for candidates from their section. According to Haven,

> our people, or those who ought to be ours are disunited[,] broken up—
> fragmentary. . . . [Many North Americans] sink, so far, every other consideration in the Nebraska issue or folly and thereby become as essentially allied to Republicanism as if they were its born heirs and sole representatives. . . .
> Our members from the South [are] pulling just as hard the other way. . . . I have been fighting . . . [the North Americans] on the one hand & the extreme Southern men on the other hand & between the two I am very nearly crushed out.

Although the House was still deadlocked after the first few days of balloting, most northern and southern nativists refused to support candidates from the opposing section, eliminating the possibility that a National American would win the speakership.[10]

During these first few days of voting, Campbell led all anti-slavery candidates. Known for a "vanity and conceit [that] over topped all else," Campbell undoubtedly believed that support from National Americans would eventually win him the speakership. Campbell had taken an active (albeit behind-the-scenes) role in directing Ohio Know Nothing operations. Consequently, most Republicans feared that a Campbell victory would benefit the American party more than the Republican, so they quickly organized to block the Ohioan's prospects. These Republicans preferred to support Banks, who had apparently joined the Know Nothings only to win re-election to Congress, and had not participated either publicly or privately in the Order's operations since then.[11]

9. Campbell to Isaac Strohm, May 24, 1855, Strohm Papers, OHS; Campbell to Chase, Nov. 5, 1855, Richard Mott to Chase, Nov. 11, 1855, Salmon P. Chase Papers, LC; Chase to Campbell, Nov. 8, 1855, Campbell Papers, OHS; S. W. Parker to Samuel Galloway, May 16, 1855, Galloway Papers, OHS; J. D. Audens to Isaac Sherman, Oct. 1, 1855, Sherman Papers, Private Collection.

10. Haven to Fillmore, Dec. 6, 1855, Fillmore Papers, SUNY-O; Haven to Ullmann, Dec. 13, 1855 (quotation), Ullmann Papers, NYHS.

11. Quotation is from handwritten note by William Schouler, written after the speakership contest, on the back of Campbell to Schouler, July 6, 1852, Schouler Papers, MHS. Banks was actually lucky to be in Congress at all, because Know Nothings supported him only after their original choice declined the nomination. See Robert M. Taylor, Jr., "Reverend Lyman Whiting's Test of Faith," *Historical Journal of Massachusetts* 12 (1984): 90–103.

Although such blatant opportunism often injured a politician, in Banks's case it helped, because it convinced Republicans that Banks cared little for nativism, and that as Speaker he would act primarily as a Republican. This convinced influential New York editors Horace Greeley and Thurlow Weed to lobby for Banks, and their efforts convinced many anti-slavery congressmen to switch their allegiance to him. Consequently, after five days and twenty-three dead-locked ballots, Campbell reluctantly consented to withdraw from the contest.[12]

Fusionist Know Nothings quickly switched to Banks, leaving moderates and those conservatives who had supported Campbell with a dilemma. If they cast their ballots for Banks, they would further weaken the independence of the American party and lend credibility to Republican claims that only the Republican organization could effectively combat the Slave Power. If they held out for a candidate dedicated to Know Nothingism, however, they risked alienating their constituents, who were growing impatient with the stalemate and had come to see the speakership battle as a test of will between North and South. At first, many of these wavering Know Nothings cast their votes for a variety of potential compromise candidates, hoping that Republicans might drop Banks. But with Republicans determined to stand firmly behind their candidate and northern public opinion supporting this resolve, most North Americans eventually fell in line behind Banks. With the "South Americans stand[ing] their ground so stiffly," reported one conservative, "I hardly see what can be done by the Northern men but abide by Banks." The support of these nativists enabled Banks to come within six votes of victory by the end of the second week of balloting. However, a stubborn cadre of forty-one National Americans (including thirteen Northerners) continued to cast their ballots for Henry M. Fuller of Pennsylvania, so as the House ended its second week of balloting, an end to the deadlock was not in sight.[13]

Despite pleas from Republicans and North Americans, the northern National Americans opposing Banks refused to drop Fuller. He is "equally as good an anti-Nebraska man as Mr. Banks," they insisted, and by electing Fuller the Order could advance anti-Nebraskaism and Americanism without condoning the extremism represented by Banks and his party. However, during a debate on December 19 concerning the Order's position on slavery, this argument lost most of its force. Asked whether he would vote to restore the Missouri Compromise, Fuller equivocated, then said that he would not because further "agitation" of the slavery question would cause more harm than good. It is unclear whether Fuller made his statement out of conviction or out of loyalty to Section Twelve, which had declared the slavery issue "settled."

12. *CG*, 34th Congress, First Session, 11 (all subsequent citations refer to this Congress and Session unless otherwise noted); Schouler to the Editor, Cincinnati *Gazette*, April 18, 1856; Fred Harvey Harrington, "The First Northern Victory," *Journal of Southern History* 5 (1939): 191–93.

13. *CG*, 12–26; F. W. Prescott to Amos A. Lawrence, Dec. 22, 1855, Amos A. Lawrence Papers, MHS. On a typical ballot at this time (the fifty-eighth), Banks received 106 votes, William A. Richardson (the Democratic candidate) 73, and Fuller 41, with five votes cast for other candidates.

Whatever his reasoning, the New York *Herald* correctly noted that Fuller's revelation "changed the whole aspect of things." What little sympathy had existed in the North for Fuller and his supporters vanished, because Fuller's revelation left Banks as the only candidate who favored repeal of the Kansas-Nebraska Act. Only five North Americans continued to vote for Fuller at this point, yet those who deserted him switched not to Banks but to a variety of hopeless candidates.[14]

As the speakership deadlock dragged on into January, most Northerners could not understand how representatives who claimed to oppose the Kansas-Nebraska Act could continue to oppose Banks, the only anti-Nebraska candidate in the field. Petitions circulated calling for the resignation of the "dough-face" Know Nothings, and newspaper columns overflowed with denunciations of their recalcitrance. North American newspapers attempted to distance themselves from the holdouts, reminding their readers that an overwhelming majority of North American congressmen supported Banks and condemning "Fuller's disgraceful surrender to Southern demagogues." Yet with each passing day, resentment toward the Know Nothings grew stronger, while respect for the Republican party increased. Still, the National Americans refused to budge. "My course is onward," vowed National American J. Scott Harrison (son of the former President), "lead tho it may to my political destruction."[15]

Another month passed, yet by the end of January the House seemed no closer to electing a Speaker than it had been eight weeks earlier. An option that had existed from the start was to change House rules to allow a plurality to elect the Speaker. Democrats had adamantly resisted such an option since early December, believing that it would ensure Banks's selection, but they eventually concocted a plan that they thought would win them a plurality of the votes. On February 1, Democrats presented a new candidate for Speaker, William Aiken of South Carolina. Observers did not initially understand the Democratic move, but they soon realized that Aiken had not attended the Democratic speakership caucus, and was therefore not bound by the caucus pledge to oppose the Know Nothings. At first, the plan seemed to have the desired effect, because Fuller made a speech urging his supporters to switch to Aiken. Furthermore, on separate attempts to elect the Speaker by resolution, Aiken received more votes than Banks. The next morning, with many Democrats thinking that they could elect Aiken, the plurality rule won approval.[16]

14. Scranton *Herald*, Dec. 22, 1855; *CG*, 54–55; New York *Herald* quoted in New York *Mirror*, Dec. 20, 1855; J. Scott Harrison to Benjamin Harrison, Dec. 28, 1855, Benjamin Harrison Papers, LC.

15. Chambersburg *Transcript*, Jan. 30, 1856 (quotation); Hamilton [Ohio] *Intelligencer*, Jan. 3, 1856; Pottsville *Miner's Journal*, Dec. 15, 22, 1855, Jan. 19, 26, 1856; J. Scott Harrison to Benjamin Harrison, Dec. 16, 28 (quotation), 1855, Benjamin Harrison Papers, LC; William W. Valk, *Letter of Mr. Valk . . . on the Occurrences Which Have Prevented an Organization of the House of Representatives of the Thirty Fourth Congress* (Washington, 1856).

16. Alexander H. Stephens to Linton Stephens, Feb. 1, 1856, in Richard M. Johnston and William H. Browne, *Life of Alexander H. Stephens* (Philadelphia, 1878), 305–6; Harrington, "First Northern Victory," 200–201.

Although many Democrats now believed that they would capture the Speakership, they soon discovered that they had stumbled into a carefully laid trap. Several National Americans from the North had purposely misled the Democrats, voting for Aiken in order to entice Democrats to support the plurality rule. After recognizing the ruse, some Democrats tried to rescind the plurality rule, but with many of their party's members tiring of the stalemate, the motion failed. While nearly all South Americans voted for Aiken on the final ballot, National Americans from the North voted either for Fuller or Campbell or abstained, enabling Banks to defeat Aiken, 103 to 100. After 63 days and 133 ballots, the most protracted speakership contest in American history had finally come to an end.[17]

Although the new Speaker was a Know Nothing and had been elected primarily with Know Nothing votes, Banks's victory was disastrous for the American party, because the public interpreted it as a Republican triumph. North Americans attempted to change this perception, cheering Banks's victory as heartily as the Republicans and pointing out that the refusal of the northern National Americans to support Aiken had secured Banks the speakership. But the public saw Banks's triumph as part of a northern movement that put anti-slavery above all other issues, a movement they identified as Republicanism. The speakership election also provided the boost Republicans needed to invigorate their new party, thereby further injuring the American party. "We have got our party formed[,] consolidated and established" declared Giddings after Banks's victory. Weed agreed that in the wake of the speakership contest, "the Republican party is now inaugurated." In contrast, the resentment generated by the National Americans during the speakership contest made "Americanism" a term of opprobrium in the North. Politicians who had scrambled to join Know Nothing lodges a year earlier now hurried to distance themselves from the Order. Know Nothing congressman James Thorington of Iowa, for example, felt obligated to inform his constituents that he did not sympathize "with the so-called American party as exhibited on the floor of this Congress."[18] Finally, the fact that the speakership contest became a struggle between North and South persuaded many Northerners to abandon the idea of establishing a national Know Nothing party. When the contest became close, nearly all the South Americans voted for Aiken, convincing most moderate Know Nothings that only an avowedly northern party could hope to counteract southern unanimity. A Boston Know Nothing told Banks that because of the cooperation between southern Know Nothings and Democrats, more Northerners "are opening their eyes to the wickedness of the pro-slavery men," and this was "fast accomplishing among our people a fusion"

17. *CG*, 337; G. Bailey to Chase, Feb. 21, 1856, Chase Papers, LC; Jacob Broom to Banks, Aug. 11, 1858, cited in Harrington, "First Northern Victory," 201 n. 55.

18. Giddings quoted in William E. Gienapp, *The Origins of the Republican Party, 1852–1856* (New York: Oxford Univ. Press, 1987), 247; Weed to Banks, Feb. 3, 1856, Banks Papers, LC; Ronald F. Matthias, "The Know Nothing Movement in Iowa" (Ph.D. diss., University of Chicago, 1965), 121.

that "no action of parties here could secure." Although this Know Nothing had previously opposed fusing with the Republicans, he now supported a "union of all men [opposed] to southern dictation or 12th sectionism." In the wake of the speakership contest, thousands of moderate Know Nothings came to the same conclusion.[19]

Events in Washington had thus entirely changed Know Nothing prospects. After the November elections and the Cincinnati convention, it seemed likely that conservatives and moderates would combine forces to make the American party a viable and potentially successful national organization. But during the speakership contest, moderate Know Nothings had instead joined forces with the fusionists to help elect Banks. In addition, the speakership contest had led most North Americans to identify with the fusionist faction of their organization. Unless the National Americans could find some way to recapture the support of the moderates, whose commitment to fusion was still tenuous, the American party would lose most of its northern supporters. National Americans hoped that the party's presidential nominating convention, scheduled to convene in Philadelphia just two weeks after Banks's victory, would provide the opportunity to reinvigorate their organization.

Although the Know Nothing party had undergone many changes since it burst on the American political scene in 1854, the front-runner for its presidential nomination had always been Millard Fillmore. Early support for the ex-President among Know Nothings was not the result of Fillmore's sympathy for nativism. In fact, Fillmore had done nothing during his long political career to suggest that he endorsed the Know Nothings' anti-immigrant agenda. But the earliest Know Nothings had emphasized patriotism and national unity as much as anti-Catholicism, and veteran nativists believed that Fillmore's devotion to the Union (as demonstrated during the crisis of 1850) would enable him to defuse sectional tensions. As early as June 1854, when the Order still had relatively few adherents, most Know Nothings supported Fillmore for president. At that time, Haven informed his former law partner that "the Know Nothings are determined to concentrate on you & make you the next Prest." Reports from other Know Nothing strongholds also indicated that veteran nativists overwhelmingly preferred Fillmore for the presidency.[20]

Fillmore did not initially plan to join forces with the Know Nothings. With anti-slavery Whigs poised to enter the Republican party, Fillmore's faction (known as the "Silver Grays" or National Whigs) believed that conservatives would finally regain control of the Whig party. In October 1854, Silver Gray leader Francis Granger informed Fillmore that immediately after the Novem-

19. L. Benker to Banks, Dec. 24, 1855, Banks Papers, IISHL.

20. E. Winslow to Charles Sumner, June 27, 1854, Sumner Papers, HU; Haven to Fillmore, June 29, 1854 (quotation), J. Randolph to Fillmore, Sept. 26, 1854, Henry Timison et al. to Fillmore, Oct. 2, 1854, James W. Hale [president of first Know Nothing lodge] to Fillmore, March 4, 1856, Fillmore Papers, SUNY-O.

ber elections, he would issue a call for a January convention that would "reinstate the Whig Party on its old [conservative] platform." Silver Grays thought that this convention would revive their political fortunes and re-establish the National Whigs as a national political force.[21] After the 1854 elections, however, the Silver Grays began to have second thoughts. Know Nothing strength in those elections, and the number of Silver Grays who voted for the Order's tickets, surprised National Whig leaders. "There is hardly a school house or cross roads or black smiths shop but the boys have an organization there," Haven reported excitedly, and he believed that "they will be found as plentiful or more so in Va, Kentucky, Tennessee & Mississippi than they are in N.Y." With this new party gaining members so quickly, many Silver Gray leaders suggested that National Whigs abandon attempts to revive the Whig party and instead join forces with the Know Nothings. "Shall we fight as the *'National Whigs,'* or as the *'American Party'*"? asked Alexander Mann, a Rochester Silver Gray, in the wake of the 1854 contests. "My own impressions incline me to the latter designation. Would we not gain everything and lose nothing by adopting it, & thus avail ourselves of the resistless Know Nothing element?" Although Silver Grays did not like everything about the Order, they believed it could, as Haven put it, "be worked . . . into a national fabrick which should be of service" to National Whigs.[22]

Although most Silver Gray leaders had adopted this view by the end of 1854, Fillmore was still hesitant. His reluctance stemmed in part from the Order's secrecy, which the ex-President believed would retard its growth and popularity. Fillmore also abhorred the Free Soilers who dominated the organization in places such as Massachusetts, and feared that the Order might become an anti-slavery vehicle. In addition, although he probably approved of the mild nativism that had tinged the Whig party, Fillmore lacked enthusiasm for the Order's strident anti-Catholicism. At one point in 1855, Fillmore criticized "the corrupting influence which the contest for the foreign vote is exciting upon our elections," asserting that "our country should be governed by American-born citizens." But this letter, obviously written for publication and aimed at impressing Know Nothings, exaggerated Fillmore's devotion to Americanism.[23] Although he tried to make it appear otherwise, the enrollment of a daughter in a Catholic school and his generous donations for the construction of Catholic churches demonstrated that Fillmore did not sympa-

21. Francis Granger to Fillmore, Oct. 24, 1854, E. R. Jewett to [Fillmore], Oct. 24, [1854], Fillmore Papers, SUNY-O; New York *Times*, Nov. 1, 1854.
22. Haven to Fillmore, Jan. 10, 1855 (first quotation), Dec. 9, 1854 (final quotation), Fillmore Papers, SUNY-O; A. Mann to Ullmann, Nov. 16, 1854, Ullmann Papers, NYHS.
23. Fillmore to Dorothea Dix, Oct. 30, 1856, in Charles M. Snyder, ed., *The Lady and the President: The Letters of Dorothea Dix and Millard Fillmore* (Lexington: Univ. of Kentucky Press, 1975), 258; Fillmore to Edward Everett, Dec. 12, 1854, April 7, 1855, Everett Papers, MHS; Fillmore to Isaac Newton, Jan. 3, 1855, *Millard Fillmore Papers, Volume Two*, ed. Frank H. Severance (Buffalo: Buffalo Historical Society, 1907), 347–49 (quotation).

thize with the militant Protestantism that inspired most American nativists. Throughout his political career, Fillmore had worked to achieve harmony and consensus, and he valued religious amity as much as sectional tranquility. It was not nativism, but rather his belief that Know Nothingism provided the "only hope of forming a truly national party, which shall ignore this constant and distracting agitation of slavery," that finally persuaded Fillmore to link his political future with that of the Know Nothings.[24]

Haven admitted to Fillmore that "the forms and mode of admission I imagine are somewhat puerile, nay they may for all I know border on foolishness. . . ." This posed a serious problem for Fillmore, because men of his social standing rarely joined such organizations. "It cannot be that he has undergone the initiatory humiliations," commented one blue-blooded Whig concerning Fillmore's dilemma. Indeed, the ex-President was reluctant to sneak through the back door of some Odd Fellows Hall to undergo initiation with the rest of the lodge. Haven eventually provided the solution. "If you choose to enlist," he told Fillmore in early January 1855, "I can make them dispense with any usual proceedings, I think, and make them send a man quietly to your house or chambers to attend to the business." This was the course that Fillmore eventually followed. As he later described it, "I finally overcame my scruples and at a council in my own house, previous to my departure to Europe, I was initiated into the Order. . . ."[25]

Although political odds-makers quickly installed Fillmore as the prohibitive favorite to win the Know Nothing presidential nomination, support for the ex-President weakened as anti-slavery, pro-temperance lodge members began to outnumber veteran nativists in Know Nothing councils. Many of these Know Nothings were fusionists who intended to quit the Order before the presidential election and cared little about the party's nomination. But moderates who envisioned the Know Nothings as a permanent anti-slavery, anti-Catholic party opposed Fillmore, and many of them instead supported the candidacy of New York businessman George Law. Born in 1806 in upstate New York, Law represented to antebellum Americans what Rockefeller, Vanderbilt, and Carnegie would to the postbellum world. Leaving his family farm at age eighteen, Law labored as a hod carrier at a canal site. He worked his way up to stone-cutter, and then mason, and by age twenty-one he had become a contractor, building a small canal lock. Soon Law had developed a

24. Robert J. Rayback, *Millard Fillmore: Biography of a President* (Buffalo: Buffalo Historical Society, 1959), 408–9; Fillmore to Alexander H. H. Stuart, Jan. 15, 1855 (quotation), Stuart Papers, University of Virginia.

25. Fillmore left for a tour of Europe early in 1855 and did not return to the United States until mid-1856. Haven to Fillmore, Dec. 9, 1854, Jan. 10, 1855, Fillmore Papers, SUNY-O; Robert C. Winthrop to Everett, Nov. 16, 1854, Everett Papers, MHS; T. G. White to Andrew Langdon, Dec. 8, 1898, in Rayback, *Fillmore*, 396 (not quoted); Fillmore to Dix, Oct. 30, 1856, in *The Lady and the President*, 281.

successful contracting business, specializing in canal and railroad construction. As a businessman he seemed to have the Midas touch. After moving to New York City, he bought a failing bank and turned it into one of the city's largest. He also acquired a struggling railroad and transformed it into a money-maker. Next Law entered the steamship business, and he soon dominated the field.[26]

Law was a political neophyte, but realizing that much of Know Nothingism's popularity resulted from public resentment toward professional politicians, he portrayed himself as a patriotic outsider who would rescue the ship of state from corrupt politicos. In an obvious reference to Law, a nativist newspaper explained that it favored "a common sense business man" for the presidency "in preference to some country attorney, debauched by bar-room politics, and the tool of pot-house politicians."[27] The support Law received from the New York *Herald* was almost as important to his candidacy as his reform image. Although it could not match Greeley's *Tribune* in national circulation, James Gordon Bennett's *Herald* was the most widely read newspaper in New York City, and one of the most influential (especially among Democrats and independents) in the nation. Although not a nativist, Bennett constantly criticized government corruption, and he believed that by electing Law president the Know Nothings might initiate wide-ranging political reform. Hoping to create the same kind of youthful exuberance that had characterized the "Young America" movement a few years earlier, Bennett referred to Law as "Live Oak George" and called for the creation of "Live Oak" clubs to promote his candidacy. Although most veteran nativists supported Fillmore, some climbed aboard the Law bandwagon, including New York's Bayard Clark, Philadelphia's Lewis C. Levin, and the Know Nothings' first national president, James Barker. While other politicians such as Texan Sam Houston were also mentioned as possible Know Nothing presidential nominees, especially when the Order first burst upon the scene, by the spring of 1855 the race for the American party nomination had narrowed to Fillmore and Law.[28]

Fillmore's supporters, at first confident that their candidate would win the Know Nothing nomination easily, began to worry as enthusiasm for Law grew during 1855, particularly within the press. Actually, Law had gained many of his newspaper endorsements simply by purchasing the journals in question.

26. *A Sketch of the Events in the Life of George Law, Published in Advance of his Biography* (New York, 1855); "George Law," *Dictionary of American Biography* (New York: Charles Scribner's Sons, 1943), XI, p. 815.

27. New York *Mirror* quoted in Boston *Bee*, Aug. 9, 1855. Law disseminated his political views in a widely reprinted letter to Pennsylvania's Know Nothing legislators. See New York *Herald*, March 5, 1855.

28. New York *Herald*, May 9, June 2, 1855; Philadelphia *Sun* [Levin's newspaper], quoted in New York *Herald*, June 13, 1855; V. Ellis to Ullmann, July 9, 1855, Ullmann Papers, NYHS.

Nevertheless, those advocating Fillmore's candidacy worried that a public ignorant of this fact might interpret this support as part of a popular ground-swell.[29] However, Law's candidacy eventually began to founder. Most anti-slavery men soured on Law when his allies voted for Section Twelve at the Know Nothings' 1855 convention. Furthermore, the methods employed by Law's handlers embarrassed reform-minded Know Nothings, who interpreted his large campaign expenditures as an attempt to "buy" the presidency. As one Know Nothing newspaper put it, Law "is without doubt a good financier, a shrewd, active, business man and in general a go-ahead-on-the-high-pressure principle Yankee[,] but our government is neither a broker's shop, a contractor's office, or a locomotive engine, is not suited to his capacities and though it might be to him a profitable speculation to be President of the United States, it would be to the people, ruinous."[30] These factors so injured Law's candidacy that by December 1855, one of Fillmore's lieutenants was able to report that the Law men were "pretty well *whipped*." Yet Law's supporters mounted one last offensive, spending money freely in a desperate attempt to secure delegates to the Know Nothings' presidential nominating convention. "His partizans are active, bold, and confident, and their operations are very extensive," noted a surprised Washington Hunt on the eve of the convention. "I did not suppose it possible, but I begin to suspect that his nomination at Phila[delphia] is not so impossible."[31]

Know Nothings from across the nation flocked to Philadelphia in February 1856 to choose the American party's presidential nominee. Following the advice of the North American convention, the National Council convened four days prior to the nominating convention, "for the purpose of *harmoniz-ing* the party, and *healing* the breach occasioned by the enactment of the '12th section.' " Yet the futility of this task soon became apparent. At first, the Council voted to replace Section Twelve with a pledge (written by veteran Massachusetts nativist Alfred B. Ely) to "abide by the principles and provisions of the Constitution of the United States" concerning slavery, "yielding no more and claiming no less." Although this new slavery plank seemed ambiguous, northern delegates liked it because it did not require acquiescence to the Kansas-Nebraska Act. Southerners, who had voted almost unani-

29. Haven to Fillmore, June 29, Dec. 6, 1855, March 2, 1856, Fillmore Papers, SUNY-O; D. D. Barnard to Hamilton Fish, Feb. 29, 1856, Fish Papers, LC; S. H. Hammond to Ullmann, April 24, 29, 1855, Ullmann Papers, NYHS; New York *Express* quoted in Boston *Bee*, March 5, 1856.

30. Youngstown *True American*, March 28, 1855; Harrisburg *Herald*, March 10, 1855; L. S. Parsons to Ullmann, Nov. 17, 1855, Ullmann Papers, NYHS; Hartford *Courant*, June 11, 1855 (excerpt from Norwich *State Guard*, quotation), Jan. 29, 1856.

31. S. Sammons to Ullmann, Nov. 24, Dec. 19, 1855; James Thompson to Ullmann, Dec. 26, 1855 (quotation), Jan. 27, 1856, J. P. Faurot to Ullmann, Jan. 31, 1856, Ullmann Papers, NYHS; New York *Times*, Dec. 14, 1855; Washington Hunt to Hamilton Fish, Feb. 7, 1856, Fish Papers, LC.

mously against it, were outraged, and threatened to abandon the party unless the new plank was rescinded.[32]

The following day, however, northern conservatives joined forces with the Southerners to undo the previous day's action. This coalition won approval of an entirely new platform, one previously adopted by District of Columbia Know Nothings. Written by Washington *American Organ* editor Vespasian Ellis, the new platform did not vary substantially from the old document. In place of Section Twelve, though, the Washington platform called for "the maintenance and enforcement of all laws constitutionally enacted until said laws shall be repealed, or shall be declared null and void by competent judicial authority." Ellis thought that Northerners would endorse this substitute, because it removed all mention of slavery from the party's platform (as many Northerners had originally advocated) and no longer called the Kansas-Nebraska Act the "final and conclusive settlement" of the slavery issue. But northern Know Nothings realized that their constituents would interpret the new slavery plank as a tacit endorsement of the Nebraska bill. It might seem odd that the convention should change course so abruptly, adopting two different platforms in two days. However, the minority of Northerners who supported Ellis's proposal after having voted for Ely's did so because they thought that southern defections over Ely's platform would destroy the party. Despite their misgivings about Ellis's proposal, they considered it "a test vote [to decide] whether we should continue as an American party, or disband in confusion and forever disgraced. . . ." As a result, the Ellis platform won approval, even though most northern delegates opposed it. Thus, the National Council, called to mollify Northerners, left most of them as angry and frustrated as before.[33]

Know Nothings had hoped that by restricting the platform debate to the National Council they could present a harmonious façade at their nominating convention. Yet when that meeting convened on February 22 in National Hall, there was little fraternal concord in evidence. Acrimonious debate immediately broke out over the seating of delegates. As in 1855, two Louisiana organizations—one admitting Creole Catholics and the other excluding them—competed for recognition. Pennsylvania had also sent two delegations, one representing the regular organization and the other appointed by the councils that had seceded from the state organization when it repudiated Section Twelve. Attempting to forge a compromise, the Committee on Credentials suggested that the convention seat the anti–Section Twelve Pennsylvania delegation (which pleased the North) and the Catholic Louisiana delegation (as the

32. Thomas Spooner, "To the State Council," January 3, 1856, Cincinnati Public Library; New York *Times*, Feb. 21, 1856. Northern delegates voted 103 to 18 in favor of this resolution, while Southerners voted 41 to 3 against it.

33. New York *Times*, Feb. 22, 1856 (quotation); V. Ellis to Ullmann, March 2, 1856, Ullmann Papers, NYHS; W. P. Simpson [Ohio delegate] to the Editor, St. Clairsville [Ohio] *Independent Republican*, March 20, 1856 (quotation). The new platform was adopted by a 108 to 77 margin.

South demanded). The convention proceeded in chaotic fashion as it debated the committee's recommendations. "Members ran about the hall as if they were mad," reported the New York *Times*, "and roared like bulls." When the convention finally endorsed the Committee's recommendations at three in the morning, neither side was happy. Veteran nativists complained that seating the Catholic delegates had "*unamericanized* the American party," while a number of Southerners walked out, insisting that they would not participate unless Section Twelve was reinstated.[34]

At the start of the second day's proceedings, former governor Richard K. Call of Florida stated that he too could not remain in the convention unless Section Twelve was restored, and bedlam broke loose as Call began exiting the hall. With tears streaming down his cheeks, Know Nothing president E. B. Bartlett pleaded with Call and his fellow Southerners to stay, and surprised everyone by moving that the convention adjourn until July. Many pro-Fillmore Know Nothings had initially favored postponing the nomination, in part because they wanted more time to evaluate the political situation, but primarily because an early nomination would leave too much time for Fillmore's opponents to attack him.[35] When a second delegate proposed delaying the nomination until the summer,

> the Convention returned again to its accustomed confusion with greater gusto than ever before. Almost every delegate was seized with a sudden desire to test the strength utmost of his lungs, and a fish-peddler from New-York added his modicum of voice to the general roar. After that you might have combined the bellowings of all the bulls of Bashan without perceptibly increasing the aggregate roar.[36]

With many Fillmore supporters already predisposed to adjourn, one would have expected the motion to carry easily. But on the previous day, a delegate at the Republican convention then meeting in Pittsburgh had read aloud a telegraph sent from Philadelphia by Ohio Know Nothing president Thomas Spooner. "The American Party are no longer united," Spooner reported, no doubt referring to the contentious conclusion of the National Council. "Raise the Republican banner. Let there be no further extension of slavery. The Americans are with you."[37] Republicans cheered wildly when they heard Spooner's message, but when word of it reached Philadelphia, the mood at the Know Nothing convention changed perceptibly. The Americans feared

34. New York *Times*, Feb. 23, 1856; Kenneth Rayner to Ullmann, June 2, 1856, Ullmann Papers, NYHS.

35. Washington *American Organ* quoted in Albany *State Register*, Sept. 12, 1855; J. P. Faurot to Ullmann, Nov. 15, 1855, Ullmann Papers, NYHS; F. W. Prescott to Amos A. Lawrence, Dec. 17, 1855, Lawrence Papers, MHS; Haven to Fillmore, Jan. 20, 1856, N. K. Hall to Fillmore, Feb. 4, 1856, Fillmore Papers, SUNY-O; Hartford *Courant*, Feb. 18, 1856.

36. New York *Times*, Feb. 25, 1856. For evidence that this description was not an exaggeration, see George Norris to John M. Clayton, Feb. 23, 1856, Clayton Papers, LC.

37. Telegraph quoted in Hartford *Courant*, Feb. 23, 1856; Spooner to Chase, Feb. 5, 1856, Chase Papers, LC.

that Spooner's telegraph was part of a plot to divide the party, so that northern nativists would be "switched off onto the Republican track before the [American] convention reassembled" in July as proposed. Realizing that the Republicans "would be glad to have this convention break up" and that adjournment seemed tantamount to dissolving the party, the delegates ended the second day's session by defeating the motion to adjourn.[38]

The convention did not meet on Sunday, but resumed its deliberations on Monday morning. When Parson William G. Brownlow of Tennessee moved to proceed with the presidential nomination, Edmund Perkins of Connecticut rose to protest. The northern delegates would leave the convention if it began making nominations, he pledged, because northern voters would not support the party's nominee unless its platform explicitly opposed slavery above the Missouri Compromise line. Despite Perkins's threat, the delegates voted 151 to 51 to begin the nomination process, at which point most of the delegates from New England, and some from Pennsylvania, Ohio, Illinois, and Iowa, left the hall. With most of the anti-slavery delegates absent, Fillmore out-polled Law 179 to 24 (with 40 votes scattered), at which point Fillmore was declared the party's nominee. The convention then chose Andrew Jackson Donelson of Tennessee (Jackson's nephew) as their vice presidential nominee, and adjourned.[39]

That evening the seceders from the North met at the Merchants' Hotel to plot strategy. They drafted a "Declaration of Principles" that condemned the convention's refusal to demand restoration of the Missouri Compromise and insisted that "the admission . . . of the delegates from Louisiana, representing Roman Catholic constituents, absolved every true American from all obligations to sustain the actions" of the gathering. While the sixty-seven delegates in attendance unanimously endorsed this part of the address, they divided over what future action to take. The proposed declaration called for the delegates to re-convene in New York on June 12 to make their own presidential nomination, but fusionists led by Spooner and Iowa's William Penn Clarke complained that a separate North American nomination would divide the North and make victory in the presidential election impossible. However, most of those present felt that if the bolters did not maintain their separate identity, the Republican party would quickly absorb the Know Nothings. As a result, the plan for the North American convention was ratified with only four dissenting votes.[40]

Some northern Know Nothings applauded Fillmore's nomination. A Pennsylvania journal called him "an American, a truly national man, and a statesman

38. Haven to Ullmann, Feb. 29, 1856 (quotation), Ullmann Papers, NYHS; speeches of J. M. Keith and Alfred B. Ely in Boston *Bee*, March 3, 7 (quotation), 1856; D. O. Kellogg to Fillmore, Feb. 29, 1856, Haven to Fillmore, March 2, 1856, Fillmore Papers, SUNY-O.

39. New York *Times*, Feb. 26, 1856; William B. Hesseltine, ed., *Trimmers, Trucklers & Temporizers: Notes of Murat Halstead from the Political Conventions of 1856* (Madison: State Historical Society of Wisconsin, 1961), 3–7.

40. New York *Times*, Feb. 26, 1856; Hesseltine, *Trimmers, Trucklers & Temporizers*, 10–11. The seceding New York delegates (all Law supporters) arrived well after the meeting had begun, so they issued a separate protest.

of recognised ability." Responding to northern displeasure with the new platform, the New York *Express* insisted that Fillmore's "administration of the
Government for nearly three years is 'platform' enough for any reasonable
man." Those Northerners who believed that "no question must be allowed to
disturb the peace and harmony of the country" predicted sure victory for the
Fillmore ticket.[41]

Despite these endorsements, most northern Know Nothings refused to
support the ex-President. "At almost any other time we would have hailed the
nomination of Millard Fillmore with delight," commented one Indiana newspaper. It refused to do so, however, because "he has been nominated upon a
slavery extension platform. . . . [The slavery issue] cannot be ignored and we
will support no one who is disposed to ignore it." A leading Iowa Know
Nothing likewise explained that "I am an American, and expect to stick to
that party & its principles, but I will not vote for any man who is not opposed
to the extension of slavery." One of the most remarkable attacks on Fillmore's
nomination came from the Albany *State Register*. For more than a year the
State Register had argued that Republicans exaggerated the importance of the
slavery issue. But after Southerners at Philadelphia forced through a pro-
slavery platform and dictated the nomination of the "dough-faced" Fillmore,
the *Register*'s editor admitted that he had been lying to his readers:

> All political action, all political principles, all political policy, every political
> movement, begins and ends with Slavery. It is the Alpha and Omega of every
> sect, every party, and every creed. It controls every Southern vote, is the
> burthen of every Southern speech, the guide of every Southern man's
> footsteps;—and we of the North must be, are compelled, whether we will or
> not, to be for it or against it. There is no longer a middle course—no neutral
> ground. We have struggled against this conviction till we can struggle no
> longer. . . .

Believing that Fillmore had pressed "the American party into the service of
slavery," most northern Know Nothings repudiated his nomination.[42]

Doubt about Fillmore's dedication to the anti-slavery cause was not the
only reason that northern Know Nothings opposed his candidacy. Many cited
his lack of record as a nativist. "Surely there was time enough in which to say
something, or do something to testify his sympathy with the American movement," insisted the *State Register*. The admission of Catholic delegates from
Louisiana and the removal of all anti-Catholic rhetoric from the platform
proved to another Know Nothing journal that "Americanism" had become "a
secondary . . . issue" with the party. An Ohio editor called "slavery and

41. Pottsville *Miner's Journal*, March 1, 1856; New York *Express*, Feb. 26, 1856; New York
Mirror, Feb. 26, 1856; St. Clairsville [Ohio] *Independent Republican*, March 13, 1856 (quotation); Philadelphia *News*, Feb. 27, 1856.

42. Aurora [Indiana] *Standard* quoted in Carl F. Brand, "The History of the Know Nothing
Party in Indiana," *Indiana Magazine of History* 18 (1922): 270; Matthias, "Know Nothing Movement in Iowa," 158 n. 1; Albany *State Register*, Feb. 29 (final quotation), March 3 (block
quotation), 1856.

political Romanism . . . the two great evils" threatening the nation, stating that he could not support Fillmore because he and his platform ignored these issues. Asserting that "the mighty arm of our noble order has been prostituted to subserve the interests of papal power and slavery aggression," Ohio Know Nothing leader Thomas Ford called upon northern nativists to divorce themselves "from the hydra-headed monsters of Popery and Slavery" and renounce Fillmore's nomination.[43]

The depth of negative reaction to Fillmore's nomination shocked not only conservative Know Nothings but Republicans as well. Fillmore's nomination initially left Thurlow Weed "ill at ease," but after witnessing the near universal condemnation of his candidacy, the Republican strategist admitted that he had overestimated the ex-President's appeal. Banks likewise reported from Washington that "here the nomination of Fillmore is dead," predicting that not a single Know Nothing congressman who had supported him for Speaker would endorse Fillmore. Another Republican reported that "Fillmore's nomination has knocked all the breath out of K Nism in the North."[44]

Despite this initial negative reaction, Americans who supported Fillmore's nomination believed that northern nativists would eventually embrace his candidacy. Massachusetts textile magnate Amos A. Lawrence predicted that with no viable alternative, northern Know Nothings would eventually "fall into line and throw up their hats for Fillmore."[45] But with condemnations of Fillmore's nomination emanating from all over the North, rumors soon spread that he would decline the nomination. These rumors gained such credence that they impeded campaign organization, and the ex-President's handlers were mortified when Fillmore wrote from Europe that he would not formally accept the nomination for several months. Haven and others implored the ex-President to accept immediately, before the campaign suffered further damage. Luckily, an ice storm had prevented Fillmore from traveling on to Russia, or he would not have received these notes for months. When Fillmore returned to Paris, however, he found the correspondence, and hastily sent off his acceptance letter.[46] With Fillmore in Europe and out of touch

43. Albany *State Register*, Feb. 29, 1856; Jamestown [New York] *Journal*, March 7, 1856; Steubenville *True American*, March 5, 1856; Thomas H. Ford to Ohio Know Nothing Deputies, March 4, 1856, quoted in Steubenville *True American*, Aug. 13, 1856.

44. Weed to Seward, Feb. 27 (quotation), March 5, 15, 1856, T. Cary to Seward, May 1, 1856, Seward Papers, UR; E. Dodd to Weed, March 13, 1856, Hamilton Fish to Weed, March 22, 1856, Weed Papers, UR; Banks to Isaac Sherman, March 1, 1856, Sherman Papers, Private Collection; E. P. Smith to Henry C. Carey, March 17, 1856 (quotation), Carey Papers, HSP; J. Sanborn to Banks, April 9, 1856, Banks Papers, LC.

45. Lawrence to Henry E. Davies, Feb. 26, 1856 (quotation), S. J. Dana to Lawrence, Feb. 26, 1856, Lawrence Papers, MHS; Haven to Ullmann, Feb. 29, April 3, 1856, Ullmann Papers, NYHS.

46. Haven to Ullmann, April 3, 1856, Ullmann Papers, NYHS; I. Sherman to Banks, April 4, 1856, Banks Papers, LC; Haven to Fillmore, April 24, 1856, John P. Kennedy to Fillmore, May 31, 1856, Fillmore Papers, SUNY-O; Fillmore to Kennedy, May 6, 24, 1856, Kennedy Papers, Enoch Pratt Free Library; Fillmore to Alexander H. H. Stuart, May 21, 1856, Stuart Papers, University of Virginia.

with the rapidly changing political situation, and his candidacy widely condemned even in party strongholds, the Know Nothings' presidential campaign was obviously in serious trouble.

As Fillmore's campaign foundered, Republicans began to receive word that disgruntled nativists were flocking to the Republican organization. From Massachusetts came the news that the Fillmore nomination "has divided the K.N.'s in the Legislature down to the very roots, & . . . a goodly number of them . . . only wait the signal to join the Republicans." A disgruntled George Law promised Thurlow Weed that he would aid the Republican cause, and an Ohio Know Nothing pledged that nativists from his state would "look only to the Republican organization for advice."[47] Despite these promises of assistance, it soon became apparent that rather than join the Republican party, many northern nativists would adhere to the North American organization created by those who had seceded from the presidential nominating convention. Republicans disagreed about how to gain the support of these independent-minded nativists. Some, including William H. Seward and George Julian, insisted that their party should make no concessions to the Know Nothings. But a majority believed that Republicans ought to unite with the nativists. Republicans had hinted at this policy in February when their Pittsburgh convention ignored calls for the adoption of a resolution censuring Know Nothingism. They also omitted the word "Republican" from the official announcement of their presidential nominating convention, reasoning that an invitation to all "opposed to the repeal of the Missouri Compromise" would make North Americans feel more welcome. However, most North American leaders did not think Republicans had gone far enough, and they continued preparations for their separate nominating convention.[48]

Connecticut's spring election provided a clear signal that the North Americans would not disband voluntarily. Theoretically, the movement of anti-slavery Know Nothings into the Republican party should have proceeded smoothly in Connecticut. Anti-slavery sentiment was particularly strong among Connecticut Know Nothings, with one of the party's leaders noting that "Americanism in this state appears to be imbued with the spirit of Republicanism." The state's leading nativist journal, the Hartford *Courant*, sought a harmonious union of the anti-Democratic forces, calling "Republicanism and Americanism . . . a smart pair of yankee twins" that sought essentially identical goals. But Connecticut Know Nothings were determined to control any fusion among the state's anti-slavery forces and tried to force Republicans to nominate incumbent Know Nothing William T. Minor for governor. Some Republicans sanctioned such a move, noting that "*it is from them that our*

47. Seth Webb, Jr., to Sumner, quoted in Gienapp, *Origins of the Republican Party*, 262; Law to Weed, Aug. 12, 1856, Weed Papers, UR; Haven to Ullmann, Feb. 29, 1856, Ullmann Papers, NYHS; John Paul to Chase, Feb. 24, 1856, Chase Papers, HSP.

48. Gienapp, *Origins of the Republican Party*, 265–70; Frederick Seward, *Seward at Washington as Senator and Secretary of State*, 2 vols. (New York, 1891), II, pp. 270–71.

strength is to come." Yet most Republican leaders refused to support Minor. Instead, they nominated Gideon Welles, an outspoken critic of nativism. The Americans then re-nominated Minor. Americans and Republicans did agree to combine forces in most legislative races, but as Welles noted, the Know Nothings dictated the nomination of "every Senator in . . . [all] twenty-one districts, conceding not a single one to the Republicans."[49] On election day, Connecticut voters demonstrated that they still considered the North Americans a viable alternative to the Republican party. Minor trounced Welles, out-polling his Republican rival by four to one. Democratic candidate Samuel Ingham actually fell just 700 votes short of winning the election, but lacking a majority, the contest was thrown to the legislature, which re-elected Minor.[50] The fact that an overwhelming majority of Connecticut's anti-Democratic voters preferred the Know Nothings should have encouraged North American independence. Yet as one nativist noted, Ingham's near victory convinced most Know Nothings of "the *necessity* of *complete union* of the anti-Administration forces in order to succeed in the presidential campaign." The Connecticut election proved that Know Nothingism still held significant appeal with the electorate, but it also added impetus to the movement to unite the North American and Republican forces.[51]

The Connecticut results were somewhat unique, as North Americans in most places offered little resistance to becoming Republicans. In New Hampshire, for example, most Know Nothings had been either Free Soilers or anti-slavery Whigs, and most of the Order's leaders there had considered their organization a "halfway house" on the road to Republicanism. It therefore came as no surprise that the New Hampshire American party renamed itself the "American Republican" party in early 1856, and its emphasis on anti-slavery rather than anti-Catholicism indicated that its sympathies rested primarily with Republicanism. In Rhode Island, too, the gubernatorial candidate who had won election in April 1855 as an "American" ran in 1856 as an "American Republican," and even the state's Know Nothing organ, the Providence *Transcript*, soon began referring to his administration as Republican. In Indiana, once the stronghold of Know Nothingism in the Midwest, most Know Nothings had also become Republicans by this time. Although allotted thirteen delegates to the 1856 American party presidential nominating convention, only three Indianans bothered to attend, and only one would participate in the upcoming North American convention. However, the state's anti-Democratic fusion convention, dominated by Know Nothings, did send dele-

49. Fra[nci]s Gillette to Chase, Feb. 18, 1856, Chase Papers, LC; Hartford *Courant*, March 6, 1856; Gienapp, *Origins of the Republican Party*, 276–77; Gideon Welles to F. S. Wildman, May 17, 1856, Welles Papers, CHS. See also Robert D. Parmet, "The Know Nothings in Connecticut" (Ph.D. diss., Columbia University, 1966), 183–90.

50. Ingham won 32,704 votes (49%), Minor 26,108 (39%), Welles 6,740 (10%), and Whig John A. Rockwell 1,251 (2%). *Tribune Almanac* (1857): 45; Hartford *Courant*, April 24, 1856.

51. Dwight Loomis to Lucius Hendee, April 12, 1856, quoted in Parmet, "Know Nothings in Connecticut," 191.

gates to the *Republican* presidential nominating convention, reflecting the shift of Indiana nativists into the Republican camp. Only conservatives from southern Indiana continued to resist fusion. They maintained the American organization and endorsed Fillmore's candidacy. The Fillmore nomination convinced many Northerners that the Order had abandoned its former anti-slavery stance, and hastened their entry into the Republican ranks.[52]

The forces pushing North Americans into the Republican party received additional impetus in May from the "sack" of Lawrence, Kansas, and the caning of Senator Charles Sumner. On May 21, a posse of several hundred pro-slavery men attacked the town of Lawrence, known as the headquarters of the territory's free-state movement. The mob destroyed the presses of the town's two anti-slavery newspapers, burned the Free State Hotel, and went on a drunken spree of looting and vandalism. Just a day earlier, Massachusetts senator Charles Sumner had concluded a speech in the Senate chamber enti-tled "The Crime Against Kansas." During the long oration Sumner had in-sulted many prominent Southerners, including Senator Andrew P. Butler of South Carolina. Sumner's uncharacteristically vehement speech may have been inspired by fears that he would lose his seat when he came up for re-election that winter. Rumors had recently circulated that Know Nothings planned to replace Sumner with Gardner, and Sumner may have made the speech—his first important address in some time—in order to win support for a second term. In any case, convinced that his family's honor had been sullied, South Carolina congressman Preston Brooks, a distant relative of Butler, sought out Sumner after the Senate adjourned on May 22. Finding the senator at his desk, Brooks began beating Sumner with his cane. By the time Republi-can congressmen managed to restrain Brooks, Sumner lay unconscious in a pool of blood.[53]

The sack of Lawrence and the caning of Sumner outraged most Northern-ers, including Know Nothings. "The brutal outrage on Senator Sumner, and the pro-slavery ruffians of Kansas, have made in the North an hundred free-soilers, where yesterday there existed one," commented a leading nativist journal in Pennsylvania. Edward Everett—who though not a Know Nothing was a Fillmore supporter—likewise lamented that the Sumner-Brooks affair "will do more to strengthen the abolition party than any thing that has yet occurred." Many Know Nothing lodges officially denounced Brooks's attack. Members of Know Nothing Council 432 in Worcester even resolved to travel

52. Manchester *American*, Feb. 9, 1856; Thomas R. Bright, "The Anti-Nebraska Coalition and the Emergence of the Republican Party in New Hampshire, 1853–1857," *Historical New Hampshire* 27 (1972): 79–80; Gienapp, *Origins of the Republican Party*, 280–81; Hartford *Courant*, March 15, 1856; James W. Stone to Banks, April 23, 1856, Banks Papers, LC; Carl F. Brand, "The History of the Know Nothing Party in Indiana," *Indiana Magazine of History* 18 (1922): 271–75.

53. David M. Potter, *The Impending Crisis, 1848–1861* (New York: Harper and Row, 1976), 199–210; David Donald, *Charles Sumner and the Coming of the Civil War* (New York: Knopf, 1961), 270, 275–76, 278–89.

to Washington if necessary to defend Massachusetts congressmen from "Southern assassins." More important to National Americans, however, was the recognition that the attack on Sumner had seriously damaged Fillmore's chances for election. Many newspapers that supported Fillmore ignored the assault, perhaps realizing that any mention of the incident would aid the Republican cause. A few months later, Fillmore himself admitted that "Brooks' attack on Sumner has done more for Frémont [the Republican presidential nominee] than any 20 of his warmest friends . . . have been able to accomplish."[54]

The attack on Sumner, the sack of Lawrence, displeasure with the Fillmore nomination, the belief that northern unity was necessary to defeat the Democrats, and a growing realization that the Republican party would become the main rival of the Democrats convinced most North Americans to cooperate with the Republicans. In fact, most North American leaders wanted to nominate the leading Republican candidate, California's John C. Frémont, at the upcoming North American convention in June. However, a number of obstacles stood in their way. A few North American leaders did not want to cooperate with the Republicans at all. They preferred to make their own nomination, in an attempt to force the Republicans to accept a North American nominee. Others favored forging a coalition with the Republicans, but only if the Republicans offered a quid pro quo.[55] The most serious problem, however, involved timing. The North Americans were scheduled to gather a few days before the Republican convention in Philadelphia, and Republicans were anxious to avoid the appearance that the North American convention had dictated the Republican nominations. Republicans therefore asked the North Americans to postpone their convention and send a committee of North Americans to Philadelphia instead. This would enable the Republican convention to make its nomination first, after which the North Americans could ratify it.[56] But North Americans balked at this proposal, fearing that they would lose both face with the public and leverage with the Republicans. Finally, Republicans devised a complicated plan that satisfied North American leaders. Isaac Sherman, a mutual friend of Frémont and Nathaniel Banks, suggested to the Speaker that "the K.N.s nominate you on the 12th of

54. Pottsville *Miner's Journal*, June 7, 1856; Edward Everett Diary, May 25, 1856 (quotation), Everett to Mrs. Charles Eames, June 21, 1856, Everett Papers, MHS; Hartford *Courant*, May 31, 1856 (quotation); E. A. Warden to Seward, May 28, 1856, Seward Papers, UR; Boston *Bee*, May 22–24, 1856; Johnstown *Cambria Tribune*, May-Sept. 17, 1856; Fillmore to William A. Graham, Aug. 9, 1856, Graham Papers, University of North Carolina, Chapel Hill.

55. Jamestown [New York] *Journal*, March 28, 1856; S. M. Allen to Banks, May 31, 1856, Francis S. Edwards to Banks, June 4, 1856, Banks Papers, LC.

56. Edwin D. Morgan to James Bunce, April 17, 18, May 9, 1856 (letterbook), Morgan Papers, NYSL; Schuyler Colfax to Alfred Wheeler, May 1, 1856, Colfax Papers, LC; Isaac Sherman to Banks, May 12, 1856, Russell Sage to Banks, May 31, 1855 [1856], Banks Papers, LC; Gienapp, *Origins of the Republican Party*, 329–30; Fred Harvey Harrington, "Fremont and the North Americans," *AHR* 44 (1939): 842–48.

June for President and some Whig like [ex-Pennsylvania] Gov. Johns[t]on for Vice President and then you decline the moment the Republican convention at Philadelphia has nominated Frémont? Could we not have an understanding of this kind which would virtually give the K.N.s the nomination of the Vice President?" Banks informed Sherman that he would abide by the Republican plan, and on the eve of the North American convention, Republicans felt confident that they would dictate its outcome.[57]

When the North American convention commenced on June 12, most observers agreed that Republicans would control the proceedings. "Thurlow Weed and his set have a pretty long finger in the pie," commented the New York *Herald*, and a number of delegates met with Weed to formulate strategy before the meeting began. A message inviting a committee of North Americans to attend the Republican convention was greeted with enthusiasm, suggesting that many delegates sympathized with the Republican strategy. It soon became clear that most delegates supported Frémont, but the possibility that they might nominate him instead of Banks horrified Republicans, who feared that "the foreigners of Iowa[,] Illinois and Wisconsin will leave us en masse" if the Know Nothings nominated Frémont first. Enthusiasm for Frémont among North Americans reflected, in part, the desire to resist Republican dictation. Many North Americans, insulted that Republicans cared more about immigrants than nativists, wanted to disrupt the Republican scheme by nominating Frémont first. Frémont had met with a delegation of North Americans before the convention, and his assurance that " 'he sympathised with them, and should not appoint any foreigners to office,[']" also contributed to his surprising strength. Although the convention adjourned for the weekend after two days of debate, many believed that when the delegates re-convened, still days before the Republican convention, Frémont would win the nomination.[58]

Republicans were having trouble executing their plan because word of it had leaked out before the start of the convention. Banks's floor manager, Stephen M. Allen, explained to the Speaker that "*conservative Americans*" were afraid that "*you would not accept*—but would decline in favor of another candidate . . . thereby sinking the American party or forcing them to go back to Fillmore."[59] Many of these North Americans actually preferred Banks, but upon learning of his deal with the Republicans, they decided to support Supreme Court Justice John McLean (Frémont's chief rival for the Republican nomination). Although McLean was not a Know Nothing, many North

57. Isaac Sherman to Banks, May 4, May 24 (quotation), June 14, 1856, James W. Stone to Banks, June 14, 1856, Banks Papers, LC.

58. New York *Herald*, June 13 (quotation), 14, 15, 1856; Isaac Sherman to Banks, June 10, 1856 (quotation), S. M. Allen to Banks, June 12 (quotation), 15, 1856, Banks Papers, LC; Hartford *Courant*, June 13, 1856; "editorial correspondence," Jamestown [New York] *Journal*, June 20, 1856 [the *Journal*'s editor was a delegate to the convention].

59. George Law, William H. Johnston, and Thomas R. Ford to Banks, June 10, 1856, Horace H. Day to Banks, June 11, 1856, S. M. Allen to Banks, June 11, 12, 15 (quotation), 1856, Banks Papers, LC.

Americans preferred him to Frémont because he had expressed sympathy for nativism in the past and was perceived to be less intimate with the party's radicals than Frémont. McLean's active role in the Methodist church (a denomination heavily represented in Know Nothing lodges) further enhanced his popularity with the North Americans, as did the belief that he could out-poll Frémont in Pennsylvania, the state which many politicians believed would decide the election.[60]

To win over McLean's supporters, Banks issued assurances (through Allen) that he would not decline the North American nomination. Allen's belief that Banks *would* accept the nomination also worked in the Speaker's favor, for his earnest work on Banks's behalf probably swayed many wavering delegates. Banks may have misled Allen to add credibility to his candidacy, but it is also conceivable that the ambitious Banks was thinking of double-crossing the Republicans and forcing himself upon the Philadelphia convention.[61] Perhaps fearing such a possibility, Republicans tried to delay the North American nomination as long as possible, and their efforts had prompted the weekend adjournment. Disgusted with Republican control of the convention, a small group of delegates seceded when it re-convened on Monday and nominated Commodore Robert Stockton of New Jersey for President and North Carolina's Kenneth Rayner as his running-mate. Sensing the growing restlessness of the North Americans, fusionists realized that they could no longer delay the nomination. The convention quickly nominated Banks for President, and unanimously endorsed Johnston for Vice President. The meeting then adjourned until the 19th, allowing a committee of North Americans to accept the Republicans' invitation to attend their convention. Although many North Americans felt betrayed by the fusionists, most had become reconciled to their position and were content to await consummation of the bargain that would make Johnston the Republican vice presidential candidate.[62]

The North American delegation received a rude shock at the Republican convention in Philadelphia. When a communication from the North American committee came before the convention, anti-nativists led by Ohio's Joshua R. Giddings convinced the delegates to table it. Ignoring the North Americans, the convention proceeded with its business, adopting a platform and then nominating Frémont for President. After Frémont's nomination, a conference committee was established to discuss the vice presidency with the North American committee. The Know Nothings expected Republicans to live up to

60. E. Joy Morris to John M. Clayton, May 11, 1856, Clayton Papers, LC; McLean to Hector Orr [a prominent veteran nativist from Philadelphia], Nov. 25, 1854, McLean to Robert A. Parrish, March 3, 1855 (draft), Chauncey Shaffer to McLean, May 31, 1855, Alfred B. Ely to O.U.A. Executive Committee, July 15, 1856, McLean Papers, LC; McLean to J. Teesdale, Nov. 2, 1855, March 5, 1856, McLean Papers, OHS.

61. F. S. Edwards to Banks, June 4, 1856, A. Wakeman to Banks, June 6, 1856, S. M. Allen to Banks, June 14, 15, 1856, Ezra Clark, Jr., to Banks, June 14, 1856, Banks Papers, LC.

62. New York *Express*, June 17, 1856; New York *Herald*, June 17, 1856; Jamestown [New York] *Journal*, June 20, 1856.

their end of the bargain by nominating Johnston, but Pennsylvania Republicans vetoed Johnston's selection. The conferees suggested other Pennsylvanians with links to the Order, but Republicans would not accept Simon Cameron, and Know Nothings would not endorse David Wilmot. At two in the morning, the two sides gave up and adjourned. Having failed to reach an agreement with the North Americans, the Republicans went ahead with the vice presidential nomination the next morning, choosing William L. Dayton, a New Jersey senator unaffiliated with the Order.[63]

North Americans were furious at the disrespect shown them at Philadelphia. The Boston *Bee* complained that the Republicans had been "discourteous in the extreme, if not downright insulting," while Ford said that the North Americans had been "spurned like dogs." Disgusted with their treatment and with the Republican refusal to adhere to the bargain, many North Americans suggested that they leave their original ticket in the field.[64] This sentiment might have carried the day, reported one North American leader, "but for Col Frémont's frank conversation on Thursday night [the evening before the North American convention resumed] with a few of us and the pledge given, that Mr. Dayton's name should be withdrawn from the ticket and that of Gov. Johnston substituted. With this understanding we succeeded in calming the angry and excited delegates." Thus, when the North Americans convention re-convened on the 20th, the delegates announced that "because the safety of the Republic required it," they would ignore the Republicans' insults and replace Banks with Frémont. With three cheers for Frémont and Johnston, the North American convention adjourned, confident that the Republicans would drop Dayton and finally effect a union of the Republican and North American forces.[65]

Only half a year earlier, the Know Nothings had appeared poised to heal their sectional divisions. The North American convention in Cincinnati had made gestures of reconciliation toward the national organization, and most Know Nothing leaders in the North had opposed fusing with the Republicans. But the speakership contest changed everything. Northerners now equated sectional compromise with "dough-faceism" and viewed the National Americans as accomplices to the Slave Power. The Know Nothings' February convention in Philadelphia further alienated Northerners, as the nomination of Fillmore

63. Schuyler Colfax to Edwin D. Morgan, July 8, 1856, Morgan Papers, NYSL; New York *Herald*, June 19, 20, 1856; New York *Tribune*, June 21, 1856.

64. Boston *Bee*, June 21, 1856; Hartford *Courant*, June 21, 1856 (quoting Ford); Allen to Banks, June 21, 1856, George Law to Banks, June 23, 1856, Banks Papers, LC; E. C. Baker [Massachusetts North American delegate] in William G. Bean, "Party Transformation in Massachusetts with Special Reference to the Antecedents of Republicanism, 1848–1860" (Ph.D. diss., Harvard University, 1922), 342.

65. Z. K. Pangborn to Banks, June 25, 1856 (quotation), Banks Papers, LC; Francis H. Ruggles and Lucius G. Peck to Executive Committee of the Republican Party, June 30, 1856, Gideon Welles Papers, LC; Hartford *Courant*, June 21, 1856 (quotation); Worcester *Transcript*, June 21, 23, 1856.

and the refusal to endorse restoration of the Missouri Compromise convinced most northern Know Nothings that their national organization was hopelessly misguided. The caning of Sumner and the sack of Lawrence further decreased enthusiasm for an independent nativist organization and convinced North American leaders to strike a bargain with the Republicans. To add insult to injury, the Republicans reneged on their deal with the North Americans concerning the vice presidency, although it still seemed possible that the Republicans might replace Dayton with Johnston. On the eve of the Know Nothings' first Philadelphia convention, it had appeared certain that the Order would elect the next President. Now, just thirteen months later, the North Americans had been reduced to an auxiliary of the Republican party, while the popularity of the National Americans had also declined precipitously. Looking back upon their disastrous year, Kenneth Rayner realized, as did all Know Nothings, that "the cursed question of '*slavery*' is at the bottom of all our troubles."[66]

66. Rayner to Ullmann, June 2, 1856, Ullmann Papers, NYHS.

9

The Know Nothings and the Presidential Election of 1856

On June 22, 1856, after a fifteen-month tour of Europe, American party presidential candidate Millard Fillmore arrived in New York. Although the power and popularity of the Know Nothings had declined precipitously during Fillmore's absence, a warm welcome greeted the former President. Fireworks exploded as Fillmore's ship entered the harbor, Know Nothings fired fifty-gun salutes from both New York and New Jersey, and a committee of New York dignitaries presented him with keys to the city. American party officials did not arrange such festivities merely to demonstrate Fillmore's popularity. Nineteenth-century election etiquette discouraged overt campaigning by political candidates, but Know Nothing leaders realized that Fillmore could make impromptu remarks to the crowds that gathered to celebrate his return without breaching decorum. To provide Fillmore with many such speaking opportunities, his backers arranged similar ceremonies all along the route to his home in Buffalo.[1]

The speeches Fillmore delivered during his journey revealed how sharply the goals of the American party differed from those espoused during its heyday in late 1854 and early 1855. Instead of criticizing the political power of Catholics and immigrants, Fillmore attacked those who disturbed the harmony of the Union. He condemned "the present agitation" of the slavery issue, "which distracts the country and threatens us with civil war," and insisted that these conditions had been "recklessly and wantonly produced" by the adoption of the Kansas-Nebraska Act. Although the Democrats had initiated the crisis, Fillmore blamed the Republicans for the persistence of sectional hostility. He noted that the Republicans had "for the first time" nominated Northerners for both the presidency and vice presidency, "with the avowed purpose of electing these candidates by suffrages of one part of the

---

1. Robert J. Rayback, *Millard Fillmore: Biography of a President* (Buffalo: Buffalo Historical Society, 1959), 405–6.

Union only, to rule over the whole United States." Fillmore promised that the American party would restore sectional harmony by favoring neither North nor South, insisting that "I know only my country, my whole country, and nothing but my country."[2]

In the wake of the caning of Charles Sumner and the sack of Lawrence, however, such arguments possessed far less appeal for northern voters, and nothing illustrates this better than the criticism Fillmore received following his address at Albany. In a speech on the steps of the capitol, Fillmore asked whether Republicans "can have the madness or the folly to believe that our Southern brethren would submit to be governed by" a sectional, anti-slavery party. He predicted that the South would not, and charged the Republicans with "moral treason" for persisting in a movement that—if successful—would cause civil war. Although Fillmore intended only to dramatize the implications of a Republican victory, many Northerners believed that the ex-President had condoned southern secession. Newspapers throughout the North denounced Fillmore's comments, and both his supporters and detractors recognized that his remarks had cost the ex-President many votes. Instead of aiding his cause, Fillmore's speaking tour demonstrated that the ex-President was out of touch with the northern political sentiment and that his campaign there had little chance of success.[3]

Fillmore's failure to gain support with his "pro-Union" speeches reflected the depth of sectional polarization caused by the Kansas-Nebraska Act, the sack of Lawrence, and the caning of Sumner. Yet despite indications that sectional reconciliation was unlikely, Know Nothing campaigners continued to make pro-Unionism the centerpiece of their campaign. According to an Indiana campaign document, "either [John C. Frémont or Democrat James Buchanan] would, necessarily, be a sectional President," while "Mr. Fillmore, who is the only conservative candidate," would "inculcate between the citizens of all parts of our Union a brotherly affection." The appeal of this argument was counteracted to some extent by its negativity. Rather than promising positive accomplishments, the Americans were in effect pledging not to make a bad situation worse. This sometimes led to embarrassing campaign statements, such as that made by Buffalo's James O. Putnam, who backhandedly endorsed Fillmore by predicting that his "administration, if not brilliant, will be safe." Yet most American campaigners managed to express the Union-saving theme in positive terms. Erastus Brooks, for example, insisted that Fillmore would bring a return to "those good old times" when "no voice . . . was ever raised . . . against all COMPROMISE." Of "all men in the country," insisted Brooks, "Mr. Fillmore is the fittest to restore order out

2. *Speeches of Millard Fillmore at New York, Newburgh, Albany, Rochester, Buffalo, &c.* (n.p., 1856), 5, 11–12.
3. *Speeches of Millard Fillmore*, 12; John Read to William H. Seward, July 15, 1856, Seward Papers, UR; Amos A. Lawrence to Linus B. Comins, July 26, 1856, Fillmore to Lawrence, Aug. 17, 28, 1856, Amos A. Lawrence Papers, MHS; Joseph W. Robbins to Fillmore, Sept. 4, 1856, Fillmore to F. Cunningham, Sept. 17, 1856, G. L. Staples to Fillmore, Oct. 8, 1856, SUNY-O.

of chaos." The Americans contended that their party would break down "the barriers of extremism on either side" and return the nation to the sectional harmony that had existed when Fillmore last occupied the White House.[4]

Fillmore's supporters also insisted that his previous presidential experience made him the candidate most capable of restoring sectional harmony. His "enlightened patriotism and unerring judgment conducted us happily over the violent commotions" of the crisis of 1850, explained one campaign pamphlet. In contrast, Frémont's only political experience was a seventeen-day stint representing California in the United States Senate. Furthermore, an army court-martial had convicted Frémont of mutiny, and the Americans charged that only the influence of his father-in-law, Missouri senator Thomas Hart Benton, had saved Frémont from being thrown out of the army. Frémont's only qualifications for the presidency, said one Know Nothing, were "that he was born in South Carolina, crossed the Rocky Mountains, subsisted on frogs, lizards, snakes and grasshoppers, and captured a woolly horse." The American party insisted that only Millard Fillmore possessed the necessary experience to forge a new sectional compromise.[5]

The American party also argued that Kansas and Sumner—the Republicans' favorite campaign themes—were in fact false issues. Fillmore's backers asserted that Republicans circulated unsubstantiated reports of violence and death in Kansas for partisan purposes, and that many emigrants went to Kansas to provoke confrontations. A settler who "minded his own business," said the Americans, did not experience problems in the territory. In a typical account, one pro-Fillmore newspaper reported that an arrested free-soiler in Kansas had been offered his freedom by the pro-slavery authorities, but had refused to leave the jail, because he said that " 'the interest[s] of the Republican party require that I should remain under arrest.' " Another American campaign speaker asked, "are we to lose our senses because a few 'border ruffians' of Missouri have perpetrated outrages, not uncommon in all border life?"[6] Although they mentioned it much less frequently, Fillmore's supporters also suggested that Sumner's injuries were far less severe than Republicans admitted. Republicans had convinced Sumner that he was more sick than he really was, suggested one letter to the New York *Express*, so that the party

4. *Address of the Fillmore State Convention to the People of Indiana* (New Albany, Ind., 1856), 16; James O. Putnam, *American Principles: A Speech Delivered at a Fillmore and Donelson Ratification Meeting in Rochester, March 3d, 1856* (n.p., 1856), 16; Erastus Brooks, *Speech of Hon. Erastus Brooks at Hartford, Conn., July 8, 1856. Mr. Fillmore's Claims on Northern Men and Union Men* (n.p., 1856), 2; "Address to the People of the United States from the Fillmore State Committees of New York, Pennsylvania, Massachusetts, and Kentucky," in Rising Sun [Indiana] *Visitor*, Oct. 25, 1856.

5. Thomas C. Ware, *Address of Thomas C. Ware, President of the State Council of Ohio. Delivered May 29th, 1856* (n.p., n.d.), 2 (quotation), OHS; Oscar F. Moore, *Letter of Hon. O. F. Moore to His Constituents* (Washington, 1856), 5 (quotation); Putnam, *American Principles*, 2.

6. Rising Sun [Indiana] *Visitor*, Oct. 4, 1856; Newark *Eagle* and Fredonia *Advertiser* in Greene [New York] *Chenango American*, Nov. 15, 1855 (quotation), Sept. 25, 1856 (quotation); Putnam, *American Principles*, 15 (quotation); Philadelphia *Times*, Sept. 22, 1855.

could create hysteria similar to that fomented by the Anti-Masonic party after William Morgan's disappearance in 1826. Americans said that by exaggerating the troubles in Kansas and the injuries to Sumner, Republicans prevented voters from considering the "true" issues of the 1856 campaign.[7]

The American party also contended that Frémont could not possibly win a majority in the electoral college, and that Northerners should consequently vote for Fillmore to prevent Buchanan from carrying the election. With Frémont certain to lose every southern state, he had to triumph in nearly all the non-slave states to capture the presidency. Republicans admitted that they could not win California, which meant that Frémont had to win Pennsylvania (a state the Republicans had barely organized at the time of Frémont's nomination) plus three of four other "doubtful" states: Connecticut, New Jersey, Indiana, and Illinois. With Democrats having won easy 1855 victories in Pennsylvania, New Jersey, and Illinois, the Americans argued that Frémont "has no mathematical chance of election. . . . It is either Fillmore or Buchanan." The Americans hoped that if Republicans understood the futility of their effort, ex-Know Nothings might vote for Fillmore and help the American party triumph in November.[8]

With the Fillmore campaign concentrating on these issues, critics scoffed that the American party no longer cared about nativism. Yet the party had not completely abandoned its anti-immigrant principles. In a speech at Newburgh, New York, Fillmore had asserted that

> Americans should govern America. I regret to say that men who come fresh from the monarchies of the old world, are prepared neither by education, habits of thought, or knowledge of our institutions, to govern America. The failure of every attempt to establish free government in Europe, is demonstrative of this fact; and if we value the blessings which Providence has so bounteously showered upon us, it becomes every American to stand by the Constitution and the laws of his country, and to resolve that, independent of all foreign influence, Americans will and shall rule America.

At other stops on his tour Fillmore made similar although briefer endorsements of "Americanism." Such statements may seem surprising, in light of Fillmore's previously mentioned reluctance to endorse militant nativism. But Fillmore was undoubtedly responding to the advice of his handlers. Solomon G. Haven had warned the ex-President that his statements should be "strong[ly] American, and a little Protestant," because the Know Nothings "have the only live politics of the day, and you must satisfy them first, 2d, & last." Fillmore's statements on this issue satisfied even the most diehard nativists. A pleasantly surprised Thomas R. Whitney (founder of the Order of United Americans)

7. *Express* quoted in Laura A. White, "Was Charles Sumner Shamming, 1856–1859," *New England Quarterly* 33 (1960): 300.

8. New York *Express*, Aug. 20, 1856, in Russell McClain, "The New York *Express*: Voice of Opposition" (Ph.D. diss., Columbia University, 1955), 211 (quotation); Lewis C. Levin, *The Union Safe! The Contest Between Fillmore and Buchanan! Fremont Crushed!* (New York, 1856), 6; Ware, *Address*, 4; St. Clairsville [Ohio] *Independent Republican*, Oct. 30, 1856.

thanked Fillmore for the "frank endorsement of the American platform" since his return. "I am glad that you have planted yourself so emphatically upon the American principles," concurred veteran Pennsylvania nativist Jacob Broom after learning of the Newburgh speech. According to Broom, those remarks had helped Fillmore win support among many " 'old guard' Native Americans, who supposed that you were an 'old line' politician and would look upon our Am[eri]can principles only incidentally." The many references made in the party's campaign documents to the threat posed by immigrants and Catholics also demonstrate that the Know Nothings had not totally dropped nativism from their agenda.[9]

Know Nothing efforts to prove that Frémont was a Catholic provide additional evidence that the American party had not fully discarded its anti-Catholicism. The Americans did not invent this charge; in fact, rumors of Frémont's Catholicism had spread privately within Republican ranks prior to his nomination. But after Frémont's selection at Philadelphia, pro-Fillmore newspapers (led by Erastus Brooks's New York *Express*) made the allegation public. Quickly discovering the effectiveness of the charge, the *Express* devoted more and more space to Frémont's religious background and transformed it into a major campaign issue.[10]

Although Frémont was actually an Episcopalian (albeit an apparently non-practicing one), circumstantial evidence lent credence to the Know Nothings' charge. Frémont's father was a French Catholic, the candidate's marriage to Jessie Benton had been conducted by a priest, and he had sent his adopted daughter to a Catholic school. To these facts (which Frémont did not deny), the Americans added countless "proofs" of their own. A woman from St. Louis stated that Frémont had regularly attended Catholic mass when he lived in that city. A New York City alderman insisted that he had seen Frémont cross himself with holy water at the cathedral in Washington. Several army veterans testified that Frémont had practiced Catholicism while residing in California, and the Americans eagerly reprinted articles from Catholic newspapers in Boston, New York, and St. Louis that identified Frémont as a Catholic.[11]

At first, Frémont's supporters believed that the "Catholic issue" would

9. *Speeches of Millard Fillmore*, 10–11 (quotation), 13, 17; Haven to Fillmore, May 11, 25, 1856, Whitney to Fillmore, July 21, 1856, Broom to Fillmore, June 30, 1856, W. S. Tisdale to Fillmore, July 8, 1856, Fillmore Papers, SUNY-O; Levin, *The Union Safe*, 4; Ware, *Address*, 5; Putnam, *American Principles*, 7–12; Hiram Ketchum, *Connecticut Aroused! Great Demonstration at New Haven. Speech of the Hon. Hiram Ketchum* (New Haven, 1856), 4–11; Brooks, *Speech at Hartford*, 3–5.

10. William E. Gienapp, *The Origins of the Republican Party, 1852–1856* (New York: Oxford Univ. Press, 1987), 368; G. Wright to I. Sherman, Sept. 24, 1856, Sherman Papers, Private Collection; New York *Express*, July–Nov., 1856; Edwin D. Morgan to Thomas B. Carroll, July 30, 1856, Morgan Papers, NYSL.

11. *Fremont's Romanism Established* (n.p., 1856); *Colonel Fremont's Religious History. The Authentic Account. Papist or Protestant, Which?* (n.p., 1856); *J. C. Fremont's Record. Proof of His Romanism* (n.p., 1856).

have little impact on the presidential contest. "It is too ridiculous an accusation . . . to affect the vote of any man," insisted the Hartford *Courant*. However, the charge soon gained credence among many voters. Thurlow Weed found that "the Catholic story is doing much damage," while a Rhode Island Republican reported that in his vicinity the accusation was "swallowed as gospel truths—alienating from [Frémont's] support hundreds [or] thousands" of voters. Former Know Nothings were especially cognizant of the rumor's damaging effects. Schuyler Colfax claimed that of "the hundreds of letters" he received from the Midwest, "scarcely any omits a reference to the fact that the Catholic story injures us materially, both in keeping men in the Fillmore ranks who ought to be with us, & in cooling many of our own friends who fear from Col. F's silence & the cloud of rumors on the subject in K.N. papers, that there may be some truth in it." In another letter Colfax warned that "these Catholic reports must be extinguished, or we shall lose Pa, N.J., Inda., Conn. & Lord knows how many more states." Simon Cameron expressed his concerns about the rumor to Horace Greeley, and by August ex-Know Nothing Thaddeus Stevens predicted that "the cry of Fremont's Catholicism has . . . lost us the Nation."[12]

The Catholic charge gained such widespread acceptance in part because Republicans initially made no effort to deny it. "I am opposed to conceding even to notice the New York *Express* . . . though they still declare him a Catholic," explained Republican national chairman Edwin D. Morgan. "This is intended to hurt and perhaps it does but if Frémont should deny it over his own signature they would make some other charge." Frémont adviser Isaac Sherman agreed that while "it is true that Col. F. is not a Catholic . . . it would be highly imprudent to authorize any person to deny the charge." Yet as damage reports continued to pour in during the summer, Republican leaders finally decided to respond by issuing pamphlets refuting the allegation.[13] By this point, however, much of the damage was irreversible. The Know Nothings had diligently collected and published the "proofs" of Frémont's Catholicism since July, and stump speakers had concentrated on this issue as well. Immediately recognizing the potential impact of the Catholic charge, New York Know Nothing president Stephen Sammons had recommended that letters be written to "each of the Methodist, Baptist, and other religious organs on the subject of Frémont's Catholicism & gotten into those papers by hook or by crook[,] for love or for money. This would drive the best nail in his

12. Hartford *Courant*, July 17, 1856; Weed to Morgan, Aug. 9, 1856, Morgan Papers, NYSL; James Walker to Salmon P. Chase, Sept. 22, 1856, Chase Papers, LC; Colfax to John Bigelow, Aug. 29, 1856, Bigelow Papers, NYPL; Colfax to Francis P. Blair, Sr., Aug. 15, 1856, quoted in Gienapp, *Origins of the Republican Party*, 370; Greeley to Cameron, Sept. 15, 1856, Cameron Papers, LC; Stevens to E. D. Gazzam, Aug. 24, 1856 (copy), Edward McPherson Papers, LC.

13. Morgan to Thomas B. Carroll, July 30, 1856 (quotation), Morgan Papers, NYSL; Colfax to Sherman, Aug. 5, 1856, Sherman to N. Davis, Sept. 21, 1856 (quotation), Sherman Papers, Private Collection; Truman Smith to Thaddeus Stevens, Aug. 18, 1856, Stevens Papers, LC; *Col. Frémont Not a Roman Catholic* ([New York, 1856]); *Frémont A Protestant* (n.p., 1856).

political coffin." The Know Nothings definitely damaged the Republican campaign with the Catholic charge, because, as the New York *Mirror* noted, "tens of thousands of the more bigoted Protestants persist in the belief, after all denials, that Col Fremont is a little fishy on the Catholic question."[14]

Although the prominence of the Catholic charge has obscured the fact, observers were essentially correct when they asserted that the American party had dropped nativism from its agenda. "Do you notice that KNism has utterly sunk all discussion of its leading principles," wrote New York Republican E. Pershine Smith to a Pennsylvania colleague. "It has nothing to say against foreigners, and its only allusion to Catholicism is in connection with the charge against Fremont."[15] A comparison of the Know Nothing campaigns of 1854 and 1856 demonstrates the accuracy of Smith's observation. With conservative Whigs now firmly in control of the Know Nothings, American party campaign documents ignored issues that eighteen months earlier had formed the core of the Order's agenda. These included the twenty-one-year delay before naturalization, bans on the importation of paupers and convicts, the disbanding of immigrant militia units, continued use of the Bible in public schools, a prohibition on the use of public tax dollars for parochial education, and the implementation of church property laws that would prevent Catholic leaders from controlling large amounts of real estate. Absent as well was the promise of political reform, for the Americans no longer presented their organization as an alternative to the professional politicians and corrupt parties that dominated American politics. Anti-slavery and temperance, key factors in the Know Nothings' 1854 triumphs, had also been jettisoned. In sum, the American party of 1856 was but a pale shadow of the original Know Nothing movement.

The American party platform of 1856 bore so little resemblance to the original Know Nothing agenda because most of the Northerners who had shaped the organization supported Frémont. Most North Americans justified this stance on the grounds that Northerners could no longer tolerate southern aggression. A Know Nothing newspaper in upstate New York that had previously counseled compromise with the South admitted that "the events of the last two years have proved the folly of all this policy. . . . With every new concession on the part of the North comes new demands on the part of the South, until association in politics with southern men, is equivalent to stultification and disgrace. . . . The Thirteen Millions of Free White citizens of the North," concluded its editor in explaining his endorsement of Frémont, "have long enough been governed

14. V. Ellis to [J. Scott Harrison], Sept. 3, 1856, Harrison Papers, LC; Sammons to Fillmore, July 24 (quotation), 28, 1856, Fillmore Papers, SUNY-O; N. Sargent to Ullmann, July 15, 1856, S. C. Busey to Ullmann, Aug. 11, Sept. 1, 1856, Ullmann Papers, NYHS; Cincinnati *Times* in St. Clairsville [Ohio] *Independent Republican*, Oct. 16, 1856; New York *Mirror* quoted in Gienapp, *Origins of the Republican Party*, 371.

15. E. P. Smith to Henry C. Carey, Oct. 31, 1856, Carey Papers, HSP.

and tyrannized by Three Hundred and Fifty Thousand Slave-holders." Know Nothings most often cited the caning of Sumner and the sack of Lawrence as the events that made it necessary to abandon the national Know Nothing movement. These incidents, noted the Gettysburg *Star and Banner*, "have aroused a popular feeling throughout the North without precedent in our National History. The settled, fixed purpose of the Southern politicians to convert the National Government into an engine for the furtherance of the purposes of Slavery propagandists, can no longer be doubted." As a result, the *Star and Banner* retracted its endorsement of Fillmore and instead called on Know Nothings to support Frémont. Even many conservatives, who had seemed incapable of supporting a Republican candidate just months earlier, decided that they could no longer ignore southern provocation:

> After fighting the battle of the South for twelve long years, defending its political rights, domestic institutions, social character, manners and habits on all occasions, recent occurrences have convinced us that the time has come for the North, with its superior numbers, intelligence, wealth and power, to take a stand, firm and fixed as its granite hills, against the threatening, bullying, brow-beating, skull-breaking spirit of the South—a spirit that tramples on Compromise; violates the sacred freedom of parliamentary debate; and murders the settlers upon our common soil for simply opposing, by voice and vote, the fastening of slavery upon a free and virgin Territory. . . . However mischievous and detestable the sentiments promulgated by [the Republicans] may be, they have never resorted to bullets and bludgeons to carry their points, or to silence their opponents.

Most northern Know Nothings concluded that "the sectional issue, distasteful as it is to most of us, must be met" by uniting with the Republicans to elect Frémont.[16]

Know Nothings also cited their desire to protect "free labor" from competition with slave labor as further justification for temporarily setting aside the Know Nothing agenda. Like most Republicans, Frémont's Know Nothing supporters rarely attacked the "peculiar institution" itself, concentrating instead on the deleterious effect of slavery on the economic well-being of whites. A Frémont victory, promised the Pottsville *Miner's Journal*, would mean "NO MORE NEGRO STATES TO DEGRADE FREEMEN AND WHITE LABOR." The Hartford *Courant* worried that should Buchanan prevail, "the aristocratical institutions of the South *that make* LABOR A DEGRADATION will become permanent in this country." Fillmore Americans called such appeals spurious because they insisted that immigrants—not southern slaves—posed the greatest threat to the economic welfare of North-

16. Jamestown [New York] *Journal*, July 4, 1856 (quotation); Gettysburg *Star and Banner*, June 27, 1856 (quotation); Pottsville *Miner's Journal*, June 28, July 26, 1856; New York *Mirror*, July 19, 1856 (quotation); Hartford *Courant*, June 25, 1856 (quotation); Muscatine *Journal* quoted in Ronald F. Matthias, "The Know Nothing Movement in Iowa" (Ph.D. diss., University of Chicago, 1965), 122.

erners. But North Americans frequently cited the importance of "free labor" in explaining their support for Frémont.[17]

Their emphasis on the slavery issue did not mean that the North Americans had abandoned all hopes of implementing their nativist agenda. But they contended that because the threat posed by the Slave Power had momentarily become greater than that presented by "political Romanism," Americanism should become secondary until Congress settled the slavery-extension issue. Know Nothings "deny none of their peculiar doctrines" by supporting Frémont, argued the Hartford *Courant*. "They merely lay them aside temporarily for the support of a higher and more noble object, and one which presses more immediately on the attention of freemen—the EX-CLUSION of slavery from the TERRITORIES. When this object is attained and the laws and compromises of the past are fixed where they stood in 1853, then the distinctive objects of each of the old parties can be pursued." An Indiana newspaper likewise asserted that Know Nothing "doctrines . . . are, in our judgment, right and proper, but now is not the time the people wish to consider them, and they will not rust by being postponed a few years. This question of slavery must be met, and met now." North Americans insisted that such a stance was not hypocritical, because "opposition to the aggressions of the slave power" had pervaded the Order from its rise in 1854. Know Nothings were merely postponing one aspect of their platform to insure the success of another.[18]

North Americans also believed that once the slavery issue was settled, Frémont would be more responsive than Fillmore to the Order's nativist agenda. Nativist newspapers throughout the North reported that Frémont had assured Know Nothing leaders of his sympathy with their movement. In comparison they portrayed Fillmore as a "parlor Know Nothing" who had never attended a lodge meeting and who had accepted membership in the Order merely to gain the American party's nomination. As a result, said North Americans, nativists would find Fillmore "less disposed to carry out the great principles of the American party than Col. Fremont will be." Frémont, of course, had never set foot in a Know Nothing council either, but North Americans contended that because "the great mass of the Republican party is composed of those who have [previously] acted with the American party," the Republicans were more likely to implement nativist laws than the Fillmore Americans, who were merely conservative Whigs with a new name. Such statements represented more than campaign rhetoric. Veteran Massachusetts nativist Jonathan Peirce stated privately that if Frémont "is elected no aliens or Roman Catholics will be retained in office." Even the Catholic Bishop of

17. Pottsville *Miner's Journal*, Sept. 27, 1856; Hartford *Courant*, Oct. 11 (quotation), 24, 1856; Harrisburg *Herald*, Sept. 5, 1856.

18. Hartford *Courant*, June 20 (quotation), Aug. 22, 1856; Terre Haute *Express*, July 21, 1856 (quotation); Boston *Bee*, Aug. 29, 1856 (quotation); Steubenville *True American*, June 25, 1856; Vincennes [Indiana] *Gazette*, July 28, 1856; Fort Wayne *Times*, June 21, 1856; D. B. Ogden to Fillmore, June 27, 1856, Fillmore Papers, SUNY-O.

Buffalo believed that the Republicans had replaced the Americans as the most anti-Catholic political party.[19]

Frémont's promise to replace Republican vice presidential nominee William L. Dayton with North American choice William F. Johnston had convinced many nativists that Republican professions of sympathy with Know Nothingism were sincere. However, the failure of Republicans to substitute quickly Johnston for Dayton produced the first strains in the Republican–North American coalition. Republicans had hoped that "the imbroglio about the Vice Presidency" would somehow take care of itself, but it soon became clear that this issue might significantly damage the Frémont campaign. Efforts to set up "Frémont Clubs" were stymied because Republicans wanted to establish "Frémont and Dayton" clubs, while North Americans would join only "Frémont" or "Frémont and Johnston" organizations. Republicans realized that Know Nothing speakers would play a crucial role in attracting nativists to Frémont's candidacy, but when popular Ohio Know Nothing Thomas H. Ford discovered that Republicans had not withdrawn Dayton, he canceled his initial campaign appearances. Although many Know Nothings seemed willing to accept Dayton for the sake of "Freedom and Frémont," the Massachusetts Know Nothing State Council that convened on July 1 in Springfield endorsed Frémont and Johnston. The Connecticut and Rhode Island state councils soon followed suit.[20]

The North Americans felt justified in demanding Dayton's withdrawal. After all, they had made a deal with the Republicans and, despite being humiliated at the Republican convention, had carried out their half of the bargain by nominating Frémont. Republican leaders, including Frémont himself, had promised to replace Dayton with Johnston. Without some gesture by the Republicans to appease nativists, said the North Americans, Frémont would lose Pennsylvania and perhaps Connecticut and New Hampshire as well.[21] Although each of these assertions was valid, the North Americans labored under several significant handicaps. First, their national chairman, Francis H. Ruggles, had no national political experience, and as a result the North American organization lacked strong and capable leadership. Second,

19. Boston *Bee*, July 1, 1856; Frémont to Thomas Ford et al., quoted in New York *Mirror*, July 1, 1856; Steubenville *True American*, Aug. 13, 1856 (quotation); Jamestown [New York] *Journal*, April 4, 18, 1856; New York *State Register*, Oct. 24, 1856 (quotation); Terre Haute *Wabash Express*, Aug. 6, 1856 (quotation); Jonathan Peirce to Nathaniel Banks, Feb. 25, 1856 (quotation), Banks Papers, LC.

20. Edwin D. Morgan to Gideon Welles, June 28, 1856, Morgan to Russell Sage, June 28, 1856, Morgan to Joshua Giddings, July 2, 1856, Colfax to Morgan, July 8, 1856 (quotation), Morgan Papers, NYSL; Worcester *Transcript*, July 12, 1856; Hartford *Courant*, June 27, 1856; James W. Stone to Weed, July 8, 1856, Weed Papers, UR.

21. Francis H. Ruggles to the Executive Committee of the Republican Party, June 30, 1856, Ruggles to Edwin D. Morgan, July 15, 1856, in Boston *Bee*, Sept. 16, 1856; Z. K. Pangborn to Banks, June 25, 1856, Banks Papers, LC; N. P. Sawyer to Francis H. Ruggles, July 7, 1856, Nathaniel P. Banks Papers, IlSHL; Worcester *Transcript*, June 23, 1856; Steubenville *True American*, June 25, 1856.

as Connecticut Republican James Bunce put it, most rank-and-file Know Nothings did not "care one straw about Dayton or Johns[t]on, but will have union for Fremont & Freedom." Bunce exaggerated the extent of this feeling, for many North Americans believed that only by offering them the vice presidency could Republicans demonstrate that they truly sympathized with the Know Nothing agenda. But many others saw the vice presidential question as an insignificant squabble amongst greedy leaders. Finally, North American efforts to secure the vice presidency suffered when word got out that Johnston was willing to decline the nomination in return for patronage. "The Ex Governor obviously wants to *sell out*," reported one Pennsylvania Republican, and with Dayton stubbornly rejecting all suggestions that he voluntarily step aside, Johnston's greed weakened the North American bargaining position. Thus, although Ruggles and other North American leaders felt that Republicans owed them the vice presidential nomination, Ruggles made little headway in his attempt to win it for Johnston.[22]

The vice presidential situation also presented a dilemma for Ruggles's Republican counterpart, Edwin D. Morgan. If Morgan officially refused to drop Dayton, it would anger nativists and perhaps push them into the Fillmore camp. But if Morgan convinced Dayton to decline, Frémont might lose the votes of Protestant immigrants and other Republicans who abhorred nativism. Morgan therefore came to the conclusion that the best response to the North Americans was no response, so he simply ignored the letters he received from Ruggles. Thurlow Weed agreed in principle with Morgan's strategy, because, he said, "I don't see what good can come of answers to such letters." However, Weed convinced Morgan that some sort of reply was necessary to avoid insulting the North Americans. So when Ruggles sent a note asking why the Republicans had not responded to the North Americans' latest proposal—that both Dayton and Johnston withdraw in favor of a third, mutually agreeable candidate—Morgan sent Ruggles a personal note stating that an official reply would harm Frémont's candidacy. Apparently anxious to avoid the embarrassment of an official rejection, Ruggles apologetically answered that his previous note had been sent by mistake, and should be ignored. The Republicans had clearly gained the upper hand in the vice presidential battle.[23]

The next test of Morgan's strategy came in Connecticut. With the North Americans making no progress in negotiating Dayton's withdrawal, Connecticut Know Nothings decided to force the issue by calling a convention to select a

22. Bunce to Morgan, Aug. 1, 1856, Thomas Williams to Morgan, June 26, 1856 (second quotation), Dayton to Morgan, June 30, 1856, Morgan Papers, NYSL; Dayton to Israel Washburne, Jr., July 12, 1856, Washburne Papers, LC; Gienapp, *Origins of the Republican Party*, 384; S. M. Allen to Banks, June 15, 1856, Banks Papers, LC.

23. Francis H. Ruggles to the Executive Committee of the Republican Party, June 30, 1856, Ruggles to Edwin D. Morgan, July 15, 1856, in Boston *Bee*, Sept. 16, 1856; Morgan to Welles, July 9, Aug. 8, 1856, Welles Papers, LC; Weed to Morgan, Aug. 3, 1856, Morgan to Weed, Aug. 8, 1856, Morgan to Dayton, Aug. 8, 1856, Morgan Papers, NYSL.

Frémont and Johnston electoral ticket. Connecticut Know Nothings contended that the results of the state's spring elections, in which they out-polled the Republicans by nearly four to one, proved that "the American party is the great dominant party in this State, and *should have precedent over the Republican party, and be allowed to call the Convention to nominate an electoral ticket.*" But the Republicans refused to be bullied. Insisting that "the great body of the Americans" had "no attachment to the Party," Republicans called their own nominating convention to meet the same day as the Know Nothing gathering. In the end, enthusiasm for Frémont enabled the Republicans to triumph. Despite the opposition of Nehemiah D. Sperry and other Know Nothing leaders, the American convention voted to cooperate with the Republicans and create a joint electoral ticket made up of three Know Nothings and three Republicans. Welles reported to Morgan that "on the subject of the vice presidency they are considered as unpledged, which means they will vote for Dayton." By outmaneuvering the North Americans in Connecticut, where the nativists had recently enjoyed great success, the Republicans proved that as an independent political movement, Know Nothingism was quickly disintegrating.[24]

The result in Connecticut also guaranteed Dayton's eventual triumph in the battle for the vice presidential nomination, because if the North Americans could not impose Johnston upon the Republicans in one of the Know Nothings' strongholds, then Johnston's cause was obviously hopeless. In order to speed the inevitable, Morgan bypassed the recalcitrant Ruggles and wrote directly to Johnston. "The past we cannot recall," said Morgan in reference to Dayton's nomination at Philadelphia, "but for the future something may be done." Elaborating a bit on this thinly veiled promise, Morgan noted that Johnston's influence was such that "a just party will not permit [it] to go unrewarded." Before he would step down, Johnston insisted upon meeting with Frémont. Morgan reported afterward that "though I know no promise was made to him, the Col said in case of his election he should give all his friends who participated in it fair play." Apparently satisfied, Johnston wrote a letter to Ruggles dated August 29 declining the North American vice presidential nomination.[25]

But in a fittingly complicated ending to this power struggle, Ruggles refused to accept Johnston's declination, telling Johnston that his withdrawal would "endanger the success of Col. Fremont in some States, while it would not be productive of good in any quarter." Johnston then wrote back to Ruggles to retract his letter of withdrawal. In the meantime, a group of renegade North Americans, angry that the Republicans had reneged on their

24. Robert D. Parmet, "The Know Nothings in Connecticut" (Ph.D. diss., Columbia University, 1966), 225–26 (quotation), 230; James Babcock to Welles, July 12, 1856 (quotation), Welles Papers, LC; Welles to Morgan, June 27, Aug. 20 (quotation), 1856, Morgan Papers, NYSL; Gienapp, *Origins of the Republican Party*, 384–85.

25. Morgan to Johnston, Aug. 6, 1856, Johnston to Morgan, Aug. 13, 1856, Morgan Papers, NYSL; Morgan to Welles, Sept. 1, 1856, Welles Papers, LC; Johnston to Ruggles, Aug. 29, 1856, in New York *Express*, Sept. 13, 1856.

promise to drop Dayton, released to the press copies of Ruggles's unanswered letters to Morgan as well as Johnston's original letter of withdrawal in the hope that insulted Know Nothings would return to the Fillmore camp. Ruggles responded by publishing the letter in which Johnston announced his decision to remain in the race.[26] By this time, however, the public had grown tired of the vice presidential squabble, and many North American newspapers that had once insisted upon Johnston as Frémont's running-mate now expressed little interest in the issue. Frémont's candidacy, they concluded, should take precedence over a relatively insignificant inter-party feud. Yet some North Americans newspapers continued to endorse "Frémont and Johnston" for the remainder of the campaign. In fact, Ruggles never officially accepted Johnston's withdrawal, and Johnston never wrote a new letter of withdrawal after rescinding his first one. But it really did not matter, because by this point most North Americans had accepted the fact that Dayton would remain as Frémont's running-mate.[27]

The important support North Americans lent to the Frémont campaign demonstrated that the vice presidential question had become a non-issue. North Americans were the most sought after of all Frémont campaign speakers, and Henry Wilson, Nathaniel Banks, Anson Burlingame of Massachusetts, and Chauncey Shaffer of New York delivered countless speeches for Frémont. Important North Americans also wrote letters for publication renouncing Fillmore's candidacy, and these played a key role in attracting Know Nothings to the Frémont ticket. George Law's repudiation of Fillmore was particularly influential, as was that of New Jersey's Ephraim Marsh, who had presided at the convention that nominated Fillmore. Even North American leader Thomas H. Ford, who had initially refused to endorse Frémont because of the vice presidential dispute, agreed to use his influence to persuade pro-Fillmore newspapers to switch to Frémont.[28] Not all North Americans remained loyal to Frémont. Citing the Republicans' failure to drop Dayton for Johnston, a group of New York North American leaders returned to the Fillmore camp. Frémont's failure to endorse explicitly the Know Nothings'

26. Ruggles to the Editor, Sept. 13, 1856, New York *Times*, Sept. 15, 1856; Ruggles and Lucius Peck to the Members of the American Party, in New York *Times*, Sept. 17, 1856 (quotation); S. M. Allen et al. to the Editor, Sept. 12, 1856, in New York *Express*, Sept. 13, 1856.

27. Further complicating a reconstruction of the vice presidential struggle are the entries in the Republican National Committee's account book indicating that the Republicans paid $300 to Ruggles in late August and $500 to Johnston in late October. It seems unlikely that the payment to Ruggles was a quid pro quo for Johnston's resignation, because if this had been the case, Ruggles would probably not have rejected Johnston's withdrawal. On these payments, see Gienapp, *Origins of the Republican Party*, 386.

28. Morgan to John Doane, Aug. 25, 1856, Morgan Papers, NYSL; George Law to Weed, Aug. 12, 1856, E. Dodd to Weed, Sept. 8, 1856, F. W. Paul to Weed, Sept. 11, 1856, Morgan to Weed, Oct. 4, 1856, Weed Papers, UR; John Wentworth to Isaac Sherman, Sept. 1, 1856, Sherman Papers, Private Collection; *"North American" Documents. Letters from Geo. Law, Ephraim Marsh, & Chauncey Shaffer* (n.p., 1856); *Geo. Law and Chauncey Shaffer's Reasons for Repudiating Fillmore and Donelson* (New York, 1856); Ephraim Marsh, *Reasons for Going for Fremont* (n.p., 1856).

nativist tenets also prompted veteran Massachusetts nativist Alfred B. Ely to lead a bolt of Bay State Know Nothings. Yet these were relatively isolated incidents, and overall, North Americans made significant contributions to the Frémont campaign.[29]

Many North Americans justified their support of Frémont on the grounds that Fillmore could not possibly win the election. There was not "a single State," they said, "that Mr. Fillmore has the remotest chances of carrying." But Fillmore's strategists insisted that their candidate could win Kentucky, Louisiana, North Carolina, Maryland, Delaware, California, New York, and Massachusetts, all of which the Americans had carried in 1855. If the Americans could hold these states, and add Missouri and Tennessee (where the Know Nothings had come close to victory in 1855) and Pennsylvania (where nativism was rampant and the Republican party barely formed), Fillmore would capture 139 electoral votes, just nine short of a majority. Once it became clear that Frémont had no chance, the Americans expected that other northern states, desperate to prevent Buchanan's triumph, would join the rush to Fillmore and secure the ex-President's victory.[30]

Yet the futility of Fillmore's strategy became apparent as the various state campaigns got under way, and in no state were the ex-President's hopes dashed more quickly than in Massachusetts. National Americans had felt especially confident about the Bay State because their ticket had swept the 1855 elections despite the bolt of anti-slavery Know Nothings to the Republican party. The fact that the Massachusetts State Council had not repudiated Fillmore's nomination at their spring convention (as had Know Nothings in every other New England state) also encouraged National Americans. Actually, the State Council that met in Boston on March 4 had not ratified Fillmore's nomination either, opting instead to postpone their decision "until assured that they [Fillmore and Donelson] do heartily endorse our American principles." But with Fillmore having embraced nativism in his Newburgh speech, National Americans undoubtedly expected the State Council to endorse the former President at their July meeting.[31]

Despite these promising signs, Fillmore's supporters failed to reckon with opposition from the state's most powerful Know Nothing, Governor Henry J. Gardner. The ambitious Gardner had spent much of 1855 positioning himself for the Know Nothings' vice presidential nomination, but once Sam Houston

29. James R. Thompson to Fillmore, Sept. 17, 19, 25, 1856, circular entitled "North American Convention" enclosed in Horace H. Day to Fillmore, Sept. 19, 1856, Fillmore Papers, SUNY-O; Boston *Ledger* [edited by Ely], July 30, 1856; Hartford *Courant*, Aug. 13, 1856.

30. Pottsville *Miner's Journal*, Aug. 23, 1856; Solomon Haven to Fillmore, March 2, April 24, 1856, Humphrey Marshall to Fillmore, July 10, 1856, Fillmore Papers, SUNY-O; Richmond *Whig* quoted in Hartford *Courant*, May 20, 1856; Philadelphia *News*, Sept. 2, 1856.

31. Boston *Bee*, March 5, 6, 8, 1856; William G. Bean, "Party Transformation in Massachusetts with Special Reference to the Antecedents of Republicanism, 1848–1860" (Ph.D. diss., Harvard University, 1922), 339–40 (quotation).

(the only southern ex-Democrat with whom a northern ex-Whig such as Gardner could be paired) faded from the race, Gardner's candidacy collapsed. Gardner then turned his eye toward the Senate seat occupied by Charles Sumner. Sumner had done little to distinguish himself during his first five years in office, but the assault by Preston Brooks transformed the senator into a living martyr, and guaranteed his re-election. Precluded from national office, Gardner decided to seek a third term as governor, but at this point his ambitions began to clash with those of the National Americans. Sensing that he could not win re-election on a ticket with the increasingly unpopular Fillmore, Gardner decided to oppose the ex-President's candidacy in late June, just days before the Massachusetts Know Nothings gathered to make their endorsement. Gardner's move shocked the National Americans, because his organ, the Boston *Bee*, had enthusiastically supported Fillmore ever since his nomination. Without Gardner's well-organized machine backing him, Fillmore stood no chance to win ratification, and the Know Nothings who gathered in Springfield on July 1 endorsed Frémont and Johnston instead.[32]

In fact, Gardner slyly utilized the vice presidential dispute to ensure his re-election. According to former Know Nothing James W. Stone, the governor and his associates insisted that "they would be glad to secure the change to *Dayton* if they could obtain as a *quid pro quo*, the State Government." Otherwise, the North Americans would run a separate electoral ticket, thus dividing the Frémont vote and possibly costing him the state. Some Republicans wanted to call Gardner's bluff, believing that the governor would not risk public condemnation for splitting the Frémont vote once North Americans in other states had agreed to support Dayton. Contending that "Gardner is possessed by the most ultra and offensive Americanism," these Republicans also feared that an endorsement of the governor would drive away the Protestant immigrants who held the balance of power in closely contested Midwestern states. Yet having underestimated Gardner's strength in 1855, and worried that they would be "damned" in the public eye should the loss of Massachusetts cost Frémont the election, Republican leaders decided to accede to Gardner's demands. The Republicans did not actually nominate Gardner, but guaranteed his re-election by making no state nominations whatsoever. In return, the North Americans agreed to support the Frémont and Dayton electoral ticket and promised not to oppose Republicans in certain congressional districts.[33] By managing to prevent the Republicans from opposing them in the state election, Massachusetts Know Nothings demonstrated that they still wielded considerable power. Yet by switching to Frémont, Gardner emasculated Fillmore's Massachusetts cam-

32. David Donald, *Charles Sumner and the Coming of the Civil War* (New York: Alfred A. Knopf, 1960), 270–76; Boston *Bee*, July 2, 3, 1856; Gienapp, *Origins of the Republican Party*, 387.

33. James W. Stone to Weed, July 8, 1856, Weed Papers, UR; Charles W. Upham to Isaac Sherman, June 10, 1856 (quotation), Sherman Papers, Private Collection; John R. Mulkern, *The Know-Nothing Party in Massachusetts: The Rise and Fall of a People's Movement* (Boston: Northeastern Univ. Press, 1990), 148–50; Gienapp, *Origins of the Republican Party*, 387–88.

paign. Fillmore diehards did eventually establish their own organization, nominating a state ticket headed by cotton dealer George W. Gordon, but neither Gordon nor Fillmore could possibly carry the state. Although the Know Nothings remained a potent force in the state's politics, by August it was clear that Massachusetts, one of the keys to Fillmore's electoral strategy, was hopelessly lost.[34]

The Fillmore campaign experienced similar difficulties in New York. Only once in American history had a victorious presidential candidate not triumphed in New York, so each of the three parties made special efforts to carry that all-important state.[35] At the Democratic national convention in Cincinnati, for example, party leaders forced New York Democrats to end the long-standing feud that had split the Democracy into "Hard" and "Soft" factions. That the two leading candidates for the Know Nothing presidential nomination were New Yorkers was likewise no coincidence, because, as one Southerner put it before the Know Nothing nominating convention, "all agree that New York *must* be carried, and the South . . . will go for whoever it is believed *can* carry N. York." National Americans had expected New York to be their strongest northern state. Unlike those in the rest of the North, the New York Know Nothing organization had never been dominated by anti-slavery men, so it suffered only minimal defections when the national organization adopted platforms that equivocated on the slavery issue. Fillmore backers also believed that the nomination of Erastus Brooks (who had gained notoriety in 1855 during the church property dispute with Archbishop John Hughes) as the party's gubernatorial candidate would boost the ex-President's prospects. Speaking of Brooks, New York American party president Stephen Sammons advised Fillmore that "there is no man in the State around whom the Protestant Element (which say what we please is the very back bone of our organization) will gather as about him." As a result, most National Americans confidently predicted that the American party would carry New York come November.[36]

As the campaign proceeded, however, Fillmore Americans discovered that they had overestimated their strength in New York. The speakership contest, the caning of Sumner, and the sack of Lawrence had caused many more defections to the Republicans than the Americans had originally realized, prompting Fillmore to complain that "if Freemont [*sic*] is elected, he will owe his election

34. Mulkern, *Know Nothing Party in Massachusetts*, 150; *The Record of George William Gordon* (Boston, 1856).

35. Only in 1812, when James Madison defeated New York's De Witt Clinton, did a victorious presidential candidate fail to carry New York.

36. V. Ellis to Ullmann, Feb. 17, 1856 (quotation), Ullmann Papers, NYHS; A. H. Wells to Fillmore, July 15, 1856, Sammons to Fillmore, Aug. 5, 1856 (quotation), Fillmore Papers, SUNY-O; Fillmore to Andrew J. Donelson, July 10, 1856, Donelson Papers, LC; Edward M. Cornell to Lawrence, Sept. 9, 1856, Amos A. Lawrence Papers, MHS; Buffalo *Commercial Advertiser*, Aug. 8, 1856; Edward Everett to Hiram Ketchum, July 12, 1856, Everett Papers, MHS.

entirely to the troubles in Kansas, and the martyrdom of Sumner. . . . The Republicans ought to pension Brooks for life." Furthermore, although the North American movement in New York involved a relatively small percentage of the party's members, it decimated the organization upstate, especially in western New York, formerly a stronghold of the Order.[37] The Know Nothings did retain significant influence in some areas, however, especially in the lower Hudson Valley. "Andes[,] which ought to be strongly Republican, is almost exclusively Know Nothing," reported one Delaware County Republican, and an operative informed Seward that Tompkins County remained a "Hot Bed of Know Nothingism." But the paucity of such statements indicated that many former Know Nothings had abandoned their organization for the Republican party. Those defections, combined with the large number of New York Democrats switching to Frémont, clearly put the Republicans in the lead in that state.[38]

The disappointing reaction to the nomination of Erastus Brooks for governor added to the Americans' troubles in New York. Brooks's opposition to liquor prohibition damaged his candidacy to some degree, but his role in spreading the rumor of Frémont's Catholicism injured his popularity most. Anti-Catholic zealots who had once praised Brooks for his "manly" opposition to Hughes now condemned him for sabotaging the anti-slavery movement with fabricated stories of Frémont's Catholicism. At the conclusion of the campaign, a newspaper that had once championed Brooks's cause reported that "henceforth the name of Erastus Brooks will be mentioned only as a lesson to teach the young adventurer in politics, how wretched a thing, he, who seeks personal advancement through the instrumentality of unblushing falsehood, may become." In fact, Brooks's failure to generate enthusiasm for the American ticket, despite his anti-Catholic credentials, demonstrated how thoroughly anti-slavery had overpowered anti-Catholicism as the motivating factor for most anti-Democratic voters. Recognizing this, one Republican remarked that even "if Fremont were 20 Catholics he would [still] carry New York."[39] Although many National Americans insisted until election day that Fillmore would triumph in his home state, more perceptive

37. Fillmore to William A. Graham, Aug. 9, 1856, Graham Papers, University of North Carolina; Ira Peck to Seward, Aug. 4, 1856, Seward Papers, UR; Henry S. Randall to Henry D. Gilpin, June 10, 1856, filed with Gilpin to Buchanan, June 27, 1856, Buchanan Papers, HSP.

38. S. C. Johnson to Weed, July 7, 1856 (quotation), John Haxtun to Weed, Aug. 4, 1856, Weed Papers, UR; A. Johnson to Seward, July 19, 1856, J. Kendall to Seward, Aug. 11, 1856 (quotation), Seward Papers, UR; S. G. Haven to Fillmore, July 15, 1856, Fillmore Papers, SUNY-O; Morgan to Cornelius Coles, July 10, 1856, Morgan Papers, NYSL.

39. Edward C. Delevan to "Dear Sir," May 22, 1856, Delevan to Fillmore, Sept. 18, 1856, Horace H. Day to Fillmore, Sept. 19, 1856, Anna Ella Carroll to Fillmore, Sept. 23, 1856, Fillmore Papers, SUNY-O; Allan Nevins and Thomas H. Milton, eds., *The Diary of George Templeton Strong*, 4 vols. (New York: Macmillan, 1952), II, pp. 290, 303; Hartford *Courant*, Oct. 28, Nov. 15 (quotation), 1856; Martin I. Townsend to Isaac Sherman, Sept. 3, 1856 (quotation), Sherman Papers, Private Collection.

observers realized that like Massachusetts, New York was "eminently safe" for Frémont.[40]

Fillmore's troubles in the North resulted in part from the American party's dismal showing in the South's August elections. Decisive defeats in Kentucky, North Carolina, and Missouri convinced most voters that Fillmore's candidacy was hopeless, and that votes cast for him in November would be "wasted." Many Fillmore supporters switched to Buchanan at this point, and although most such conversions occurred in the South, some Northerners (mostly conservative Whigs) also threw their support to the Pennsylvanian. On the eve of the southern contests, a Philadelphian had warned Fillmore that "many of our good staunch friends say that unless the South shows strong indications of giving you . . . support they will vote for Buchanan to save the Union." Other National Americans joined the Frémont campaign at this juncture. Ephraim Marsh, who had presided at the convention that nominated Fillmore, cited the southern results prominently in the letter announcing his repudiation of Fillmore. "Shall we of the North cling to Mr. Fillmore," asked Marsh, "after he has been deliberately abandoned by the South, while those [Southerners] most earnest for his nomination [at Philadelphia] are supporting Mr. Buchanan?"[41] Although the editor of the Americans' California organ advised Fillmore that "the best possible face is put upon this news," the southern results convinced most voters that Fillmore could not possibly win the election and further depleted the already thin American party ranks.[42]

By early autumn, then, it had become evident that Fillmore could not win a majority in the electoral college. Yet his staunchest advocates did not give up hope. While admitting that their candidate could no longer carry enough states to win the election outright, they insisted that if Fillmore could win just a few states, no candidate would capture a majority of the electoral votes, in which case the House of Representatives would decide the election. Because a majority of the representatives had at one time been affiliated with Know Nothing lodges, National Americans insisted that "Fillmore will be President should the election be thrown to the house." However, Fillmore backers overestimated their strength in Congress, because many (if not most) congressmen who had once belonged to Know Nothing lodges had subsequently severed their ties to the Order. The National American candidate for Speaker never polled more than forty-one votes, so Fillmore was unlikely to control a majority of the congressional delegations. Despite its improbability, the slim

40. S. G. Haven to Lawrence, Oct. 6, 1856, Amos A. Lawrence Papers, MHS; Morgan to James Nye, July 9, 1856 (quotation), Morgan Papers, NYSL.

41. Isaiah Fuller to Fillmore, Aug. 7, 1856 (quotation), Haven to Fillmore, Aug. 15, 1856, Fillmore Papers, SUNY-O; Philadelphia correspondent in New York *Tribune*, May 2, 1856; Hartford *Courant*, Sept. 1, 22 (quotation), 1856.

42. James Allen to Fillmore, Sept. 19, 1856, Fillmore Papers, SUNY-O; New York *Mirror*, Aug. 9, 1856; George E. Baker to Seward, Aug. 11, 1856, Seward Papers, UR.

chance that Fillmore might throw the election into the House prevented many voters from abandoning his apparently hopeless candidacy.[43]

Many Republicans had initially believed that their party stood no chance in the presidential election of 1856. But with Fillmore's campaign floundering, some Frémont supporters came to the conclusion that their candidate might carry the election after all. Yet Republicans realized that Frémont's apparently comfortable lead in most northern states "will avail nothing in the doubtful states of Pennsylvania, Indiana, and Illinois. These three states and particularly Pennsylvania will be the great battle ground on which the contest must be decided." Pennsylvania certainly was the key, because as mentioned earlier, Frémont had to win that state if he hoped to win the election. Furthermore, Pennsylvania would hold its state election in October, and as one of Frémont's advisors put it, "if we carry a majority there it will be increased by thousands in November and will make a perfect stampede of the Buchaniers in all the other Northern States." On the other hand, if they lost Pennsylvania in October, it would convince voters that Frémont had no chance and ensure Buchanan's election. Frémonters thus threw all their resources into the Pennsylvania state campaign, hoping that a victory there would provide the final surge necessary to elect their candidate.[44]

Frémonters faced a daunting task in Pennsylvania. Anti-Democratic forces controlled northern and western Pennsylvania, but the Republican party had barely organized in the more populous southern portion of the state, where Stevens reported that "Americanism is [still] the deepest feeling." The Republican movement had failed to catch on in Pennsylvania in part because Know Nothings had sabotaged the Republicans' initial efforts in the state by infiltrating the Republican state committee. Pennsylvania's endemic factionalism also hindered the Republicans, as the feud that had split the Know Nothings into ex-Whig and ex-Democratic factions continued in the Republican ranks. Many residents of southern Pennsylvania had relatives in the South or had once lived there themselves, so in that region the Republicans' anti-southern ideology held little appeal. Philadelphia's close economic ties to the slave states likewise impeded Republican recruiting, because many Philadelphians feared that a Republican victory would at best bring southern economic retaliation against northern merchants, and at worst a civil war that would sever all trade between the sections. In addition, Pennsylvania's Republican state committee was particularly inept, and its members squandered time and money while the well-oiled Democratic machine efficiently advanced its

43. J. D. Colver to Ullmann, Aug. 30, 1856, Ullmann Papers, NYHS; Henry A. Wise to Everett, Sept. 11, 17 (quotation), Oct. 7, 1856, Everett Papers, MHS; Fillmore to John P. Kennedy, Oct. 26, 1856, Kennedy Papers, Enoch Pratt Free Library.
44. Ovid Miner to Seward, June 16, 1856, D. M. Nagle to Seward, July 20, 1856 (quotation), Seward Papers, UR; F. P. Blair, Jr., to Isaac Sherman, Sept. 5, 1856 (quotation), L. F. Foster to James F. Babcock, Sept. 17, 1856, Sherman Papers, Private Collection.

party's cause. Finally, a Democratic defeat in October in no way guaranteed a Republican victory in November, because while the Americans and Republicans had created a common ticket for the October election, Fillmore and Frémont would divide the anti-Democratic vote in the national contest.[45] Republicans hoped that an anti-Democratic victory in October would convince National Americans to switch from Fillmore's hopeless candidacy to Frémont's, or at least persuade the Americans to form a common electoral ticket. Yet many Pennsylvania Americans (as well as conservative Whigs) had vowed never to aid the "radical" Republicans, even by supporting a fusion electoral ticket. With the Republicans facing this variety of obstacles, a Frémont victory in Pennsylvania seemed impossible.[46]

Confronting such a daunting task, Republicans resolved to employ every available means to convert Pennsylvania's Fillmore Americans to Frémont. Relaying the sentiments of Henry B. Stanton, who headed the Republican speakers' bureau, one Frémonter told another that success in Pennsylvania would "depend upon persuading the Fillmore men some, dragooning them some, & cheating them some—all which methods he thought would be faithfully tried." The Republicans' primary strategy was, in the words of Simon Cameron, to "convince the people that Fremont can be elected and that Fillmore, as is the truth, has not the shadow of a chance." Frémonters supplemented this strategy with elements of deception, dispatching Thaddeus Stevens and Thomas H. Ford to southern Pennsylvania to purchase the support of pro-Fillmore newspapers. "I negotiated with the leading American editor of York who was doing much mischief; indeed was keeping 4000 Fillmore men from both the state and electoral ticket," reported Stevens. "He is to change his course and have $350." Stevens spent $4000 in this manner, and Ford, who was authorized to spend $5000, mortified Republican leaders by expending nearly twice that sum. Republicans hoped that these editorial conversions would create the impression that National Americans were abandoning Fillmore and prompt a final surge that would lift the anti-Democratic ticket to victory.[47] On election day, however, the Frémonters fell just short of their goal, as the Demo-

45. On why the Fillmore men agreed to a fusion with the Republicans for the state election when they opposed cooperation for the national contest, see Isaac Hazlehurst to Fillmore, Oct. 2, 1856, Fillmore Papers, SUNY-O.

46. Thaddeus Stevens to Dr. E. D. Gazzam, Aug. 24, 1856 (copy), Edward McPherson Papers, LC; W. H. Hutter to Buchanan, Sept. 20, 1856, Buchanan Papers, HSP; E. D. Morgan to Simon Cameron, Aug. 20, 1856, Cameron Papers, DCHS; E. Pershine Smith to Henry C. Carey, Oct. 30, 1855, Carey Papers, HSP; Henry R. Mueller, *The Whig Party in Pennsylvania* (New York: Columbia Univ. Press, 1922), 231; William Dusinberre, *Civil War Issues in Philadelphia, 1856–1865* (Philadelphia: Univ. of Pennsylvania Press, 1965), 19; Gienapp, *Origins of the Republican Party*, 394–400.

47. E. P. Smith to H. C. Carey, Sept. 7, 1856 (quotation), Thaddeus Stevens to Carey, Sept. 24 (quotation), 30, 1856, A. Rood to Carey and "Mr. Fry," Oct. 9, 1856, Carey Papers, HSP; Simon Cameron to Edwin Morgan, Aug. 18, 1856, Morgan Papers, NYSL; Thomas H. Ford to Dear Sir, Sept. 12, 1856, Morgan to Weed, Oct. 7, 1856, Weed Papers, UR; Morgan to Gideon Welles, Oct. 8, 1856, Welles Papers, LC; Gienapp, *Origins of the Republican Party*, 399.

cratic slate of candidates defeated the American/Republican "Union" ticket by fewer than 3000 votes.[48]

At this point, most Frémonters conceded that their candidate could not win the presidential election. Charles Francis Adams recognized that Republicans "must bid adieu to any idea of success" in November, and Thurlow Weed admitted defeat as well. Other Frémonters, however, believed that if Republicans and Americans united on a common electoral ticket, they might yet carry Pennsylvania in November. These optimists incorrectly assumed that Fillmore voters would willingly vote for a ticket that aided Frémont. As mentioned earlier, many Americans and Whigs had promised to vote for Buchanan if the Americans joined forces with the Republicans. One Pennsylvania American told Fillmore that he had voted for the Democratic state ticket in October in order to repudiate all association with "Abolitionists," and that "there are very many who have felt compelled to act likewise." This Philadelphian concluded that "Buchanan has gained thousands of votes in our state in consequence of the party fusion," and those Whigs and Americans who could not bring themselves to vote for a Democrat probably abstained altogether.[49] Other American party members balked at aiding Frémont because of the Catholic question. The Americans had not emphasized this issue in Pennsylvania out of fear that it would hurt the anti-Democratic ticket in October, but the charge made a strong impact in Pennsylvania nonetheless. "This State is lost to Fremont if he does not come out with a letter over his own signature denying that he is a Catholic," predicted one Pennsylvanian, and others agreed that the charge "has unquestionably lost us thousands of votes." Still, in Pennsylvania and other states where the election seemed close, Republicans stepped up efforts to create fusion tickets with the Americans in a desperate effort to salvage their campaign.[50]

Such efforts produced few tangible results. In New Jersey, Republicans had initiated fusion negotiations because they realized that Frémont could not carry this conservative state independently. "We have New York on one side, & Phila. on the other, with a large cotton interest in Newark, where they manufacture almost everything for a Southern market," wrote Dayton, explaining the hopeless situation. Although some Know Nothings advocated the creation of a fusion ticket, the opposition of key New Jersey Americans such as Charles D. Deshler blocked the fusion movement. Deshler believed that

48. The Democratic candidate for canal commissioner (the top post on the ticket) won 212,886 votes (50.3%), while the Union candidate captured 210,111 (49.7%). *Tribune Almanac* (1857): 49.

49. Charles Francis Adams Diary, Oct. 17, 1856, Adams Papers, MHS; Weed to Cameron, Nov. 12, 1856, Cameron Papers, LC; B. England to Fillmore, Oct. 17 (quotation), 1856, Fillmore Papers, SUNY-O; Henry C. Carey to [George?] Morey and [?] Smith, Oct. 19, 1856, Carey Papers, HSP; William Chace to Welles, Oct. 21, 1856, Welles Papers, LC.

50. N. Sargent to Fillmore, Oct. 12, 1856, Fillmore Papers, SUNY-O; Thaddeus Stevens to E. D. Gazzam, Aug. 24, 1856, Edward McPherson Papers, LC; G. Wright to Isaac Sherman, Sept. 24, 1856 (quotation), Sherman Papers, Private Collection; Henry C. Carey to J. Goodrich, [Nov. 1856?] (quotation), attached to Goodrich to Carey, Oct. 16, 1856, Carey Papers, HSP.

while fusion might enable Fillmore to win a portion of New Jersey's seven electoral votes, cooperation with the Republicans "would almost certainly cost us the entire electoral vote of one or more of the Southern States, now quite certain for us."[51]

Fusion efforts also failed in Indiana. "The Southern portion of our state was settled by people from North Carolina, Kentucky, & Tennessee, and [they] are ignorant," lamented Indiana Republican chairman John Defrees. "The infernal Catholic *lie* prejudices them against Col. Fremont, and it will be hard to get them to vote for him." Indiana Democrats reported gleefully that the Americans and Republicans "fight each other with the same animosity" previously reserved for the Democrats, and that, as a result, victory "will be so easy that it is hardly worth while for us to make an effort."[52] Nonetheless, Indiana Americans suggested that the two groups form a fusion ticket with eight Frémont and five Fillmore electors, but Republicans rejected the proposal, because as Schuyler Colfax explained, "we were satisfied that we should be weaker with this Fusion than without—as it would alienate all the foreign vote & would not bring more than half the Fillmore vote to us at any rate." Another proposal acceptable to Republicans (and sanctioned by American leaders in New York) was scuttled when the leading Indiana American, Richard W. Thompson, refused to endorse it. Illinois Americans and Republicans also failed to agree upon a fusion arrangement.[53]

Only in Pennsylvania did the two anti-Democratic parties form a fusion ticket. At first, a fusion agreement had seemed unlikely, because American party leaders in Philadelphia adamantly opposed any cooperation with the Republicans. But it soon became clear that Americans in the remainder of the state favored fusion, and on October 21 conferees from both sides agreed to a fusion formula.[54] Under the complicated arrangement, the two sides main-

51. William L. Dayton to Isaac Sherman, Oct. 1, 1856, Sherman Papers, Private Collection; Joseph Randolph to Fillmore, June 28, Sept. 1, Oct. 29, 1856, Charles D. Deshler to Fillmore, July 17 (quotation), Oct. 24, 27, 1856, Fillmore Papers, SUNY-O; F. S. Evans to Weed, Sept. 10, 1856, Weed Papers, UR.

52. John Defrees to Isaac Sherman, Oct. 29, 1856, Schuyler Colfax to Sherman, Nov. 1, 1856, Sherman Papers, Private Collection; P. M. Kent to William H. English, July 5, [1856] (quotation), W. Newkirk to English, July 19, 1856 (quotation), English Papers, IndHS; Carl F. Brand, "The History of the Know Nothing Party in Indiana," *Indiana Magazine of History* 18 (1922): 284–86.

53. Colfax to Defrees, Oct. 27, 1856, in Roger Van Bolt, "The Rise of the Republican Party in Indiana, 1840–1856," *Indiana Magazine of History* 47 (1951): 115; "Steeltrap" [James R. Thompson] to Fillmore, Nov. 1, 1856, Richard W. Thompson to Fillmore, Nov. 10, 1856, Fillmore Papers, SUNY-O; Defrees to Isaac Sherman, Oct. 29, Nov. 1, 8, 1856, Sherman Papers, Private Collection.

54. E. R. Jewett to Fillmore, Oct. 12, 1856, Alfred B. Ely to Fillmore, Oct. 13, 1856, William R. Wilson to Fillmore, Oct. 14, 1856, R. C. Himes to Fillmore, Oct. 20, 1856, Edmund Blanchard to Fillmore, Oct. 22, 1856, Fillmore Papers, SUNY-O; Stephen Miller to Cameron, [endorsed Aug. 28, 1856], Cameron Papers, DCHS; Cameron to Isaac Sherman, Sept. 5, 1856, Sherman Papers, Private Collection; Morgan to Welles, Oct. 15, 18, 22, 1856, Welles Papers, LC; Philadelphia *News*, Oct. 18, 20, 1856; Pottsville *Miner's Journal*, Oct. 25, 1856; Alexander McClure, *Old Time Notes of Pennsylvania*, 2 vols. (Philadelphia, 1905), I, pp. 259–60;

tained separate tickets, but twenty-six of the twenty-seven electors would be identical. Frémont and Fillmore would serve as the twenty-seventh electors, which would allow voters from each side to make their preference known when they voted. If the joint ticket carried Pennsylvania, the state's electoral vote would be divided in a proportion equal to the number of votes cast for each ticket, but if the state's electoral vote could provide the margin of victory for either candidate, then all twenty-six votes (the twenty-seventh would be split and thus lost) would be cast for that candidate.

All hopes that the Pennsylvania fusion ticket would prevent a Buchanan victory there were dashed when the American state chairman, John P. Sanderson, repudiated the arrangement and announced that the original slate of Fillmore electors would remain in the field. Americans would therefore choose either the fusionist "Fillmore Union" ticket or the non-fusion "Fillmore Straight" ticket when they ventured to the polls on election day. Sanderson's decision outraged Republicans and those Americans who supported fusion, and when popular North Carolina American Kenneth Rayner arrived to campaign for the Fillmore Union ticket, pressure on the anti-fusionists to drop the Straight ticket increased.[55] At this point only the consent of Fillmore himself could have persuaded the anti-fusionists to withdraw the Straight ticket. In response to last-minute pleas from both sides, the ex-President advised the anti-fusionists to "do as our friends there think best," but since he knew that the Straight men opposed fusion, this response was tantamount to an endorsement of their position. The continued division of the anti-Democratic forces on the eve of the election guaranteed a Buchanan victory in Pennsylvania.[56]

The refusal of Fillmore supporters in the lower North to endorse fusion might seem illogical, but Fillmore and his advisers believed that fusion in the North would help Frémont more than the Americans. They reasoned that fusion would inflate Frémont's electoral tally, while Fillmore's gains would be offset by the loss of southern states, whose voters would shun Fillmore if he cooperated with the Republicans. Fillmore calculated that he already controlled enough states to force the election to the House, and that consequently it made no sense to endorse fusion. This was a risky strategy, because if Fillmore made no fusion and did poorly in the South, the election would never reach the House. But Americans were willing to take this chance because they believed that a poor showing by Frémont would destroy the Republican party and leave the Americans as the Democrats' only viable national competitor. Conversely, Americans insisted that fusion would ruin their party's hopes of future political success. Pennsylvania's Henry D. Moore charged that those

55. *The American Party Sold to Buchanan* (Philadelphia, 1856); McClure, *Old Time Notes*, I, p. 260; Address of Philadelphia [pro-fusion] Americans in Clearfield [Pennsylvania] *Raftsman's Journal*, Oct. 29, 1856; Philadelphia *News* [edited by Sanderson], Sept. 3, Oct. 22, 1856; A. Cummings to Weed, Oct. 28, 31, 1856, Weed Papers, UR.

56. Andrew Stewart to Fillmore, Oct. 25, 1856, Isaac Hazlehurst to Fillmore, Oct. 30 [with a copy of Fillmore's response (quotation) on the back, dated Nov. 1], Nov. 1, 1856, K. Rayner to Fillmore, Nov. 3, 1856 (with a copy of Fillmore's response on the back), Fillmore Papers, SUNY-O.

"in the Republican Party who are urging us to this course" are doing so not because "*they* believe we could carry the State by it, but because they *know* it would destroy our Nationality as a Party!" Others agreed that fusion was a Republican plot "to disorganize our party."[57] Finally, Americans contended that cooperation with a sectional party was antithetical to the tenets of Americanism. Fillmore told Rayner after the election that fusing with the Republicans in Pennsylvania would have "violat[ed] one of the fundamental principles of our party, which was to be a *national Union party.*" Moore also advised that the Americans should concede Pennsylvania "rather than lose our identity as a National conservative party." Although Republicans charged that Fillmore voters wanted Buchanan to win the presidency, principle and strategy dictated their actions.[58]

On election day, the electorate proved how faulty Fillmore's strategy had been. He carried only one state, Maryland, while Buchanan captured all the remaining slave states, plus California, Illinois, Indiana, Pennsylvania, and New Jersey, and with them the election. In the South, Fillmore actually fared relatively well, winning 44 percent of the vote. In fact, with a change in a few thousand votes in Kentucky, Louisiana, and Tennessee, Fillmore would have carried those states and thrown the election into the House. In the North, however, Fillmore captured only 13 percent of the vote, and Frémont won all the Know Nothings' previous strongholds in New England by wide margins. The Americans did retain strength in some non-slave areas. Gardner won re-election in Massachusetts, guaranteeing that the Know Nothings would remain a force in that state's politics. In New York, Erastus Brooks captured 22 percent of the vote in the gubernatorial election, and won a plurality in several downstate counties. Pennsylvania Americans controlled 18 percent of the vote in 1856, and in Philadelphia they outnumbered Republicans by three to one. In Connecticut, too, Know Nothings still exerted significant influence, but seemed certain to wield it within the Republican organization, rather than as an independent force. Americans in New Jersey, Indiana, Illinois, and California would also hold the balance of power in future elections in those states. Nonetheless, there could be no doubt that as a national political movement, the American party was dead.

The two American organizations offered a variety of explanations for their defeats. One National American insisted that "the cry 'of no chance for Mr. Fillmore' hamstrung the Party completely." Parson William G. Brownlow of Tennessee blamed his fellow Southerners for the party's setback, lamenting

57. Fillmore to John P. Kennedy, Oct. 25, 1856, Kennedy Papers, Enoch Pratt Free Library; W. A. Glanville to Fillmore, Oct. 21, 1856, Horace H. Day to Fillmore, Oct. 26, Nov. 1, 1856, Henry D. Moore to Fillmore, Oct. 31, 1856, Alfred B. Ely to Fillmore, Nov. 4, 1856, Richard W. Thompson to Fillmore, Nov. 10, 1856, *To the Friends of Fillmore and Donelson in Lancaster County*, broadside (quotation), filed under "[1856]," Fillmore Papers, SUNY-O; Philadelphia *News*, Oct. 28, 1856.

58. Fillmore to Rayner, Nov. 14, 1856, Fillmore Papers, Buffalo and Erie County Historical Society; Henry D. Moore to Fillmore, Aug. 2, 1856, Fillmore Papers, SUNY-O.

that although Fillmore had sacrificed his popularity in the North to maintain his standing in the South, "thousands went over to Buchanan, who disliked to vote for him, but were induced to believe that it was necessary to defeat Fremont." Donelson, on the other hand, blamed Fillmore's northern supporters, who foolishly allowed their hatred of the Republicans to interfere with the fusion efforts in the key northern states. These factors, however, explained only why Fillmore had captured a single state, instead of three or four. As to why the American party had not dominated the election, as its members had arrogantly predicted two years earlier, there was only one answer: the sectional crisis. Just when the American party would appear to make some headway in the campaign, explained Sammons, "some new piece of actual or reputed" news would "come up from Kansas" and cause its adherents to "return to the other parties." Although Sammons overstated the Americans' losses during the campaign, his assessment of the Republican party was particularly perceptive. "The Republican leaders have been successful in keeping the attention of the community directed towards Democratic iniquities, until, taking advantage of a combination of things[,] a deep seated and almost vindictive antipathy has been concentrated over the entire North towards the South." He astutely concluded that "there can be no quiet" until the South makes "full atonement . . . in some satisfactory way."[59]

North Americans, on the other hand, blamed the Republicans' failure to endorse the North American vice presidential candidate for Frémont's defeat. The Lowell News asserted that the ticket of Frémont and Johnston "would have swept New Jersey, Pennsylvania, and California" and thus carried the election, and the Boston Bee agreed that the North American ticket would have easily defeated Buchanan. North Americans were not the only ones who came to this conclusion. Republicans such as Thurlow Weed asserted afterward that "the first, and as I still think fatal error, was in not taking a Vice President in whose nomination the North Americans would have concurred cordially."[60] Yet it seems likely that Frémont would have lost the election even with Johnston as his running-mate. Despite the vice presidential controversy, Frémont carried the states—such as New York, Massachusetts, and Connecticut—in which nativism was still a major force in the American party and where the vice presidential dispute generated the most intra-party animosity. In the northern states that Buchanan won, most Fillmore voters spurned Frémont not because he lacked nativist credentials, but because they perceived the Republican party to be a radical, sectional organization.

At the conclusion of 1856, then, the American party obviously had no future in the North. As one Republican rejoiced, the American party "has been

59. R. Graves to Fillmore, Nov. 13, 1856, W. G. Brownlow to Fillmore, Nov. 13, 1856, A. J. Donelson to Fillmore, Oct. 25, 1856, S. Sammons to Fillmore, Nov. 7, 1856, Fillmore Papers, SUNY-O.

60. Boston Bee, Nov. 7, 11 (quoting Lowell News), 1856; Jamestown [New York] Journal, Nov. 14, 1856; Weed to Cameron, Nov. 12, 1856, Cameron Papers, LC.

killed dead, dead, never, never to rise again." Yet the American party's influence would not die so quickly. After all, cautioned the New York *Times*, "no sentiment, or conviction, which has the power to create such a party in so short a time, can perish or lose its vital force so suddenly." Furthermore, the American party at the end of 1856 was composed of two somewhat distinctive components: pro-Union conservatives and diehard nativists. It seemed certain that most nativists would eventually join the Republican party, because the Democrats continued to embrace immigrants and denounce the Know Nothings. But the future of the conservatives was far less certain. Because these Americans were concentrated in the midwestern states which still eluded the Republicans, they would determine the fate of the anti-slavery party and the legacy of the Know Nothing movement.[61]

61. C. S. Henry to Seward, Nov. 6, 1856, Seward Papers, UR; New York *Times*, Nov. 18, 1856.

10

The Know Nothings and
Republican Ascendancy, 1857–1860

The American party continued to decline precipitously after the presidential canvass of 1856, contesting its final election in 1859. Under ordinary circumstances, the swift and predictable demise of a third political party would merit minimal attention. But because scholars agree that the flow of Fillmore voters into the Republican party carried Abraham Lincoln to victory in 1860 (and thus helped precipitate the Civil War), they have thoroughly scrutinized the dissolution of the American party. Two widely divergent interpretations have emerged concerning how the Republicans managed to convert the Americans. One emphasizes Republican endorsements of nativism. Historians espousing this view point to Republican enactment of voting restrictions and church property laws as the *quid pro quo* with which the Republicans attained the support of former Know Nothings.[1] The other questions whether these laws should be considered concessions to the Americans and contends that such legislation played only a minor role in convincing Fillmore voters to become Republicans.[2] An examination of the context in which Republicans enacted nativist legislation in the late 1850s and of political conditions in the closely contested states where no such laws were passed indicates that while

1. William E. Gienapp, "Nativism and the Creation of a Republican Majority in the North before the Civil War," *Journal of American History* 72 (1985): 529–59; Joel Silbey, " 'The Undisguised Connection,' Know Nothings into Republicans: New York as a Test Case," in Silbey, *The Partisan Imperative: The Dynamics of American Politics Before the Civil War* (New York: Oxford Univ. Press, 1985), 127–65; Michael F. Holt, *Forging a Majority: The Formation of the Republican Party in Pittsburgh, 1848–1860* (New Haven: Yale Univ. Press, 1969), 222; Ronald P. Formisano, *The Birth of Mass Political Parties: Michigan, 1827–1861* (Princeton: Princeton Univ. Press, 1971), 284–87.

2. Eric Foner, *Free Soil, Free Labor, Free Men: The Ideology of the Republican Party before the Civil War* (New York: Oxford Univ. Press, 1970), 226–60; Richard H. Sewell, *Ballots for Freedom: Antislavery Politics in the United States, 1837–1860* (New York: Oxford Univ. Press, 1976), 275; David M. Potter, *The Impending Crisis, 1848–1861* (New York: Harper and Row, 1976), 259.

Republicans did make a more concerted attempt to woo nativists than some historians have admitted, such efforts did not convince most Fillmore voters to join the Republican party. The moderation of their position on slavery and the endorsement of a more stringent protective tariff won Republicans the support of most Fillmore voters, and transformed the Republicans into the nation's dominant political organization.

Although observers expected the American party to disintegrate after the 1856 election, its leaders insisted that they had no plans to disband the organization. "The American party, slaughtered to all human appearance, is not dead," announced an Ohio newspaper, while the Worcester *Transcript* agreed that "the future existence of the American party is a fixed fact." Pointing out that it took the Whig party a decade to elect its first President, these optimists contended that Fillmore's poor showing was no cause for alarm. "When the [slavery] excitement has abated, and the people come coolly and calmly to deliberate," predicted a New York journal, "they will perceive the full value of the American policy." Privately, too, most American leaders exuded confidence. "I think the Republican vote was accidental last fall," Solomon G. Haven told Fillmore, adding that "the causes which produced it are nearly extinct already. If our boys can hold on two years . . . one side or the other will come to our party."[3]

The naïveté of these diehard Americans became evident in June 1857, when the leaders of the American party gathered in Louisville for their last national convention. The site of the meeting was significant, because by convening for the first time in a slave state, party leaders admitted that their power base had shifted from the northeast to the border states. The presence of only one New Englander at the convention confirmed this change. After re-adopting their 1856 platform (without the planks criticizing the Pierce administration), the delegates selected an executive committee to coordinate party operations. By abolishing the office of party president and replacing it with an executive committee, the Americans destroyed the last vestiges of their fraternal past. Furthermore, by canceling future annual meetings (they empowered the executive committee to call a convention should one became necessary), American party leaders indicated that they expected individual state organizations to initiate the party's revival.[4]

With Know Nothing Henry J. Gardner beginning his third term as governor, American party leaders hoped that Massachusetts would initiate their

3. Hillsborough [Ohio] *American Citizen*, March 28 (quotation), Sept. 19, 1857; Boston *Bee*, Nov. 14 (quotation), 17, 1857; Seneca Falls *American Reveille* in St. Clairsville [Ohio] *Independent Republican*, Nov. 20, 1856 (quotation); R. Graves to Fillmore, Nov. 13, 1856, Jacob Broom to Fillmore, Dec. 15, 1856, Haven to Fillmore, Jan. 3, 1857, Fillmore Papers, SUNY-O; A. H. Lippitt to J. Scott Harrison, Jan. 15, 1857, Jacob Broom to Harrison, July 16, 1857, J. Scott Harrison Papers, LC; J. P. Faurot to Daniel Ullmann, Nov. 15, 1856, Ullmann Papers, NYHS.

4. New York *Herald*, June 4, 5, 1857; Robert D. Parmet, "The Know Nothings in Connecticut" (Ph.D. diss., Columbia University, 1966), 275.

organization's renaissance. Nativism, after all, still exerted a potent influence in Massachusetts. However, these Know Nothings failed to grasp the essentially weak position of the American party there. Most of the state's nativists were North Americans who had voted for Frémont in 1856. They had no desire to perpetuate an independent American party, preferring instead to exercise their influence within the Republican organization. Although they called themselves "Frémonters" rather than Republicans, they did so not because they intended to maintain a separate organization, but in the belief they might wield more influence by maintaining the threat of independent action.

Developments during the 1857 Massachusetts legislative session convinced many North Americans that they had been far-sighted in maintaining the option for independent action. Two constitutional amendments of particular interest to the Americans came before the state's lawmakers in 1857, both of which had been approved by the previous legislature. One made the ability to read and write a qualification for voting, while the other prescribed that naturalized citizens wait fourteen years before gaining the franchise. The second amendment mattered far more to Americans than the first. In 1855, when the Know Nothings had controlled virtually every seat in the legislature, they had not ratified the reading and writing amendment. In contrast, the effort to impose a waiting period before immigrants could vote lay at the heart of the Know Nothing agenda. Know Nothings had advocated a twenty-one-year hiatus between naturalization and voting, insisting that it took this long to "Americanize" immigrants, but had substituted the fourteen-year proposal to gain Republican support in 1856.

Republicans dominated the legislature in 1857, and because they had no objection to the literacy amendment, it won approval by an overwhelming margin.[5] However, many Republicans opposed the fourteen-year amendment. Some condemned the proposal on moral grounds, calling it "bigoted" and "proscriptive." Others denounced it as inexpedient, predicting that thousands of German immigrants would abandon the Republican party if its Massachusetts members supported the proposal.[6] Consequently, the Republican-controlled senate refused even to consider the fourteen-year amendment, although, in an attempt to appease nativists, it passed a new amendment mandating a two-year interval. The house, with a greater concentration of nativists, substituted fourteen years for the senate's two, but the 161 to 110 vote in favor fell short of the two-thirds' majority necessary for approval. Hoping to reach a compromise with the senate, some lawmakers proposed a five-year waiting period, but dedicated nativists—angry that their fourteen-

5. The vote in the House was 226 to 43, and in the Senate 30 to 5. *Debates and Proceedings in the Massachusetts Legislature* (1857): 146, 176–77; Boston *Bee*, March 16, 1857.

6. Worcester *Spy* quoted in Boston *Bee*, March 20, 1857; Edward L. Pierce, *Effect of Proscriptive or Extreme Legislation Against Foreigners in Massachusetts and New England* (Boston, 1857).

year proposal had been derailed—refused to support the measure, and it failed to win even a simple majority.[7]

Americans bitterly denounced the Republicans for defeating the fourteen-year amendment. North Americans claimed that they had supported Republican legislative candidates in the 1856 elections only after receiving assurances that Republicans would endorse the fourteen-year bill. Americans also asserted that under a logrolling arrangement, they had agreed to support Charles Sumner's re-election to the Senate in return for Republican pledges to back the fourteen-year proposal. Republicans denied the existence of any such bargains. Some anti-nativist Republicans feared that "to quiet honest nativism," they might eventually have to enact the two-year amendment, but they hoped that because of the legislature's action, all such proposals had been "killed stone dead, as they deserve."[8]

The defeat of the fourteen-year amendment indicated to nativist Republicans that anti-nativists would ignore them when formulating policy. Nativists' suspicions were further aroused when the Republican state nominating convention, scheduled for June 24 in Worcester, "was called in such a way as to exclude all Americans from it."[9] Some nativists wanted to respond to these insults by retaining the American party as an independent organization and renominating Gardner. Most North Americans, however, believed that such a strategy would be disastrous, reasoning that if they abandoned the anti-slavery coalition, anti-nativists would gain firm control of the Republican party. Consequently, anti-Gardner nativists formulated a plan aimed at forcing the Republicans to nominate North American Nathaniel Banks, Jr., for governor. Former Know Nothings believed that with Banks as governor, the Republican party would be unable to snub nativists or ignore their agenda.

The North Americans executed their plan flawlessly. First, the influential Boston *Bee* began to boom Banks for governor. A few days later, the *Bee* printed a call for an American nominating convention to be held on June 16, eight days before the Republican gathering. Moses G. Cobb, chairman of the American state executive committee, denounced this call as "wholly unauthorized," but admitted privately that he could do nothing to stop it. Predictably, this "informal" American convention nominated Banks.[10] To this point many Republicans were thrilled with the action of the renegade North Americans. Republicans in Congress had used Banks's candidacy for Speaker to wean northern Know Nothings from the American party, and they believed that as a candidate for governor he would serve the same function. Republicans considered Banks more a Republican than a Know Nothing and were convinced that

7. *Debates and Proceedings in the Massachusetts Legislature* (1857): 310–12, 326, 348, 391–92, 400–403; Boston *Bee*, March 18, 31, April 8, 29, May 27, 28, 1857.

8. Boston *Bee*, March 18, 19, 20, 21, 24, 27, April 3, 6, 1857; Edward L. Pierce to Charles Sumner, May 10, 1857, Sumner Papers, HU; Worcester *Spy* quoted in Boston *Bee*, March 20, 1857; D. W. Alvord to Francis Bird, June 2, 1857, Bird Papers, HU.

9. Boston *Bee*, June 5, 1857.

10. Boston *Bee*, June 1, 2, 3, 5, 9 (quotation), 1857.

he had joined the Order out of expediency, rather than a dedication to nativism. Banks had reinforced this perception by helping Frémont gain the North American presidential nomination. Republicans also believed that Banks would not accept the American nomination until after his selection by the Republicans (thus avoiding the appearance that nativists had dictated his selection). Therefore, although many Republicans wished that "Banks was not tinged with KNism," most welcomed his nomination as a means of finally unifying the anti-slavery forces in Massachusetts.[11]

As anti-nativist Republicans congratulated themselves on the imminent surrender of the North Americans, Banks stunned them by accepting the American nomination before the Republican convention. The frank endorsement of Americanism in Banks's acceptance letter especially angered the anti-nativists. They threatened to bolt the Republican convention if Banks won its nomination, increasing the likelihood of a close contest for the gubernatorial nomination. When the Republicans convened at Worcester, however, it became apparent that only a small portion of Massachusetts Republicans were dedicated anti-nativists. Banks won the gubernatorial nomination by an overwhelming majority, capturing 337 out of 431 votes cast. Gardner, refusing to retire gracefully, became the candidate of the anti-fusion Fillmore Americans when a second American convention nominated him for governor. With the support of both the Republicans and North Americans, Banks easily defeated both Gardner and the Democratic nominee in the November election.[12]

Upon taking office, Banks announced that he would "cheerfully concur" with any changes made in voting qualifications—a direct reference to the movement to restrict immigrant voting. The legislative committee created to study the matter (headed by former Massachusetts Know Nothing president John W. Foster) recommended a constitutional amendment that would bar immigrants from voting until two years after naturalization. Many former Know Nothings complained that the measure was a pale imitation of their original twenty-one-year proposal, but their efforts to lengthen the waiting period on the house and senate floors were repulsed by Republicans. Although the two-year amendment passed by wide margins in both the house and senate, restricting immigrant voting was so sensitive an issue that more

11. D. W. Alvord to Bird, June 2, 3, 4, 5, 7, 14 (quotation), 1857, Bird Papers, HU; Amos A. Lawrence to [Charles D.] Robinson, June 6, 1857, Amos A. Lawrence Papers, MHS. The fact that American newspapers felt obliged to make excuses for Banks's past disloyalty to the American cause after he received the gubernatorial nomination demonstrates that he was perceived to be more of a Republican than an American. See, for example, Boston *Bee*, June 11 (quoting Westfield *News Letter*), July 3, 1857.

12. Boston *Bee*, June 19, 20, 23, July 1, Sept. 11, 17, 22, 23, 24, Oct. 5, 15, Nov. 2, 1857; Lowell *American Citizen*, Sept. 24, 1857; Banks, *The Great Questions of National and State Politics* (Boston, 1857); *Facts for the People*, broadside, MHS; J. W. Foster to Banks, June 23, 1857, Banks Papers, IISHL; Edward L. Pierce to Salmon P. Chase, Aug. 3, 1857, Chase Papers, LC; Edward L. Pierce to Sumner, "September 1857," Sumner Papers, HU; William G. Bean, "Party Transformation in Massachusetts with Special Reference to the Antecedents of Republicanism, 1848–1860" (Ph.D. diss., Harvard University, 1922), 358–67.

than half the house members absented themselves rather than record their position on the matter.[13]

The two-year amendment gained overwhelming legislative approval in 1859 without the abstentions that had tainted its ratification in 1858, suggesting that the issue had become less controversial.[14] After the legislature adjourned, however, anti-nativist Republicans launched an intensive campaign to defeat the amendment when the voters decided its fate in May. Although they admitted that the naturalization laws were often abused, the amendment's opponents insisted that less proscriptive means existed to ameliorate the problem. They also claimed that the measure would alienate German immigrants in the closely contested midwestern states. "Nothing could be more ill-timed and impolitic," wrote William Cullen Bryant to Banks, and Horace Greeley's New York *Tribune* predicted that "its adoption . . . might even defeat the election of a Republican President in 1860."[15] In contrast, supporters of the amendment contended that the sentiments of 1,000,000 northern nativists should take precedence over those of 100,000 German immigrants in the west. They also asserted that anti-nativist Republicans had promised to accept this mild version of the original twenty-one-year proposal as a compromise, and denounced their subsequent opposition as a thinly veiled attempt to stamp out nativism within the Republican party. Proponents claimed that the measure would end the practice of illegally naturalizing immi-

13. The Massachusetts legislature did not print journals for either 1858 or 1859, so I have relied on the scrapbook in the Boston Public Library which contains newspapers reports of their daily proceedings. For the two-year amendment in 1858, see debates of Feb. 3, 4, 10, 11, 12, 16, 19, 20, 1858, Massachusetts Legislative Scrapbook, Rare Book Room, BPL. The quotation from Banks's message is in *Massachusetts Senate Documents* (1858): no. 1, pp. 16–17. The vote by party breaks down as follows:

1858 House Vote on Massachusetts Two-Year Amendment

	Republicans	*Americans*	*Democrats*	*Party Unknown*	*Total*
Yes	78	12	0	7	97
Absent	65	22	22	11	120
No	1	2	15	2	20

Source: Party affiliations from election results printed in Boston *Courier* in the days after the 1857 election; votes from Boston *Advertiser*, Feb. 13, 1858.

14. Debates of Feb. 4, 7, 8, 18, 1859, Massachusetts Legislative Scrapbook, Rare Book Room, BPL; Caleb Cushing, *Speeches on the Amendment of the Constitution of Massachusetts, Imposing Disabilities on Naturalized Citizens of the United States* (Boston, 1859).

15. William Slade to Banks, March 8, 1859, W. C. Bryant to Banks, April 25, 1859, S. Bowles to Banks, May 2, [1859], Banks Papers, IISHL; H. Kreismann to Banks, April 2, 1859, Banks Papers, LC; Edward L. Pierce to Chase, April 28, 1859, Chase Papers, LC; Boston *Courier*, April 19 (minutes of public meeting featuring Carl Schurz), 28 (with letter of Henry Wilson opposing the amendment), May 7 (quoting the *Tribune*), 1859; Springfield *Republican*, April 27, May 3, 6, 1859; F. I. Herriott, "The Germans of Iowa and the 'Two-Year' Amendment of Massachusetts," *Deutsch-Americanische Geschichtsblätter* 13 (1913): 202–308.

grants immediately before elections in return for their votes. "No party would buy up votes two years ahead," argued the amendment's advocates. "It would not pay. There would be quite too much uncertainty as to where the new made voters would be after the lapse of two years." Republicans opposing the amendment believed that if Banks recommended its defeat, voters might reject it at the polls. But the governor, who had praised the measure in his 1859 annual message, remained silent, and in May voters ratified the amendment by a wide margin.[16]

Historians have long debated the significance of the Massachusetts two-year amendment. Joel Silbey has called it "a climactic example of the association of nativist sentiment with the Republican party." Dale Baum, on the other hand, has argued that nativists were not influential in the Massachusetts Republican party by 1859, and Eric Foner has likewise asserted that "far from demonstrating the connection between Republicanism and nativism, the two-year amendment indicated that even in Massachusetts nativism was dying out as a political force."[17] Yet while nativism *had* greatly diminished by 1859— both within the Republican party and as an independent political force— passage of the two-year amendment attests to nativism's continuing influence within the Massachusetts Republican organization. After all, this overtly nativist amendment was ratified by two Republican-dominated legislatures, and Republican legislators voted for the measure to an even greater degree than their American counterparts.[18]

Nonetheless, any inference that Republicans enacted the two-year amendment in an attempt to draw Fillmore voters into their party is unwarranted. By the time the two-year amendment came up for consideration before the 1859 legislature, nearly all Massachusetts nativists had already joined the Republican party. Banks, who had attracted only 47 percent of the vote in 1857, captured 61 percent when he won re-election in 1858, thereby assuring Republican control of Massachusetts politics. Those who remained in the Massachusetts American party after 1858 stressed preservation of the Union over nativism, and after that year's election an American leader admitted that "the number of us who hold" these " 'national' views is so small, or else we are so

16. Boston *Atlas and Bee*, Feb. 9, April 12 (quotation from letter signed "A Subscriber to the Worcester *Spy*"), 1859; Charlestown *Advertiser*, May 7, 1859; Boston *Journal*, April 28, 29 (letter signed "H."), May 3 (letter in response to Wilson's written by Amasa Walker), 1859; Boston *Courier*, May 4, 1859; J. Z. Goodrich to Banks, April 27, 1859, Banks Papers, IISHL; Edward L. Pierce to Sumner, April 18, May 31, 1859, Albert G. Browne to Sumner, June 28, 1859, Sumner Papers, HU; Edward L. Pierce to Chase, May 30, 1859, Chase Papers, LC; Bean, "Party Transformation in Massachusetts," 371; Baum, *Civil War Party System*, 44–48.

17. Silbey, *The Transformation of American Politics, 1840–1860* (Englewood Cliffs, N.J.: Prentice-Hall, 1967), 14–15; Gienapp, "Nativism and the Creation of a Republican Majority," 551, 557–58; Baum, *Civil War Party System*, 47; Foner, *Free Soil*, 253.

18. Fifty-four percent of House Republicans voted for the amendment in 1858, while only 33 percent of the Americans cast affirmative ballots. See fn. 13 above. Because there were so few Americans in the 1859 legislature, a statistically significant comparison for that session is not possible.

dull, that we may be left out of the account without being missed." Why then, if they did not need to court outsiders, did the Republicans pass the two-year amendment? Republicans enacted it because nativists within the party demanded it and because anti-nativists failed to convince the rest of the party to oppose it. Thus, the two-year amendment was not a Republican concession designed to attract Fillmore voters, and its revision from twenty-one years to two attests to the declining appeal of nativism. Nevertheless, its addition to the state constitution indicates that anti–immigrant sentiment still influenced politicians and voters in Massachusetts.[19]

As in Massachusetts, most Connecticut voters who had supported Frémont had once been Know Nothings. But despite their numerical strength, Connecticut nativists had relinquished their dominant role among the anti-Democratic forces in the summer of 1856, when Republicans succeeded in forcing the North Americans to accept William L. Dayton as their vice presidential nominee. "You see how they turned tail in the matter of the Vice Presidency," noted New Haven Republican James F. Babcock. "They swallowed every thing because the Republicans walked directly over them." Babcock predicted that a similarly firm stance in 1857 would result in the destruction of the American party. Republicans failed to realize, however, that North American enthusiasm for Frémont—not Know Nothing weakness—had brought about the Republican victory in the vice presidential dispute. This became evident when the "Union" nominating convention met in New Haven in January 1857.[20] The gubernatorial nomination went to the American choice, Alexander H. Holley, instead of Republican William A. Buckingham. Americans also controlled nominations on the local level, dictating nearly every candidate for state senator, probate judge, and sheriff. On election day in April, Holley narrowly defeated his Democratic opponent.[21]

In the aftermath of this triumph, Americans believed that they would continue to control the Union organization. Holley's recommendation that the legislature enact a constitutional amendment instituting a waiting period before naturalized citizens could vote also cheered nativists. Yet it soon became evident that nativism was losing its political influence in Connecticut. First, the legislature ignored Holley's call to restrict immigrant voting. Next,

19. Lawrence to [N. Sargent], Dec. 1858 (letterbook), Amos A. Lawrence Papers, MHS. Although Lawrence was replying to a query from Sargent about the possibilities of creating a new conservative party dedicated to anti-sectionalism, his response provides an accurate picture of American strength after the 1858 contest.

20. The gathering was referred to as the "Union" convention because both the Americans and the Republicans refused to participate in a convention organized by the other party. Americans hoped that this neutral organization would form the basis for a national fusion between Americans and Republicans, whereas Republicans believed that once they achieved control of the party, they could change its name to "Republican."

21. Parmet, "Know Nothings in Connecticut," 239–71 (240 for Babcock quotation); Mark Howard to Gideon Welles, Feb. 21, 1857, Moses Pierce to Welles, Feb. 19, March 13, 30, 1857, Welles Papers, LC.

the subsequent Union party convention denied him renomination, choosing Buckingham instead. In an attempt to placate disgruntled Americans, the platform included a call for a literacy test and a condemnation of ballot-box frauds, but when Americans attempted to add nativist rhetoric to the document, Republicans rebuffed them. Americans insisted that they would not cooperate with an organization that ignored their principles, and called their own convention. However, their first three nominees for governor all declined the honor, forcing the embarrassed nativists to recant their words of defiance and endorse Buckingham. His victory in the April 1858 election doomed the independent American party to extinction in Connecticut.[22]

In the wake of the 1858 Connecticut election results, most American party leaders who had refused to join the Republicans now made their way into that party. The 1858 legislature demonstrated that nativists had not lost all their influence when it granted initial approval to constitutional amendments imposing a one-year wait before naturalized citizens could vote and a literacy test on all voters. By this time, however, such gestures of conciliation to nativists had become increasingly infrequent. Republicans no longer called themselves the "Union" party to appease Americans, and demonstrated the significance of this change by removing the two mild nativist planks from their platform in 1859. When the nativist amendments came before the legislature in that year, Republicans vigorously opposed them and caused their overwhelming defeat. Although some former Americans had complained that the Republicans "hate the very smell of a man who *has ever been a Know Nothing,*" Republicans did not ostracize them from the party. They were simply too numerous to be ignored. In fact, Republicans made former Know Nothing congressman John Woodruff their state chairman in 1859, and replaced him in 1860 with former Know Nothing president Nehemiah D. Sperry, who as late as 1858 had supported an independent American party. The state chairman was responsible for organizing election campaigns, and although chairmen did not wield the patronage that came with elective office, their control over the party purse strings made them quite influential. Such appointments indicated that Republicans still worried about placating former Know Nothings. Yet Connecticut Republicans converted them to Republicanism without making concessions to their nativism.[23]

New York Republicans made a stronger effort to woo Americans than their Massachusetts or Connecticut counterparts, but these efforts were hindered by anti-nativists and produced a negligible impact on the dissipation of the American party. New York was the last place one would have expected to find Republicans courting Know Nothings. Frémont had easily carried the state in 1856, and under the leadership of Senator William H. Seward, the New York Republican party had consistently condemned nativism. But politi-

22. Parmet, "Know Nothings in Connecticut," 272–300.
23. Parmet, "Know Nothings in Connecticut," 301–19, 324; Welles to O. S. Ferry, Dec. 2, 1857 (quotation), Welles Papers, CHS.

cal analysts realized that in 1857 Republican popularity would decrease, primarily because "Soft" Democrats who had supported Frémont in 1856 were bound to vote Democratic in the upcoming state contest. The conduct of the 1857 legislature further damaged Republican prospects. In an obvious grasp for patronage, this Republican-controlled body stripped New York City of most of its power of self-government and enacted an unpopular liquor license law as well.[24] As a result, the Democratic ticket defeated the Republicans in the state's November election, while the Americans ran a distant third.[25]

In the aftermath of their 1857 defeat, Horace Greeley and other New York Republicans called for fusion with the Americans to improve Republican prospects in future contests. New York's Republican governor, John A. King, apparently endorsed this strategy, informing Seward in early 1858 that "I recognized the great object of the American party by recommending a [voter] Registry Law in my message." The legislature failed to act on King's proposal, but the strong support the measure received from Republicans convinced many Americans that, as their New York president put it, "we Republicans and Americans have a common interest." In order to facilitate fusion, Americans scheduled their fall convention for the same date and location as the Republicans'. Committees from both parties conferred and agreed upon terms for fusion: Republicans promised to insert planks into their platform endorsing a registry law and a waiting period before naturalized citizens could vote, to moderate their anti-slavery rhetoric, and to split the state nominations with the Americans. In return, the Americans would dismantle their organization and join the Republican party. Following the advice of Seward and Weed, however, the full Republican convention rejected the fusion proposal, adopting instead a more radical anti-slavery plank and choosing an all-Republican ticket. The Republicans left the two nativist planks in place, but the Americans scoffed at this token gesture and nominated their own ticket.[26]

Why did Republicans renege on their agreement with the Americans?

24. Edward K. Spann, *The New Metropolis: New York City, 1840–1857* (New York: Columbia Univ. Press, 1981), 384–400.

25. Thomas J. Curran, "The Know Nothings of New York" (Ph.D. diss., Columbia University, 1963), 266–69; Louis Dow Scisco, *Political Nativism in New York State* (New York: Columbia Univ. Press, 1901), 226–31; Albany *Statesman* quoted in Steubenville *True American*, Nov. 19, Dec. 2, 1857; Brooklyn *Star* quoted in Steubenville *True American*, Nov. 18, 1857; New York *Sunday Dispatch* quoted in St. Clairsville [Ohio] *Independent Republican*, Nov. 19, 1857, and in Steubenville *True American*, Dec. 2, 1857; F. Hawley to "Dear Children," Nov. 23, 1857, James Hawley Papers, LC.

26. John A. King to Seward, Feb. 1, 1858, King Papers, NYSL; Gustavus Scroggs quoted in Curran, "Know Nothings of New York," 270; New York *Times* and *Tribune*, Sept. 9, 10, 11, 1858. Silbey and Gienapp describe these planks as meaningful concessions made to the Americans, but ignore the demeaning manner in which they were proffered. When viewed in the proper context—as part of the slap in the face the Americans received at the convention—it becomes evident that the planks did not represent a significant concession to the Americans. Silbey, " 'The Undisguised Connection,' " 145–47; Gienapp, "Nativism and the Creation of a Republican Majority," 549.

Some scholars have suggested that Weed wanted to maintain Seward's distance from nativism in order to preserve his presidential prospects, but Weed was probably motivated to an equal extent by the belief that most Americans would join the Republican party even without a deal. Whatever the case, Weed's strategy succeeded, because the Republicans carried the 1858 election, and it appears that most Americans who left their party in that year voted Republican.[27] However, the Republican margin of victory was still uncomfortably slim; most Americans remained attached to their party; and the Americans still held the balance of power in the state.

When the New York legislature convened in 1859, the registry law was once again on the agenda. But by this point, both Americans *and* Republicans desired passage of a registry law. "The undeniable fact," commented the New York *Times*, is "that nine-tenths of [the Republican] party desire a Registry, and insist on its enactment." The legislature passed a registry law that spring, but filled it with loopholes that limited its effectiveness. First, the law required voter registration only in New York City and county. Second, a voter *could* register in advance, but might circumvent this requirement if he furnished a witness to testify to his qualifications. Observers immediately recognized that the law would never accomplish the "purification of the ballot-box" sought by the Americans. As the New York *Times* noted:

> It invites [those who currently vote fraudulently] to register their names beforehand; but knowing their repugnance to this premature exposure, it kindly permits them to vote without it. Their sole chance is at the polls, where the crowd and the hustle so effectually favor their designs. Not one of that class will take the trouble to place his name on the list. That would be an act of verdancy entirely unworthy of him. But he will go with a friend, as the new law requires, and when the rush is greatest, will force in his ballot by his own oath and that of his confederate. The only difference to him between the new law and the old is that two oaths are to be henceforth required instead of one. But as he can reciprocate, there will be no great difficulty in finding a swearing friend to back his claim.

27. A comparison of the 1857 vote (for secretary of state) with that of 1858 (for governor) suggests that most defecting Americans voted Republican:

New York Election Returns

	Republican	American	Democrat
1857	177,425 (40%)	66,882 (15%)	195,482 (44%)
1858	247,953 (46%)	60,880 (11%)	230,513 (43%)

Source: Tribune Almanac (1858): 52, (1859): 45.

Of course, a comparison of the two elections does not prove that Americans shifted primarily to the Republicans in 1858. Americans might have become Democrats, while Democrats became Republicans. But my analysis of these returns is confirmed by contemporary observers as well as the ecological regression estimates made by Silbey and Gienapp. This same caveat applies to all the voting tables that follow.

Instead of calling the new law a registry, the *Times* concluded that it ought to be known as an act to increase "in the smallest practicable degree the difficulties of illegal voting."[28]

Some American organs applauded the new registry law despite its deficiencies, but the most influential American party journal, the New York *Express*, condemned the statute. That the Republicans would enact such a useless measure should not surprise anyone, commented the *Express*, because the registry bill "promised in the Republican convention . . . was only a milk and water law, and the milk was extracted and the water left, as soon as the convention adjourned." The *Express* wished "it understood for one that we do not regard the bill passed by the Legislature in any true sense a Registry Law." Consequently, the law had little impact on Republican efforts to woo Americans. Many abandoned the dying organization, but others decided to retain their independence until the other parties recognized that "Americanism . . . is an element which must be taken into serious account in all of their future calculations."[29] The Americans realized that the Republicans would carry the state in 1859 if the Americans continued to run a third ticket. Consequently, the Americans decided to endorse five Republicans and four Democrats, to demonstrate that they still held the balance of power. The success of their ticket (eight of its nine candidates were elected) confirmed that the registry law had not brought about the surrender of the Americans. The Americans would remain independent, insisted one of their organs, until the Republicans "meet us on an honorable footing."[30] Because they insulted the Americans at their 1858 convention, and because the registry law they passed was intentionally ineffectual, Republican efforts to court Fillmore voters with nativist legislation had little impact on the dissolution of the American party in New York.

Like their New York counterparts, Americans in Ohio appeared to hold the balance of political power after the 1856 election.[31] Ohio's governor, Salmon P. Chase, planned to seek re-election in 1857, primarily because a successful campaign would enhance his presidential aspirations. However, a portion of the American party had vehemently opposed Chase in 1855. Many of the governor's advisors, fearing that renewed American opposition might lead to his defeat, urged Chase to decline renomination in order to protect his chances for the presidency. Others suggested that the Republicans make con-

28. New York, *Laws* (1859): 895–902; New York *Times*, March 30, 1859, quoted in Silbey, " 'The Undisguised Connection,' " 151; *Times* quoted in Boston *Courier*, April 19, 1859.

29. New York *Express* quoted in Boston *Courier*, April 19, 1859; Canandaigua *Ontario Repository* quoted in Ithaca *American Citizen*, Aug. 17, 1859.

30. Curran, "Know Nothings of New York," 279–84; Scisco, *Political Nativism in New York State*, 235–38; Ithaca *American Citizen*, Nov. 16, 1859. The head of the Republican ticket in 1859 received 251,139 votes (50%), the Democrat 227,304 (45%), while the average difference between the Republicans who were and were not supported by the Americans (the only way to determine the size of their vote) was 24,813 (5%). *Tribune Almanac* (1859): 45; Silbey, "Undisguised Connection," 157.

31. Frémont had polled 187,497 votes (49%), Buchanan 170,874 (44%), and Fillmore 28,126 (7%).

cessions to the Americans, in order to secure a fusion of the two parties and ensure Chase's re-election.[32]

As in Massachusetts and Connecticut, the concession both sides had in mind was a constitutional amendment to extend the period before immigrants could vote, in this case by one year. The Americans supported the proposal, as did the many former Know Nothings who had become Republicans in 1855 and 1856. Yet while Chase wanted to retain the support of anti-slavery nativists, he also sought to maintain good relations with Ohio's Protestant German immigrants. Consequently, Chase worked to kill the one-year amendment, and in the house it failed to win the three-fifths' majority necessary for approval.[33] Realizing that some gesture of conciliation to nativists was necessary, Chase reluctantly agreed to back two other measures instead. One, a church property law, mandated that lay boards of trustees hold the title to church property. Because Catholics were the only religious denomination in America that did not already follow this practice, the discriminatory nature of the law was unmistakable. Furthermore, German Protestants were vehemently anti-Catholic, so by allowing such a measure to pass, Chase actually improved his standing with Protestant German immigrants.[34]

The second measure endorsed by Chase involved modification of Ohio's voting laws. Ohio Republicans were particularly anxious to amend their election laws, because they believed that the "importation" of Irish railroad gangs had defeated Know Nothing-turned-Republican Samuel Galloway in the 1856 Columbus congressional race. But Chase, ever cautious of his standing with German voters, refused to sanction a voter registration law. Acting at his behest, the legislature instead modified the existing voting code, although it made only two significant changes. First, in addition to the requirement that voters reside in the state for thirty days, they would now have to live in the town in which they voted for twenty days (thus preventing the situation that had purportedly defeated Galloway). Second, voters if challenged would be required to produce their naturalization papers for inspection by a judge, although if the voter stated that the documents had been lost, a simple oath to that effect would suffice. One historian recently cited

32. Eugene H. Roseboom, *The Civil War Era, 1850–1873*, vol. IV of *The History of the State of Ohio*, ed. Carl Wittke (Columbus: Ohio State Archaeological and Historical Society, 1944), 325.

33. Fifty-three Ohio House members voted in favor of the one-year amendment, while 50 opposed it. All the affirmative votes were cast by Republicans, while 19 Republicans voted against it. Ohio, *House Journal* (1857): 434–35; Ohio, *Senate Journal* (1857): 289; James Noble to J. Scott Harrison, Feb. 15, 1857, Harrison Papers, LC; John B. Weaver, "The Decline of the Ohio Know-Nothings, 1856–1860," *Cincinnati Historical Society Bulletin* 40 (1982): 238–39.

34. Ohio, *House Journal* (1857): 478; Ohio, *Acts* (1857): 110–12; Weaver, "Decline of the Ohio Know-Nothings," 238; Patrick J. Dignan, *A History of the Legal Incorporation of Catholic Church Property in the United States (1784–1932)* (Washington: Catholic Univ. Press, 1933), 202.

this "stringent voter-registration" law as evidence of the Republicans' efforts to woo Know Nothings. But inasmuch as this law did not require voters to register, and made only these two relatively minor changes to the voting laws (one of which was negated by a major loophole), such a characterization seems unjustified. In fact, the bill was so mild that it received overwhelming bipartisan support, with only four legislators in the house and senate combined voting against it. If the bill had been perceived to contain nativist overtones, Democrats would have opposed it, as they had the one-year amendment, so their support suggests that the measure held little appeal for nativists.[35]

That this was the case is confirmed by the reactions of the Americans themselves. The voting act did not impress the Americans, and they insisted that if the Republicans had truly valued their cooperation, they would have passed the one-year amendment. According to an American organ, the amendment's failure proved that the Republicans could not be trusted to support the American agenda, because Republicans took no action without considering "what beer-sucking foreigner it pleased or offended." Nativists within the Republican party expressed similar sentiments. Thomas H. Ford, Chase's lieutenant governor and the leading ex-Know Nothing within the Republican organization, realized that despite the impression created by passing the church property law, Ohio Republican leaders were methodically working to destroy nativist influence within their party. "Every living man connected however remotely with the *American* organization is dead with the Republicans," complained Ford, and "a united determination to crush out everything coming from that quarter is everywhere manifest."[36] Events at the Republican state nominating convention verified Ford's allegations, because Ford and all but one of the other Know Nothings who had run with Chase in 1855 were dropped from the 1857 ticket. The renomination of even the one Know Nothing was probably disingenuous because the candidate, Jacob Blickensderfer, had been involved in a scandal concerning the awarding of canal contracts, and was thus certain to lose. According to one observer, the nominations demonstrated that the Republicans "have ceased to recognize Know Nothingism as an element to be recognized or conciliated."[37] Because Republicans assumed this hostile attitude toward Ohio's nativists, the Americans ran their own candidate, Philadelph Van Trump, for governor. Although Chase managed to win re-election, he did so by the most narrow of margins, and a comparison of the election results with those of the presidential contest of 1856 indicates that few Fillmore voters had cast

35. Ohio, *Acts* (1857): 136–38; Gienapp, "Nativism and the Creation of a Republican Majority," 549; Ohio, *House Journal* (1857): 327; Ohio, *Senate Journal* (1857): 286.

36. Hillsborough [Ohio] *American Citizen*, April 11, 1857; Ford to Chase, Aug. 4, 1857, Chase Papers, LC.

37. Cincinnati *Commercial* quoted in Hillsborough [Ohio] *American Citizen*, Aug. 22, 1857.

Chase ballots.[38] The one anti-Catholic law passed by the legislature had thus done little to draw Americans into the Republican camp. Taken out of context, it appears to be a significant concession made by Republicans to win American support. In fact, it was a mere gesture designed to obscure the Republicans' overarching goal—destruction of nativist influence within their party.

Rather than appeal to the Americans' nativism, and thereby damage their image with immigrant voters, Ohio Republicans attempted to attract Fillmore voters by appealing to their conservatism. To this end, they nominated two former Fillmore supporters for Congress in 1858: Thomas Corwin, who had served as Fillmore's secretary of the treasury, and Carey Trimble, son of the Americans' 1855 gubernatorial nominee. The choice of Corwin is particularly instructive. Republicans did not fear losing Corwin's district, which they controlled solidly. Their motivation in supporting Corwin is revealed in a condition attached to his nomination—that he must make extensive speaking tours, not only in Ohio but also in neighboring states with significant concentrations of Fillmore voters. During the 1858 campaign and in subsequent years, Corwin campaigned in all the doubtful Republican states, assuring conservatives that their views would be respected within the Republican organization and emphasizing that only the Republicans could make the alterations in tariff rates that Whigs sought. Some Republicans worried that Corwin's nomination was meant to "bring down our doctrines and position to the Fillmore level." Yet by essentially espousing nullification of the fugitive slave law in their 1859 platform, Ohio Republicans reclaimed their reputation as the most radical Republican organization in the Midwest. Their platform in that year also condemned the Massachusetts two-year amendment, removing any suspicion that nativism still wielded significant influence in the party. However, by devices such as the nomination of Corwin and Trimble, Ohio Republicans

---

38. Roseboom, *Civil War Era*, 324–29; Weaver, "Decline of the Ohio Know-Nothings," 239–41; E. Lippitt to J. Scott Harrison, Jan. 15, 1857, Harrison Papers, LC; Thomas C. Ware to My Dear Sir, in Steubenville *True American*, May 13, 1857; Hillsborough [Ohio] *American Citizen*, June 6, Aug. 8, 15, 22, 1857; St. Clairsville [Ohio] *Independent Republican*, June 11, July 23, Aug. 20, 1857; John J. Brasee to Chase, Aug. 28, 1857, Chase Papers, LC. Votes in the two elections were cast as follows:

Ohio Voting

	Republican	American	Democrat
1856	187,497 (49%)	28,121 (7%)	170,874 (44%)
1857	160,541 (49%)	10,135 (3%)	159,060 (48%)

Source: Tribune Almanac (1858): 59.

secured the support of enough Fillmore voters to insure their electoral success in 1858, 1859, and 1860.[39]

It was in Pennsylvania that the Americans posed the greatest threat to Republican success. Fillmore captured a larger percentage of the vote in Pennsylvania than in any other northern state, and received especially strong support in southeastern counties such as Philadelphia, where he out-polled Frémont by more than three to one. Conservative Whigs had accounted for most of the American vote, and Republicans realized that they would have to convert these Whig diehards if they hoped to win Pennsylvania in the future. In order to facilitate American conversions, Republican leaders again agreed to participate in the anti-Democratic coalition known as the "Union party." Although Republicans were determined to control the Union organization, they felt that retaining this name would make their party seem less radical and slavery-oriented. As expected, Republicans dominated the 1857 Union convention in Harrisburg. Rather than choose a gubernatorial candidate who appealed to both Republicans and Americans, as many had expected, the convention nominated David Wilmot, whom North Americans had rejected as a compromise vice presidential choice in 1856, and who the Philadelphia *North American* characterized as "a Republican, pure and simple." The convention did offer the Americans some concessions. Former Know Nothings received two of the three remaining positions on the ticket, and the platform contained one plank condemning fraudulent voting and another criticizing the naturalization of those owing allegiance to a "foreign supremacy." Yet Republicans were pleased with the convention's outcome, because they had made the ticket "as distinctively Republican as possible without slapping the Americans squarely in the face."[40]

With the Union movement in the hands of the Republicans, Americans decided to hold their own convention. For governor they nominated Isaac Hazlehurst, a leading Philadelphia American who had seceded from the Pennsylvania Know Nothing organization when it repudiated Section Twelve and had led the opposition to the fusion presidential ticket in 1856. The American

---

39. Michael F. Holt, *The Political Crisis of the 1850s* (New York: Wiley, 1978), 209 (quotation); Daryl Prendergaft, "Thomas Corwin and the Conservative Republican Reaction," *Ohio Archaeological and Historical Quarterly* 57 (1948): 1–23; Roseboom, *The Civil War Era*, 30, 337–38; Corwin to James S. Pike, Sept. 24, 1858, in Pike, *First Blows of the Civil War* (New York, 1879): 426–27.

40. John F. Coleman, *The Disruption of the Pennsylvania Democracy, 1848–1860* (Harrisburg: Pennsylvania Historical and Museum Commission, 1975), 106–7 (including *North American* quotation); C. Maxwell Myers, "The Rise of the Republican Party in Pennsylvania, 1854–1860" (Ph.D. diss., University of Pittsburgh, 1940), 158–62; James Cooper to Thaddeus Stevens, March 22, 1857, Stevens Papers, LC; Russell Errett to Salmon P. Chase, March 14, 1857, Chase Papers, HSP; Wilmot to Samuel Calvin, April 30, 1857, Calvin Papers, HSP; Philadelphia *North American*, March 27, 1857 (platform); Alexander McClure, *Old Time Notes of Pennsylvania*, 2 vols. (Philadelphia, 1905), I, p. 300 (quotation).

platform stressed adherence to the Union, condemned congressional interference with slavery in the territories, endorsed a more stringent protective tariff, called for modification of the naturalization laws, and demanded that the Bible remain in the school curriculum. To counter the appeal of the American ticket, the Union forces emphasized the nativism of their candidates. In response to a letter sent by nativists to each Union candidate, Wilmot condemned the interference of the Catholic hierarchy in the nation's political affairs and asserted that native-born Americans deserved preference in government offices.[41] This statement had little impact, however, because the Americans' main objection to Wilmot was his radicalism on the slavery issue. Even the banking crisis that developed in the final weeks of the campaign failed to aid Wilmot's candidacy. Normally the calls for a higher tariff that accompanied the panic would have hurt the Democrats, traditionally proponents of low tariff rates. Yet the Union forces could not take advantage of this opportunity, because during his tenure in Congress, Wilmot, then a Democrat, had also voted against higher tariffs.[42] By emphasizing his party's high tariff platform, Hazlehurst managed to retain the loyalty of most Fillmore "Straight" voters, and consequently the Democratic slate easily defeated the Union ticket.[43]

Despite their defeat in 1857, prospects for the Democrats' opponents seemed bright in 1858. The financial panic had a devastating effect on Pennsylvania's coal- and iron-producing regions, and the public blamed the panic's persistence on Democratic opposition to a higher tariff. Buchanan's attempt to end the Kansas controversy by forcing the pro-slavery Lecompton constitution through Congress was also particularly damaging to Pennsylvania Democrats, because they could not easily distance themselves from the policies of Buchanan, the state's most prominent Democrat. Furthermore, the Americans had demonstrated a new willingness to fuse with the Republicans during

41. Philadelphia *News*, June 4, 1857; Charles B. Going, *David Wilmot, Free-Soiler: A Biography of the Great Advocate of the Wilmot Proviso* (New York, 1924), 732–36.

42. Coleman, *Disruption of the Pennsylvania Democracy*, 107–9; Myers, "The Rise of the Republican Party in Pennsylvania," 163–78; Malcolm R. Eiselen, *The Rise of Pennsylvania Protectionism* (Philadelphia: Univ. of Pennsylvania Press, 1932), 241–46.

43. A comparison of the 1856 and 1857 results indicates that the Americans retained most of the Fillmore "Straight" vote, and won a portion of the Fillmore "Fusion" voters as well:

Vote for President and Governor in Pennsylvania

	1856	1857
Republican/Union	147,251 (32%)	146,136 (40%)
Fillmore Union	56,039 (12%)	–
Fillmore Straight/American	26,303 (6%)	28,132 (8%)
Democratic	230,101 (50%)	188,887 (52%)

Sources: Coleman, *Disruption of the Pennsylvania Democracy*, 172–73 (1856 results); *Tribune Almanac* (1858): 53.

the spring mayoral election in Philadelphia. In that contest, Republicans and Americans had formed a single organization and elected Alexander Henry mayor on a platform that emphasized the tariff and minimized slavery. The two organizations used the Philadelphia example to cement their relations on a state-wide basis, renaming themselves the "People's party," the name used by the Philadelphia fusionists. The differences between the Union and People's parties were clearly visible in their platforms. While the 1857 Union platform had vigorously endorsed the right of Congress to exclude slavery from the territories, the People's document of 1858 merely condemned the administration's Kansas policy. Americans were also conciliated with planks calling for a strong protective tariff, purity of the ballot box through strict enforcement of the naturalization laws, and a ban on the immigration of criminals. Republicans maintained control of the nominations, however, installing prominent free-soiler John M. Read as the candidate for justice of the supreme court, while nominating a former Know Nothing for a position that was to be abolished soon after the election.[44] Yet by broadening their platform and softening their anti-slavery rhetoric, Pennsylvania Republicans transformed their party from an anti-slavery vehicle to a broad-based organization that all opponents of the Democracy could support. As a result, the People's party easily defeated the Democrats in the 1858 election.[45]

The Democrats' loss of Pennsylvania in 1858 paved the way for the Republicans' presidential triumph in 1860 and has therefore come under intense scrutiny by historians. Scholars traditionally attributed the Democratic defeat to the Lecompton controversy, but have recently cited either the tariff issue or the accession of nativist voters as the proximate cause of the People's victory.[46] In truth, these three factors often worked in concert to such a degree

44. Philadelphia *North American*, July 16, 1858.

45. Bruce Collins, "The Democrats' Loss of Pennsylvania in 1858," *Pennsylvania Magazine of History and Biography* 109 (1985): 514–24; Coleman, *Disruption of the Pennsylvania Democracy*, 110–16; Myers, "The Rise of the Republican Party in Pennsylvania," 197–99. The vote broke down as follows:

Vote for Governor and Supreme Court Judge in Pennsylvania

	Union/People's	*Democratic*	*American*
1857	146,136 (40%)	188,887 (52%)	28,132 (8%)
1858	198,117 (54%)	171,130 (46%)	–

Source: Tribune Almanac (1858): 53; (1859): 52.

46. Allan Nevins, *The Emergence of Lincoln*, 2 vols. (New York, 1950), 400–402; William Dusinberre, *Civil War Issues in Philadelphia, 1856–1865* (Philadelphia: Univ. of Pennsylvania Press, 1965), 79; Collins, "The Democrats' Loss of Pennsylvania in 1858," 499–536; Coleman, *Disruption of the Pennsylvania Democracy*, 117–18; David E. Meerse, "The Northern Democratic Party and the Congressional Elections of 1858," *Civil War History* 19 (1973): 119–37; James L. Huston, *The Panic of 1857 and the Coming of the Civil War* (Baton Rouge: Louisiana State Univ. Press, 1987), 143–72.

that separating them is quite difficult. For example, when a Pennsylvania congressman called for "protection to *everything American against everything foreign*," he was referring to the tariff, but in language sure to appeal to nativists as well. Furthermore, the People's party often linked the tariff and slavery questions. They argued that Democratic candidates who vowed to increase the tariff could never deliver on such promises, because the Slave Power, whose representatives in Congress allegedly controlled that party, opposed raising the tariff. Only by repudiating the Slave Power's northern allies, said the People's party, could Pennsylvanians gain the tariff protection they desired.[47]

Although the interaction of these issues obscures the relative importance of each, it seems clear that concessions to nativists were not responsible for the People's party's stunning victory. The People's ticket of 1858 offered nativists nothing more than had the Union ticket in 1857. Both contained a mixture of nativist and non-nativist candidates, and both platforms included mild nativist planks. On slavery and the tariff, however, the two organizations differed immensely. While the Union party had made the controversial claim that Congress could exclude slavery from the territories and placed the state's best known anti-slavery radical at the head of its ticket, the People's platform merely made vague criticism of the Buchanan administration's Kansas policy. Although the Union organization had made a last-minute attempt to take advantage of the tariff issue (an effort nullified by the presence of an anti-protection candidate at the head of its ticket), the People's party made protection the centerpiece of its campaign. The People's party did not delete nativism from its platform; in fact they retained their nativist planks in 1859 and 1860. Yet it was primarily the moderation of their anti-slavery agenda and the expansion of their platform to include protectionism that won them the support of Pennsylvania's Fillmore voters.

Republicans in the remaining doubtful states utilized similar strategies, using the tariff and a moderation of their anti-slavery position to attract former Fillmore supporters. In New Jersey, the anti-Democratic forces followed the example of their Pennsylvania neighbors, creating an "Opposition" party that stressed the tariff issue. Only in the vicinity of Camden, a stronghold of nativism, did the Americans maintain an independent organization. In the rest of the state, however, emphasis on the tariff question convinced most Americans to cooperate with the Republicans, and allowed Opposition candidates to capture every New Jersey congressional seat.[48] In Indiana, Republicans drastically modified their anti-slavery posi-

---

47. *CG*, 36th Congress, First Session, 1844, quoted in Foner, *Free Soil*, 203.

48. Charles M. Knapp, *New Jersey Politics During the Period of the Civil War and Reconstruction* (Geneva, N.Y.: W. F. Humphrey, 1924), 1–28; Huston, *Panic of 1857*, 143–44; New York *Tribune*, Sept. 23, 27, Oct. 25, Nov. 4, 1858; New York *Times*, Oct. 7, 1858; Reynell Coates, *To the Americans of West Jersey in the Congressional Canvass in the First District* (n.p., 1858). A

tion in 1858, dropping their call for no more slave states and instead endorsing popular sovereignty to settle the slavery question. This strategy won the Republicans many converts in southern Indiana, where Fillmore had outpolled Frémont in 1856.[49] The Illinois Republican party, as one of its leaders noted, had been "under the control of moderate men, and conservative influences" from its inception in 1856, so little modification of the party's image was necessary in that state. While Illinois Republicans did not dilute their anti-slavery agenda, they consistently nominated moderate or conservative candidates for state office in order to attract the Whig/Americans of southern ancestry who lived in central and southern Illinois and had voted for Fillmore.[50]

By 1860, then, Republicans had won the support of most northern Fillmore voters without making significant nativist concessions. In Massachusetts, passage of the two-year amendment reflected the influence of nativists already in the Republican party, not an effort to woo Americans. The laws enacted in Ohio are also a poor indicator of relations between the Republicans and nativists, because they did not mollify nativists and were passed at a time when Ohio Republicans were systematically ridding their party of nativist influence. In New York, although Republicans did try to attract American support by enacting a registry law, the ineffectual statute had little impact on the electoral balance. Nativist platform planks also had little to do with the accession of Fillmore voters into the Republican party in Pennsylvania.

Events at the Republican national nominating convention of 1860 confirmed that Republicans no longer worried about losing the Americans' allegiance. Republican nativists won a partial victory in the fact that Seward, their

---

comparison of the aggregate vote for Congress in 1858 and President in 1856 suggests that most Americans supported the Opposition ticket:

New Jersey Voting

	Republican/Opposition	*American*	*Democratic*
1856	28,338 (29%)	24,115 (24%)	46,943 (47%)
1858	50,001 (52%)	3,793 (4%)	41,500 (44%)

Source: Tribune Almanac (1859): 54.

It should be noted that two of the congressional candidates supported by the New Jersey Opposition were anti-Lecompton Democrats, and this left the possibility that some 1858 Opposition voters might vote Democratic in the future.

49. Carl F. Brand, "The History of the Know Nothing Party in Indiana," *Indiana Magazine of History* 18 (1922): 296–99; George Julian, *Political Recollections, 1840–1872* (Chicago, 1884), 167; Elmer D. Elbert, "Southern Indiana Politics on the Eve of the Civil War" (Ph.D. diss., Indiana University, 1967), 26–77.

50. Orville H. Browning to Lyman Trumbull quoted in Foner, *Free Soil*, 198; Roy P. Basler, ed., *The Collected Works of Abraham Lincoln*, 7 vols. (New Brunswick: Rutgers Univ. Press, 1953), II, pp. 476–81, 503, 523–24, III, pp. 335–36.

arch-enemy, failed to capture the presidential nomination, and the enmity nativists held for Seward undoubtedly played a role in his rejection at Chicago. Thaddeus Stevens justified his opposition to the New Yorker on the grounds that "Pennsylvania will never vote for a man who favored the destruction of the common school system in New York to gain the favor of Catholics and foreigners." Others agreed that nativist opposition contributed to the New Yorker's defeat.[51] Yet it was Seward's radicalism—not his opposition to nativism—that doomed his candidacy to failure. As former Know Nothing Richard M. Corwine noted in justifying his support of Lincoln, "we can not elect extreme men. Moderation in their past life & present views, must mark them, or we can not elect them." An Illinois Republican likewise demonstrated that the American party had become synonymous with conservatism, not nativism, when he wrote that "we must carry the american or conservative element in the middle states." Seward lost the nomination because delegates from the lower North such as Corwine were convinced that Seward could not carry those doubtful states, all of which contained significant concentrations of conservative Fillmore voters. Lincoln, perceived to be a moderate, would deliver their votes, while Seward, the radical, could not. Letters from throughout the nation reported as much after Lincoln's nomination, and even Fillmore's own organ, the Buffalo *Commercial Advertiser*, which would never have supported Seward, endorsed Lincoln.[52]

In fact, Lincoln's nomination gave the Republicans a standard-bearer who opposed nativism as strongly as Seward. Lincoln wrote to his friend Joshua Speed in 1855:

> I am not a Know-Nothing. That is certain. How could I be? How can anyone who abhors the oppression of negroes, be in favor of degrading classes of white people? Our progress in degeneracy appears to me to be pretty rapid. As a nation, we began by declaring that "*all men are created equal.*" We now practically read it "all men are created equal, *except negroes.*" When the Know-Nothings get control, it will read "all men are created equal, except negroes, *and foreigners, and catholics.*" When it comes to this I should prefer emigrating to some country where they make no pretence of loving liberty— to Russia, for instance, where despotism can be taken pure, and without the base alloy of hypocrisy.

51. R. Hosea to Salmon P. Chase, May 18, 1860, Chase Papers, LC; McClure, *Old Time Notes*, I, p. 399; James G. Blaine, *Twenty Years of Congress*, 2 vols. (Norwich, Conn.: 1884–86), I, pp. 165–66; Gienapp, "Nativism and the Creation of a Republican Majority," 553–54; Charles Granville Hamilton, *Lincoln and the Know-Nothing Movement* (Washington, 1954), 8–9; Frederick Bancroft, *The Life of William H. Seward*, 2 vols. (New York: Harper & Brothers, 1900), 535 (quotation).

52. Reinhard H. Luthin, *The First Lincoln Campaign* (Cambridge, Mass.: Harvard Univ. Press, 1944), 140–47; Corwine to Lincoln in Basler, *Lincoln Works*, IV, p. 48; H. Kreismann to Banks, April 2, 1859 (quotation), Banks Papers, LC; Schuyler Colfax to Lincoln, May 26, 1860, S. P. Hanscom to [W. Kellogg], May 26, 1860, W. Kellogg to Lincoln, May 26, 1860, Lincoln Papers, LC. Even the Fort Wayne *Times*, one of Indiana's leading Know Nothing organs, opposed Seward's nomination not because of his treatment of Catholics, but because of his radicalism. See Fort Wayne *Times*, April 12, 18, May 2, 1860.

Although Lincoln made this indictment of Know Nothingism in private correspondence, he expressed essentially the same sentiment publicly in 1859. In response to a letter from a group of German-Americans seeking his opinion on the Massachusetts two-year amendment, Lincoln stated:

> I am against it's adoption in Illinois, or in any other place, where I have a right to oppose it. Understanding the spirit of our institutions to aim at the *elevation* of men, I am opposed to whatever tends to *degrade* them. I have some little notoriety for commiserating the oppressed condition of the negro; and I should be strangely inconsistent if I could favor any project for curtailing the existing rights of *white men*, even though born in different lands, and speaking different languages from myself.

Consequently, few nativists supported Lincoln at the Chicago convention. Most preferred either Edward Bates, a Missouri Whig who had supported Fillmore in 1856, or Ohio's John McLean, whose nativism had made him a favorite of former Know Nothings at the Republicans' 1856 gathering. Although nativist opposition may have played a secondary role in ruining Seward's presidential aspirations, Lincoln's triumph over Bates and McLean indicates that by this point, nativists wielded little power in the Republican party.[53]

Incorporation of the anti-nativist "Dutch Plank" into the Republican national platform provides further evidence that Republicans no longer felt obliged to cater to nativist sentiment. Republican conventions in Ohio, Wisconsin, and Iowa had passed resolutions condemning the Massachusetts two-year amendment, and German-Republicans demanded that the party endorse these measures in its national statement of principles. The Republicans decided to address the immigrants' concerns in their fourteenth plank, which stated that "the Republican party is opposed to any change in our naturalization laws, or any state legislation by which the rights of citizens hitherto accorded to immigrants from foreign lands shall be abridged or impaired; and in favor of giving a full and efficient protection to the rights of all classes of citizens, whether native or naturalized, both at home or abroad." Nativist Republicans predicted that the "Dutch Plank" would cause former Know Nothings to bolt the party, and a few did leave. "According to the *new tests* of Republicanism, I regard myself as *resolved out of that party*," asserted Lewis D. Campbell of Ohio. In another letter, Campbell attributed the Republicans' anti-nativist course to "the *crushing out* policy which Greeley, Dr [Gamaliel] Bailey, Seward, Weed, et al. got up in 1855." Know Nothings had magnanimously agreed to sublimate their nativist agenda in order to promote the anti-slavery cause, yet Republicans repaid them with "the complete *Dutchif*ication of the Republican party, and a *new platform* in favor of *alien suffrage*. This is progress with a vengeance!" Nevertheless, few

---

53. Lincoln to Speed, Aug. 24, 1855, Lincoln to Theodore Canisius, May 17, 1859, in Basler, *Lincoln Works*, II, p. 323, III, p. 380; F. I. Herriot, "The Premises and Significance of Abraham Lincoln's Letter to Theodore Canisius," *Deutsch-Americanische Geschichtsblätter* 15 (1915): 181–254. It is possible that nativists did have enough influence in Republican ranks to veto Seward's nomination, but not enough to force their choice upon the convention.

nativists followed Campbell's example. A Pennsylvania Republican reported that "there is some squirming among our Americans at the Fourteenth Resolution," but predicted that nativists would support the Republican nominees. "The Americans feel humiliated by a section of the platform, because it strikes directly at them," concurred a Connecticut Republican, "yet they have reluctantly swallowed the pill." Although Lincoln received numerous reports of nativist displeasure with the "Dutch Plank," a significant revolt by nativist Republicans never materialized.[54]

Despite the Dutch Plank, former Know Nothings played an important role in Lincoln's campaign. Daniel Ullmann was in great demand as a speaker in New York, New Jersey, and southeastern Pennsylvania. James O. Putnam of Buffalo, like Ullmann a Fillmore supporter in 1856, gave speeches aimed at conservatives whom Lincoln found "truly admirable." Although Ullmann and Putnam concentrated on the slavery issue and the sectional crisis in their addresses, former Know Nothings referred to nativism on occasion. Gustavus A. Scroggs, president of the New York American party, called upon Know Nothings to support the Republican candidates because "that party has already inaugurated some of the reforms which were principles embraced in our political creed, and it has given sanction to others, which, if carried out, would go a great length towards accomplishing the aims of our political action." Richard W. Thompson and Thomas Corwin also made significant contributions to the Lincoln campaign by reassuring conservatives in the lower North that the Republican party respected their views.[55]

The popularity of the "Wide Awake" political clubs during the election of 1860 also reflected the continuing influence of Know Nothingism. While it was common for political parties to form clubs during presidential campaigns in order to create enthusiasm for the ticket and to aid with local organization, the

54. *Proceedings of the First Three Republican Conventions* (Minneapolis, 1893), 137–40; Lewis D. Campbell to the editor of the Hamilton *Intelligencer*, quoted in Cincinnati *Commercial*, Aug. 14, 1860 (quotation); Campbell to Isaac Strohm, July 18, 1860 (quotations), Strohm Papers, OHS; Joseph Casey to L. Swett, May 26, 1860 (quotation), David Davis Papers, IlSHL; James F. Babcock to Mark Howard, Aug. 4, 1860 (quotation), Howard Papers, CHS; Elihu Washburne to Lincoln, May 20, 1860, James E. Harvey to Lincoln, May 21, 1860, Z. K. Pangborn to Josiah Lucas, May 22, 1860, Lyman Trumbull to Lincoln, May 22, 1860, Schuyler Colfax to Lincoln, May 26, 1860, John D. Defrees to Lincoln, May 26, 1860, Nehemiah D. Sperry to Lincoln, May 27, 1860, Richard Corwine to Lincoln, May 28, 1860, Lincoln Papers, LC; Foner, *Free Soil*, 257–58.

55. Ullmann, *Speech of Hon. Daniel Ullmann of New York at the Lincoln and Hamlin Ratification Meeting in Newark, New Jersey, June 12, 1860* (n.p., n.d.); Ullmann to Edwin D. Morgan, July 11, 1860, Morgan Papers, NYSL; A. K. McClure to Ullmann, July 18, 1860, George W. Curtis to Ullmann, Sept. 23, 1860, Ullmann Papers, NYHS; Putnam, *Americans Repudiate Fusion! Speech of the Hon. James O. Putnam, Against the Sale of the American Party to the Douglas Democracy. Delivered in Rochester, August 8, [1860]* (n.p., n.d.); Lincoln to Putnam, July 28, 1860, in Basler, *Lincoln Works*, IV, p. 89; Gustavus A. Scroggs, *The Duty of Americans. Speech of General G. A. Scroggs (President of the American State Council) at the American Meeting Held at Aurora, Erie Co., N.Y., Aug. 4, 1860. And of George B. Babcock, and of James O. Putnam, in Reply to Ex-Governor Hunt* (Buffalo, 1860), 5; Richard W. Thompson, *To the Conservative Men of Indiana* (n.p., n.d.), broadside collection, Indiana University Library; Lincoln to Thompson, July 10, 1860, in Basler, *Lincoln Works*, IV, pp. 82–83; Charles Roll, *Colonel Dick Thompson, the Persistent Whig* (Indianapolis: Indiana Historical Bureau, 1948), 159–65; Prendergaft, "Thomas Corwin," 10–23.

Wide Awake organizations that supported Lincoln differed from these, and were suspiciously similar to Know Nothing lodges. Like the Know Nothings, Wide Awakes participated in elaborate initiation rituals. In fact, probably referring to the vigilance necessary to repulse the encroachments of the Catholic Church, nativists had often described themselves as "wide awakes."[56] The success of the Know Nothings had demonstrated that fraternal organizations attracted members more readily than conventional political clubs, so Republicans utilized the forms of Know Nothingism to arouse enthusiasm for Lincoln's candidacy.[57]

Of course, not all former Know Nothings endorsed Lincoln. Some, especially those who had previously been Democrats, supported the candidacy of Illinois senator Stephen A. Douglas. However, most Fillmore voters who opposed Lincoln joined the Constitutional Union party. Organized in 1860 as a vehicle to unite conservative Whigs, Americans, and southern opponents of the Democratic party, the Constitutional Union party pledged to preserve the Union by ignoring the slavery question. Former Know Nothings such as Erastus Brooks, Jacob Broom, and Nathan Sargent helped create the new party, and the American party's national executive committee, dormant since early 1857, resurrected itself in order to endorse the new organization. At its convention in Baltimore, the Constitutional Union party nominated John Bell of Tennessee for President and Edward Everett of Massachusetts for Vice President. Most of the party's advocates realized that Bell could not win a majority in the electoral college, but they hoped that he would capture enough states to force the election into the House, where they predicted that Bell would triumph as the compromise candidate.[58]

The Constitutional Union party in the North was run almost exclusively by former Know Nothings. Besides Brooks and Broom, other prominent Americans active in the party included John A. Rockwell and Ezra Clark of Connecticut, Charles D. Deshler of New Jersey, and J. Scott Harrison, Edward Ball, and Philadelph Van Trump of Ohio. Most of the remaining American newspapers endorsed Bell and Everett, praising their "conservative," "national" views. On rare occasions, the Constitutional Unionists attempted to attract support with nativist rhetoric. Deshler's New Jersey newspaper insisted that former Know Nothings could not support the Republicans because that party bid for the votes of "the infidel Germans, who hate our public schools, the holy Sabbath, and who pretend to teach Americans how to rule America." An American newspaper in Ohio likewise predicted that the

56. See for example *The Wide-Awake Gift: A Know-Nothing Token for 1855, Edited by "One of 'Em"* (New York, 1855).

57. Luthin, *First Lincoln Campaign*, 173–74; Julius G. Rathbun, " 'The Wide Awakes': The Great Political Organization of 1860," *Connecticut Quarterly* 1 (Oct. 1895): 327–35; Glenn C. Howland, "Organize! Organize! The Lincoln Wide-Awakes in Vermont," *Vermont History* 48 (1980): 28–32.

58. John B. Stabler, "A History of the Constitutional Union Party: A Tragic Failure" (Ph.D. diss., Columbia University, 1954), 301–492, 520; N. Sargent to Amos A. Lawrence, Dec. 4, 1858, Lawrence to Sargent, "December 1858," Amos A. Lawrence Papers, MHS; James Randolph to J. Scott Harrison, June 27, 1860, Harrison Papers, LC.

"dutch plank, . . . insolently dictated" by the Germans, would cost the Republicans thousands of votes. Know Nothings in the Lincoln camp attempted to refute this charge. Scroggs pointed out that "the national union convention never uttered a syllable, either by resolution, address or otherwise, in any way signifying that it endorsed or approved a single principle or doctrine of the American party. Neither are its nominees representatives of the American party." Nativist Constitutional Unionists replied that the party had left these issues out of its platform to promote the unity of action necessary to save the Union, and that only the election of its candidates would insure the successful implementation of the tenets of Americanism.[59]

On election day, the support Lincoln received from former Fillmore voters played an important role in the Republicans' victory. In New York and New England, only about half of the Fillmore supporters who voted in 1860 cast ballots for Lincoln, with the remainder voting primarily for the Constitutional Union ticket. Republicans already controlled these states, so this rate of conversion allowed them to maintain their majorities in that region. In the doubtful states of Pennsylvania and the Midwest, election returns confirmed the observation of Lincoln's law partner that "the 'old line Whigs' " who had voted for Fillmore "are . . . going almost unanimously and wildly for Lincoln." For the most part, these results merely confirmed the voting trends that had taken shape in 1858. Despite the formation of the Constitutional Union party, which created a new pro-Union alternative for former Fillmore voters, Americans who had converted to Republicanism after 1856 remained loyal to their new party. Of course, Fillmore voters were not the only voters who switched to the Republican party between 1856 and 1860. Many Protestant immigrants joined the anti-slavery party during this period, and the Dred Scott decision and Lecompton controversy drove some Democrats into the Republican fold as well. However, converts from the American party outnumbered those from other sources, and they proved decisive in the doubtful states that had eluded Frémont in 1856, but which propelled Lincoln to victory in 1860.[60]

Once the Civil War began, nativism in the United States diminished perceptibly. As John Higham has noted, "now the foreigner had a new prestige; he

59. Baum, *Civil War Party System*, 51; Holt, *Forging a Majority, 288;* Curran, "Know Nothings of New York," 287–88; Ithaca *American Citizen*, May 16, 1860; Terra Haute *Wabash Express*, Aug. 8, 1860; Russell McClain, "The New York *Express*: Voice of Opposition" (Ph.D. diss., Columbia University, 1955), 229–34; St. Clairsville [Ohio] *Independent Republican*, April 28, May 17, June 14 (quotation), 1860; Paul Hallerberg, "Charles D. Deshler, Versatile Jerseyman" (M.A. thesis, Rutgers University, 1939), 115–119; Scroggs, *Duty of Americans*, 2. The quotation from Deshler's paper actually dates from before the nomination of the presidential candidates, but reflects an editorial theme that continued during the campaign.

60. Herndon quoted in William E. Gienapp, "Who Voted for Lincoln?," in John L. Thomas, ed., *Abraham Lincoln and the American Political Tradition* (Amherst: Univ. of Massachusetts Press, 1986), 65. My estimate of the proportion of Fillmore voters who supported Lincoln is also based on Gienapp's ecological regression statistics, although as mentioned earlier, a simple comparison of raw voting figures for each state leads one to the same conclusions.

was a comrade-at-arms." However, anti-Irish sentiment revived quickly in 1863 in the aftermath of the New York City draft riots. The brutality with which the predominantly Irish rioters attacked the city's black inhabitants prompted an outpouring of rage against the Irish even more virulent than that displayed during the height of Know Nothingism. Some insisted that once the North had subdued the southern rebels it would have to subdue its Irish inhabitants as well, and a few New Yorkers proposed that the Know Nothings be revived to deal with the Irish menace. Still, isolated events such as the draft riots could not counteract the more fundamental decline of nativism during the Civil War.[61]

In the postbellum period, anti-Catholicism ebbed and flowed primarily in response to educational controversies, as it had before the rise of the Know Nothings. The first such dispute arose in New York in 1869, when "Boss" William M. Tweed introduced a bill in the legislature to allow public financing of parochial schools. When the measure failed to win approval, Tweed implemented his plan by quietly amending the New York City tax laws. Protestants were outraged when they discovered the change, and the controversy, which dragged on until the mid-1870s, prompted *Harper's Weekly* artist Thomas Nast to create his famous depiction of "The American River Ganges," in which Catholic prelates emerge from the water in the form of alligators to devour helpless American schoolchildren. School funding disputes also erupted in New Jersey and Ohio in the mid-1870s.[62]

It might seem surprising that a new nativist political movement did not emerge in this period, inasmuch as similar controversies had prompted the creation of the American Republican party in the 1840s and the Know Nothings in the 1850s. In fact, Daniel Ullmann did attempt to resurrect the American party during the height of the school dispute. Yet while nativists created new fraternal orders and revived others at this time, few shared Ullmann's enthusiasm for organizing an independent political organization. One veteran nativist explained to Ullmann that "when I think how the American party was swindled . . . & how badly we were sold out by the political tricksters, I do not feel at all anxious to be a campaigner for a third party again. It appears to me that those [anti-Catholic] principles can be only carried out thru' the Republican party." Events seemed to justify the nativists' confidence in the Republicans. In an address delivered in Des Moines, President Ulysses S. Grant demanded a constitutional amendment banning the expenditure of public taxes to finance parochial education. Such a measure gained approval

61. John Higham, *Strangers in the Land: Patterns of American Nativism, 1860–1925,* 2nd ed. (New York: Atheneum, 1973), 12–13; New York *Times,* Oct. 13, 1863; Allan Nevins and Milton H. Thomas, eds., *The Diary of George Templeton Strong* (New York: Macmillan, 1952), 340–43.

62. John W. Pratt, *Religion, Politics, and Diversity: The Church-State Theme in New York History* (Ithaca: Cornell Univ. Press, 1967), 195–200; [Charles H. Pullen], *Miss Columbia's Public School; Or, Will It Blow Over? By A. Cosmopolitan. With 72 Illustrations by Thomas Nast* (1871; rpt., Freeport, N.Y.: Books for Libraries Press, 1969); Higham, *Strangers in the Land,* 28–30; *Harper's Weekly,* Sept. 30, 1871; Morton Keller, *The Art and Politics of Thomas Nast* (New York: Oxford Univ. Press, 1968), 159–62.

in the House in 1876, but fell two votes short of the necessary two-thirds' majority in the Senate. In 1882, however, Republicans in Congress succeeded in enacting another of the Know Nothings' most sought-after "reforms"—a ban on the immigration of convicts and paupers.[63] Minister Samuel D. Burchard's famous characterization of the Democrats as the party of "Rum, Romanism, and Rebellion" during the 1884 presidential campaign confirmed that anti-Catholicism still motivated many American voters.[64]

By this time, however, anti-radicalism had replaced anti-Catholicism as the driving force behind American nativism. When nativists revived the American party in 1886, they cited as their goal "the exclusion of the restless revolutionary horde of foreigners who are now seeking our shores from every part of the world." Even the fraternal orders, which had originated as anti-Catholic organizations, had begun by the 1880s to concentrate their attacks on the "Anarchists and all that class of heartless and revolutionary agitators" who come to America "to terrorize the community and to exalt the red flag of the commune above the Stars and Stripes." Also, economics overshadowed religion in the nativist movement after 1880, as labor leaders pressed for immigration restriction as a means to improve the wages of native-born workers. Only the American Protective Association, formed in 1887, continued to emphasize anti-Catholicism above these new issues, and although the group attracted as many as 500,000 members by the mid-1890s, its political influence never approached that of the Know Nothings.[65]

By the turn of the century, then, nativism had been transformed into a movement that most antebellum Americans would have found utterly alien. Yet Know Nothingism had left an indelible legacy. First, the Know Nothing movement helped destroy the second American party system. In the west, the Whig party disintegrated in the wake of the Kansas-Nebraska Act. In the east, however, the Whigs retained significant strength, and many members predicted that if the party could maintain its popularity in that region, they could eventually revive their organization as an anti-slavery party. But by winning a

63. Ullmann letterbook, Feb.-Dec., 1871, William F. Chapman to Ullmann, Nov. 26, 1875 (quotation), Ullmann Papers, NYHS; *Congressional Record*, 44th Congress, 1st Session, 5189–92, 5453–61, 5580–95; Higham, *Strangers in the Land*, 29, 44.

64. Coincidentally, the minister originally scheduled to address this Republican campaign gathering in New York was not Burchard, but Otis H. Tiffany, formerly president of the Pennsylvania Know Nothings. At the last moment, however, some of the ministers at the gathering complained about the process by which Tiffany had been chosen to speak. As a compromise, the group decided to allow the oldest minster present to address the audience, and thus the task fell to the unprepared Burchard. The circumspect Tiffany would undoubtedly have delivered a tasteful speech, but Burchard's scandalous remarks caused some of the Irish-Americans who had flocked to James G. Blaine's candidacy (because of the anti-English reputation he had earned as secretary of state) to reconsider. Because a change of fewer than 600 votes would have given Blaine New York and the election, it is likely that Burchard's remarks cost Blaine the presidency. McClure, *Old Time Notes*, I, pp. 242–43.

65. Higham, *Strangers in the Land*, 30–32, 49–50, 54–58 (quotations), 62, 70–72, 80–87; Donald L. Kinzer, *An Episode in Anti-Catholicism: The American Protective Association* (Seattle: Univ. of Washington Press, 1964).

surprisingly large vote in New York, a majority of the anti-Democratic ballots in Pennsylvania, and a record-breaking landslide in Massachusetts, the Know Nothings demonstrated that the Whig party was hopelessly moribund. This convinced politicians and voters to abandon the Whig party, thus shattering the partisan alignment that had defined American politics for twenty years.

The success of the Know Nothings also demonstrated that religious bigotry was widespread in nineteenth-century America. As we have seen, many joined the Order primarily as a means to combat the Slave Power or to enact temperance legislation, and these Know Nothings lacked the proscriptive zeal of the veteran nativists who founded the organization. Yet few of these "less dedicated" nativists questioned the veterans' contention that Catholicism was a misguided and dangerous religion or doubted that the political power of its adherents ought to be curtailed. Antebellum Americans were driven to this conclusion primarily by their belief that Protestantism defined American society, and that Catholicism was fundamentally incompatible with Protestant values. Although racism and the fear of radicalism would eventually displace anti-Catholicism as the foundation of American nativism, most latter-day nativists would look back fondly upon the Know Nothing era as the heyday of their movement.

Finally, the infusion of American party members into the Republican party after 1856 transformed the Republicans into the nation's dominant political party. Republicans converted Fillmore voters in the doubtful states primarily by modifying their stance on slavery and expanding their platform to include calls for increased tariff protection. In some instances Republicans also courted Americans by endorsing nativist legislation, but in most cases (such as New York and Ohio) these gestures were disingenuous or ineffectual. Nativism did not disappear from the American political scene. On the contrary, Massachusetts Republicans ratified their controversial two-year amendment, and the People's party in Pennsylvania retained modest nativist planks in its platform until the end of the decade. Thus, while it may be an exaggeration to say that the Republicans converted the Americans "without having to embrace a particle of the nativists' platform," the thrust of this statement is essentially correct. The Republican party secured the allegiance of most Fillmore voters without making meaningful concessions to their nativism.[66]

The frequency with which Know Nothings became prominent Republicans illustrates the relative ease with which this transition occurred. Lincoln appointed Connecticut Know Nothing president Nehemiah D. Sperry to the postmastership of New Haven. Holding that position until the end of the century (except during the Cleveland administrations, when he served in Congress), Sperry became one of the wealthiest and most respected residents of the city. Other Know Nothings advanced their careers in the Republican party with patronage appointments under Lincoln. Nathan Sargent, who spread rumors of Frémont's Catholicism and helped create the Constitutional

66. Sewell, *Ballots for Freedom*, 275.

Union party, was named commissioner of customs. Simon Cameron became secretary of war, and John P. Sanderson, who as chairman of the Pennsylvania American state committee prevented a complete fusion of the Fillmore and Frémont electoral tickets, captured the chief clerkship of that department.[67] Pennsylvania's Know Nothing governor, James Pollock, was made director of the United States Mint at Philadelphia, where he used his influence to have "In God We Trust" added to American currency. Americans also earned their fair share of diplomatic posts. Anson Burlingame became minister to China, where he negotiated an important treaty in 1868. In addition, Pennsylvania American leader E. Joy Morris was appointed minister to Turkey, Thomas Corwin occupied a similar post in Mexico, and James O. Putnam landed the consulate at Le Havre. Indiana's Richard W. Thompson was also rewarded with patronage appointments, and eventually became secretary of the Navy under President Rutherford B. Hayes. Some Know Nothings earned fame in the Union army, such as Daniel Ullmann, who commanded Louisiana's black Union troops.[68]

Former Know Nothings did not rely on patronage, however, to advance their political careers. Pennsylvania Know Nothing leader Stephen Miller emigrated to Minnesota, where his ability to address the state's German immigrants in their native tongue helped him become governor in 1864. Francis W. Palmer, a leading New York North American, moved to Iowa and became a prominent Republican, and eventually served as postmaster of Chicago and public printer of the United States. The Grant administration best exemplifies the ease with which Know Nothings made the transition into the Republican party. Grant himself had been a Know Nothing, and although he insisted in his memoirs that he had joined solely out of curiosity, his actions suggest that he endorsed the Order's agenda. In his private letters, for example, Grant complained that immigrants held too many government offices, and we have seen that as President he proposed a constitutional amendment prohibiting government funding of parochial schools. Although voters knew nothing of Grant's affiliation with the Order until after he left office, his Vice Presidents, Schuyler Colfax and Henry Wilson, had both been prominent Know Nothings. Most

67. Ironically, Sanderson became a national hero for his role in exposing the activities of another secret society, the pro-southern Order of American Knights, during the Civil War. Wood Gray, *The Hidden Civil War: The Story of the Copperheads* (New York, 1942), 196–97; James G. Wilson and John Fiske, eds., *Appleton's Cyclopaedia of American Biography* (New York, 1888), V, p. 386.

68. Harry J. Carman and Reinhard H. Luthin, *Lincoln and the Patronage* (New York: Columbia Univ. Press, 1943), 55, 58–59, 81, 85, 88, 101, 237, 253, 328; *Dictionary of American Biography* (New York: Charles Scribner's Sons, 1943), XVII, p. 456; Robert Sobel and John Raimo, eds., *Biographical Directory of the Governors of the United States, 1789–1978*, 4 vols. (Westport, 1978), III, p. 1308; Neill F. Sanders, " 'Fairness, and Fairness Only': Lincoln's Appointment of James O. Putnam as Consul at Le Havre," *Lincoln Herald* 87 (1985): 76–82; Ralph Basso, "Nationalism, Nativism, and the Black Soldier: Daniel Ullmann, A Biography of a Man Living in a Period of Transition, 1810–1892" (Ph.D. diss., St. John's University, 1986), 279–91.

Know Nothings never attained such high office, but the fact that many did become important politicians proves that Know Nothing membership was not an impediment to one's advancement in American politics.[69]

Know Nothings who refused to join the Republican party tended to enjoy less success in politics. Henry J. Gardner became a Democrat in 1863, but like other nativists who joined the Democratic party, Gardner discovered that a nativist background was a liability in a party that depended so heavily on immigrant votes. As a result, Gardner was forced to quit politics and return to his dry-goods business. Of all the Know Nothings who became Democrats, only Erastus Brooks gained any fame, first when the government halted distribution of his New York *Express* for its purported "Copperhead" proclivities, and later in 1883 when, as an assemblyman from Staten Island, Brooks earned public sympathy after a young colleague named Theodore Roosevelt repeatedly insulted him during legislative debates. For the most part, though, Know Nothing leaders who did not become Republicans remained aloof from both major parties. Dedicated nativists such as Daniel Ullmann devoted themselves to the perpetuation of secret nativist organizations, confident that a nativist political party would eventually dominate American politics.[70]

Ullmann's enduring belief that the American party could be revived suggests that he did not understand why it had failed. To some extent, of course, the Know Nothing party declined for reasons its leaders could not control. The Crimean War, which broke out soon after the Order burst onto the American scene, caused immigration to decrease sharply, because the resulting labor shortage convinced many potential emigrants to remain in Europe. With immigration diminishing perceptibly, Americans felt less incentive to join a nativist organization.[71] The Know Nothings were also hurt by the fact that, as their Ohio president put it, "the novelty of our movements are no longer a source of perplexity to our opponents, nor has it any longer the charm to lure away those who are ever ready to be led away by any new or

69. Miller to Simon Cameron, Feb. 15, 1859 (misfiled as 1857), Cameron Papers, DCHS; Sobel and Raimo, *Biographical Directory of Governors*, II, p. 775–76; Palmer to Weed, Sept. 30, 1858, Weed Papers, UR; *Biographical Dictionary of the United States Congress, 1774–1989* (Washington, 1989): 1607; Grant, *Personal Memoirs of U. S. Grant* (1885; rpt., New York: Grosset & Dunlap, 1962), 107; William S. McFeely, *Grant: A Biography* (New York: Norton, 1981), 69; Ernest A. McKay, *Henry Wilson: Practical Radical* (Port Washington, N.Y.: Kennikat Press, 1971), 227–28.

70. Baum, *Civil War Party System*, 69, 94; Sobel and Raimo, *Governors of the United States*, II, p. 706; Robert S. Harper, *Lincoln and the Press* (New York: McGraw-Hill, 1951), 251–55; William H. Harbaugh, *The Life and Times of Theodore Roosevelt* (rpt., New York: Oxford Univ. Press, 1981), 34; Ullmann to [?], April 10, 1871, Ullmann to Richard C. Corwine, n.d. [May 1871], Ullmann to C. Adams, May 20, 1871, Ullmann to "My Dear Sir," Oct. 9, 1871, Ullmann to Cortland Parker, March 12, 1872, Thomas B. Hammer to Ullmann, July 3, 1874, Hammer to Thomas G. Baker, July 3, 1874, Baker to Ullmann, July 6, 1874, J. W. Beekman to Ullmann, Dec. 28, 1874, George R. Babcock to Ullmann, Sept. 28, 1875, Ullmann Papers, NYHS.

71. Know Nothings noticed the drop in immigration. See for example the New York *Express*, July 31, Sept. 15, 1855.

novel movement." Many Americans voted for Know Nothings once for novelty, but had no intention of ever supporting the party's candidates again.[72]

The nature of the Know Nothings' rise to prominence also played an important role in their subsequent decline. As the New York *Times* noted, "the party had no childhood; it came into existence endowed at once with all the vigor and strength of manhood." Consequently, the Know Nothings lacked experienced leaders who knew how to operate a large political organization. "Know Nothingism presents the phenomenon of a powerful party without leaders," commented the New York *Herald*, "a splendid army without so much as a single field officer." The lack of leaders did not worry Know Nothings, because they believed that it would insure that their party remained responsive to the will of its members. A letter to the Boston *Bee* boasted that "the American party is *emphatically* a party of the people." It "has no leaders, and desires none."[73] Yet this leadership vacuum severely impaired the Know Nothings' ability to compete with other political parties. For example, it helped exacerbate the factionalism that plagued the Know Nothings during their short career. Without acknowledged and respected leaders, the Know Nothings lacked an influence that other parties used to repair rifts and rally their forces behind key legislation. This, in turn, contributed to some of the Know Nothings' embarrassing legislative defeats, such as their failure to elect a senator in Pennsylvania. Finally, because they promised to provide the experience that the Order seemed to lack, office-seekers from other parties were able to infiltrate the Order. Many Know Nothings ascribed their decline to the "cliques of unprincipled politicians [who] crept in, assumed the leadership of the Order and perverted its movements to their own selfish purposes."[74]

Diehard nativists who expected the American party to revive acknowledged these problems in hindsight, and promised to avoid them when the nativist movement reorganized. However, they failed to recognize that other factors, which they could not overcome, had prevented the Know Nothings from becoming a permanent political party. First, these diehard nativists erroneously assumed that the hundreds of thousands of votes cast for Know Nothing candidates in late 1854 and early 1855 reflected the true strength of support for their radical anti-immigrant agenda. Yet as we have seen, many Northerners joined the Know Nothings primarily in response to the slavery and temperance issues, or as a means to escape their old parties during the disintegration of the second party system. Many saw the purpose of the Order

72. Thomas Spooner, *Report of the President of the State Council of Ohio, June 5, 1855* (n.p., n.d.), 10.

73. New York *Times*, Sept. 17, 1857; New York *Herald*, June 10, 1855; "A True American" in Boston *Bee*, Sept. 27, 1855; Jamestown [New York] *Journal*, April 4, 1856.

74. Troy *Family Journal*, Sept. 15, 1855 (quotation); Rayner to Ullmann, March 7, 1855, June 2, 1856, Ullmann Papers, NYHS; Cincinnati *Gazette*, Jan. 13, 1855, quoted in John B. Weaver, "Nativism and the Birth of the Republican Party in Ohio, 1854–1860" (Ph.D. diss., Ohio State University, 1982), 52–53; letter to the editor, Hartford *Times*, March 15, 1855; Cincinnati *Times*, July 26, 1855.

as "the disorganization of the old, . . . corrupt parties,—& the weaning of those who were attached to them . . . ; this being now accomplished to a sufficient degree, . . . that reason for a secret order no longer remains." For these Know Nothings, the Order served merely as "a *half-way house*—a *stopping place on the road*" to their new political parties.[75] Dedicated nativists failed to understand this, and thus could not comprehend why subsequent nativist organizations failed to enjoy the unprecedented success of the Know Nothings.

One should not infer, however, that these less-dedicated Know Nothings opposed the Order's nativist tenets. On the contrary, even these voters sympathized with the party's anti-Catholic agenda. Why then, while American bigotry toward the Irish and Catholics continued, did the Know Nothings and subsequent nativist organizations fail to establish themselves as permanent political forces? Although historians have offered a number of explanations,[76] the answer lies primarily in the fact that while many Americans held nativist views, few voters made nativism a priority when they went to the polls. Nativism competed with sectional, economic, and local issues for the attention of voters, and these other questions usually carried precedence with the electorate. Under certain circumstances, though, nativism could move to the forefront of American political debate. Such was the case in 1854, when immigration reached unprecedented levels; religious disputes concerning education and church property erupted across the North; the most important nativist organization became associated with other popular movements, such as anti-slavery, temperance, and political reform; and, most important, the incipient disintegration of the Whig party created the opportunity for the fraternal order to attract more voters. These circumstances allowed a nativist political party, which usually failed to attract significant followings outside of large cities, to flourish briefly in the mid-1850s.

This still fails to explain why, under the ideal conditions existing in 1854 and 1855, the Know Nothing movement proved to be so fleeting. Ironically, it was the slavery question, which initially helped attract Northerners to the Order, that eventually destroyed the Know Nothings. "The principle cause . . . of our strength becoming weakened was the unlooked for Kansas question," noted

75. Youngstown *True American*, March 21, 1855; Henry S. Randall to D. Gilpin, June 10, 1856, filed with Gilpin to James Buchanan, June 27, 1856, Buchanan Papers, HSP.

76. Eric Foner has explained this apparent contradiction by distinguishing between "cultural" nativism, which held a consistent appeal, and "political" nativism, which only flourished under certain conditions. Others have contended that Foner's argument "makes an artificial distinction between cultural and political nativism," and instead contend that nativists continued to vent their anti-foreign animus through the Republican party. I agree that the distinction between cultural and political nativism can be misleading, but find that Foner's critics exaggerate the extent to which the Republican party embraced nativism. Although some Republicans continued to espouse nativism and push for its inclusion in their platform, *most* recognized that nativism was a liability, and succeeded in removing it from the party agenda after 1860. Foner, *Free Soil*, 260; William E. Gienapp, *The Origins of the Republican Party, 1852–1856* (New York: Oxford Univ. Press, 1987), 421; Holt, *Political Crisis of the 1850s*, 179.

one of the remaining Know Nothing organs in 1858. "This assumed a prominence which commanded the attention of the public, and . . . overshadowed in
a measure the question of Americanism." Some Northerners had believed that
the Know Nothings could function as both an anti-Catholic and anti-slavery
party, but when their June 1855 convention produced a platform that asked
Americans to accept the Kansas-Nebraska Act, Northerners demonstrated
where their priorities lay by abandoning the Know Nothings for the anti-slavery
Republican party. Most anti-slavery veterans had predicted that their ideology
would eventually overpower that of the Know Nothings. As one put it, "neither
the Pope nor the foreigners ever can govern the country or endanger its liberties, but the slavebreeders and slavetraders *do* govern it, and threaten to put an
end to all government but theirs. Here is something tangible to go upon, an
issue which . . . will . . . surely succeed in the long run."[77] Most Northerners
arrived at the same conclusion during the mid-1850s, and this, more than
anything else, doomed the Know Nothing movement.

77. [Greene, New York] *Chenango American*, Oct. 28, 1858; Charles A. Dana to Henry C.
Carey, Nov. 27, [1856?], Carey Papers, HSP.

Appendix

The purpose of this appendix is to explain, in more detail than is feasible in the footnotes, the methods used for compiling and categorizing the occupational and property data presented in Chapters 2 and 6. The most difficult task concerned the classification of the occupations. Luckily, my task in this regard was much simpler than that confronted by those examining occupational mobility, who are forced to make judgments on the relative status of various occupations. Because I was comparing the jobs held by two different groups of workers, rather than deciding whether a single worker's change of jobs marked a step up or down in the employment ladder, no such problem presented itself, and as long as I grouped both those Know Nothings and non–Know Nothings who pursued the same occupation in the same occupational category, my purpose—to present a means for comparing the jobs held by both groups—would be served.

Because I often found conflicting information concerning a Know Nothing's occupation, I had to determine which sources were most credible. In the end, I created the following hierarchy, from most to least reliable: Know Nothing minute-books, 1855 state census, city directory, 1850 federal census, 1860 federal census. I trusted the 1855 census more than city directories because one can not be sure that the directories were updated each year, while the information from the census was likely to come from a family member who would know what occupation the Know Nothing pursued. The 1850 census was given precedence over the 1860 census because that information was gathered closer (four years versus six) to the time that most Know Nothing lodges were formed.

A much more difficult problem concerned the classification of job titles whose meaning was unclear. In most cases, my rule was to be consistent with both Know Nothings and non–Know Nothings, so that even if a mistake was made, it would be reflected equally in both the Know Nothing and non–Know Nothing categories. The occupations which most frequently presented such a problem were those of "shoe manufacturer," "railroad conductor," "overseer," and, to a much lesser extent, "machinist." Most shoemakers simply called themselves "bootmakers" or sometimes "shoemakers." However, some called themselves "boot manufacturer," and I soon discovered that this term was utilized by both simple bootmakers and those who owned huge shoemaking factories. In these cases, I conducted additional research, and in every instance I was able to determine with relative certainty (through wealth statistics in the census, or when those were inconclusive through city directories) which category these workers belonged in. Such research was also conducted to determine the placement of those calling themselves things such as "soda water manufacturer," "faucet manufacturer," and so forth. As to "railroad conductor," this was a term used both by those who collected tickets on a train, and those who owned the railroad, so I used the same method for determining their status as was used for the shoe "manufacturers." Every once in a while, this problem developed with the term "machinist," because some men who owned huge machine works worth hundreds of thousands of dollars referred to themselves by this misleading name, and I used the same method to resolve such situations.

The term "overseer" was also one that could be frustratingly ambiguous, because while a "poor house overseer" is most likely a lower-status white-collar job, a foundry overseer was probably someone who had trained as a founder, and who was probably required to be on the shop floor and assist with the manual labor at times. Consequently, overseers in such industries were grouped with the skilled workers, while those such as the poor house overseer were categorized with lower-status white-collar workers.

Finally, I must warn scholars against trying to use these statistics to make certain comparisons concerning the distribution of workers within a given occupational category or industry. The control groups were constructed entirely from the census, in order to eliminate as many of those who were not qualified for Know Nothing membership as possible. In contrast, nearly all the Know Nothing occupations in Worcester, and many in East Boston and Portland, were found in the city directories. This is an important distinction because in most cases the city directories were more specific about a person's occupation than was the census. Thus, one finds with the Worcester Know Nothings some bootmakers, some boot crimpers, some boot "treers," some boot "clickers," and so forth, while in the census nearly everyone in the shoe industry is simply listed as a "bootmaker." When I found these census "bootmakers" in the directory, I usually found them listed by one of the more specialized titles that I had found for the Know Nothings. Thus, one should not infer from the differences in job titles listed below that Know Nothings in the shoe industry tended to hold more lower-paying, specialized jobs than did members of the control group, whose designation simply as "bootmakers" might suggest that they still performed all facets of the shoe-making process. A valid comparison *can* be made of the proportion of Know Nothings and non–Know Nothings in the shoe trade, which reveals that a nearly identical number of Know Nothings and non–Know Nothings were employed in this industry. The same situation presents itself in East Boston, because although the census and the directory describe jobs with different degrees of specificity, one finds the same proportion of mariners in both the Know Nothing and control-group ranks.

With those caveats in mind, here then are the occupations that comprise each category of each occupational chart presented in Chapters 2 and 6. The

East Boston Know Nothing professionals consisted of two lawyers, two doctors, a minister, and an accountant. The Know Nothing merchants consisted of 12 grocers, seven lumber dealers, six salesmen, five provisions dealers, four stove dealers, three coal dealers, junk dealers, traders, and contractors, two merchants, shoe dealers, furniture dealers, dry goods dealers, and fish dealers, and one shoe store owner, linseed oil manufacturer, liquor dealer, lobster dealer, grain dealer, boardinghouse owner, chair dealer, druggist, and clothing dealer. The lower-status white-collar Know Nothings included 31 clerks, four agents, two depot masters, bookkeepers, newspaper reporters, and brokers, and one appraiser, ballast officer, draughtsman, inspector of ballast and lighters, linseed oil mill overseer, music teacher, salt works superintendent, shipping master, teacher, theater prop man, and truant officer. The skilled workers consisted of 52 carpenters, 39 ship carpenters, 27 caulkers, 26 machinists, 23 ship joiners, 21 shipwrights, 20 painters, 18 engineers, 14 housewrights, 13 mariners, 13 blacksmiths, 11 coopers, nine pile drivers, seven masons, seven moulders, six bakers, six lightermen, six sail makers, five cabinet makers, four sawyers, four master boat builders, three spar makers, ship smiths, shoemakers, pilots, pattern makers, piano makers, brass founders, restorators, and stone cutters, two tailors, tinsmiths, stair builders, riggers, joiners, paper hangers, mast makers, forgemen, portrait painters, printers, pump and block makers, and gas fitters, and one boiler maker, bridge builder, butcher, car builder, coppersmith, daguerrotypist, ferryman, fisherman, gas maker, hatter, helmsman, iron founder, last maker, leather measurer, music printer, planer, puddler, roller, undertaker, upholsterer, wheelwright, and wood turner. Unskilled Know Nothing laborers included 20 teamsters, eleven laborers, five watchmen, four policemen, three expressmen, two coachmen, two stevedores, and one boat keeper, ferry toll taker, lamp lighter, messenger, porter, and stable keeper.

The East Boston control group professionals consisted of five doctors, one lawyer, one minister, and one civil engineer. The merchants included 10 grocers, four salesmen, four shoe dealers, three contractors, three dry goods dealers, two fish dealers, and one clothing dealer, druggist, fruit dealer, furnishing goods dealer, hardware dealer, ice man, junk dealer, liquor dealer, lumber dealer, merchant, oil dealer, and provisions dealer. The lower-status white-collar workers included nine clerks, three bookkeepers, two brokers, and one assessor, auctioneer, custom house worker, inspector, railroad superintendent, shipping master, and student. The skilled workers in the control group consisted of 40 ship carpenters, 23 carpenters, 18 caulkers, 15 mariners, 14 machinists, 13 ship joiners, 10 masons, seven engineers, seven painters, six blacksmiths, six pile drivers, four ferrymen, four shoemakers, three boat builders, carriage makers, printers, and shipwrights, two bakers, mastmakers, oil makers, riggers, ship smiths, tailors, and overseers, and one boilermaker, bookbinder, brass founder, brickmaker, brushmaker, carver, candle maker, boat captain, cooper, coppersmith, fireman, gas fitter, house joiner, iron founder, last maker, lathe maker, lighterman, lobsterman, miller, moulder, musician, naval officer, omnibus driver, paper hanger, paper ruler, piano maker, pilot, planer, portrait painter, restorator, sailmaker, sawyer, stair builder, tinsmith, trunk maker, and upholsterer. The unskilled laborers included 16 teamsters, four laborers, four watchmen, three policemen, two stablers, two expressmen, and one courier, ferry toll taker, gate tender, lamp lighter, and milkman.

The Worcester Know Nothing professionals included four accountants, four ministers, three physicians, one architect, one county treasurer, and one dentist. The merchants and manufacturers consisted of 11 grocers, four clothing dealers, four shoe dealers, two boot manufacturers, flour dealers, leather dealers, lumber dealers, merchants, and refreshment room owners, and one bonnet and fancy goods seller, coal dealer, corn dealer, crockery merchant, fur store owner, furniture dealer, hardware dealer, hat store owner, manufacturer, shoe tools seller, stove dealer, thread store owner, variety store owner, and victualler. Lower-status white-collar workers included 21 clerks, five agents, two surveyors, and one baggage master, bookkeeper, city treasurer, missionary, real estate agent, teacher, and ticket salesman. Worcester Know Nothing skilled workers consisted of 44 carpenters, 42 machinists, 11 bootmakers, 10 boot clickers, eight cabinet makers, seven carriage makers, six plow makers, five boot crimpers, boot treers, painters, and pattern makers, four tinsmiths, three aeolian and seraphine makers, three blacksmiths, boot finishers, masons, wheelwrights, and wire drawers, two boot bottomers, daguerrotypists, engineers, machinists' tool sellers, tailors, and watchmakers, and one armorer, baker, belt maker, butcher, carriage trimmer, cloth finisher, cordwainer, cutter, engraver, foundry overseer, gas fitter, gilder, hair dresser, harness maker, miller, moulder, paper hanger, percussion press maker, printer, pump and block maker, saw maker, shoe shop overseer, silverware maker, stair builder, stone cutter, trunk maker, undertaker, wood measurer, wood turner, and wood worker. The unskilled laborers included 10 hospital attendants, three coachmen, three couriers, three laborers, two expressmen, two teamsters, two watchmen, and one freight handler.

The Worcester control group professionals included four lawyers, four ministers, three dentists, two physicians, and one accountant, county treasurer, professor, and veterinarian. The merchants and manufacturers consisted of seven grocers, six merchants, two manufacturers, two peddlers, two provisions dealers, and one chemist, coal dealer, hotel keeper, lumber dealer, marble dealer, music store owner, restaurateur, tobacconist, and victualler. Lower-status white-collar workers included 16 clerks, five bookkeepers, three agents, two cashiers, two railroad conductors, two secretaries, and one auctioneer, broker, collector, editor, freight agent, gas agent, railroad agent, student, and teacher. Skilled workers consisted of 38 carpenters, 37 machinists, 26 bootmakers, 13 painters, eight masons, eight wire workers, six blacksmiths, five armorers, four butchers, engineers, mechanics, printers, and tailors, three carders, three clickers, three pattern makers, two jewelers, moulders, sash and blind makers, and tinsmiths, and one baker, basket maker, bootcrimper, boottreer, brickmaker, cabinet maker, carriage maker, carver, chair maker, coal weigher, confectioner, cook, crockery maker, fireman, gas fitter, gem smith, ladder maker, miller, overseer, paper hanger, pistol maker, plow maker, railroad repairer, reed maker, saw maker, shuttle maker, slater, soda water manufacturer, stair builder, type founder, watchmaker, weaver, and wheelwright. The unskilled laborers included 18 laborers, and one courier, factory operative, hackman, porter, stable keeper, and waiter. Farmers included one gardener.

The Portland Know Nothing professionals included four lawyers and one minister. The merchants and manufacturers group consisted of five traders, four chemists, four grocers, two clothing dealers, two dry goods dealers, two provisions dealers, and one bookseller, flour dealer, express service owner, furniture dealer, lumber dealer, merchant, shoe-store owner, stove dealer, and tobacconist. The lower-status white-collar workers consisted of six clerks, two bookkeepers, and one auctioneer. The skilled workers included three carpenters, three mariners, two blacksmiths, cigar makers, coopers, harness makers, and jewelers, and one bootmaker, carriage maker, confectioner, cordwainer, crockery maker, daguerrotypist, edge tool maker, gilder, joiner, mason, painter, printer, rope maker, and umbrella maker. The unskilled laborers consisted of one coachman, ferry tollman, laborer, provisions packer, stable keeper, teamster, and watchman.

The Portland control group professionals included three dentists, three lawyers, three doctors, two ministers, and one civil engineer. The merchants and manufacturers category consisted of 16 grocers, 14 merchants, eight traders, four clothing dealers, four dry goods dealers, three boarding house owners, three railroad conductors, three stove dealers, two chemists, corn dealers, lumber dealers, and provisions dealers, and one fur dealer, hay dealer, lamp dealer, peddler, publisher, shoe dealer, tavern keeper, tobacconist, toy shop owner, victualler, and oyster dealer. The lower-status white-collar group consisted of 19 clerks, two editors, two teachers, and one agent, alms house keeper, auctioneer, baggage master, bank teller, bookkeeper, broker, collector, custom house worker, depot master, harbor master, real estate agent, and student. Skilled workers in the Portland control group included 55 mariners, 18 carpenters, 17 joiners, 13 painters, 12 blacksmiths, 11 coopers, 11 masons, nine printers, seven machinists, seven sail makers, seven ship carpenters, six fishermen, five cordwainers, four hat makers, four tailors, three bakers, bootmakers, harness makers, iron founders, and tinsmiths, two boat builders, book binders, caulkers, chair makers, confectioners, and hair dressers, and one boat maker, boiler maker, brass founder, cabinet maker, captain, carriage maker, carriage trimmer, carver, chandler, cigar maker, coppersmith, corn measurer, crockery maker, edge tool maker, engineer, boatman, gilder, distiller, jeweller, linman, mast maker, pile driver, pilot, rock blower, rope maker, ship joiner, shipwright, silversmith, stone cutter, umbrella maker, upholsterer, wheelwright, whip maker, and wood turner. The unskilled laborers consisted of 15 laborers, six teamsters, three coachmen, two stable keepers, two waiters, one domestic, one expressman, one mailman, and one steward.

The Canandaigua Know Nothing professionals included eight lawyers, four ministers, and four doctors. The merchants and manufacturers consisted of 11 merchants, four grocers, three tavern keepers, two chemists, and one coal dealer, hotel owner, lumber dealer, produce dealer, restaurateur, salesman, shoe dealer, saddle dealer, and stage proprietor. Canandaigua's Know Nothing lower-status white-collar workers included 15 clerks, three agents, two railroad conductors, two students, and one bookkeeper, editor, street commissioner, railroad overseer, and saloon keeper. The skilled workers included 13 carpenters, seven blacksmiths, six tailors, five painters, four shoemakers, four engineers, four masons, three brickmakers, butchers, carriage makers, harness makers, machinists, printers, tanners, and tinsmiths, two jewelers, two joiners, two mechanics, and one bartender, bookbinder, carriage trimmer, cooper, fireman, gunsmith, musician, silver plater, and wagon maker. The unskilled laborers consisted of eight laborers, four teamsters, and one courier, baggage man, gate tender, watchman, and turnkey.

Canandaigua control group professionals included six lawyers, three doctors, one banker, and one minister. The merchants and manufacturers consisted of six merchants, five grocers, two produce dealers, one bookseller, one lumber dealer, and one tobacconist. The lower-status white-collar workers included eight clerks, three agents, three teachers, and one boardinghouse keeper, ex-sheriff, street commissioner, railroad conductor, railroad trackmaster, and student. The skilled workers included 11 carpenters, seven blacksmiths, seven painters, six shoemakers, three tailors, three wagon makers, two cabinet makers, coopers, engineers, harness makers, machinists, masons, saddlers, and tinsmiths, and one artist, bartender, basket maker, brickmaker, captain, carriage maker, coppersmith, gardener, lumberman, mechanic, printer, seaman, silver plater, tanner, and telegraph operator. The unskilled laborers consisted of 28 laborers, three teamsters, one stable keeper, and one mailman.

For the occupational figures concerning Know Nothing officeholders, the New Hampshire Know Nothing professionals included 12 lawyers, 11 doctors, four ministers, two dentists, one accountant, and one civil engineer. The merchants and manufacturers consisted of 11 merchants, five manufacturers, three lumber dealers, two railroad conductors, and one bookseller, boot manufacturer, druggist, grocer, hotel keeper, and trader. The lower-status white-collar workers consisted of three clerks, two overseers, two teachers, and one agent, cashier, postmaster, student, state treasurer, and sheriff. Skilled workers included nine carpenters, seven bootmakers, four machinists, three blacksmiths, two sawyers, and one book binder, glove maker, hat maker, joiner, mason, millman, millwright, printer, seaman, tanner, tinsmith, undertaker, and watchmaker.

The New Hampshire control group professionals included 18 lawyers, eight doctors, one civil engineer, and one minister. The merchants and manu-facturers consisted of 15 merchants, four lumber dealers, two railroad conduc-tors, two store keepers, and one clothing dealer, contractor, iron foundry owner, grocer, and manufacturer. Lower-status white-collar workers included two clerks, two postmasters, one agent, one cashier, and one overseer. The skilled laborers consisted of six carpenters, four shoemakers, three machin-ists, three tanners, two blacksmiths, two carriage makers, two pilots, and one caulker, cooper, harness maker, iron founder, musical instrument maker, pa-per maker, marble worker, and sawyer. The unskilled laborers group con-tained one laborer. Two gentlemen were classified as farmers.

The Connecticut Know Nothing professionals included nine lawyers, six doctors, and one minister. The merchants and manufacturers consisted of 22 manufacturers, 15 merchants, and one bookseller, lumber dealer, railroad president, and stove manufacturer. The lower-status white-collar workers con-sisted of three teachers. The skilled workers included nine mechanics, four mariners, three joiners, two tanners, printers, masons, and hatters, and one blacksmith, carriage trimmer, carpenter, machinist, and saw handle maker.

The Connecticut control group professionals included 12 lawyers, two ministers, and one doctor. The merchants and manufacturers category is com-prised of 16 manufacturers, 15 merchants, one express service owner, one bleacher, and one stage proprietor. The lower-status white-collar group con-sisted of one agent, one ship master, and one "public servant." The skilled workers included five mechanics, three blacksmiths, and one engineer, shoe-maker, cabinet maker, carriage maker, hatter, bell founder, millwright, ship carpenter, and watch maker.

New York Know Nothing professionals included three lawyers and one doctor. The merchants and manufacturers consisted of seven merchants, three forwarders, and one stage proprietor. The lower-status white-collar workers included two teachers, one editor, and one author. The skilled workers con-sisted of one carpenter.

The New York control group professionals included 17 lawyers and five doctors. The merchants and manufacturers consisted of 15 merchants, and one contractor, forwarder, hotel keeper, lumber dealer, manufacturer, and nursery owner. The lower-status white-collar workers included one auction-eer, one broker, and one clerk. The skilled workers consisted of four mechan-ics, one jeweller, one mariner, and one tailor.

The Indiana Know Nothing professionals included 17 lawyers, six physi-cians, four ministers, and one dentist. Merchants and manufacturers consisted of four merchants, and one contractor, hotel keeper, lumber dealer, and nursery owner. The lower-status white-collar workers included two editors. The skilled workers consisted of one blacksmith, carpenter, gunsmith, and millwright.

The Indiana control group professionals included 12 lawyers and four doctors. The merchants and manufacturers consisted of six merchants and one livestock dealer. The lower-status white-collar workers included one clerk, one editor, and one teacher. The skilled workers consisted of two carpenters, two tanners, one cooper, and one miller.

The Pennsylvania Know Nothing professionals included ten lawyers, three doctors, and one banker. The merchants and manufacturers consisted of four merchants, and one grocer, manufacturer, publisher, shoe dealer, and receiver of railroad commissions. The lower-status white-collar workers included four clerks, two collectors, and one justice of the peace. The skilled workers consisted of one printer and one potter. The unskilled category consisted of three laborers.

The Pennsylvania control group professionals included 12 lawyers and one dentist. The merchants and manufacturers consisted of five merchants, and one coal dealer, transporter, grocer, hotel keeper, liquor dealer, lumber dealer, manufacturer, and receiver of railroad commissions. The lower-status white-collar workers included two clerks, and one editor, justice of the peace, student, surveyor, and superintendent of finance. The skilled workers consisted of two carpenters, one artist, and one flangeman. The unskilled laborer category included one laborer.

For the statistics concerning property, I sought to insure that the Know Nothing figure was not artificially increased because transient Know Nothings would not be found, while the control group would contain whichever transients happened to be in town when the census was taken. Consequently, the control groups for Worcester and East Boston consist of a random sampling of native-born citizens of voting age as of 1854 who appeared in the manuscript state census of 1855 and were still found in the city either five years earlier (in the case of Worcester) or five years later (in the case of East Boston). For Portland (whose control group is the same as that used above for occupations) and Canandaigua (whose control group consists of a random sampling of native-born citizens at least 25 years old in 1860, the youngest age of any Know Nothing in that year), such a system could not be used, because no 1855 census was conducted in Maine, while the 1855 census taker in Canandaigua seems to have neglected to record most households. Thus, the figures from East Boston are most reliable, because they were compiled with both an accurate control group and the more informative census. However, because most Portland Know Nothings were found in the census (of those who were not, most were actually merchants, not workingmen), those figures are probably relatively accurate. In addition, although the Canandaigua figures overall may make the Know Nothings appear more wealthy than they really were, those figures for merchants and farmers, two groups that were not very transitory, are probably accurate. Finally, the figures concerning Canandaigua farmers include those categorized as "farm laborers" by the census taker.

Bibliography

This bibliography does not list every source utilized in the preparation of this book. Instead, I have listed those works that I relied upon most heavily for information, or that influenced my conception of Civil War–era politics and culture. Those who wish to examine a more extensive list, especially of anti-Catholic literature and Master's theses, should consult my doctoral dissertation, "Nativism and Politics: The Know Nothing Party in the Northern United States" (Columbia University, 1990).

KNOW NOTHING RECORDS

American Party Ritual. Rare Book Room, University of Rochester.
Constitution and By-laws of the Order. Adopted, May, 1855. Indianapolis, 1855. Indiana State Library.
Constitution of the S.C. of the State of Connecticut. Adopted Sept. 7, 1854. Hartford, 1854. Connecticut State Library.
Constitutions of the State and Subordinate Councils of Wisconsin. Milwaukee, 1855. State Historical Society of Wisconsin.
Ethan Allen Council [Canandaigua, New York] Minute Book. Ontario County Historical Society.
Know Nothing Party [?] Membership List, Maine Historical Society.
Rituals of the First and Second Degrees. [n.p., n.d.]. State Historical Society of Wisconsin.
Sub-Council 5 [East Boston] Minute Book. Solomon B. Morse, Jr., Papers. Massachusetts Historical Society.
Sub-Council 23 [Worcester, Massachusetts] Membership List and Scrapbook. Worcester Historical Museum.
Sub-Council 49 [Worcester] Minute Book. American Antiquarian Society.

RECORDS OF OTHER NATIVIST ORGANIZATIONS

Guard of Liberty [Harrisburg] Minute Book. Pennsylvania State Archives.
Order of United Americans Scrapbook, New York Public Library.

MANUSCRIPTS

Adams Family Papers, Massachusetts Historical Society
Archdiocesan Records, University of Notre Dame Archives
Nathaniel P. Banks, Jr. Papers, Library of Congress

Nathaniel P. Banks, Jr. Papers, Illinois State Historical Library
Beekman Family Papers, New-York Historical Society
William Bigler Papers, Historical Society of Pennsylvania
Francis Bird Papers, Harvard University
James Bishop Papers, Rutgers University
Jeremiah S. Black Papers, Library of Congress
James G. Blaine Papers, Library of Congress
Samuel Bowles Papers, Yale University
James Buchanan Papers, Historical Society of Pennsylvania
Edmund Burke Papers, Library of Congress
Simon Cameron Papers, Library of Congress
Simon Cameron Papers, Dauphin County Historical Society
Lewis D. Campbell Papers, Ohio Historical Society
Henry C. Carey Papers, Gardiner Collection, Historical Society of Pennsylvania
Salmon P. Chase Papers, Historical Society of Pennsylvania
Salmon P. Chase Papers, Library of Congress
William Penn Clarke Papers, Iowa State Department of History and Archives.
John M. Clayton Papers, Library of Congress
Schuyler Colfax Papers, Indiana Historical Society
Schuyler Colfax Papers, Indiana State Library
Schuyler Colfax Papers, Indiana University
Schuyler Colfax Papers, Northern Indiana Historical Society
Schuyler Colfax Papers, Library of Congress
John Covode Papers, Library of Congress
Will Cumback Papers, Indiana University
Richard H. Dana Papers, Massachusetts Historical Society
John G. Davis Papers, Indiana Historical Society
Charles D. Deshler Papers, Rutgers University
Andrew J. Donelson Papers, Library of Congress
William H. English Papers, Indiana Historical Society
Edward Everett Papers, Massachusetts Historical Society
Millard Fillmore Papers, Buffalo and Erie County Historical Society
Millard Fillmore Papers, State University of New York at Oswego
Hamilton Fish Papers, Library of Congress
Oren Follett Papers, Cincinnati Historical Society
Benjamin French Papers, Library of Congress
Samuel Galloway Papers, Ohio Historical Society
Joshua Giddings Papers, Library of Congress
Joshua Giddings Papers, Ohio Historical Society
Joseph Gillespie Papers, Illinois State Historical Library
Horace Greeley Papers, Library of Congress
Horace Greeley Papers, New York Public Library
Whiting Griswold Papers, Library of Congress
J. Scott Harrison Papers, Library of Congress
Joseph Hawley Papers, Library of Congress
Lucius J. Hendee Papers, Connecticut Historical Society
Washington Hunt Papers, New York State Library
John P. Kennedy Papers, Library of Congress
Amos A. Lawrence Papers, Massachusetts Historical Society

Lewis C. Levin Papers, Henry E. Huntington Library
Abraham Lincoln Papers, Library of Congress
John McLean Papers, Library of Congress
Edward McPherson Papers, Library of Congress
Horace Mann Papers, Massachusetts Historical Society
William Marcy Papers, Library of Congress
Sidney D. Maxwell Diary, Cincinnati Historical Society
William Medill Papers, Library of Congress
Edwin D. Morgan Papers, New York State Library
Godlove S. Orth Papers, Indiana State Library
Kenneth Rayner Papers, University of North Carolina, Chapel Hill
John Rockwell Papers, Henry E. Huntington Library
William Schouler Papers, Massachusetts Historical Society
William H. Seward Papers, University of Rochester
Horatio Seymour Papers, New York State Library
Isaac Sherman Papers, Private Collection
Matthew Simpson Papers, Library of Congress
Thaddeus Stevens Papers, Library of Congress
Isaac Strohm Papers, Cincinnati Historical Society
Isaac Strohm Papers, Ohio Historical Society
Charles Sumner Papers, Harvard University
Richard W. Thompson Papers, Illinois State Historical Library
Richard W. Thompson Papers, Indiana State Library
Richard W. Thompson Papers, Indiana University
Richard W. Thompson Papers, Lincoln National Life Foundation
Richard W. Thompson Papers, Rutherford B. Hayes Library
Allen Trimble Papers, Ohio Historical Society
Allen Trimble Papers, Western Reserve Historical Society
Lyman Trumble Papers, Illinois State Historical Lbrary
Lyman Trumble Papers, Library of Congress
Daniel Ullmann Papers, New-York Historical Society
Elihu B. Washburne Papers, Library of Congress
Israel Washburne, Jr., Papers, Library of Congress
Thurlow Weed Papers, University of Rochester
Gideon Welles Papers, Connecticut Historical Society
Gideon Welles Papers, Library of Congress
Henry Wilson Papers, Library of Congress
Joel Wilson Papers, Henry E. Huntington Library

As is evident from my footnotes, some of these collections were more useful than others. The two that are by far the most important for a study of the Know Nothings are those of Daniel Ullmann and Millard Fillmore. The Ullmann collection is the only one that contains detailed information on the critical summer and autumn of 1854, while the Fillmore Papers at the State University of New York at Oswego provide insight into the thoughts of those leaders of the American party who still remained loyal to the organization after Fillmore's nomination in 1856. Of the other Know Nothings listed above, many followed the party's dictates of secrecy by destroying most their correspondence concerning the Order. Those Know Nothings whose papers contain the most information on the party are Nathaniel P. Banks, Jr., Simon Cameron,

Lewis D. Campbell, Will Cumback, Charles D. Deshler, J. Scott Harrison, Amos A. Lawrence, and Godlove S. Orth. A few non–Know Nothings were particularly well informed concerning the workings of the Order, and their papers, if used with caution, provide additional information concerning the Know Nothing party. The most useful of these collections were those of the Beekman Family, William Bigler, James Buchanan, William H. Seward, Charles Sumner, and Thurlow Weed.

NEWSPAPERS

Because so few Know Nothing manuscript collections are extant, scholars must rely upon newspapers for most information concerning the party. Luckily, enough Know Nothing journals have survived to enable the historian to track all but the early history of the party. The Boston *Bee* was the party's Massachusetts organ, but should be supplemented with the Worcester *Transcript*, whose editor belonged to a Worcester lodge, as well as the Boston *Know Nothing*, the Boston *American Patriot*, and the Boston *Ledger*, all edited by veteran nativists. The Know Nothings' Connecticut organ was the Hartford *Courant*. Also see the New Haven *Palladium*, whose editor James F. Babcock quickly moved into the Republican party. Other newspapers useful to the study of Know Nothingism in New England include the Manchester, New Hampshire, *American*, the Providence, Rhode Island, *Tribune*, and the Ellsworth, Maine, *American*.

A variety of New York Know Nothing newspapers are available to scholars. The most important, in my opinion, is the Albany *State Register*, whose columns reflect the mixture of nativism, temperance, and anti-slavery that made the Order so popular in the North. Unfortunately, half of the New York State Library's run of the journal has inexplicably found its way into the attic of the Davenport Library in Bath, New York. However, those interested in understanding Know Nothingism in the North will find making the trip to Bath well worth the effort. Among the many other New York Know Nothing newspapers, those I found most useful were the New York *Express*, co-edited by Know Nothing leader Erastus Brooks; the Albany *Statesman*, which became the capital's pro-Fillmore organ when the *State Register* refused to support him; the Jamestown *Journal*, edited by a leading North American; the New York *Crusader*, published by a fervently anti-Catholic Italian immigrant; as well as the Greene *Chenango American*, the Ithaca *American Citizen*, and the Rochester *American*.

As with New York, those studying Pennsylvania Know Nothingism must examine a variety of newspapers in order to understand each of the state's Know Nothing factions. The most important journal is the Harrisburg *Herald*, whose editor Stephen Miller was a party leader. The Philadelphia *News*, edited by the chairman of the party's pro-Fillmore state committee, is another important source. Other newspapers of particular value in understanding Pennsylvania Know Nothingism are the Clearfield *Raftsman's Journal*, Gettysburg *Star and Banner*, the Johnstown *Cambria Tribune*, the Philadelphia *Times*, the Philadelphia *Sun* (edited by veteran nativist Lewis C. Levin), the Pittsburgh *Times*, the Pittsburgh *Dispatch*, and the Pottsville *Miner's Journal*.

Because there were fewer factions vying for control of the Know Nothings in the Midwest, a shorter list of newspapers suffices for those states. In Ohio, I found the Cleveland *Express*, the Cincinnati *Times*, the Hillsboro *American Citizen*, the St. Clairsville *Independent Republican*, the Steubenville *True American*, and the Youngstown *True American* to be the most useful. Indiana Know Nothingism can be traced through the columns of the Fort Wayne *Times* (whose editor was a leading North

American), the New Albany *Tribune*, the Rising Sun *Visitor*, and the Vincennes *Gazette*. In Illinois, few newspapers openly endorsed the Know Nothings before the nomination of Fillmore, but scholars can glean some information from the Chicago *Literary Budget*, whose editor served as the Order's state president. In Wisconsin, the Milwaukee *American* served as the party organ. A list of approximately 300 additional northern newspapers that at some point supported the American party can be found in my doctoral dissertation, cited above.

Although those investigating the Know Nothings should rely upon these Know Nothing newspapers rather than those published by the party's enemies, a few journals not affiliated with the Order provided valuable information. Most important in this regard are the New York *Times*, New York *Tribune*, and New York *Herald*. These papers were especially useful for coverage of Know Nothing conventions, particularly during the Order's early, secretive stages. Other non–Know Nothing newspapers that aided my research were the Harrisburg *Telegraph*, the Columbus *Ohio Statesman*, the Cincinnati *Commercial*, and the Boston *Advertiser*.

BOOKS AND PAMPHLETS

After newspapers, books and pamphlets (primarily the latter) were the primary means by which the Know Nothings disseminated information about the Order and its intentions. As far as the origins of the Order are concerned, the most important work is Thomas R. Whitney, *A Defence of the American Policy* (New York, 1856). Whitney, a founder of the Order of United Americans and later a Know Nothing congressman, played a key role in the OUA's takeover of the Know Nothings, and consequently was privy to more information concerning the early operations of the Order than virtually anyone else. Anna Ella Carroll's *The Great American Battle; or, the Contest between Christianity and Political Romanism* (New York, 1856) also contains information on the early years of the Order, as does *The Sons of the Sires; A History of the Rise, Progress, and Destiny of the American Party, and Its Probable Influence in the Next Presidential Election* (Philadelphia, 1855) and John Hancock Lee, *The Origin and Progress of the American Party in Politics* (Philadelphia, 1855).

In addition to these works, a number of exposés appeared soon after the Order's appearance, claiming to contain secret information concerning the origins of the organizatrion. Of these, the only one that seems authentic is *The History of the Rise, Progress & Downfall of Know-Nothingism in Lancaster County by Two Expelled Members* (Lancaster, Pa., 1856). The others, including *A Complete Exposure of the Order of "Know Nothings"; Being a Revelation of All the Signs, Secrets, Peculiarities, Plans and Operations of the Mysterious Body. By One of the "Expelled"* (Philadelphia, 1854), *Exposition of the Mysteries and Secrets of the Order of "Know Nothings": . . . by a Late Member of the Order* (New York, 1854), *The Know Nothings. An Exposure of the Secret Order . . . ; the Most Ludicrous and Startling Yankee "Notion" Ever Conceived* (New York, 1854), *The Ritual of the Order of Know Nothings, with the Initiation Oaths Taken by James Pollock, Now Governor of Pennsylvania* (n.p., n.d.), and William Swinson, *An Expose of the Know Nothings, Their Degrees, Signs, Grips, Passwords, Charges, Oaths, Initiations* (Philadelphia, 1854), all contain enough inaccuracies to imply that they are either pure fabrications printed to earn quick profits from a curious public, or partisan publications designed to inspire the party's enemies.

Information concerning the principles of the Know Nothings' early leaders is much easier to uncover than are the details of its origins, because at one point or another most of the Order's original leaders addressed the issues of the day in speeches before the OUA. The most revealing are Alfred B. Ely, *American Liberty, Its Sources,—Its Dangers,—and the Means of Its Preservation* (New York, 1850), a speech by a veteran Massachusetts nativist; Charles D. Deshler, *"The Great American Middle Class." An Address Delivered Before the Order of United Americans, of Newark, N.J., in Library Hall, on . . . February 22, 1855* (New York, 1855), by a longtime New Jersey nativist who served as the Order's national corresponding secretary; and Whitney's *Defence of the American Policy* cited above. Other addresses by important veteran nativists affiliated with the Know Nothings include Lewis C. Levin, *Speech of Mr. L. C. Levin, of Pennsylvania, on the Subject of Altering the Naturalization Laws . . . December 18, 1845* (Washington, 1845), as well as three by Pennsylvanian Jacob Broom: *An Address Delivered at Castle Garden, February 22, 1854, Before the Order of United Americans* (New York, 1854), *An Address Delivered at the First Presbyterian Church, Jersey City, July 4th, 1854, Before the Order of United Americans* (New York, 1855), and *Defense of Americanism. Speech of Hon. Jacob Broom, of Pennsylvania; Delivered in the House of Representatives, August 4, 1856* (Washington, 1856). Those seeking more information concerning Whitney's views can refer to three of his speeches: *An Address on the Occasion of the Seventh Anniversary of the Alpha Chapter, Order of United Americans* (New York, 1852), *The Union of the States: An Oration Delivered Before the Order of United Americans . . . February 22, 1855* (New York, 1855), and *Church and State; Speech . . . in Congress July 28, 1856* (Washington, 1856).

Veteran nativists were not the only Know Nothings to publicize their views through pamphlets. Daniel Ullmann's *The Course of Empire* (New York, 1856) provides particularly valuable insight into how the Know Nothings' conception of nationhood shaped their political agenda. His views on the issues of the day are also set forth in *Civil and Religious Liberty. An Address at Wilmington . . . July 4, 1855* (n.p., n.d). For the views of two other conservative Whigs-turned-Know Nothings, see Thomas C. Ware, *Address of Thomas C. Ware, President of the State Council of Ohio. Delivered May 29th, 1856* (n.p., n.d), and Erastus Brooks, *American Citizenship and the Progress of American Civilization; An Oration Delivered Before the Order of United Americans . . . February 22d, 1858* (New York, 1858).

Unfortunately, few of the less-conservative Know Nothings, who stressed anti-slavery and temperance in addition to nativism, published detailed accounts of their conception of the movement's agenda. The president of the Pennsylvania Know Nothings, Otis H. Tiffany, advocated the anti-slavery cause in many of his speeches, but his only published work, *Lecture on the Cultivation of the Christian Elements of Republicanism* (Carlisle, Pa., 1855), concentrates on the perceived threat to republicanism posed by the Catholic Church. The views of anti-slavery Know Nothings are better illustrated in the writings of Ohio Know Nothing president Thomas Spooner, such as his *Report of the President of the State Council of Ohio, June 5, 1855* (n.p., n.d.), and his *To the State Council*, a circular dated January 3, 1856, in the Cincinnati Public Library. Perhaps the best indication of how northern Know Nothings blended the slavery issue with anti-Catholicism is Anson Burlingame, *Oration by Hon. Anson Burlingame, Delivered at Salem, July 4, 1854* (Salem, 1854). However, because these are the only works that reflect what was, in my opinion, the point of view held by most northern Know Nothings, they must be supplemented with speeches and editorials from Know Nothing newspapers in order to understand more fully how the Order made use of the slavery and temperance issues. For the efforts of ministers to assert more influence in politics, a movement that aided Know Nothing recruitment, see Rev. Samuel Harris, "Politics and the Pulpit," *New Englander* (May 1854), and Daniel C. Eddy, *The Commonwealth: Political Rights of Ministers; A Sermon Preached on Fast Day, April 4, 1854* (n.p., n.d).

Many of the pamphlets containing Know Nothings' speeches were issued in order to justify the members' actions in various legislative debates. In New York, most attention focused on the church property controversy. See George Babcock, *Remarks of Mr. Babcock, of Erie, on the Roman Catholic Church Property Bill: In the Senate, June 24, 1853, Upon the Motion to Strike Out the Enacting Clause of the Bill* (Albany, 1853); Erastus Brooks, *Speech of Hon. E. Brooks on the Church Property Bill* (New York, 1855); James O. Putnam, *Ecclesiastical Tenures* (Albany, 1855); W. S. Tisdale, ed., *The Controversy between Senator Brooks, and "† John," Archbishop of New York, over the Church Property Bill* (New York, 1855). Hughes's response to the Order's charges can be found in John Hughes, *Brooksiana* (New York, 1855). Other issues of interest to Know Nothings in the New York legislature are addressed in Brooks's *Speech of Hon. Erastus Brooks in the Senate, Feb. 7th, 8th, & 13th, 1855, the Lemmon Slave Case and Slavery—Secret Societies and Oaths—Grounds of Opposition to Mr. Seward—the Common Schools of New York—the Pure Franchise—A Better System of Naturalization—American Ambassadors Abroad—American Rulers at Home* (n.p., 1855). The motivations of those Know Nothings who supported Seward's election can be found in *United States Senatorial Question* (Albany, 1855).

In Massachusetts, pamphlets appeared concerning a variety of legislation enacted by the Know Nothings. On the effort to remove Judge Edward G. Loring because of his acquiescence to the fugitive slave law, see *Report of the Committee on Federal Relations, to Whom Were Referred Petitions for, and Remonstrances Against the Removal of Edward G. Loring* (Boston, 1855); James W. Stone, *Removal of Judge Loring. Remarks of James W. Stone in the Massachusetts House of Representatives, April 13, 1855* (Boston, 1855); John L. Swift, *Speech of John L. Swift, Esq., on the Removal of Edward G. Loring . . . Delivered in the Massachusetts House of Representatives, Tuesday, April 10, 1855* (Boston, 1855). The Order's Massachusetts opponents published a number of pamphlets addressing other legislative action taken by the Know Nothings. Charles Hale condemned the Know Nothings' efforts to limit office-holding to native-born citizens in *All Men Are Born Equal. Speech of Charles Hale, in the House of Representatives of the Massachusetts Legislature, March 27, 1856, on a Proposition for Amending the Constitution to Deprive Persons of Foreign Birth of the Right to Hold Office in Massachusetts* (Boston, 1856). The actions of the Massachusetts Nunnery Committee are denounced in Hale's *"Our Houses Are Our Castles": A Review of the Proceedings of the Nunnery Committee of the Massachusetts Legislature: And Especially their Conduct . . . on Occasion of the Visit to the Catholic School in Roxbury, March 26, 1855* (Boston, 1855), as well as *The Convent Committee, Better Known as the Smelling Committee, in the Exercise of Their Onerous and Arduous Duties at the Ladies Catholic Seminary, Roxbury* (Boston, 1855). After the 1856 election, anti-nativist Republicans attempted to thwart the passage of a constitutional amendment mandating a waiting period after naturalization before immigrants could vote with Edward L. Pierce, *Effect of Proscriptive or Extreme Legislation Against Foreigners in Massachusetts and New England* (Boston, 1857), and Caleb Cushing, *Speeches on the Amendment of the Constitutional Convention of Massachusetts, Imposing Disabilities on Naturalized Citizens of the United States* (Boston, 1859). For two campaign documents that criticize the Know Nothings' legislative performance, see S. P. Hanscom [a Know Nothing-turned-Republican], *To His Excellency Henry J. Gardner, Governor of the Commonwealth of Massachusetts* (n.p., [1855]), and [Gideon Haynes], *Facts for the People. The American State Convention. Governor Gardner's Speech Reviewed. Letters of Hon. Timothy Davis and Hon. Gideon Haynes* (Boston, 1856).

Pennsylvania Know Nothings did not issue as many publications as their New York and Massachusetts counterparts. However, the circulars issued by both sides in the senatorial debate, and found in the Cameron Papers at the Library of Congress, are quite revealing. In addition, Alexander McClure's *Old Times Notes of Pennsylvania*, 2 vols. (Philadelphia, 1905), is extremely informative.

The school controversies that developed in the early 1850s also inspired a variety of publications. Two written by Know Nothings are James N. Sykes, *Common vs. Catholic Schools. A Discourse Delivered . . . Nov. 24, 1853* (Boston, 1853), and Daniel Ullmann, *Amendments to the Constitution of the United States. Non-Sectarian and Universal Education . . . Remarks of Daniel Ullmann in Response to the Sentiment: Our Common Schools, the Glory of Our Republic, Undefiled by Sectarianism, Our Hope and Boast; They Shall Be Maintained* (New York, 1876), and although Ullmann's treatise was published twenty years after his Know Nothing involvement, it undoubtedly reflects views that he held in the 1850s as well. Other works touching upon the school issue include J. Kelly and A. W. McClure, *The School Question: A Correspondence between Rev. J. Kelly . . . and Rev. A. W. McClure, Jersey City* (New York, 1853), Henry S. Randall, *Decision . . . on the Right to Compel Catholic Children to Attend Prayers, and to Read or Commit Portions of the Bible, as School Exercises* (n.p., [1853]), George B. Cheever, *The Right of the Bible in Our Public Schools* (New York, 1854), Richard H. Dana, Jr., *The Bible in Schools. Argument of Richard H. Dana, Jr.* (Boston, [1855]).

Although Know Nothings wielded less influence in Congress than in many state capitals, events in Washington prompted them to publish a number of pamphlets, and despite the fact that many of them are difficult to track down, they provide important insight into the difficulties the party encountered there. National Americans defended their actions in the speakership contest in Oscar F. Moore, *Letter of Hon. O. F. Moore to His Constituents* (Washington, 1856), William W. Valk, *Letter of Mr. Valk . . . on the Occurrences Which Have Prevented an Organization of the House of Representatives of the Thirty-fourth Congress* (Washington, 1856), and Thomas R. Whitney, *Political. Letter from Mr. Whitney, of New York, to His Constituents* (Washington, 1856). When the National Americans were criticized for not supporting Republican attempts to bar slavery from Kansas, they responded with Moore's *Speech of Hon. Oscar F. Moore, of Ohio. Practical Legislation for the Troubles in Kansas* ([Washington], 1856), Valk's *Speech on the Contested Kansas Election, Given March 17, 1856* (n.p., n.d), and Bayard Clark's *Speech of Hon. Bayard Clark, of New York, on the Senate Kansas Bill, and in Defence of the American Party. Delivered in the House of Representatives July 24, 1856* (Washington, 1856).

Besides these speeches, a number of more general publications were issued espousing the Know Nothing cause, although I tended to utilize these works less often than those discussed in the previous paragraphs because it is impossible to determine the extent to which these primarily anonymous works reflected Know Nothing opinion. See *An Alarm to Heretics; Or, an Exposition of Some of the Evils, Villainies and Dangers of Papacy, Also a Vindication of and an Outline of the True American Platform*

(Philadelphia, 1854); *A Constitutional Manual for the National American Party. In Which Is Examined the Question of Negro Slavery in Connexion with the Constitution of the United States. By a Northern Man, With American Principles* (Providence, R.I., 1856); John Denig, *The Know Nothing Manual* (Harrisburg, 1855); *Know Nothing Platform: Containing an Account of the Encroachments of the Roman Catholic Hierarchy on the Civil and Religious Liberties of the People in Europe, Asia, Africa and America, Showing the Necessity of the Order of Know Nothings* (Philadelphia, n.d); *Principles and Objects of the American Party* (New York, 1855); Sam C. Crane, *Facts and Figures for Native-Born Americans* (Ithaca, 1856); *Startling Facts for Native Americans Called "Know Nothings," or a Vivid Presentation of the Dangers to American Liberty, to Be Apprehended from Foreign Influence* (New York, 1855); *The Wide-Awake Gift: A Know-Nothing Token for 1855, Edited by "One of 'Em"* (New York, 1855).

One such publication which I did use quite extensively, however, was *The Know Nothing Almanac and True American's Manual* (New York, 1854, 1855, 1856). The publisher of this work obviously coordinated his efforts with National American leaders such as Erastus Brooks and Jacob Broom, and in terms of nativism, the *Know Nothing Almanac* is the best single source for understanding the worldview of the Order's members. I also relied a great deal upon John P. Sanderson's *Republican Landmarks. The Views and Opinions of American Statesmen on Foreign Immigration* (Philadelphia, 1856), in part because his role as president of the Pennsylvania Fillmore State Committee confirms his influence.

Although the pamphlets and newspapers listed here provide the student of Know Nothingism with insight into every facet of Know Nothingism, I found it necessary to consult additional anti-Catholic tracts—ones not necessarily written by Know Nothings—in order to understand the nuances of nineteenth-century anti-Catholicism. Of particular importance is Alessandro Gavazzi, *The Lectures Complete of Father Gavazzi* (New York, 1854), containing the speeches of the apostate priest who inspired much of the hostility to papal nuncio Gaetano Bedini. Another extremely useful book is Edward Beecher, *The Papal Conpiracy Exposed and Protestantism Defended in the Light of Reason, History, and Scripture* (Boston, 1855), a lengthy diatribe written by a member of the most prominent family of American ministers. However, I found that Civis [pseud.], *Romanism Incompatible with Republican Institutions* (1844; rpt., New York, 1854), was the single best source for understanding the groundings of nineteenth-century anti-Catholicism. Other particularly revealing works include John McClintock, *The Temporal Power of the Pope* (New York, 1855), John C. Pitrot, *Review of the Speech of Hon. J. R. Chandler of Pennsylvania on the Political Power of the Pope* (Boston, 1855), and D. G. Parker, *A Compilation of Startling Facts; or, Romanism Against Republicanism* (Chicago, 1856).

For the scholar who wishes to consult additional anti-Catholic tracts, those that provide the most insight into the issues of most importance to Know Nothings include Thomas Bayne, *Popery Subversive of American Institutions* (Pittsburgh, 1856); Samuel C. Busey, *Immigration: Its Evils and Consequences* (1856; rpt., New York, 1969); Rufus W. Clark, *Romanism in America* (Boston, 1855); John Cumming, *Lectures on Romanism, Being Illustrations and Refutations of the Errors of Romanism and Tractarianism* (Boston, 1854); Joel T. Headley [a prominent New York Know Nothing], *History of the Persecutions and Battles of the Waldenses* (New York, 1850); William S. Plumer, *Rome Against the Bible, and the Bible Against Rome; or, Pharisaism, Jewish and Papal* (Philadelphia, 1854); *Romanists Disqualified for Civil Power; Proved from the Decrees of the Council of Trent* (New York, 1855); Napoleon Roussell, *Catholic and Protestant Nations Compared in Their Threefold Relations to Wealth, Knowledge, and Morality* (Boston, 1855); John F. Weishampel, *The Pope's Stratagem: "Rome to America!" An Address to the Protestants of the United States, Against Placing the Pope's Block of Marble in the Washington Monument* (Philadelphia, 1852). The literature on convents is particularly extensive, but of those published during the heyday of Know Nothingism, I found three to be particularly useful: Thomas F. Caldicott, *Hannah Corcoran: An Authentic Narrative of Her Conversion from Romanism; Her Abduction from Charlestown, and the Treatment She Received During Her Absence* (Boston, 1853); *The Escaped Nun; Or, Disclosures of Convent Life and the Confessions of a Sister of Charity* (New York, 1855); and Charles W. Frothingham, *Six Hours in a Convent; Or, the Stolen Nuns*, 8th ed. (Boston, 1855).

It is also important to recognize that most of the Know Nothings' proposals for dealing with the Catholic and immigrant "menaces" had been suggested years earlier by previous nativist organizations. See Samuel F. B. Morse, *Imminent Dangers to the Free Institutions of the United States through Foreign Immigration* (New York, 1835); Morse, *Foreign Conspiracy Against the Liberties of the United States* (New York, 1835); *A Brief Examination of the Expediency of Repealing the Naturalization Laws* (New Orleans, 1840); *Arguments Proving the Inconsistency and Impolicy of Granting to Foreigners the Right of Voting* (Philadelphia, 1844); *Address to the People of the State of New York by the General Executive Committee of the American Republican Party of the City of New York* (New York, 1844); *A Brief View of the Origin and Object of the Native American Party. By a Native American* (Philadelphia, 1844); *Facts for the People. Condition of the Country. Frauds of the Old Parties by Means of the Foreign Vote* (New York, 1845); *Party Spirit and Popery: Or; The Beast and His Rider* (New York, 1847).

Despite the depth of anti-Catholicism in antebellum America, those who had gained control of the Know Nothing party by the presidential campaign of 1856 tended to focus on issues other than nativism in their campaign documents. For the speeches of the candidate himself, see *Fillmore on the Great Questions of the Day. The Arrival, Reception, Progress, and Speeches of Millard Fillmore* (New York, 1856), *Mr. Fillmore at Home. His Reception at New York and Brooklyn, and Progress Through the State to his Residence in Buffalo* (n.p., 1856), and *Speeches of Millard Fillmore at New York, Newburgh, Albany, Rochester, Buffalo, &c. Also Evidences of Fremont's Romanism* (New York, 1856). Two campaign biographies also appeared: Ivory Chamberlain, *Biography of Millard Fillmore* (Buffalo, 1856), and [Edwin Williams], *The Life and Administration of Ex-President Fillmore* (New York, 1856). Of the dozens of other pro-Fillmore publications, those I found most useful were Erastus Brooks, *Speech of Hon. Erastus Brooks at Hartford, Conn., July 8, 1856. Mr. Fillmore's Claims on Northern Men and Union Men* (New York, 1856); James Brooks, *Defence of President Fillmore* (New York, 1856); Hiram Ketchum, *Connecticut Aroused! Great Demonstration at New Haven. Speech of the Hon. Hiram Ketchum* (New Haven, 1856); James O. Putnam, *American Principles; A Speech Delivered at a Fillmore and Donelson Ratification Meeting in Rochester, March 3d, 1856* (n.p., n.d.); Lewis C. Levin, *The Union Safe! The Contest Between Fillmore and Buchanan! Fremont Crushed!* (New York, 1856); *Proceedings of the Fillmore and Donelson New Jersey State Convention. Speeches of Hon. J. F. Randolph, Hon. Hiram Ketchum, and Com. R. F. Stockton* (n.p., 1856); *Buchanan's Political Record. Let the South Beware!* (Washington, 1856). Fillmore supporters in Pennsylvania attempted to prevent defections to Frémont with *The Great Fraud by Which Pennsylvania Is Sought to*

Be Abolitionized (n.p., 1856). Finally, charges that Frémont was a Catholic were spread in *Colonel Fremont's Religious History. The Authentic Account. Papist or Protestant, Which?* (n.p., 1856); *Fremont's Romanism Established* (n.p., 1856); *The Popish Intrigue: Fremont a Catholic!!!* (n.p., 1856).

Those North Americans who endorsed Frémont responded to these charges with publications of their own. See *Geo. Law and Chauncy Shaffer's Reasons for Repudiating Fillmore and Donelson* (New York, 1856); Ephraim Marsh, *Reasons for Going for Fremont* (n.p., 1856); *North American Documents. Letters from Geo. Law, Ephraim Marsh, & Chauncey Shaffer* (n.p., 1856). For the all-important Pennsylvania contest, they issued *The American Party Sold to Buchanan* (Philadelphia, 1856) and *Facts for the People No. 1. The Conspiracy of the Fillmore Leaders to Elect Buchanan* (n.p., n.d).

After the election of 1856, Know Nothing candidates rarely bothered to issue campaign pamphlets. Republicans, on the other hand, financed a number of publications designed to persuade Fillmore voters to support Lincoln in 1860, including James O. Putnam, *Americans Repudiate Fusion! Speech of the Hon. James O. Putnam, Against the Sale of the American Party to the Douglas Democracy. Delivered in Rochester, August 8* (n.p., n.d.); Gustavus A. Scroggs, *The Duty of Americans. Speech of General G. A. Scroggs, President of the American State Council at the American Meeting Held at Aurora, Erie Co., N.Y., Aug. 4, 1860. And of George B. Babcock, and of James O. Putnam, in Reply to Ex-Governor Hunt* ([New York, 1860]); Daniel Ullmann, *Speech of Hon. Daniel Ullmann of New York at the Lincoln and Hamlin Ratification Meeting in Newark, New Jersey, June 12, 1860* (n.p., n.d.).

Finally, although I did not make extensive use of the works of southern Know Nothings, two publications by southern nativists are particularly useful for understanding Know Nothingism in the North. Charles Gayarre's *Address on the Religious Test to the Convention of the American Party Assembled in Philadelphia on the 5th of June, 1855* (New Orleans, 1855) is a speech delivered by one of the Louisiana Catholic Know Nothings who was barred from the party's 1855 Philadelphia convention. In addition, Kenneth Rayner's *Reply to the Manifesto of Hon. Henry A. Wise* (Washington, 1855) is important both because it concerns the key Virginia state election of 1855 and because Rayner possessed more influence with northern Know Nothings than any other southerner.

SECONDARY SOURCES

The standard work on immigration to America before the Civil War is Marcus Lee Hansen's *The Atlantic Migration, 1607–1860* (Cambridge, 1940). However, in order to gain a more detailed understanding of the phenomenal influx of Europeans into the United States from 1845 to 1854, one must consult books that concentrate on specific ethnic groups. The best such work is Kerby A. Miller, *Emigrants and Exiles: Ireland and the Irish Exodus to North America* (New York, 1985), which provides fascinating detail on the conditions that drove one-quarter of Ireland's inhabitants to America, but is less useful for those seeking to understand the lives led by the newcomers in the United States. For that subject, the best work is still Oscar Handlin, *Boston's Immigrants: A Study in Acculturation* (New York, 1959). Other studies dealing with Irish immigration are Cecil Woodham-Smith, *The Great Hunger: Ireland, 1845–1849* (New York, 1962), and Oliver MacDonagh, "The Irish Famine Emigration to the United States," *Perspectives in American History* 10 (1976): 357–446.

and James M. Berquist, "The Concept of Nativism in Historical Study Since *Strangers in the Land*," *American Jewish History* 76 (1986): 125–41.

As far as early American nativist groups are concerned, the first such organization of significance is examined in Leo Hershkowitz, "The Native American Democratic Association in New York City, 1835–1836," *New-York Historical Society Quarterly* 46 (1962): 41–59. For their more popular successors, see Ira M. Leonard, "The Rise and Fall of the American Republican Party in New York City, 1843–1845," *New-York Historical Society Quarterly* 50 (1966): 151–92; Herbert I. London, "The Nativist Movement in the American Republican Party in New York City During the Period 1843–1847" (Ph.D. diss., New York University, 1966); Carl F. Siracusa, "Political Nativism in New York City, 1843–1848" (Ph.D. diss., Columbia University, 1965). Unfortunately, the only lengthy study of the American Republicans in Pennsylvania is Leonard Tabachnik, "Origins of the Know-Nothing Party: A Study of the Native American Party in Philadelphia, 1844–1852" (Ph.D. diss., Columbia University, 1973), a disappointing work. The inadequacies of Tabachnik's work can be partially remedied by consulting Michael Feldberg, *The Philadelphia Riots of 1844: A Study in Ethnic Conflict* (Westport, 1975), a thorough and insightful work. Another excellent study of the Philadelphia violence is David Montgomery, "The Shuttle and the Cross: Weavers and Artisans in the Kensington Riots of 1844," *Journal of Social History* 5 (1972): 411–46, although I do not find its conclusions applicable to the Know Nothings. Wilfred J. Bisson, *Countdown to Violence: The Charlestown Convent Riot of 1834* (New York, 1989), recounts the story of an earlier anti-Catholic riot. Much has been written on the educational controversies that helped the American Republicans gain adherents. The most thorough study is Vincent P. Lannie, *Public Money and Parochial Education: Bishop Hughes, Governor Seward, and the New York School Controversy* (Cleveland, 1968), although John W. Pratt's *Religion, Politics, and Diversity: The Church-State Theme in New York History* (Ithaca, 1967) looks at this issue over a longer period of time. Seward's motives for making his controversial school proposal are also discussed in Glyndon G. Van Dusen, "Seward and the School Question Reconsidered," *Journal of American History* 52 (1965): 313–19. Additional information on pre–Know Nothing nativist political organizations is contained in Lee Benson, *The Concept of Jacksonian Democracy: New York as a Test Case* (Princeton, 1961), and Sean Wilentz, *Chants Democratic: New York City and the Rise of the American Working Class, 1788–1850* (New York, 1984), which discusses the participation of workingmen in the early nativist organizations. More work in this area is needed, especially a study of the Order of United American Mechanics, of which we know virtually nothing.

Of the lengthier general works on the Know Nothing party, few are very good. Carleton Beals, *Brass Knuckle Crusade: The Great Know-Nothing Conspiracy* (New York, 1960), is a sensationalistic tome that betrays little understanding of the organization. J. Humphrey Desmond, *The Know-Nothing Party, a Sketch* (Washington, 1904), is of interest only because it was written by a notable Catholic journalist. Adina Cheree Carlson, "Order, the Secret, and the Kill: The Rhetoric of the Know Nothing Party" (Ph.D. diss., University of Southern California, 1985), posits an interesting but unpersuasive thesis concerning the Know Nothings' underlying message. George N. Kramer, "A History of the 'Know Nothing Movement'" (Ph.D. diss., University of Southern California, 1936), is of no value to modern scholars.

The best short history of the Know Nothings is Michael F. Holt's "The Antimasonic and Know Nothing Parties," *History of U.S. Political Parties*, ed. Arthur M. Schlesinger, Jr. (New York, 1973), vol. I, 575–737. In addition, Holt's "The Politics of

Impatience: The Origins of Know Nothingism," *Journal of American History* 60 (1973): 309–31, is the most frequently cited work on the causes of the Know Nothings' success. Although I have benefited enormously from the latter study, I found Holt's attribution of Know Nothing popularity to the rapidity of social change ultimately unconvincing, especially in light of my findings concerning the socio-economic bases of the party. Two other works of significance are William G. Bean, "An Aspect of Know Nothingism—The Immigrant and Slavery," *South Atlantic Quarterly* 23 (1924): 319–34, and Stephen E. Maizlish, "The Meaning of Nativism and the Crisis of the Union: The Know Nothing Movement in the Antebellum North," in *Essays on American Antebellum Politics, 1840–1860*, eds. Stephen E. Maizlish and John J. Kushma (College Station, 1982), the only studies that sufficiently emphasize the role of the Order's anti-slavery reputation in its success.

Other short works of value for studying the Know Nothings include Harry J. Carman and Reinhard H. Luthin, "Some Aspects of the Know-Nothing Movement Reconsidered," *South Atlantic Quarterly* 39 (1940): 213–34, which underestimates the importance of nativism to the party. Dale T. Knobel, "Know Nothings and Indians: Strange Bed-fellows?," *Western Historical Quarterly* 15 (1984): 175–98, examines Know Nothing use of Indian terminology, but in reality the Know Nothings had dispensed with the use of such terms before most Americans joined their lodges. Richard Carwardine, "The Know-Nothing Party, the Protestant Evangelical Community and American National Identity," in *Religion and National Identity: Papers Read at the Nineteenth Summer Meeting and the Twentieth Winter Meeting of the Ecclesiastical History Society*, ed. Stuart Mews (Oxford, England, 1982), 449–63, is a short piece on a subject that requires further study, although some additional information can be gleaned from Terry Carter's doctoral thesis cited above, as well as Cecil S. H. Ross, "Pulpit and Stump: The Clergy and Know Nothings in Mississippi," *Journal of Mississippi History* 48 (1986): 271–82. Unfortunately, Daniel Walker Howe's "The Evangelical Movement and Political Cullture in the North During the Second Party System," *Journal of American History* 77 (1991): 1216–39, does not address the Know Nothing movement. Bertram W. Korn, "The Know-Nothing Movement and the Jews," in his *Eventful Years and Experiences: Studies in Nineteenth Century Jewish History* (Cincinnati, 1954), 58–78, is a disappointing study which merely chronicles the editorial comments of New York's Jewish newspaper.

On the vitally important question of who joined the Know Nothings, the only study is George H. Haynes, "A Chapter from the Local History of Know Nothingism," *New England Magazine* 21 (1896): 82–96. However, Haynes's work is highly misleading, because he fails to provide a valid control group with which to compare the Know Nothings. Another work purporting to examine a Know Nothing membership list, Gerald G. Eggert's " 'Seeing Sam': The Know Nothing Episode in Harrisburg," *Pennsylvania Magazine of History and Biography* 111 (1987): 305–40, actually analyzes the membership of a rival nativist group, the Guard of Liberty. W. V. Hensel once had the opportunity to examine a now lost Know Nothing minute book, but his "A Withered Twig: Dark Lantern Glimpses into the Operation of Know Nothingism in Lancaster Sixty Years Ago," *Journal of the Lancaster County Historical Society* 19 (1915): 174–81, does not analyze the lodge's membership.

Although most general works on the Know Nothing party are disappointing, a number of biographical works are of use. The standard life of the Know Nothing presidential candidate is Robert J. Rayback, *Millard Fillmore: Biography of a President* (Buffalo, 1959). Also see Robert C. Schelin, "Millard Fillmore, Anti-Mason to

Know Nothing: A Moderate in New York Politics" (Ph.D. diss., State University of New York at Binghamton, 1975), whose section on Fillmore's Know Nothing involvement has been published as "A Whig's Final Quest: Fillmore and the Know Nothings," *Niagara Frontier* 26 (1979): 1–11. Both Ernest A. McKay, *Henry Wilson: Practical Radical* (Port Washington, N.Y., 1971), and Richard H. Abbott, *Cobbler in Congress: The Life of Henry Wilson, 1812–1875* (Lexington, Ky., 1972), are capable studies of the Order's Massachusetts senator. Wilson's New Hampshire and Connecticut colleagues are the subjects respectively of Richard H. Sewell, *John P. Hale and the Politics of Abolition* (Cambridge, 1965), and Nelson R. Burr, "United States Senator James Dixon: 1814–1873, Episcopalian Anti-Slavery Statesman," *Historical Magazine of the Protestant Episcopal Church* 50 (1981): 29–72. The Know Nothings' leaders in the House of Representatives are described in William E. Van Horne, "Lewis D. Campbell and the Know Nothing Party in Ohio," *Ohio History* 76 (1967): 202–21; Willard H. Smith, *Schuyler Colfax: The Changing Fortunes of a Political Idol* (Indianapolis, 1952); Fred H. Harrington, *Fighting Politician: Major General N. P. Banks* (Philadelphia, 1948).

Biographical works on other Know Nothings include Charles Roll, *Colonel Dick Thompson, the Persistent Whig* (Indianapolis, 1948), which should be supplemented with Mark E. Neely, Jr., "Richard W. Thompson: The Persistent Know Nothing," *Indiana Magazine of History* 72 (1976): 95–122; Russell McClain, "The New York Express: Voice of Opposition" (Ph.D. diss., Columbia University, 1955), which traces the life or Erastus Brooks; Frederic A. Godcharles, "Governor James Pollack," *Northumberland County [Pa.] Historical Society Proceedings* 8 (1936): 5–39; Ralph Basso, "Nationalism, Nativism, and the Black Soldier: Daniel Ullmann, a Biography of a Man Living in a Period of Transition, 1810–1892" (Ph.D. diss., St. John's University, 1986), which concentrates on the subject's military exploits; Paul Hallerberg, "Charles D. Deshler, Versatile Jerseyman" (M.A. thesis, Rutgers University, 1939), a very useful study; Erwin Stanley Bradley, *Simon Cameron, Lincoln's Secretary of War: A Political Biography* (Philadelphia, 1966); Richard N. Current, *Old Thad Stevens: A Story of Ambition* (Madison, 1942); John A. Forman, "Lewis C. Levin: Portrait of an American Demagogue," *American Jewish Archives* 12 (1960): 150–94. In addition, short biographical sketches of James Barker, Jacob Broom, Nehemiah D. Sperry, Francis W. Palmer, John Covode, Anson Burlingame, and others can be found in the *Dictionary of American Biography* (New York, 1943).

The biographies of a few southern nativists were consulted during the course of my research. David G. Cantrell, "The Limits of Southern Dissent: The Lives of Kenneth and John B. Rayner" (Ph.D. diss., Texas A&M University, 1988), contains less on the nativist career of the South's most prominent Know Nothing than I had hoped. Another southerner who supported the Know Nothing cause is examined in Janet L. Coryell, *Neither Heroine Nor Fool: Anna Ella Carroll of Maryland* (Kent, Ohio, 1990). In addition, it should be noted that because most biographers grow to admire their subjects, many of the authors cited above argued, despite significant evidence to the contrary, that their subjects lacked devotion to the nativist tenets of the Order. Consequently, biographies must be used with both caution and a healthy dose of skepticism when the subject's dedication to Know Nothingism is questioned.

Although these biographies provided a great deal of information concerning the Know Nothings, most secondary sources that treat the Know Nothings are state or local studies. Most of the work on Know Nothingism in Maine has been done by a single author, Allan R. Whitmore. See his "Portrait of a Maine 'Know-Nothing' [William H. Chaney]," *Maine Historical Society Quarterly* 14 (1974): 1–57, as well as " 'A Guard of Faithful Sentinels': The Know Nothing Appeal in Maine, 1854–1855," *Maine Historical Society Quarterly* 20 (1981): 151–97. One can also consult William L. Lucey, "Maine in 1854: Letters on State Politics and Know Nothingism," *Records of the American Catholic Historical Society of Philadelphia* 65 (1954): 176–86.

Although New Hampshire was, after Massachusetts, the state in which the Know Nothing party fared best, no good history of the Order's activities there has been written. The lack of extensive manuscript sources and the New Hampshire Know Nothings' close cooperation with other anti-slavery forces make this a difficult but far from impossible task. Some information is available in Peter Haebler, "Nativist Riots in Manchester: An Episode of Know-Nothingism in New Hampshire," *Historical New Hampshire* 39 (1984): 121–37; Thomas R. Bright, "The Anti-Nebraska Coalition and the Emergence of the Republican Party in New Hampshire, 1853–1857," *Historical New Hampshire* 27 (1972): 57–88; Carolyn W. Baldwin, "The Dawn of the Republican Party in New Hampshire," *Historical New Hampshire* 30 (1975): 21–32, but these sources must be supplemented with newspapers in order to complete the story. In Vermont, the Know Nothings did not thrive, primarily because of the state's isolation. For this period in the state's political history, see Edward P. Brynn, "Vermont's Political Vacuum of 1845–1856 and the Emergence of the Republican Party," *Vermont History* 38 (1970): 113–23.

Know Nothingism in Rhode Island resembled in many ways the movement in New Hampshire, and as with New Hampshire, no substantive history of the party in Rhode Island has been written. Charles Stickney, *Know-Nothingism in Rhode Island* (Providence, 1894), is very short and uninformative, while Larry A. Rand, "The Know-Nothing Party in Rhode Island," *Rhode Island History* 23 (1964): 102–16, also raises more questions than it answers. Scholars can also consult John Michael Ray, "Anti-Catholicism and Know-Nothingism in Rhode Island," *American Ecclesiastical Review* 148 (1963): 27–36.

More has been written about the Know Nothings in Massachusetts than in any other state, which is only fitting considering their phenomenal success there. John R. Mulkern's *The Know-Nothing Party in Massachusetts: The Rise and Fall of a People's Movement* (Boston, 1990), contains most of the factual information one needs concerning the organization in the state. However, I found that Mulkern's argument that the "pressures of modernization" account for the Know Nothings' success there unconvincing, because although it is true that the Know Nothings fared better in the more populous and industrialized eastern portion of the state, the fact that Know Nothings in other states usually fared *better* in rural areas suggests that some other factor probably accounts for the geographic distribution of the Know Nothing vote in Massachusetts. The socio-economic background of Massachusetts Know Nothing legislators is ably analyzed in Virginia C. Purdy, "Portrait of a Know Nothing Legislature: The Massachusetts General Court of 1855" (Ph.D. diss., George Washington University, 1970). Robert M. Taylor, Jr., "Reverend Lyman Whiting's Test of Faith," *Historical Journal of Massachusetts* 12 (1984): 90–103, discusses the decision of a minister to decline a Know Nothing congressional nomination. Two works by William G. Bean are important for understanding the manner in which anti-slavery sentiment helped attract Massachusetts residents to the Order. See "Puritan versus Celt, 1850–1860," *New England Quarterly* 7 (1934): 70–89, and "An Aspect of Know Nothingism—The Immigrant and Slavery," cited above. Other works on the Massachusetts Know Nothings include George H. Haynes, "The Causes of Know Nothing Success in Massachusetts,"

American Historical Review 3 (1897): 67–82; Haynes, "A Know Nothing Legislature," *American Historical Association Report* (1896): 175–87; Haynes, "A Chapter from the Local History of Know Nothingism," cited above; Mulkern, "Scandal Behind the Convent Walls: The Know-Nothing Nunnery Committee of 1855," *Historical Journal of Massachusetts* 11 (1983): 22–34; Mulkern, "Western Massachusetts in the Know Nothing Years: An Analysis of Voting Patterns," *Historical Journal of Western Massachusetts* 8 (1980): 14–25; James Tracy, "The Rise and Fall of the Know-Nothings in Quincy," *Historical Journal of Massachusetts* 16 (1988): 1–19. I also consulted Dale Baum, *The Civil War Party System: The Case of Massachusetts, 1848–1876* (Chapel Hill, 1984), which concentrates primarily on voting patterns, and must be supplemented with William G. Bean, "Party Transformation in Massachusetts with Special Reference to the Antecedents of Republicanism, 1848–1860" (Ph.D. diss., Harvard University, 1922). Useful information can also be found in Thomas H. O'Connor, *Lords of the Loom: The Cotton Whigs and the Coming of the Civil War* (New York, 1968); Kevin Sweeney, "Rum, Romanism, Representation, and Reform: Coalition Politics in Massachusetts, 1847–1853," *Civil War History* 22 (1976): 116–37. Also see the biographies of Banks, Wilson, and Sumner cited above. A biographical work on Know Nothing governor Henry J. Gardner is badly needed, as is a stuudy of the passage of the two-year amendment.

The story of the Order in Connecticut is thoroughly and ably decribed in Robert D. Parmet, "The Know Nothings in Connecticut" (Ph.D. diss., Columbia University, 1966). His "Connecticut's Know Nothings: A Profile," *Connecticut Historical Society Bulletin* 31 (1966): 84–90, is also enlightening, although the occupational and financial data one can now gather thanks to census indexes is more revealing. C. J. Noonan, *Nativism in Connecticut* (Washington, 1938), is far less sophisticated than Parmet's study.

One of the best state studies of the Know Nothing party is Thomas J. Curran, "The Know Nothings of New York" (Ph.D. diss., Columbia University, 1963). His thoughts on the Know Nothings' role in Seward's re-election to the Senate are available in his "Seward and the Know-Nothings," *New-York Historical Society Quarterly* 51 (1967): 141–59. Also of great value is Louis Dow Scisco, *Political Nativism in New York State* (New York, 1901), which despite its age contains a great deal of useful information, especially concerning the early years of the Order. Joel Silbey's " 'The Undisguised Connection,' Know Nothings into Republicans: New York as a Test Case," in his *The Partisan Imperative: The Dynamics of American Politics Before the Civil War* (New York, 1985), is a very important study which influenced my conception of the period after 1856 immensely. Although I disagree with his conclusion concerning the ultimate impact of the Republicans' overtures to the Know Nothings, we definetely need more studies of this type. Also see F. J. Zwierlein, "Know Nothingism in Rochester, New York," *United States Catholic Historical Society Records and Studies* 14 (1920): 20–69; Richard J. Purcell and John F. Poole, "Political Nativism in Brooklyn," *Journal of the American Irish Historical Society* 32 (1941): 10–56; Felicity O'Driscoll, "Political Nativism in Buffalo," *Records of the American Catholic Historical Society* 48 (1937): 279–319.

Absolutely nothing has been writtten on the Know Nothing party in New Jersey, although some information on nativism there can be found in Douglas V. Shaw, *The Making of an Immigrant City: Ethnic and Cultural Conflict in Jersey City, New Jersey, 1850–1877* (New York, 1976). Charles Hallerberg's master's thesis on Charles Deshler, cited above, contains little information on the Order there.

The Know Nothings exerted significant influence in Pennsylvania for many years, yet few good works on the party there have been written. Warren F. Hewitt, "The Know-Nothing Party in Pennsylvania," *Pennsylvania History* 2 (1935): 69–85, is of little value. James L. Huston, "The Demise of the Pennsylvania American Party," *Pennsylvania Magazine of History and Biography* 109 (1985): 473–97, is much better, but covers only a short portion of the Know Nothings' Pennsylvania career. David R. Keller, "Nativism or Sectionalism: A History of the Know-Nothing Party in Lancaster County, Pennsylvania," *Journal of the Lancaster County Historical Society* 75 (1971): 41–100, contains some useful information. William Gudelunas, Jr., "Nativism and the Demise of Schuylkill County Whiggery: Anti-Slavery or Anti-Catholicism?," *Pennsylvania History* 45 (1978): 225–36, relies too heavily on a single newspaper in drawing his conclusions. For other interpretations, see Frank Gerrity, "The Disruption of the Philadelphia Whigocracy: Joseph R. Chandler, Anti-Catholicism, and the Congressional Election of 1854," *Pennsylvania Magazine of History and Biography* 111 (1987): 161–94; Marie J. McCann, "Nativism and the School Controversy in Pittsburgh, 1843–1860" (Ph.D. diss., Catholic University, 1960); Sister M. St. Henry, "Nativism in Pennsylvania with Particular Regard to Its Effect on Politics and Education, 1834–1860," *American Catholic Historical Society of Philadelphia, Records* 47 (1936): 5–47; Hiram H. Shenk, "The Know Nothing Party in Lebanon County [Pa.]," *Lebanon County Historical Society Papers* 4 (1906–9): 54–74. Studies which do not concentrate on the Pennsylvania Know Nothings but which were of value nonetheless include John F. Coleman, *The Disruption of the Pennsylvania Democracy, 1848–1860* (Harrisburg, 1975), a good survey of Pennsylvania politics; William E. Gienapp, "Nebraska, Nativism, and Rum: The Failure of Fusion in Pennsylvania, 1854," *Pennsylvania Magazine of History and Biography* 109 (1985): 425–71, a detailed study of the 1854 election in Pennsylvania; Michael F. Holt, *Forging a Majority: The Formation of the Republican Party in Pittsburgh, 1848–1860* (New Haven, 1969), a model of its kind; Huston, "Economic Change and Political Realignment in Antebellum Pennsylvania," *Pennsylvania Magazine of History and Biography* 113 (1989): 347–95; William Dusinberre, *Civil War Issues in Philadelphia, 1856–1865* (Philadelphia, 1965); Bruce Collins, "The Democrats' Loss of Pennsylvania in 1858," *Pennsylvania Magazine of History and Biography* 109 (1985): 499–536. A lengthy study of the Know Nothing movement in Pennsylvania would be a welcome addition to the literature.

A solid treatment of the Know Nothing party in Ohio is also needed. The Know Nothings' role in the election of Salmon P. Chase to the governorship in 1855 has been thoroughly studied by Eugene H. Roseboom in "Salmon P. Chase and the Know Nothings," *Mississippi Valley Historical Review* 25 (1938): 335–49, and William E. Gienapp in "Salmon P. Chase, Nativism, and the Formation of the Republican Party in Ohio," *Ohio History* 93 (1984): 5–39. The most useful portion of John B. Weaver's "Nativism and the Birth of the Republican Party in Ohio, 1854–1860" (Ph.D. diss., Ohio State University, 1982), is the last chapter, which has been published as "The Decline of the Ohio Know-Nothings, 1856–1860," *Cincinnati Historical Society Bulletin* 40 (1982): 235–46. Also see his "Ohio Republican Attitudes Towards Nativism, 1854–1855," *Old Northwest* 9 (1983–84): 289–305. For additional studies consult William A. Baughin, "Bullets and Ballots: The Election Day Riots of 1855," *Historical and Philosophical Society of Ohio Bulletin* 21 (1963): 267–72; Baughin, "The Development of Nativism in Cincinnati," *Bulletin of the Cincinnati Historical Society* 22 (1964): 240–55; Baughin, "Nativism in Cincinnati before 1860" (M.A. thesis, University of Cincinnati, 1963). A valuable survey of the state's politics is Stephen E. Maizlish, *The*

Triumph of Sectionalism: The Transformation of Politics in Ohio, 1844–1856 (Kent, Ohio, 1983).

For Indiana, where the Know Nothings fared better than in any other midwestern state, see Carl F. Brand, "The History of the Know Nothing Party in Indiana," *Indiana Magazine of History* 18 (1922): 47–81, 177–206, 266–306. Although Brand relies far too often on the Know Nothings' enemies for information, he brings together a significant amount of valuable data on the Order there, especially newspaper quotations and accounts of Know Nothing meetings. All the significant extant correspondence of the Order's Indiana president is presented in J. Herman Schauinger, ed., "The Letters of Godlove S. Orth, Hoosier American," *Indiana Magazine of History* 40 (1944): 51–66. Cheryl Treusdell, " 'Have You Seen Sam': In Search of the Allen County [Indiana] Know-Nothings," *Old Fort News* 44 (1980): 31–41, concentrates on the eccentric editor of the Order's Fort Wayne organ. For the election of 1854 in Indiana, scholars can also examine Roger Van Bolt, "Fusion Out of Confusion, 1854," *Indiana Magazine of History* 49 (1953): 353–90; while a useful survey is Emma Lou Thornbrough, *Indiana in the Civil War Era, 1850–1880* (Indianapolis, 1965).

The standard work on the Know Nothings in Illinois is John P. Senning, "The Know Nothing Movement in Illinois, 1854–1856," *Illinois State Historical Society Journal* 7 (1914): 7–33, which is badly in need of revision. However, the history of the party in Chicago is fairly well documented in Thomas M. O'Keefe, "Chicago's Flirtation with Political Nativism, 1854–1856," *Records of the American Catholic Historical Society of Philadelphia* 82 (1971): 131–58, and Bruce M. Cole, "The Chicago Press and the Know Nothings, 1850–1856" (M.A. thesis, University of Chicago, 1948). Also see Richard W. Renner, "In a Perfect Ferment: Chicago, the Know-Nothings, and the Riot for Lager Beer," *Chicago History* 5 (1976): 161–69, and O'Keefe, "The Catholic Issue in the Chicago *Tribune* before the Civil War," *Mid-America* 57 (1975): 227–45. In addition, neither Stephen L. Hansen, *The Making of the Third Party System: Voters and Parties in Illinois, 1850–1876* (Ann Arbor, 1980), nor Arthur C. Cole, *The Era of the Civil War, 1848–1870* (Chicago, 1922), contain much information on the Know Nothings.

A number of works illuminate the history of the Know Nothing movement in the remaining non-slave states. A survey of the subject, and one of the better works produced at Catholic University, is Sister M. Evangeline Thomas, *Nativism in the Old Northwest, 1850–1860* (Washington, 1936). Nothing has been written on Know Nothingism in Michigan, but the influence of nativism in the state's politics is well documented in Ronald P. Formisano, *The Birth of Mass Political Parties: Michigan, 1827–1861* (Princeton, 1971). For Know Nothingism in Iowa, see Ronald F. Matthias, "The Know Nothing Movement in Iowa" (Ph.D. diss., University of Chicago, 1965), a thorough survey of the subject. Joseph Schafer, "Know-Nothingism in Wisconsin," *Wisconsin Magazine of History* 8 (1924): 3–21, considers another state where, due to the heavy concentration of immigrants, the Know Nothings fared poorly. Because its peculiar politics were unlike those of any other non-slave state, I did not devote much attention to California in this volume. The standard work on the Know Nothings there is Peyton Hurt, "The Rise and Fall of the 'Know Nothings' in California," *California Historical Society Quarterly* 9 (1930): 16–49, 99–128. Also see Gerald F. Uelmen, "The Know Nothing Justices of the California Supreme Court," *Western Legal History* 2 (1989): 89–106; Leonard Pitt, "The Beginnings of Nativism in California," *Pacific Historical Review* 30 (1961): 23–38. For Oregon, consult Priscilla Knuth, "Nativism in

Oregon" (B.A. thesis, Reed College, 1945), and her "Oregon Know Nothing Pamphlet Illustrates Early Politics," *Oregon Historical Quarterly* 54 (1953): 40–53.

It is important to understand the popularity of fraternal organizations during the 1850s in order to fully appreciate the factors that led to the Know Nothings' success. Unfortunately, neither Mary Ann Clawson, *Constructing Brotherhood: Class, Gender and Fraternalism* (Princeton, 1989), nor Mark C. Carnes, *Secret Ritual and Manhood in Victorian America* (New Haven, 1989), address the Know Nothings in any detail.

Because so few good works have been written on the Know Nothings, I relied to a great extent on other works that treat the politics of the 1850s. Luckily, a number of excellent studies of the decade leading up to the Civil War have been written. The one that is by far the most valuable for those interested in the northern Know Nothing party is William E. Gienapp's *The Origins of the Republican Party, 1852–1856* (New York, 1987). Although he focuses on the Republican organization, Gienapp's belief that nativism destroyed the second party system leads him to devote a great deal of attention to the Know Nothing party. While I disagree with his interpretation of the disintegration of the second party system, his is by far the most sophisticated and persuasive of the works that emphasize the role of ethno-cultural issues in the politics of the 1850s. Another important work is Michael F. Holt, *The Political Crisis of the 1850s* (New York, 1978). David M. Potter's *The Impending Crisis, 1848–1861* (New York, 1976) elegantly addresses the key events of the period with remarkable clarity and insight. Although Potter does not discuss the Know Nothings in great detail, his comments on their activities in the North are consistently astute. Finally, Eric Foner's *Free Soil, Free Labor, Free Men: The Ideology of the Republican Party before the Civil War* (New York, 1970), contains an important discussion of the place of nativism within the Republican party. My belief that Foner's chapter on that subject was inadequate in light of subsequent research originally prompted me to undertake this study. In the end, however, I found that Foner's contention—that Republican nativism did not play a key role in the eventual accession of Fillmore voters to the Republican party—is accurate.

On the speakership contest in the Thirty-fourth Congress, which played a key role in the decline of the Know Nothings, see Fred Harvy Harringon, "The First Northern Victory," *Journal of Southern History* 5 (1939): 186–205. The Republicans' activities in this session are analyzed in Joel Silbey, "After 'The First Northern Victory': The Republican Party Comes to Congress, 1855–1856," *Journal of Interdisciplinary History* 20 (1989): 1–24. For the presidential election of 1856, Harrington's "Frémont and the North Americans," *American Historical Review* 44 (1939): 842–48, is helpful. David Potter's "The Know-Nothing Party in the Presidential Election of 1856" (M.A. thesis, Yale University, 1933) was disappointing. Abraham Lincoln's activities during that campaign can be followed in Thomas F. Schwartz, "Lincoln, Form Letters, and Fillmore Men," *Illinois Historical Journal* 78 (1985): 65–70.

A number of works relate to the controversial question of what convinced Fillmore's northern supporters to join the Republican ranks by 1860. Gienapp's "Nativism and the Creation of a Republican Majority in the North before the Civil War," *Journal of American History* 72 (1985): 529–59, contains information on this question not found in *Origins of the Republican Party*, as does his "Who Voted for Lincoln?," in *Abraham Lincoln and the American Political Tradition*, ed. John L. Thomas (Amherst, 1986). James L. Huston, *The Panic of 1857 and the Coming of the Civil War* (Baton Rouge, 1987), addresses this issue, although most of the book concentrates on Pennsylvania. David E. Meerse, "The Northern Democratic Party and the Congressional Elections of 1858," *Civil War History* 19 (1973): 119–37, and Bruce Collins, "The Democrats' Electoral Fortunes During the Lecompton Crisis," *Civil War History* 24 (1978): 314–31, convincingly argue that debate over the Lecompton constitution did not significantly alter the electoral balance. Of course, this does not necessarily mean that the Republicans' modification of their stance on the slavery issue did not induce voters to join their party. Also see Daryl Prendergaft, "Thomas Corwin and the Conservative Republican Reaction," *Ohio Archaeological and Historical Quarterly* 57 (1948): 1–23, and Elmer D. Elbert, "Southern Indiana Politics on the Eve of the Civil War, 1858–1861" (Ph.D. diss., Indiana University, 1967). On the role of nativism and immigrants in Lincoln's election, see Charles Granville Hamilton, *Lincoln and the Know-Nothing Movement* (Washington, 1954), a superficial study; F. I. Herriott, "The Germans of Iowa and the 'Two-Year' Amendment of Massachusetts," *Deutsch-Americanische Geschichtsblätter* 13 (1913): 202–308; Herriott, "The Premises and Significance of Abraham Lincoln's Letter to Theodore Canisius," *Deutsch-Americanische Geschichtsblätter* 15 (1915): 181–254; Thomas W. Kremm, "Cleveland and the First Lincoln Election: The Ethnic Response to Nativism," *Journal of Interdisciplinary History* 8 (1977): 83–105; Frederick C. Luebke, ed., *Ethnic Voters and the Election of Lincoln* (Lincoln, 1971). For Lincoln's treatment of ex–Know Nothings once he assumed the presidency, see Harry J. Carman and Reinhard H. Luthin, *Lincoln and the Patronage* (Gloucester, Mass., 1964).

Nearly all of the former Know Nothings who did not vote for Lincoln supported the Constitutional Union party's ticket. Know Nothing particpation in the party's campaign is documented in John B. Stabler, "A History of the Constitutional Union Party: A Tragic Failure" (Ph.D. diss., Columbia University, 1954), and Barry A. Crouch, "Amos A. Lawrence and the Formation of the Constitutional Union Party in 1860," *Historical Journal of Massachusetts* 3 (1980): 46–58.

In order to fully understand the Know Nothings' appeal, one must examine the various issues and controversies that concerned them. The subject that most preoccupied the Order, the nation's naturalization laws, is the subject of Frank George Franklin, *The Legislative History of Naturalization in the United States* (Chicago, 1906), and John J. Newman, *American Naturalization Processes and Procedures, 1790–1985* (Indianapolis, 1985), neither of which is truly adequate. Benjamin J. Klebaner, "The Myth of Foreign Pauper Dumping in the United States," *Social Service Review* 35 (1961): 302–9, addresses another of the Know Nothings' complaints, although he underestimates the extent of the practice. Patrick J. Dignan, *A History of the Legal Incorporation of Catholic Church Property in the United States (1784–1932)* (Washington, 1933), was more useful for my purposes than Patrick W. Carey, *People, Priests, and Prelates: Ecclesiastical Democracy and the Tensions of Trusteeism* (Notre Dame, 1987). The American reaction to these church property controversies is also detailed in James F. Connelly, *The Visit of Archbishop Gaetano Bedini to the United States of America (June 1853–February 1854)* (Rome, 1960).

Another issue of great importance to the Know Nothings was the position of Irish immigrants and the Catholic Church on slavery. Unfortunately, virtually nothing of any value has been published on this vital question. Gilbert Osofsky, "Abolitionists, Irish Immigrants, and the Dilemmas of Romantic Nationalism," *American Historical Review* 80 (1975): 889–912, is the exception in this regard, but it does not address this subject in much detail. Of the other works that deal with this question, most are apologies for the church's refusal to condemn the institution. See Cuthbert E. Allen,

"The Slavery Question in Catholic Newspapers," *United States Catholic Historical Society Records and Studies* 26 (1936): 99–169; Maria Genoino Caravaglios, *The American Catholic Church and the Negro Problem in the XVIII-XIX Centuries* (Charleston, S.C., 1974); John C. Murphy, *An Analysis of the Attitudes of American Catholics Toward the Immigrant and the Negro, 1825–1925* (Washington, 1940); Madeleine Hook Rice, *American Catholic Opinion on the Slavery Controversy* (New York, 1944). Charles P. Connor, "The Northern Catholic Position on Slavery and the Civil War: Archbishop Hughes as a Test Case," *Records of the American Catholic Historical Society of Philadelphia* 96 (1986): 37–48, is more scholarly, but was of little use for my study.

On the temperance issue, which also attracted many Northerners to the Order, the best work is Ian Tyrrell, *Sobering Up: From Temperance to Prohibition in Antebellum America* (Westport, Conn., 1979). Tyrrell, however, underestimates the importance of the anti-liquor movement to rural Know Nothings. Also see Jed Dannenbaum, *Drink and Disorder: Temperance Reform in Cincinnati from the Washingtonian Revival to the WCTU* (Urbana, 1984), an excellent case study. A study of the political activity of temperance advocates, especially in the years immediately after the Maine Law was enacted, would be a valuable contribution to the literature on antebellum politics. Useful for understanding the social and political significance of saloons to drinkers are Jon M. Kingsdale, " 'The Poor Man's Club': Social Functions of the Urban Working-Class Saloon," *American Quarterly* 25 (1973): 472–89, and W. J. Rorabaugh, "Rising Democratic Spirits: Immigrants, Temperance, and Tammany Hall, 1854–1860," *Civil War History* 22 (1976): 138–57.

In order to gain a balanced perspective on Know Nothing anti-Catholicism, it is important to understand American Catholic practices in this period. Among the works to consult are Jenny Franchot, "Roads to Rome: Catholicism in Antebellum America" (Ph.D. diss., Stanford University, 1986); Thomas H. O'Connor, *Fitzpatrick's Boston, 1846–1866: John Bernard Fitzpatrick, Third Bishop of Boston* (Boston, 1984); Patrick W. Carey, "Republicanism Within American Catholicism, 1785–1860," *Journal of the Early Republic* 3 (1983): 413–37; Frank J. Coppa, *Pope Pius IX, Crusader in a Secular Age* (Boston, 1979); Loretta Clare Feiertag, *American Public Opinion on the Diplomatic Relations between the United States and the Papal States (1847–1867)* (Washington, 1933).

The relationship of English anti-Catholicism, which in the Victorian era peaked around 1850, and its American counterpart, which reached its zenith only a few years later, is one that needs to be studied. English anti-Catholicism in this period is the subject of Robert J. Klaus, *The Pope, the Protestants, and the Irish: Papal Aggression and Anti-Catholicism in Mid-Nineteenth Century England* (New York, 1987); Walter S. Arnstein, *Protestant Versus Catholic in Mid-Victorian England: Mr. Newdegate and the Nuns* (Columbia, 1982); Homer H. Blass, "Popular Anti-Catholicism in England and the Ecclesiastical Titles of 1851" (Ph.D. diss., University of Missouri-Columbia, 1981); Frank H. Wallis, "The Anti-Maynooth Campaign: A Study in Anti-Catholicism and Politics in the United Kingdom, 1851–1869" (Ph.D. diss., University of Illinois at Urbana-Champaign, 1987); Walter Ralls, "The Papal Aggression of 1850: A Study in Victorian Anti-Catholicism," *Church History* 43 (1974): 242–56; D. G. Paz, "Anti-Catholicism, Anti-Irish Stereotyping, and Anti-Celtic Racism in Mid-Victorian Working Class Periodicals," *Albion* 18 (1986): 601–16.

Finally, although the Know Nothing movement in the South was fundamentally different than its northern counterpart, an understanding of the party's operations there is important in order to comprehend the conflicts that arose between southern and northern Know Nothings. The standard work on the subject, W. Darrell Overdyke's *The Know-Nothing Party in the South* (Baton Rouge, 1950), is uninsightful and poorly organized. Additional general studies include James H. Broussard, "Some Determinants of Know Nothing Electoral Strength in the South, 1856," *Louisiana History* 7 (1966): 5–20; Arthur C. Cole, "Nativism in the Lower Mississippi Valley," *Mississippi Valley Historical Association Proceedings* 6 (1912–13): 258–75; George M. Stephenson, "Nativism in the Forties and Fifties, with Special Reference to the Mississippi Valley," *Mississippi Valley Historical Riview* 9 (1922): 185–205; Donald W. Zacharias, "The Know-Nothing Party and the Oratory of Nativism," in *Oratory in the Old South*, ed. Waldo W. Braden (Baton Rouge, 1970), 218–33; and Randall Miller, "The Enemy Within: Some Effects of Foreign Immigrants on Antebellum Southern Cities," *Southern Studies* 24 (1985): 30–53. The most sophisticated examination of the Know Nothings in a single state—north or south—is Jean H. Baker, *Ambivalent Americans: The Know Nothing Party in Maryland* (Baltimore, 1977). Another better-than-average study is Leon Cyprian Soule, *The Know Nothing Party in New Orleans* (New Orleans, 1961).

The remaining works on southern Know Nothingism are presented in the hopes that some scholar will use them to create a modern southern counterpart to my own study: Harold T. Smith, "The Know Nothings in Arkansas," *Arkansas Historical Quarterly* 34 (1975): 291–303; Arthur W. Thompson, "Political Nativism in Florida," *Journal of Southern History* 15 (1949): 39–65; Royce C. McCrary, "John MacPherson Berrien and the Know Nothing Movement in Georgia," *Georgia Historical Quarterly* 61 (1977): 35–42; Agnes Geraldine McGann, *Nativism in Kentucky to 1860* (Washington, 1944); Philip W. Kennedy, "The Know-Nothing Movement in Kentucky: Role of M. J. Spalding, Catholic Bishop of Louisville," *Filson Club Historical Quarterly* 38 (Jan. 1964): 17–35; Wallace S. Hutcheon, Jr., "The Louisville Riots of August, 1855," *Register of the Kentucky Historical Society* 69 (1971): 150–72; Robert C. Reinders, "The Louisiana American Party and the Catholic Church," *Mid-America* 40 (1958): 218–28; W. Darrell Overdyke, "History of the American Party in Louisiana," *Louisiana Historical Quarterly* 15 (1932): 581–88; 16 (1933): 84–91, 256–77, 409–26, 608–27; Marius M. Carriere, "The Know Nothing Movement in Louisiana" (Ph.D. diss., Louisiana State University, 1977); Benjamin Tuska, *Know Nothingism in Baltimore, 1854–1860* (Washington, 1930); Cecil S. H. Ross, "Charles D. Fontaine: A Mississippi Know Nothing Leader," *Journal of Mississippi History* 48 (1986): 105–18; Ross, "Dying Hard, Dying Fast: The Know Nothing Experience in Mississippi" (Ph.D. diss., University of Notre Dame, 1982); Mary de Lourdes Gohmann, *Political Nativism in Tennessee to 1860* (Washington, 1938); Sister Paul-of-the-Cross McGrath, *Political Nativism in Texas* (Washington, 1930); Ralph A. Wooster, "An Analysis of the Texas Know-Nothings," *Southwestern Historical Quarterly* 70 (1967): 414–23; Wayman L. McClellan, "1855: The Know Nothing Challenge in East Texas," *East Texas Historical Journal* 12 (Fall 1974): 33–44; McClellan, "The Know Nothing Party and the Growth of Sectionalism in East Texas," *East Texas Historical Journal* 14 (Fall 1976): 26–36; Philip Morrison Rice, "The Know Nothing Party in Virginia, 1854–1856," *Virginia Magazine of History and Biography* 55 (1947): 61–75, 159–67; Constance M. Gay, "The Campaign of 1855 in Virginia and the Fall of the Know-Nothing Party," *Richmond College Historical Papers* 1 (1916): 309–35.

Index

Adams, Charles Francis, 97; belief in inevitability of Whig defeat (1852), 16
Aiken, William: as Democratic candidate for House Speaker, 200, 201; supported by South Americans, 201
Allen, Charles B., Know Nothing founder, xix, 20–21
Allen, Stephen M., 216, 217
American Catholic Bishops, First Plenary Council of, 24
American party, xviii; abolishes office of party president, 247; campaign tactics of, 223; charges of Catholicism against Frémont by, 223, 224; comparison of 1854 with 1856 campaign, 226; confidence of leadership despite poor showing in 1856 elections, 247; decline after 1856, 246; distinguished from Know Nothing movement, xviii; infusion of former leaders into Republican party, 273; Louisville convention (1857), 247; revival of (1886), 272; shadow of original Know Nothing movement, 226; shift of support to border states, 247; Ullmann attempts to resurrect in 1870s, 271. *See also* Know Nothing party
American Protective Association, 272
American Protestant Association, 110, 110–11n; president a Know Nothing, 81n
American Reform ticket, in Ohio (1854), 69
American Republican party: convention, 12; effect of Philadelphia riots on, 12; in election of 1852, 16; formation of, 11; name changed to Native American party, 12; success of, 11, 12
Anglican church, and Know Nothings, 49

Anti-Catholicism: as cause of Know Nothing victory in Pennsylvania (1854), 66; continues after Civil War, 271; Fillmore criticized for lack of record on, 210–11; as issue in New York (1855), 185; as Know Nothing tenet, 104; as political issue in Boston, 32; reemergence of in 1830s, 9; reflected in Ohio church-property law, 258; replaced by anti-radicalism as emphasis of American nativism, 272; role of in Massachusetts election (1854), 94
Anti-slavery sentiment: as common component of Know Nothing U.S. Senate choices, 145ff.; in Indiana election (1854), 72; as issue in Massachusetts (1854), 91; as issue in New York (1855), 185; as issue in Seward reelection, 149; Know Nothing convention split caused by, 170–73; as Know Nothing tenet, 44, 45, 106; as main impetus to growth of Know Nothing party, 100, 101; in Massachusetts (1855), 190; in Massachusetts Know Nothing legislative program, 154–56, 157; in Ohio election (1854), 70; in Pennsylvania election (1854), 66; strength of in Connecticut, 212; as U.S. Senate campaign issue in Massachusetts, 145–46. *See also* Slavery
Assimilation, Know Nothing position on, 107
Attorneys. *See* Lawyers

Babcock, James F., predicts Know Nothing demise, 253
Bailey, Gamaliel, 175
Baird, Thomas H., 59
Baker, George E., 76

Brooks, Preston, caning of Sumner by, 214. *See also* Sumner, Charles

Broom, Jacob, 154; elected to Congress, 62n; on Fillmore's nativist remarks (1856), 224; on Know Nothings as a response to the corruption of other parties, 123; as Native American presidential nominee, 14; as supporter of Constitutional Union party, 269

Brownlow, Parson William G., 209; on defeat of Fillmore, 243–44

Brownson, Orestes, on Protestantism, 112

Bryant, William Cullen, on Massachusetts two-year amendment, 251

Buchanan, James: Democratic presidential candidate, 222, 223, 227; on Know Nothing success in Pennsylvania, 53; and presidential election results, 243; presidential victory guaranteed, 240; South abandons Fillmore for, 237

Buckingham, William A., 253; American endorsement of, 254; nominated in Connecticut to replace Holley, 254

Buffalo, New York, St. Louis' Church lawsuit in, 26

Buffalo *Commercial Advertiser,* endorses Lincoln, 266

Bunce, James, on Frémont and Know Nothings, 230

Buntline, Ned, falsely claims to have created Know Nothings, 22n

Burchard, Samuel D., 272

Burlingame, Anson: appointed minister to China, 274; on Catholic support for slavery, 45; on dangers of Catholicism, 112; speeches for Frémont by, 232

Burned-Over District: Know Nothings in, 48–49; Know Nothings in 1854 New York election in, 86; Section Twelve and, 183

Burns, Anthony, 89, 155

Burwell, William M., author of Section Twelve, 167

Butler, Andrew P., 214

Buying American, Know Nothing efforts to promote, 33, 33n

California, gold discovery as cause of Whig party decline, 15

California Know Nothings, 73; carry election (1855), 194; in elections of 1854, 56–57

Call, Richard K., favors restoring Section Twelve (1856), 208

Cameron, Simon, xiii, 150; background, 151; on Frémont's supposed Catholicism, 225; and Pennsylvania Senate campaign, 151–54; unacceptable for Republican vice-presidential nomination, 218

Campbell, James, 60; appointed postmaster general, 30; blamed for Democratic mayoral defeat in Philadelphia, 54; protests against appointment of, 30; Simon Cameron's opposition to, 151

Campbell, James H., elected to Congress, 62n

Campbell, Lewis D., 69, 198, 199; on death of Whig party, 16; feels no longer welcome in Republican party, 267; Know Nothing elected to Congress, 70n; as moderate Know Nothing, 166; role in House Speaker election, 198

Campbell, William W., 77

Canal system, Pennsylvania, Know Nothing attempts to sell, 157

Canandaigua, N.Y.: age of Know Nothings in, 41 *table;* formation of Know Nothing lodge, 22; occupations of Know Nothings in, 36 *table;* 284; property ownership of Know Nothings in, 37 *table,* 38; renegade lodge in, 77–78; as typical lodge, 42; wealth of Know Nothings by occupational category in 39–40 *table,* 40; wealth of Know Nothings in, 38 *table*

Carroll Hall ticket, 22

Cass, Lewis, 18

Catholic Bible. *See* Douay Bible

Catholic Church, Roman; accused of encouraging fraud in voting, 117–18; attitudes toward education by, 113–14; Church of the Holy Trinity, 26; connections to slavery, 46; convents, 115, 137; debate over property of, 26–27, 139–40; denial of officeholding to members of, 111; electoral influence

Whig party (*continued*)
   vert to Know Nothings (1855), 184,
   185; Silver Gray faction, 202; support
   for Lincoln by ex-members, 270. *See
   also* Silver Gray Whigs
Whitney, Thomas R.: as co-founder of
   Order of United Americans, 13; Know
   Nothing elected to Congress, 84; on
   liberty and Catholicism, 113; on
   OSSB, 20–21; positive view toward
   Fillmore's nativist remarks, 223–24
Wide Awake political clubs, 268–69
Williamson, Passmore, 181
Wilmot, David, 218; nominated for governor of Pennsylvania (1857), 261–62
Wilmot Proviso, 15; Jacob Brinkerhoff
   as author/supporter of, 176
Wilson, Henry, 89, 90, 97, 141, 146–47,
   187; attempts to draw Know Nothings
   into Republican party, 187–88; campaigns for Republicans in New York,
   185; on Catholic support for oppression, 45; as Grant's vice president,
   274; Know Nothing convention intrigues by, 171; makes speeches for
   Frémont, 232; in Massachusetts Senate
   election, 146–47; opposes intense
   nativism (1855), 188; portrayed by historians, 190; withdraws from governor's race to aid Know Nothings, 91
Wise, Henry, 164; campaign versus
   Know Nothings in Virginia, 164–65
Women, involvement in nativist movement, 24n
Woodruff, John, 254
Worcester, Massachusetts: age of Know
   Nothings in, 41 *table;* length of residence of Know Nothings in, 42; occupations of Know Nothings in, 35 *table,*
   282–83; property ownership of Know
   Nothings in, 37 *table,* 38; wealth of
   Know Nothings in, 38 *table,* 40 *table*
Work force: immigrant children as pro-
   portion of, 32; immigrants as propor-
   tion of, 32
Workingmen: perceived attraction of to
   Know Nothing party, 40; Know Nothing belief that immigrants reduced status and income of, 109; Know Nothing
   laws favoring, 158–59; Know Nothing
   membership of, 35 *table,* 36, 36 *table.*
   See also Labor